Come In and Hear the Truth

Come In and Hear the Truth
Jazz and Race on 52nd Street

Patrick Burke

The University of Chicago Press Chicago and London

Patrick Burke is assistant professor of music at
Washington University in St. Louis.

The University of Chicago Press, Chicago 60637
The University of Chicago Press, Ltd., London
© 2008 by The University of Chicago
All rights reserved. Published 2008
Printed in the United States of America

17 16 15 14 13 12 11 10 09 08   1 2 3 4 5

ISBN-13: 978-0-226-08071-0
ISBN-10: 0-226-08071-4

Library of Congress Cataloging-in-Publication Data

Burke, Patrick Lawrence.
    Come in and hear the truth : jazz and race on 52nd
Street / Patrick Burke.
        p. cm.
    Includes bibliographical references and index.
    ISBN-13: 978-0-226-08071-0 (cloth : alk. paper)
    ISBN-10: 0-226-08071-4 (cloth : alk. paper) 1. Jazz—
New York (State)—New York—1931–1940—History and
criticism.
2. Jazz—New York (State)—New York—1941–1950—
History and criticism.
3. Music and race. 4. Fifty-second Street (New York,
N.Y.)
I. Title.
    ML3508.8.N5B87 2008
    781.6509747'109043—dc22
                                        2007035580

♾ The paper used in this publication meets the
minimum requirements of the American National
Standard for Information Sciences—Permanence of
Paper for Printed Library Materials, ANSI Z39.48–1992.

To Flannery and Kevin, with love and thanks

Contents

Acknowledgments {ix}   Introduction {1}   Chapter One **First for the Musicians, Then for the World** The Birth of Swing Street {13}   Chapter Two **Let's Have a Jubilee** 52nd Street Goes Commercial {33}   Chapter Three **Here Comes the Man with the Jive** Stuff Smith {60}   Chapter Four **A Little Law and Order in My Music** The John Kirby Sextet and Maxine Sullivan {89}   Chapter Five **Swingin' Down That Lane** 52nd Street at the Height of the Swing Era {112}   Chapter Six **Making It into the Big Time** Count Basie, Joe Marsala, and "Mixed" Bands {134}   Chapter Seven **This Conglomeration of Colors** Bebop Comes to Swing Street {155}   Chapter Eight **Apples and Oranges** 52nd Street and the Jazz War {180}   Conclusion **Long May It Be Remembered** {201}   Appendix **Chronology of 52nd Street Clubs** {207}   Notes {217}   Index {291}

Acknowledgments

Certainly the most gratifying aspect of this project has been the opportunity to meet dozens of friendly and generous people who helped me along the way. Foremost among them are the musicians and jazz fans who took the time to tell me about their experiences in 52nd Street's nightclubs. Dan Acosta, LeRoy Battle, Eddie Bert, Johnny Blowers, Barbara Carroll, Al Casey, Harrison Cooper, Bill Crow, Leonard Gaskin, William Gottlieb, Tom Hollyman, Robert Inman, Steve Knight, Barry Levine, Sam Levine, Lawrence Lucie, Fred Lyman, Irv Manning, Lou Mecca, Dan Morgenstern, Carline Ray, John Robinson, Artie Shapiro, Herb Shultz, Robert Stendahl, Morris Sunshine, Edwin Swanston, Billy Taylor, Al and Dot Vollmer, and Frank Zachary each responded graciously and enthusiastically to what must have seemed like a never-ending deluge of questions about 52nd Street. By e-mail or letter, on the phone, or in interview settings ranging from the Times Square Howard Johnson's to the offices of the Hearst Corporation to 52nd Street itself, they made "Swing Street" come alive for me and greatly enriched this book with their memories and insights. I owe special thanks to several. LeRoy Battle, Johnny Blowers, Al Casey, Leonard Gaskin, Lawrence Lucie, Lou Mecca, and the Vollmers welcomed me into their homes for lengthy and rewarding discussions. Robert Inman, Fred Lyman, and Herb Shultz provided me with copies of their own unpublished pieces on 52nd Street. John Robinson took me for a memorable stroll down 52nd Street in which he pointed out the sites of its long-departed clubs and described vividly what it had been like to walk down the street almost sixty years earlier. Al Vollmer showed great enthusiasm my earlier efforts into this book, I benefited from the careful reading and thoughtful comments of Flannery Burke, Jerome Camal, Ben Cawthra, Gerald Early, Phoebe Hyde, Gerald Izenberg, Bill Lenihan, Hugh Macdonald, Wayne Marshall, Karl Hagstrom Miller, Craig Monson, Dolores Pesce, Robert Snarrenberg, and Akiko Tsuchiya. At Washington University, faculty lecture series sponsored by American Culture Studies, the Center for the Humanities, and the Department of Music each allowed me to present my work to colleagues, and several guest lecture series enabled me to discuss my project at length with visitors Robin D. G. Kelley, Dan Morgenstern, and Guthrie Ramsey, each of whom offered insight and encouragement. The Modernist Studies Association, the Society for American Music, and the Society for Ethnomusicology gave me opportunities to present my work at their national conferences. Special thanks goes to friends who, in addition to intellectual engagement, graciously provided air mattresses or extra beds upon which I crashed during various research trips: Thea Browder, Ryan Carey, Todd Seguin, Diane Shinberg, Amy Staehr, and Roger White.

This book was made possible by grants from several generous institutions. My research in 2001 and 2002 was assisted by a fellowship from the Social Science Research Council's Program on the Arts with funds provided by the Rockefeller Foundation. In 2002 and 2003, the writing of my dissertation was funded by an Alvin H. Johnson–AMS 50 Dissertation Fellowship of the American Musicological Society as well as a University Dissertator Fellowship from the University of Wisconsin–Madison. In 2005, my work proceeded with assistance from a National Endowment for the Humanities Summer Stipend. (Any views, findings, conclusions, or recommendations expressed in this publication do not necessarily reflect those of the National Endowment for the Humanities.) Finally, I completed the book in 2007 as a faculty fellow of the Center for the Humanities at Washington University in St. Louis, where I benefited greatly from the friendly support of Gerald Early, Robbi Jones, Jian Leng, Barb Liebmann, and my co-fellows Gerald Izenberg and Akiko Tsuchiya.

At the University of Chicago Press, I thank Doug Mitchell for taking on this project with confidence and enthusiasm, Tim McGovern for guiding me smoothly through the publication process, and Lori Meek Schuldt for thoughtful and thorough copyediting. Charles Hersch and three anonymous readers provided valuable commentary on my book proposal and the manuscript itself. For supplying the photographs that appear in this book, I thank Frank Driggs, Ed Gottlieb, and Don Peterson. Tad Hershorn converted one of the photographs to a usable electronic format. Elliott

Goldkind and Martin Kennedy each helped transform my scrawls into immaculate, computer-notated musical transcriptions, and James Morley and Amanda Rounsaville each helped translate hand-drawn charts into the pristine graphs in the appendix.

Last but certainly not least, I thank my family. As always, my parents, Diane and Frank Burke, and my sister, Amy Burke, provided unconditional love and support and helped give me the confidence to persevere in this project. My son Kevin, born in 2006, has made life infinitely sweeter ever since. Most of all, I thank my wife, Flannery Burke, for her love, patience, and inspiration. Like many more important things, this book would not be possible without her.

Portions of chapter 1 were originally published in "Oasis of Swing: The Onyx Club, Jazz, and White Masculinity in the Early 1930s," *American Music* 24, no. 3 (Fall 2006): 320–46, reprinted by permission of the University of Illinois Press.

Introduction

On a later occasion, the bop trumpeter Dizzy Gillespie was having a vogue on the Street. In front of his club were posters advising: "Come in and Hear Dizzy." [Trumpeter Wingy] Manone attended and listened. He went back to Ryan's and posted his own sidewalk sign. It read: "Come in and Hear the Truth!"—**Robert Sylvester,** *Notes of a Guilty Bystander* (1970)

In early July 1946, a late-night wanderer in midtown Manhattan could have stopped in for a drink at the Spotlite Club, a tiny, smoky spot in the basement of a brownstone at 56 West 52nd Street. There, he or she would have heard a seventeen-piece band led by African American trumpeter Dizzy Gillespie, who was introducing his audience to a novel, harmonically and rhythmically innovative style that had recently become known as bebop.[1] When Gillespie's band took a twenty-minute break, our club-hopper could have strolled across the street to 53 West 52nd, entered another small club called Jimmy Ryan's, and listened to a quintet led by white trombonist Georg Brunis, playing in a familiar, indeed somewhat archaic, idiom that showcased collective improvisation and was usually called New Orleans style or Dixieland.[2] Rambling down the block to yet another cramped basement club, the Three Deuces at 72 West 52nd, our night owl could have heard a quartet led by black tenor saxophonist Ben Webster, a master of small-group swing famous for his hard-driving approach to up-tempo numbers and for the sensuous, breathy way he played ballads.[3] As our wanderer, by now perhaps a bit drunk despite 52nd Street's notoriously watered-down liquor, stepped out onto the sidewalk for some fresh air, he or she would have encountered a tantalizing dissonance still remembered vividly by those who were lucky enough to walk down 52nd Street at its peak: the sound of all three bands playing at once from different doorways.

Standing beneath the neon lights on Manhattan's hippest sidewalk, gazing up at the surrounding skyscrapers, and listening to an uneasy but strangely stirring blend of bebop, swing, and Dixieland, a thoughtful (if inebriated) observer would have been struck by the remarkable range of musical styles to be found on the short stretch of 52nd Street bounded by Fifth and Seventh avenues. Even a jazz novice would have noticed an obvious difference among the bands: while Brunis's and Webster's small groups were well suited for the narrow basements in which they played, Gillespie's big band barely fit into the confines of the Spotlite and almost overwhelmed its small audience with its powerful sound. If, however, like many of 52nd Street's loyal patrons, our observer was a serious jazz aficionado, he or she probably would have viewed each band as radically distinct from the others. Although each emphasized improvisation, the spiky harmonies, unpredictable rhythms, and virtuosic technical displays of Gillespie's band (and to a lesser extent Webster's) contrasted notably with the warm, cooperative bounce of Brunis's group. Moreover, the performers presented themselves to their audiences in different ways. While Webster was known primarily for his music rather than for theatrics, Brunis and Gillespie each had a reputation for clowning. Brunis, however, tended toward broad slapstick, parading around the club and sometimes playing the trombone with his foot, while Gillespie cultivated a more ironic and self-possessed, if also at times physical, brand of humor. A 52nd Street regular would also have been aware that the audience at each club varied. While the Dixieland music offered at Jimmy Ryan's attracted a relatively conservative faction of white businessmen and college students, the crowds at the Three Deuces and the Spotlite included a small number of African Americans, as well as ostentatious hipsters, both white and black, sporting goatees and sunglasses. As this book's epigraph demonstrates, arguments among musicians and audiences over their preferred brand of jazz often led advocates of Dixieland or bebop to the heights of polemical fervor. Such conflicts were not limited to matters of musical taste. Only the year before, 52nd Street's unusual tolerance of racial integration had led to police crackdowns on clubs and occasional street brawls. Although the street's atmosphere was fun and festive, battles over racial identity and artistic integrity loomed close to the surface. Weary of pondering such weighty matters, our jazz enthusiast might then have meandered down the street in search of some of 52nd Street's other performers, who on various nights in July 1946 included tenor saxophonist Coleman Hawkins, singer Billie Holiday, and pianist Art Tatum.[4]

In this book, I explore musical and racial tensions and collaborations across the history of the 52nd Street jazz scene, which while short-lived and unpretentious was nonetheless central to the history of jazz. From the mid-1930s until the late 1940s, 52nd Street was arguably the jazz capital of the world, known simply as "The Street" to a generation of musicians and their audiences. In its broad outline, the history of 52nd Street is familiar to many jazz fans and scholars, thanks largely to Arnold Shaw's engaging 1971 survey *The Street That Never Slept.*[5] The street's reputation as a center for jazz began during Prohibition with tiny, illicit speakeasies where white professional musicians gathered to socialize and to play in casual jam sessions. After the repeal of Prohibition, legal nightclubs opened on 52nd Street, featuring small ensembles of both black and white musicians whose performances combined jazz improvisation with broad comedy. By 1937, as swing music became a national sensation, 52nd Street was home to a shifting series of small clubs that drew both jazz connoisseurs and an enthusiastic general audience. Although big bands occasionally squeezed into the crowded clubs, the great majority of the groups that played on 52nd Street included seven musicians or fewer. In an era when large, highly arranged swing bands dominated the commercial music industry, 52nd Street's musicians—such as Hawkins, Holiday, and Tatum—forged a style of small-group swing that emphasized intimacy, spontaneity, and individual virtuosity. As the swing era waned in the mid-1940s, 52nd Street hosted such bebop pioneers as Gillespie and alto saxophonist Charlie Parker, who drew attention for both their challenging new style of jazz and their stance as serious modern artists. By the end of the 1940s, when 52nd Street's clubs began to close or to feature burlesque instead of jazz, the street had provided a forum for the skill and innovation of many of the most influential figures in jazz history. Many musicians who performed on the street have recalled their wonder at the range of talent that surrounded them. Pianist Marian McPartland, for example, claimed that "on 52d St., you could walk through the history of jazz," while drummer Shelly Manne remembered that "if you were a jazz historian you could have gone down there and seen and heard, with your own ears, the evolution of the music, right there on the street, and it all made sense."[6] Thus 52nd Street played an important role in jazz history as one of the key sites where the "jazz tradition" developed and progressed.

In addition to its reputation for musical innovation, 52nd Street was also significant for its role in the vanguard of a changing racial climate. By the late 1930s, 52nd Street's clubs were among the first in New York to feature racially integrated bands and to allow integrated audiences, and by the 1940s there were black-owned clubs on the street. Although these advances were countered by racist violence and police harassment, they also enabled musical and social dialogues between blacks and whites that were rare in the United States at this time. Historians of jazz in the 1930s and 1940s have taken differing views of 52nd Street's racial dynamic. Lewis A. Erenberg, for example, celebrates the street's jazz scene as a catalyst of positive change, arguing that interracial intermingling among 52nd Street's musicians was a progressive force that "created the momentum for the integration of audiences."[7] David Stowe, in contrast, points out that 52nd Street's clubs "were by no means racial utopias," as demonstrated by police action against racially "mixed" clubs during World War II.[8] While these accounts may seem contradictory, they reflect the complexity of policies and attitudes on 52nd Street, where the most conventional forms of racial discrimination and stereotyping existed alongside a radical trend toward racial integration.

While both approaches to 52nd Street's history—examining the street's significance in the development of musical style or assessing its role in changing race relations—yield important insights, they rely on assumptions about jazz and race that have recently been called into question. As historian Scott DeVeaux points out, the notion of jazz as an insular, organically developing tradition is a retrospective construction that allows historians to organize a range of styles into a compelling narrative but does not necessarily represent musical practices as they were originally perceived.[9] The idea of the "jazz tradition" obscures the ways in which music now seen as part of the jazz canon both influenced and reflected other styles of music and popular entertainment. Moreover, this notion ignores the coexistence and mutual influence of jazz styles often seen as historically distinct. In addressing 52nd Street, where jazz performers working in a variety of idioms mingled freely with one another and with musicians and entertainers from outside the jazz world, this narrative is inevitably reductive and excludes, rather than explains, social and musical complexity. Similarly, scholars in the humanities have long argued that the idea of race is an ever-changing social construction rather than an immutable, objective reality. This position is familiar to literary and cultural historians, but its implications have rarely been pursued in jazz scholarship, which too often tends to rely on rigid conceptions of "black" and "white" in categorizing musical style.[10] While racial inequities and perceptions certainly had tangible effects on 52nd Street's musicians and audiences, the street's interracial culture also helped alter the concept of race itself. A close look at 52nd Street demonstrates that, like music, the notion of race is both pervasive and elusive: although both surround us every day, their meanings can never be pinned down completely. As a place where traditional boundaries were continually challenged, 52nd Street challenges scholars to account for the instability of both musical and racial categories.

In this book, I seek to shed new light on this important moment in jazz history by telling the seemingly familiar story of 52nd Street and its music in a different way, focusing on the mutual influence between musical style and racial representation. Rather than trace the formal development of jazz on 52nd Street, I emphasize the ways in which ideas about racial identity and racial authenticity affected music's performance and reception on the street. Conversely, while I address the street's racial politics and policies, I am especially interested in how the musical culture of 52nd Street helped construct new notions of race. How did audiences on 52nd Street "hear" race as reflected in jazz? To what extent did musicians reinforce and perpetuate conventional racial stereotypes, and to what extent did they aspire to suggest novel conceptions of racial identity? By asking such questions, I want to suggest new directions not only for jazz studies but also for the broader fields of historical musicology and ethnomusicology, which, as Ronald Radano and Philip V. Bohlman point out, have often "sought to deny the racial dimension" of musical experience. Radano and Bohlman argue that music both "contributes substantially to the vocabularies used to construct race" and "fills in the spaces between racial distinctiveness"—in other words, music sometimes helps erect racial barriers and sometimes challenges and undermines them.[11] In examining 52nd Street, I trace the ways in which its musical culture both confirmed existing racial ideologies and alluded to new possibilities. An understanding of this tension is important in discussing 52nd Street, where race was a powerful idea with real political and social effects but was also a shifting, slippery construction. An investigation of this unique, complex environment can expand not only our knowledge of jazz as a musical style but also our larger understanding of how the music contributes to racial formations.

This approach to 52nd Street thus departs from more traditional accounts that view jazz exclusively in terms of musical progress or broad racial categories. Instead, I uncover the history and effects of a particular conception of authentic jazz prevalent among the street's musicians and audiences, a conception that knit together ideas about race, the commercial entertainment industry, and musical performance. 52nd Street's jazz scene was heir to a long history of stereotypes about black music and musicians. The most fundamental of these was what Ted Gioia has termed the "Primitivist Myth" of jazz studies: "a stereotype which views jazz as a music charged with emotion but largely devoid of intellectual content, and which sees the jazz musician as the inarticulate and unsophisticated practitioner of an art which he himself scarcely understands."[12] On 52nd Street, jazz was often regarded as a music that came instinctively to black performers in the form of uncontrollable, irrational improvisation that defied the restrictive conventions of mainstream popular or classical music. It is possible to view this notion of unfettered, anticommercial black musicianship in terms of white dominance and black resistance, as a belief simply imposed on African American performers by white musicians and audiences. It is more accurate, however, to see this idea as a kind of template for jazz performance within which both blacks and whites assumed a variety of attitudes, some resistant and some acquiescent. Black musicians, for example, often engaged in improvisatory flights that audiences perceived as signs of racially determined abandon, but they also countered this image with obviously premeditated, stagily artificial performance styles and carefully controlled arrangements. White performers sometimes enacted their fantasies of a carefree, spontaneous black identity in an offensive, condescending way, but they also paid genuine tribute to black musicians as conscious, rational artists. "Mixed," or interracial, groups that appeared on 52nd Street further complicated this tangle of racial ideology and dramatized it for a curious audience. Ideas of racial authenticity, then, influenced musical practice even as they were formed by it.

Addressing 52nd Street in this way reveals that jazz was part of a long tradition of representations of black identity and black musicianship. The roots of the "primitivist myth" can be traced back at least as far as Rousseau's "natural man," a symbol of uncivilized virtue based on eighteenth-century Europeans' beliefs about life among "savages."[13] In the early 1800s, similar ideas were popularized in the United States through what historian George M. Fredrickson terms "romantic racialism," a condescending ideology that ostensibly celebrated blacks for what were believed to be inherent, admirable qualities of gentleness and spirituality while denying that they could operate as full citizens in a rationally functioning society.[14] At the same time, in American musical culture, degrading images of black identity found their most enduring and notorious form in blackface minstrelsy, in which both whites and blacks took on a patently inauthentic guise while confirming a dominant, racist notion of authentic black spontaneity, natural musicality, and independence from labor structures.[15] Shortly after the Civil War, publications such as *Slave Songs of the United States* (1867) and successful black performers such as the Fisk University Jubilee Singers (founded 1871) brought African American spirituals to white audiences for whom, as Radano puts it, "the perceived purity and wholeness of the slave songs also signified what was missing in whiteness as a consequence of civilization itself."[16]

The notion that authentic blackness could fill a void in the soul of modern white civilization persisted into the twentieth century in forms that had a direct bearing on the reception of jazz. Interest in primitivism among modern art circles, as articulated in works such as critic Roger Fry's *Vision and Design* (1920), reinforced the insulting image of black artists as intuitive, irrational creators who lacked the ability to reflect critically on their art.[17] European writers such as Hugues Panassié and Robert Goffin expressed similar views in the 1930s as they founded the discipline of jazz criticism.[18] The work of these critics coincided with that of American folklorists who began to uphold the folk music of black southerners as evidence that the United States had an indigenous music independent of British influence.[19] The most notable example of this trend was the "discovery" by white folklorists John and Alan Lomax of black Louisiana songster Huddie Ledbetter, better known as Lead Belly. In 1935, the Lomaxes brought Lead Belly to New York, where they began a publicity campaign that depicted the singer as both "an authentic folk forefather" and "a savage, untamed animal."[20] Historian Francis Davis writes that Lead Belly's white liberal audiences in New York "projected quite a bit of their own emotional makeup" onto the singer, viewing him through fantasies of "mankind's sentimentalized former self, a preindustrialized American Adam."[21] As 52nd Street entered its heyday as a center for jazz in the mid-1930s, then, it was informed by a history of demeaning, primitivist ideas about black identity and black music.

At the same time, of course, there existed a rich African American tradition of challenging dominant conceptions of race to assert alternative visions of black identity. Such formulations often celebrated the ability of blacks to maintain their personal integrity in the face of a racist society. For example, the slave aphorism "Got one mind for white folk to see / 'Nother for what I know is me" suggests the presence of a secret, authentic self that is necessarily kept hidden behind a mask of subterfuge.[22] On the other hand, the implication that the mask, just as much as the authentic self, constitutes the slave's mind reveals that such resistance brings with it an internal struggle over identity. This struggle finds its best-known expression in W. E. B. Du Bois's *The Souls of Black Folk* (1903), in which Du Bois describes black Americans as living in a state of "double-consciousness" in which one is "always looking at one's self through the eyes of others" and therefore can have "no true self-consciousness."[23] As literary critic Houston A. Baker Jr. points out, however, African Americans in Du Bois's era and beyond have often found ways to turn such double-consciousness to their advantage, through either a "mastery of form" in which they take on features of the familiar minstrel persona in order to "ensure survival" while fighting racism, or a "deformation of mastery" in which they aggressively assert the value of those aspects of black culture that have been labeled "alien" and "monstrous."[24] Rather than rejecting racial stereotypes overtly, such tactics employ aspects of racist ideology in order to subtly undermine that ideology. A significant example of these strategies is the work of Harlem Renaissance intellectuals such as Alain Locke, who, as Baker points out, took on the dominant "language of RACE" in order to "convert it into a weapon and creative instrument of massed, *national, racial will*."[25] In *The Negro and His Music* (1936), Locke assented to the normally belittling notion that jazz comes naturally to blacks in order to assert that jazz is an authentically black expression in which all black Americans can take pride.[26] African Americans in this era also resisted conventional notions of race by embracing values that were supposedly foreign to blacks. Jazz scholar Burton Peretti writes that early jazz musicians "adopted one of the central principles of the European art-music tradition" by insisting on values of "individuality, and even alienation from the mainstream of musical culture" commonly associated with figures such as Beethoven.[27] Despite the continued power of racist stereotypes, then, African American musicians on 52nd Street also inherited a legacy of affirmative ideas of black identity and musicianship.

Examining 52nd Street's role in this long history of racial representation leads me to draw on the methods of ethnomusicology, cultural studies, and cultural and social history. Instead of treating jazz as a series of great performances to be analyzed and codified, I discuss it as a set of musical and cultural practices kept in perpetual motion by a network of ever-shifting social relationships among musicians and their audiences.[28] In particular, I emphasize 52nd Street's vexed role within the commercial music and entertainment industry, which many of the street's musicians and patrons strove to resist even as the street itself became a center of marketing and publicity. As DeVeaux argues, "race is inextricably linked to economics" in debates over commercialism in jazz.[29] To explore this link, I approach 52nd Street's musicians as working professionals rather than transcendent artists, and I pay attention to 52nd Street's most commercially successful and best-publicized musicians as well as its most canonical. Readers may be surprised to see that, on a street that commonly featured such icons of the jazz tradition as Fats Waller and Lester Young, public attention often fixated on now-obscure figures such as Mike Riley and Maxine Sullivan. Although I engage in analysis of the recorded performances of these and other musicians, I am concerned less with tracing the stylistic development of jazz than with exposing the music's role in creating and conveying ideas of racial identity. Moreover, I am equally concerned with 52nd Street's audiences and the marketing and advertising that lured them to the street. My sources include popular and scholarly magazines, journals, books, and newspapers; studio recordings and radio broadcasts; films and photographs; and oral history, including my own interviews and correspondence with 52nd Street's performers and patrons. It is my hope that this eclectic range of colorful material not only will shed new light on 52nd Street's racial dynamic but also will give readers a sense of the vitality, humor, and romance of the 52nd Street jazz scene.

Come In and Hear the Truth proceeds chronologically through the two decades of 52nd Street's rise and fall as a jazz hub, with eight chapters grouped into pairs. Chapters 1 and 2 address the white musicians who founded 52nd Street's jazz scene in the early to mid-1930s and the ideas about race and commerce that motivated them. Chapter 1 discusses the Onyx Club, a clandestine speakeasy that around 1930 became the first jazz venue on 52nd Street. Here, white studio musicians, who made their living playing predictable arrangements of conventional popular music, got together informally for improvised jam sessions that mimicked what these musicians saw as the earthy, uninhibited qualities of African American jazz. The connections that these musicians perceived among masculinity, black identity, spontaneous musical creativity, and an anticommercial attitude helped define the street's culture for the next two decades. In chapter 2, I turn to the period immediately following the repeal of Prohibition, when legally operated clubs on 52nd Street began to market such charismatic performers as Louis Prima and Wingy Manone to a burgeoning mass audience. Between 1934 and 1936, such musicians demonstrated that improvised jazz, which 52nd Street's first musicians had prized as resistant to the mainstream, could nonetheless become a form of popular entertainment. The popularity of these performers helped expose a wide audience to the notions of authentic black music prevalent among 52nd Street's original circle of white musicians.

Chapters 3 and 4 discuss the first African American performers to appear on 52nd Street. As black musicians began to play regularly in the street's clubs in the mid-1930s, they were forced to contend with already well-established stereotypes about their purportedly nonintellectual, unstructured, ecstatic approach to music making. Chapter 3 focuses on the performances and reception of violinist Stuff Smith, whose Onyx Club Boys became one of the most popular groups on the street in 1936 and 1937 by combining fervent, unpredictable improvisation with rambunctious comedy. While Smith's freewheeling music and happy-go-lucky stage persona sometimes appeared on the surface to conform to conventional images of natural, irrational black entertainers, I argue that a closer reading of his performances reveals an aggressive, subversive affirmation of black identity that drew on the culture of 1930s Harlem. Chapter 4 addresses the John Kirby Sextet and singer Maxine Sullivan, who succeeded Smith at the Onyx Club in 1937. Kirby and Sullivan rejected the manic stage presence and unrestrained improvisation often stereotypically associated with African American musicians, performing instead in a reserved, mannered idiom that referenced European classical and folk music. In very different ways, each group challenged the limiting notions of black musicianship that dominated 52nd Street.

Chapters 5 and 6 deal with 52nd Street at its apex of commercial success in the late 1930s and early 1940s, at the height of what has become known as the swing era. Chapter 5 considers 52nd Street's paradoxical relationship to mainstream swing. While the street, as part of an economic system that included large booking agencies and radio networks, was undeniably a part of the entertainment industry, its clubs and performers continued to present themselves as alternatives to the banal, predictable world of conventional popular music. At the same time, those aspects of 52nd Street that appeared to run counter to professionalism, such as the street's reputation as a friendly, casual refuge for hardworking musicians and its subculture of zealous record collectors, nonetheless proved profitable in marketing the street to a broad public. Chapter 6 explores the racial implications of 52nd Street's ambivalent relationship to commerce by contrasting two musicians who performed simultaneously on the street in 1938: black pianist and big-band leader Count Basie and white clarinetist Joe Marsala. While each capitalized on the notion that jazz was a liberating alternative to mainstream entertainment, each approached his music and public image differently. Basie's band was known for powerful swing and brilliant improvisation, traits that conformed to familiar stereotypes of black music, but his overt professionalism undermined these stereotypes by belying the condescending notion that black musicians were irrational, undisciplined creators. Marsala similarly highlighted improvisation and spontaneity, but, unlike Basie, he reinforced 52nd Street's dominant image of jazz as an anticommercial expression with what audiences saw as his uncompromising devotion to esoteric, authentic forms of early jazz. The chapter concludes with a discussion of interracial performances on swing-era 52nd Street, which sometimes obscured racial boundaries but sometimes highlighted them. Together, these two chapters seek to unravel the paradox of how 52nd Street's anticommercial ethos was itself commodified during the swing era even as white musicians and audiences continued to fetishize jazz and its African American creators for their supposed resistance to mass culture.

Chapters 7 and 8 address musical and social changes on 52nd Street during World War II, particularly an increasing tension over racial issues as black-owned clubs and interracial audiences began to appear on the street. Chapter 7 examines the rise of bebop on 52nd Street. Viewed as part of the history of racial representation on the street, bebop's primary innovation was the way in which it synthesized the competing traditions represented by Stuff Smith's hip stage presence and virtuosic improvisation and John Kirby's disciplined arrangements and calculated gestures toward the European canon. As bop musicians and their hipster followers provoked conservative audiences by challenging racial and sexual conventions, they simultaneously asserted their status as self-consciously modern artists rather than intuitive creators. While bebop perpetuated the stance of authentic anticommercialism common on 52nd Street, it linked that stance to artistry and intellect rather than a stereotype of inherent racial creativity. At the same time, like their predecessors, 52nd Street's bebop musicians sought ways to attract a larger audience even as their style acquired a reputation for forbidding complexity. Chapter 8 turns to the so-called Dixieland revival, which looked to the past to glorify styles of jazz associated with early twentieth-century New Orleans. Although the revival was in some respects a novel development, it also represented yet another manifestation of the notion of carefree, natural black musicianship that had been common among white musicians and audiences on 52nd Street since the days of the original Onyx Club. I address the continued attraction that Dixieland held for some audiences and musicians in the face of the assertive black modernism of bebop, and I also discuss the struggles of black Dixieland musicians to claim their own identities as artists. The famous battles between beboppers and "moldy figs" in this era were, I argue, the culmination of debates about racial representation that had informed 52nd Street's entire history as a jazz district. As collaborations among musicians associated with these competing styles revealed, however, the "jazz war" did not create an unbridgeable divide.

The conclusion addresses the period from 1946 to 1950, when 52nd Street's clubs began to go out of business or to shift from jazz to burlesque in order to survive changes in popular interest. The nostalgic discourse on the "death of the street" that pervaded media coverage in this period presaged the way in which 52nd Street itself has since become a romanticized symbol of authentic jazz.

52nd Street's musical and social influence was not limited to a small coterie of jazz musicians and listeners but extended into the wider popular culture of the United States. The improvisatory, small-group style that developed on 52nd Street in the 1930s and 1940s had a profound influence on all jazz that followed, and its performers were instrumental in popularizing the image of jazz as a virtuosic art music worthy of serious attention. Moreover, 52nd Street's musicians were among the first in the United States to demonstrate professional cooperation across racial lines, and their music, while it sometimes reinforced stereotypes, also pointed the way to novel, affirmative conceptions of race. From 52nd Street's shabby, ephemeral clubs, there emerged new visions of jazz and racial identity that had an enduring impact on American culture.

Chapter One **First for the Musicians, Then for the World** The Birth of Swing Street

On January 24, 1933, a group of New York's most sought-after studio musicians gathered for a routine recording session. During much of the session, these musicians, all white men, accompanied Viennese singer Greta Keller on popular numbers including *I'll Never Have to Dream Again* and *I'm Playing with Fire,* but they also took time to record a much less conventional performance not intended for commercial release. Trumpeter Manny Klein recalled years later that the band, led by Victor Young and including such rising jazz luminaries as Tommy and Jimmy Dorsey and violinist Joe Venuti, was "trying to cut this corny waltz" but kept making mistakes. "Finally, Victor said, 'Let's play it through. Play the worst you can. And let's get all those clinkers out of our systems.'" A 78 rpm record of this experiment, entitled *Onyx Club Revue,* was pressed in limited quantity and distributed to the members of the band; a copy also went to Joe Helbock, a white bootlegger and jazz buff who owned the Onyx Club, a 52nd Street speakeasy that served as a meeting place for these and other musicians. Even a cursory hearing of *Onyx Club Revue,* reissued on CD in 2002, reveals that this is a willfully irreverent recording. It features intentionally out-of-tune playing and nasal singing, flippant references to drinking, passages in which the musicians' barely suppressed laughter renders them almost unable to perform, a jarring and seemingly irrelevant quotation from *St. Louis Blues,* and even a series of belches into the microphone by guitarist Carl Kress. A private joke rather than a public performance, *Onyx Club Revue* allows us a rare glimpse of soon-to-be-famous musicians in an unguarded and relaxed moment, clowning for their own amusement.[1]

I begin the story of 52nd Street with *Onyx Club Revue* not to argue that this strange recording deserves to be enshrined in the jazz canon but rather because the flippant, rowdy, boys' club atmosphere that it conveys is revealing of a particular vision of white masculinity that played a profound role in the creation of 52nd Street's jazz scene in the early 1930s. At the Onyx Club, the first jazz venue on 52nd Street, young, white, male musicians strove to reject the perceived banality and pretense of mainstream pop music in favor of what they saw as the more open, vital expression to be found in African American jazz. The improvisatory creativity of jazz allowed these musicians to enact an ideal of masculine independence and self-determination that contrasted with the restrictions and limitations imposed by the music business in which they worked. Although this sense of self provided both liberation and camaraderie for the musicians of the Onyx Club, it was constructed in an environment of exclusion and misrepresentation in which women and African American men were virtually absent. 52nd Street's tenure as a jazz center thus began in a club dominated by white men, whose notions of authentic jazz were to play a persistent role in the street's culture even as its performers and audiences became increasingly diverse throughout the 1930s and 1940s.[2]

Several interrelated ideas motivated the patrons of the Onyx Club: a belief that jazz was a distinctly masculine form of musical expression; the valorization of jazz as an authentic alternative to an inauthentic commercial music industry; and a perceived connection between African American identity and anticommercial attitudes and behavior. Although these ideas derived from such important precedents as blackface minstrelsy and urban saloon culture, they took on a distinctive and influential form within the confines of the Onyx Club. The attitudes of the Onyx Club's patrons toward African American music and musicians were complex and often contradictory. The white musicians who congregated at the Onyx were deeply fascinated by African American musical practices. While these musicians all had at least some direct contact with black performers, they also were unavoidably influenced by the pervasive stereotypes of blackface minstrelsy and the broader circulation of racist imagery and beliefs in national culture. On the one hand, the Onyx circle transcended minstrel stereotypes with their overt respect for, and emulation of, the artistry and sophistication of black musicians. On the other hand, these very stereotypes, such as the idea of natural, spontaneous black musicianship, were perpetuated in the Onyx musicians' view of jazz as an authentic, immediate form of personal expression.[3] Such attitudes led white musicians at the Onyx to associate African American jazz musicians with both anticommercial values and an enviable, supposedly unfettered masculinity. The Onyx Club is thus an early example of a racial dynamic that persisted throughout the history of 52nd Street, in which racist ideologies paradoxically coexisted with sincere attempts to undermine racism.

"Strictly a Musicians' Spot"   The original Onyx Club opened at 35 West 52nd Street in Manhattan sometime between 1927 and 1930 and closed shortly before February 1934, when owner Joe Helbock responded to the recent repeal of Prohibition by opening a "legitimate" Onyx Club down the block at number 72. My lack of precision about these dates reflects the sketchy historical record of such illegal taverns as the Onyx. Although the Volstead Act prohibiting the sale of alcohol was poorly enforced in New York City—the city's police commissioner estimated in the mid-1920s that there were thirty-two thousand speakeasies in the five boroughs—drinking establishments were nonetheless illegal, and their proprietors took pains to minimize evidence of their existence. Nonetheless, it is certain that by the early 1930s, West 52nd Street's unassuming brownstones had acquired underground fame as the sites of illicit speakeasies; according to an often-cited (and perhaps apocryphal) tale, in one night humorist Robert Benchley had a drink at each of thirty-eight such establishments on the block between Fifth and Sixth avenues. The paucity of documentary evidence makes it difficult to determine whether these speakeasies featured music or any sort of live entertainment. One of the most celebrated, the 21 Club, offered fine dining and wine but does not appear to have hired entertainers. The investigative reports of the Committee of Fourteen, an antivice group, reveal that speakeasies on this block between 1927 and 1929 included the Aquarium (35 West 52nd), Club Basque (66 West 52nd), and unidentified spots at numbers 59 and 62, but these reports do not mention music or any other kind of performance. The names of some speakeasies suggest that they may have featured music: the Yacht Club was named for a popular singing group, the Yacht Club Boys, and another club, Helen Morgan's Summer Home, was named for and fronted by the famous torch singer. Broadway columnist Robert Sylvester writes that, in addition to the Yacht Club Boys and Morgan, performers in 52nd Street's speakeasies included singers

Dwight Fiske and Harry Richman, ballroom dancers Tony and Renee DeMarco, and bandleader Vincent Lopez. Other clubs emphasized informal musical novelties—Leon & Eddie's Eddie Davis sang bawdy songs full of double entendres, while at Tony's, owner Tony Soma, an avid proselytizer for yoga, was known to sing while standing on his head. Although these speakeasies may have begun to establish 52nd Street's reputation as an entertainment district as early as the 1920s, many patrons likely saw the performances merely as unrelated and unexceptional accompaniments to illicit drinking. [4]

These relatively invisible speakeasies were, ironically, hidden away within New York's most visible neighborhood: midtown Manhattan. The prosperity of the 1920s and advances in communications had made New York "the command center of a new kind of culture" based on mass media and marketing. Midtown became "the new center of life in Manhattan, as with remarkable speed an intricate, ultramodern nexus of office buildings, department stores, apartment houses, and hotels sprang up around the visionary transportation complex of Grand Central Terminal to service the city's new clean industries, including advertising, communications, public relations, retailing, and mass-market entertainment." [5] Of direct importance to these industries were new national radio networks based in midtown. NBC, the first network, made its inaugural broadcast in 1926 from the Waldorf Astoria Hotel at 34th Street and Fifth Avenue. CBS went into business the following year and in 1929 established studios at 52nd Street and Madison Avenue. [6] Midtown also encompassed the bustling Broadway theater and nightclub scene, which included such ballrooms as the Roseland (51st and Broadway) and the Arcadia (53rd and Broadway) that featured African American jazz bands. [7] Even after the stock market crash of 1929, midtown remained at the center of New York's attention with the construction of such architectural marvels as the Chrysler Building at 43rd and Lexington, completed in 1929; the Empire State Building at 34th and Fifth Avenue, completed in 1931; and Rockefeller Center, begun in 1929 and bounded during the 1930s by 48th and 51st streets and Fifth and Sixth avenues. [8]

In contrast to the flashy edifices that surrounded it, the Onyx Club was an unpretentious, relaxed spot, as this 1939 reminiscence by jazz critic Wilder Hobson suggests:

During Prohibition the Onyx was a conventional enough second-floor speakeasy whose only distinguishing characteristic was the fact that its clientele was mostly made up of dance and radio musicians, and that its entertainment

was intended to please them. You went in a brownstone basement entry and up a dark flight of stairs to the second floor where there was a door painted a dirty mottled silver with the customary Judas hole. Inside there was a shadowy hall and a couple of drinking rooms, the rear room containing a bar, one of those push-ball games, a shabby upright piano, a few tables and some wicker chairs. Many musicians used the place as a club, made telephone calls there and parked their instruments, but nothing very much happened until late in the afternoon and nothing at all like a stampede after that. I don't think there were more than ten small tables in the whole joint, and I'm certain that I never saw more than twenty-five people in the place at any one time.[9]

As Hobson points out, what made the Onyx unique was not its location, size, or decor but rather its reputation as a haven for white jazz and dance-band musicians. Before the Onyx opened, a speakeasy called Plunkett's on West 53rd Street had served this function. Trumpeter Jimmy McPartland remembered that around 1929 "that's where all the jazz musicians or the musicians around town, Jimmy [Dorsey], Tommy Dorsey, [Benny] Goodman, Bix [Beiderbecke] and all the Whiteman band, oh so many guys used to congregate there. It was our water hole so to speak." Guitarist Eddie Condon, who provided a vivid recollection of Plunkett's in his autobiography, stated that musicians conducted "all kinds of business there." Onyx owner Helbock remembered that he sometimes attended Plunkett's with musicians but went on to say, "I guess the Onyx put Plunkett's out of business. All the musicians came over once we got going." Although it is not clear why the Onyx replaced Plunkett's as the musicians' speakeasy of choice, the former soon became a central gathering point. Songwriter and pianist Hoagy Carmichael wrote that "if you sat long enough" at the Onyx, "you could meet all the jazzmen that were around New York, or hunting a job, or passing through."[10]

A list of the club's patrons, compiled from firsthand accounts, comprises many of the most commercially successful young white jazz and popular musicians in New York in the early years of the Great Depression: clarinetist Benny Goodman; guitarists Carl Kress, Eddie Lang, and Dick McDonough; pianists Roy Bargy, Walter Gross, Milt Raskin, Artie Schutt, Howard Smith, and Joe Sullivan; saxophonists Frankie Chase, Jimmy Dorsey, Bud Freeman, and Frank Trumbauer; singer and comb player Red McKenzie; trumpeters Bunny Berigan, Manny Klein, Del Staigers, and Charlie Teagarden; trombonists Tommy Dorsey, Jack Teagarden, and George Troup; and violinist Joe Venuti.[11] In 1930, the average age of these musicians was about twenty-five. Some, such as the Dorsey brothers, Lang, and Schutt, had moved to New York in the mid-1920s, where they freelanced in recording studios or worked as "hot soloists" who supplied improvised choruses for dance orchestras such as Paul Whiteman's and Paul Specht's.[12] A number of Chicago musicians, including Goodman, Sullivan, and Freeman, came to New York in 1928 after crackdowns on Chicago's cabaret speakeasies limited the possibilities for employment there.[13] The rise of talking motion pictures, which put theater musicians out of work across the country, also led many musicians to move to New York in search of employment in 1928.[14] In the aftermath of the stock market crash of 1929, still more musicians came to New York, "where most of the depression-ravaged, streamlined popular music industry was located. . . . In 1934 nearly one-fifth of all AFM [American Federation of Musicians] members [in the entire United States] belonged to New York's Local 802."[15] This influx of musicians "attempted to sign on with dance bands, radio studios, Broadway pit orchestras, and even the Muzak Corporation and other producers of 'musical environments.'"[16] Of these jobs, radio work and recording were the most lucrative and therefore the most competitive.[17] Historian Samuel Charters writes that "the studio work was monopolized by a small group of musicians who turn up on hundreds of records of every kind"; he also points out that racial discrimination by recording contractors meant this group was almost exclusively white.[18] For this elite group of musicians, the Onyx, located in the same neighborhood as "CBS (52d and Madison), NBC (711 Fifth), Radio City and . . . Broadway theaters," was a short walk for studio and theater employees in search of a drink and the company of their peers.[19] Soon after its opening, the club adopted a password for entrance that reflected its patrons' professional affiliations: "I'm from 802."[20]

As a drinking establishment that catered to members of a specific skilled profession, the Onyx was heir to a long tradition of workingmen's saloons. Saloons played an important role in the everyday lives of urban industrial workers, who forged a group identity as they bought one another drinks, joked, sang, transacted business, and relaxed in an "all-male environment of amiable sociability" that encouraged both friendly competition and fellowship.[21] Both of the latter were prominent at the Onyx, where musicians tried to "cut" one another in heated jam sessions that also served to cement loyalty and friendship. Helbock, a white jazz fan whose interest in African American music had been sparked in the 1910s and 1920s by the bands of James Reese Europe and Duke Ellington, fostered a convivial, welcoming climate at the Onyx. In addition to providing liquor, a piano, and a phonograph for his customers, Helbock stored instruments, took and forwarded telephone messages from family members and employers, and received musicians' mail.[22] These amenities and the relaxed ambience led the Onyx to become a home away from home for many musicians—radio announcer Paul Douglas remembered that in the early 1930s "the Onyx lived almost exclusively on the musicians, and the musicians lived in the Onyx."[23]

The Onyx, like earlier saloons, was patronized almost entirely by men. Its customers formed part of a larger "bachelor subculture" that was a significant presence in American cities between 1880 and 1930.[24] Historian Madelon Powers argues that in the early twentieth century "many working-class men sought the companionate ideal not in marriage, but in male peer groups" centered in saloons.[25] In these groups, men upheld an "ethic of manliness" based both on values of loyalty and fair play and on the exclusion and disparagement of women, who were rarely admitted to saloons and then only through a special "ladies' entrance" that avoided the main barroom.[26] Although the Onyx was not closed to women, their almost complete absence from primary sources on the club suggests that they occupied a peripheral place there. A 1933 profile of Carl Kress mentions that "Carl has been married just five months to a swell dame named Evelyn, whom he met at the Onyx, a rendezvous for musicians, just eighteen months ago."[27] Paul Douglas remembered in a 1938 article that a couple from New Jersey, "Mr. and Mrs. W. B. Armstrong," regularly came to the Onyx to listen to the music.[28] In a 1992 interview, Manny Klein stated simply that "different girls" would come to the club.[29] It is difficult to draw firm conclusions from such minimal evidence, but these quotations suggest that women attended the Onyx only as the companions of male musicians or listeners rather than as musicians themselves—I have found no account of the speakeasy that describes women making music there. Klein's fond recollection of an incident in which bandleader Paul Whiteman played the "big shot" by inviting a group of men from the Onyx to patronize a "cathouse" at his expense suggests that shared objectification of women was seen as one legitimate way for male musicians to cement bonds of friendship and reciprocity.[30] The prevailing vision of masculinity at the Onyx appears to have centered on homosocial rituals in which women had a place only as sexual objects rather than as equal participants.

The Onyx circle's notion of masculinity was also heavily influenced by their view of the commercial music industry in which they made their living. At the Onyx, musicians aspired to a state of masculine independence in which they resisted the conventions of the music business and upheld the value of musical and personal self-expression. This attitude was part of a larger trend in early twentieth-century American labor history. Between 1900 and 1930, "new methods of industrial management undermined the very foundation of craftsmen's functional autonomy."[31] Skilled industrial laborers in the nineteenth century often determined their own working methods and level of output and viewed managerial interference as an affront to their "manliness."[32] By the mid-1920s, however, Taylorist systems of "enforced standardization," in which workers' time and activities were systematically determined and rigorously monitored, "had found favor in almost every industry."[33] Workers responded to this development both by organizing major "control strikes" and by employing less visible tactics of shop-floor resistance, such as intentional slowdowns.[34] Although the musicians who congregated at the Onyx were employed in radio and recording studios rather than in factories, they faced a similar increase in standardization as workers in the new "capitalist culture industries," which, "unlike the cultural institutions of the nineteenth century, were built on profit, not taste."[35] These industries, in the words of C. Wright Mills, required a "stable of cultural workmen" "who bec[a]me the rank-and-file . . . of the commercially established cultural apparatus" and were expected to create a consistent product rather than to innovate.[36] Musicians in New York reacted to new labor conditions in ways similar to those of workers in other industries, both through the formally organized campaigns of AFM Local 802 and with more subtle subversions of studio discipline.[37] In this conflict between musicians and the culture industry, the Onyx played a role similar to that of other workingmen's saloons, where industrial workers "asserted their bid for independence and their right to spend their time and money as they pleased, without attempts by employers, wives, or others to restrain or reform them."[38]

To examine the significance of the Onyx in the lives of professional musicians, we must rely largely on after-the-fact recollections, which even by the mid-1930s were often cast in nostalgic, glorified terms that pitted the carefree Onyx against the repressive music industry. Samuel Charters sums up the prevailing contempt for "commercial" music in such accounts when he states that "during the first years of the Depression, while the great Harlem bands were developing the new swing styles and the Harlem musicians were reaching new levels of technical virtuosity, the white musicians around Times Square were spending more and more of their time in a dreary round of studio recording dates and network

programs." The musicians who escaped nightly to the Onyx played during the day formulaic stock arrangements of popular melodies in studio
groups such as the Broadway Bellhops and the Ipana Troubadours. Studio
jobs had many advantages; they paid well, and certainly many musicians
enjoyed performing with other skilled professionals for a large audience.
Most recollections of studio work, however, emphasize the inflexible arrangements and tedious schedule. Benny Goodman, one of the busiest of
the studio musicians, remembered that "a recognized hot man" (in other
words, a jazz musician) often "went in for that sort of work because he
made good dough and got steady work around the studios. But whenever
you met him you could tell that the work bored the pants off him, and I
have seen more than a few fellows crack up for this one reason."[39]

These "crack-ups" sometimes took the form of willfully unprofessional
or irreverent misbehavior in the studio. For example, Manny Klein, a studio freelancer and Onyx regular in the early 1930s, once put an unfamiliar mouthpiece into the trumpet of his friend Charlie Margulis so that
he would play poorly. In another incident, a radio producer and a group
of musicians including Klein conspired to turn the studio clock ahead
so that bandleader Richard Himber would begin the band's performance
early. They then played the introduction to the show as badly as possible,
much to the horror of Himber, who believed that they were already on
the air.[40] The "mistakes" that supposedly preceded the creation of *Onyx
Club Revue* might well have been intentional attempts to sabotage the
"corny waltz" that the musicians were obligated to play.[41] These mild examples of workers' resistance exemplify the "hot man's" disregard both
for the music that was being played in the studios and for the highly
structured labor system of studio work.

The Onyx Club's loyal patrons, in contrast, remembered the club as the
antidote to the studio, as a place where spontaneity and self-expression
were the norm; or, as one of its earliest chroniclers put it, as an "oasis of
swing."[42] Although not all of the patrons of the Onyx were musicians,
the club's illicit nature contributed to its reputation as an exclusive spot
where an intimate circle of musicians could play and interact freely
without the limitations imposed by a commercial audience. Paul Douglas
remembered that nonmusicians were accepted only grudgingly at the
Onyx: "your early swing fans, the alligators, were tolerated by the musicians because they knew their place, and by Helbock because they paid
well to worship."[43] Benny Goodman recalled that as late as September
1933, only a few months before the original Onyx closed, the club was
"strictly a musicians' spot, before the general public had gotten around

to it." [44] Publicist and *Down Beat* columnist Jack Egan wrote that "since the clientele at the Onyx consisted of musicians practically exclusively, they all felt at ease and never had fear of being criticized by what is commonly referred to as 'the public,' who just don't understand but like to comment anyway." [45] Douglas provides a vivid, but typical, recollection of the role of the Onyx in the lives of these musicians.

To understand the incubation of swing in the Onyx, you must understand, as far as it's humanly possible, the cats themselves. Whereas the milkman works while you sleep, the musician works while you play. All night and most of the day he's been toiling, taking direction, repeating the same bars of music. Essentially a poet, a bellyaching soul seeking expression and release from those stock arrangements in five flats, he's got to go where somebody understands him—the Onyx—where he has a chance to open his heart and blow his brains out. He always knows better than the leaders how music should be played, and here, in the company of his peers, the blower, pounder, or scraper sits in around Helbock's piano, and takes off. He gives out music with all the honesty he knows—happy music—swing music—Jam.[46]

These accounts are grounded in the idea that commercialism is the antithesis of authentic personal expression and that the purest music making, in this case represented by informal improvising, takes place only outside the strictures of the culture industry. Douglas, for example, upholds romantic conceptions of the self-expressive artist—the musician as a "poet" who needs to "open his heart"—while also valorizing vernacular informality and earthiness—the musician as a "blower, pounder, or scraper" who "blow[s] his brains out" while crowded casually around a humble piano. These ideas of authenticity are defined against mainstream commercial values, represented in Egan's discussion by the philistine public and in Douglas's by the strict leaders and "stock arrangements" of studio work.

Although Douglas and Egan were publicists and promoters of swing rather than musicians themselves, similar values had long been held by many of the musicians who gathered at the Onyx. As historian Burton Peretti illustrates, "white Chicago jazz musicians" in the 1920s, such as Bud Freeman, "sported attitudes and manners combining intellect, extravagance, and an experimental sensibility." [47] This group of musicians took an active interest in such modernist expressions as the writing of Ernest Hemingway and H. L. Mencken, the painting of Paul Cézanne, and the compositions of Igor Stravinsky, Maurice Ravel, and Gustav Holst.

Around the same time, Hoagy Carmichael and his friends in Blooming-ton, Indiana, experimented similarly with a kind of homespun modern-ism that manifested itself in "nonsensical conversation" and "eccentric group behavior." Such musicians viewed their identification with avant-garde movements as akin to their attraction to jazz, with both forming part of a larger rejection of mainstream American culture. As Peretti writes, "their interest in jazz was mixed with a desire to think and act differently."[48] Such attitudes were an important source of the Onyx crowd's resistance to the values of the commercial music industry.

As *Onyx Club Revue* reveals, however, these musicians by no means al-ways presented themselves as serious modern artists. The record begins with a brass fanfare with no apparent meter or tonal center, played in unison but out of tune and with an intentionally sour timbre. Victor Young irrelevantly yells, "Hello, Fred! . . . Hello, Joe!" and then, in a sten-torian parody of a radio announcer, proclaims, "The Onyx Club Revue!" Between each of his pronouncements, the horns interject seemingly ran-dom chords. After a four-bar introduction, the band begins its "corny waltz," an unexceptional melody in a conventional key (A-flat major) and form (ABA.) As Manny Klein later pointed out, the band plays as "flat as first-grade students," and guitarist Carl Kress belches into the microphone at the end of each phrase of the A section.[49] The B section features a de-liberately out-of-tune, badly phrased eight-bar trombone solo by Tommy Dorsey, followed by four bars of what sounds like a kazoo or perhaps a comb and then four more bars of Dorsey's trombone. After a four-bar modulation to F major, singer Will Osborne begins the second chorus of the waltz, in a nasal style intended to poke fun at popular crooner Rudy Vallee.[50] His mock-sentimental drinking song celebrates the Onyx: "Have a little drink on me, my boy / Drinks you have on me will surely bring you joy / Love will be the way it used to be / At the Onyx Club with me / Tom and Jim / And Manny too / They wind up playin' blues for you." At this point, halfway through the B section of the waltz, the band launches suddenly into a raucous version of *St. Louis Blues,* in an unexpected new key (G minor) and new meter (4/4). This brief interlude showcases the po-lyphony (a term referring to music in which multiple distinct melodies are performed simultaneously) that is characteristic of early New Orleans jazz. Manny Klein and Tommy Dorsey aggressively growl on trumpet and trombone, respectively, while clarinetist Jimmy Dorsey bends pitches in the high register in an exaggerated imitation of traditional New Orleans clarinet style. After four bars of this swinging reference to jazz tradition, Osborne mutters, "Oh, boy, what stuff," and the band returns to F major and 3/4 time for the final A section of the chorus, with Osborne singing, "So have a little drink on me, my boy / At the Onyx Club with me." At the end of this chorus, a modulation to G major sets up the coda, an instrumental version of the waltz's A section during which members of the band can be heard laughing. After the music ends, Osborne facetiously says, "You made a mistake!" to the musicians.

Onyx Club Revue draws on the irreverent humor of the bachelor subculture to satirize mainstream popular music. The performance's sophomoric, insider jokes, its references to drinking, and its mockery of crooners such as Vallee, who were often criticized at the time as "effeminate," all reflect the Onyx Club group's immersion in the masculine norms of saloon culture.[51] Moreover, *Onyx Club Revue* vividly reveals the musicians' low regard for the material that they performed on a daily basis in the studios. *Onyx Club Revue* demonstrates a standard of masculine behavior, both personal and musical, based around resistance to the perceived mediocrity and sentimentality of the commercial music industry.

Playing Black   The values of the Onyx Club circle also were closely linked to issues of race. In *Onyx Club Revue,* a moment that is particularly charged with racial significance is the surprising interpolation of *St. Louis Blues* into a nonswinging waltz. The musicians' overenthusiastic performance of the blues can easily be read as parody, but it is also revealing of their sense of their own musical allegiances. The animation and excitement that the band displays in this passage, contrasted with their lethargic, contemptuous reading of the waltz, implies that the blues engages their interests and perhaps represents their collective identity in a way that the waltz does not.[52] What did it mean for a group of insouciant white musicians to invoke *St. Louis Blues* in 1933? The blues had been a powerful symbol of black musicality in the imagination of white musicians and audiences since at least 1920, when Harlem singer Mamie Smith sparked a national "craze" for the genre. *St. Louis Blues* was associated with W. C. Handy, one of the most widely known African American composers of the era. Furthermore, the performance of *St. Louis Blues* in *Onyx Club Revue* appears to emulate specific black musicians. The polyphonic improvising of Klein and the Dorseys, for example, derives fundamentally from the music of black New Orleans bands such as King Oliver's. A more immediate source might have been Louis Armstrong's 1929 recording of *St. Louis Blues,* in which trumpeter Red Allen and trombonist J. C. Higginbotham improvise polyphonically over the tune's minor strain. Klein's growling timbre on trumpet mimics the style of African American trumpeters such as Bubber Miley, who was featured with Duke Ellington at Harlem's Cotton Club in the early 1930s and had worked with Venuti and the Dorsey brothers at a 1930 recording session. Ellington's white critics and audiences at the time heard this growling sound as a racial signifier, referring to it as "jungle music." Although it is difficult to draw precise conclusions from this brief four-bar passage, a likely interpretation suggests that these musicians construed emulation of black styles as an oppositional practice that flouted the restrictions of the music industry, represented here by the waltz.[53]

Another view of the Onyx Club musicians' interest in African American musical practices is provided by two studio recordings whose titles mention Harlem: Irving Mills and His Hotsy Totsy Gang's *Deep Harlem* (1930) and the Dorsey Brothers Orchestra's *Old Man Harlem* (1933).[54] These titles, with their references to New York's best-known African American neighborhood, suggest that the performers were self-consciously attempting to evoke images of black life or perhaps were making overt efforts to imitate black musicians. *Deep Harlem,* performed by a ten-piece band including Onyx club regulars Benny Goodman, Jack Teagarden, and Joe Venuti, comprises three distinct sections with contrasting tempi and forms, suggesting that it was intended as programmatic listening music rather than as a dance arrangement.[55] The overall form of the performance can be plotted as ABCC'A'. The A section is a medium-tempo blues in which the last four bars repeat to produce a sixteen-bar form. Here, Bix Beiderbecke's cornet states the melody while the rest of the band plays firmly on every beat. This accompaniment style was likely derived from African American musicians; compare, for example, the first and last choruses of Louis Armstrong's celebrated *West End Blues* (1928), during which pianist Earl Hines and banjoist Mancy Carr similarly play chords metronomically on every beat.[56] The B section is a sixteen-bar minor passage in the same tempo, in which Goodman plays a growling clarinet solo reminiscent of New Orleans performers and perhaps also of Ellington's "jungle style." [57] The C section consists of a faster twelve-bar blues with a four-bar introduction; the last four bars are played in half time (in other words, at half the speed of the rest of the section) with Beiderbecke's trumpet carrying the melody. This rhythmic shift recalls Louis Armstrong's *Muggles* (1928), in which Armstrong similarly ends a fast blues chorus with four bars of half time.[58] The stylistic diversity found in this titillating glimpse of "deepest Harlem" allowed these musicians to display their abilities in a variety of African American jazz idioms. *Old Man Harlem,* recorded three years later, is less eclectic but still demonstrates a range of approaches toward African American musical styles. The tune, composed by Rudy Vallee and Hoagy Carmichael, has the thirty-two-bar, AABA form that was standard for pop tunes at the time and a jaunty major-key melody that contrasts with the somber blues of *Deep Harlem*. The arrangement sometimes makes reference to older jazz styles but is often self-consciously "modern." In the third chorus, for example, a "hot" clarinet solo is backed with rapidly picked guitar chords that seem intended to imitate a banjo, both references to New Orleans practice. At other points, however, the band moves away from accenting the first and third beats of each four-beat measure—the two-beat rhythm typical of both New Orleans jazz and popular "fox-trots"—and into a swinging four-beat rhythm that stresses every beat equally, at the time a novel sound associated with Harlem bands.[59] Like *Deep Harlem, Old Man Harlem* illustrates these white musicians' knowledge of and dedication to black jazz styles and also suggests that they may have understood these styles within the exotic vision of Harlem life held by many white New Yorkers at the time.

It is unlikely, however, that these recordings are representative of what music making was actually like at the Onyx. Although, to my knowledge, no recordings were made inside the Onyx Club itself before the end of Prohibition, firsthand accounts of the club suggest that spontaneous jam sessions constituted most of the musical activity there. Wilder Hobson remembered that "along about five in the afternoon Joe Sullivan or Charley Born [Bourne] or Art Tatum would be playing the piano, but it was all so casual that if you hadn't known they were engaged by the management you might have supposed they had just dropped in and sat down." Sullivan, for example, might improvise on tunes such as his own *Gin Mill Blues* or the pop standard *Three Little Words*. As other musicians began to arrive at the club, each joined in gradually, supporting the others' solos with background figures and sometimes laying out to allow other musicians to play their instrument. Paul Douglas described one late-night session that included many of the Onyx regulars:

By the time Big Tea [Jack Teagarden] had done a hundred and sixty bars, Tommy Dorsey had arrived, and had been handed Tea's slip horn. Manny Klein had Little Tea's [Charlie Teagarden's] trumpet, Karl [*sic*] Kress was fingering McDonough's guitar. The music was still *Three Little Words,* but indelibly trademarked by those playing it. It took half a dozen choruses to get rolling. By mutual consent, each man took the lead, and took the melody apart, developed, embroidered, made it his own. Wherever he went with the music, the others stayed with him, filling in and setting tempo. There was no let-up. It made no difference in the quality of the improvisation that Roy Bargy was at the piano, Bunny Berigan blowing the trumpet, or that Frankie Chase alternated with Bud Freeman on the tenor sax. They're still talking about how Jimmy Dorsey and Benny Goodman tried to blow each other out of the place. Each man the complete master of his instrument, possessing a highly developed imagination, the result was music first for the musicians, then for the world.[60]

This description suggests that musicians at the Onyx were free to play long solo improvisations on a given tune—for example, Jack Teagarden's "hundred and sixty bars" comprise five full choruses of *Three Little Words*. These musicians did not normally have the opportunity to solo at such length in recording or radio studios.[61]

At the same time that the jam session enabled individual expression, it also encouraged musical interaction, as musicians traded instruments, backed up soloists with appropriate riffs, and engaged in friendly rivalry. Douglas, for example, mentioned both competition ("They're still talking about how Jimmy Dorsey and Benny Goodman tried to blow each other out of the place") and cooperation ("Each man had his turn to throw the theme around, while the others made background"). Mimicry sometimes provided a social connection between musicians. In a rare reference to a black musician copying a white musician at the Onyx, Hobson reported that "Charley Born [Bourne] used to imitate not only the music but the manner of a lot of other pianists and I particularly remember the rather rigid weaving of the body which was a dead ringer for Artie Schutt." Playing at the Onyx allowed musicians both to explore their individual creativity and to develop a collective musical identity rooted in mutual cooperation, competition, and imitation.[62]

Although this developing identity was informed by white musicians' imitation of African American musical and social practices, personal interactions among black and white musicians in New York often were discouraged in professional situations or fraught with tension. Segregated employment, which was the norm in radio and recording studios, prevented whites and blacks from working together professionally except in occasional "mixed" recording dates.[63] Some white musicians, such as Bud Freeman, had flouted these conventions by playing informally with black musicians on the South Side of Chicago, and they continued to seek out such opportunities in Harlem, which had become a popular destination in the 1920s for whites interested in African American culture.[64]

Historian Arnold Shaw claims that after the Onyx closed for the night, its patrons would travel as a group to Harlem "to continue jamming and drinking." Freeman recalled, perhaps somewhat defensively, that Harlem "was a marvelous village in those days. You could walk around there at 4:00, 5:00 in the morning and nobody would bother you and word was out that the white musicians were there to hear the music and everything was fine, not that they would have bothered us anyway." African American multi-instrumentalist Benny Carter later claimed that black musicians would "welcome" whites who sat in at Harlem clubs.[65]

It appears, however, that white musicians sometimes were met with suspicion or hostility when they ventured uptown. Carter qualified his statement by explaining that black musicians were "resigned" to racism in the music industry and had a "feeling" that "even the white musicians themselves couldn't do anything about it," which suggests an atmosphere of wary acquiescence rather than warm acceptance. Manny Klein remembered that Harlem had "no white people in those days—no way. If I would drive with my car, they would get mad at me. 'Keep going, you son of a bitch!' Just like that!" Hoagy Carmichael recalled an incident in a "cellar joint" in Harlem in which a "young Negro," annoyed by the stares of Carmichael's white companion, "flicked the contents of a glass of whiskey at her," and only the intercession of black pianist Willie "the Lion" Smith prevented the club from erupting into "mayhem." Saxophonist and bandleader Charlie Barnet stated that although white and black musicians "all had a ball" when they played together in Harlem, few whites actually took part, and that he had "been there when I was the only white guy." Although these recollections may reflect the apprehension and discomfort of some white musicians as much as they do the attitude of blacks, they suggest that white musicians' exposure to black music involved complex negotiations of physical space and social norms rather than uncomplicated meetings across the color line.[66]

This dynamic was reflected at the Prohibition-era Onyx, where black musicians were present only in limited numbers and within the proscribed role of hired performers. Pianists Art Tatum, Willie "the Lion" Smith, and Charlie Bourne appear to have been the only African American musicians who regularly attended the original Onyx. Although it seems that Tatum and Smith initially came to the club as patrons, both eventually became casual employees. Smith remembered that Helbock asked him, "Lion, why don't you stop by every day around five and I'll give you a little salary for your trouble?"[67] According to Herb Shultz, who interviewed Helbock in the 1960s, Tatum was paid "$45 a week and free whiskey" to appear at the Onyx.[68] The Spirits of Rhythm, a black string-and-vocal group, also were paid a salary by Helbock shortly before the repeal of Prohibition.[69] Smith fondly remembered playing with white musicians at the club, but his position as a paid employee, like that of Tatum, Bourne, and the Spirits of Rhythm, differentiated him from the white studio musicians who dropped in to socialize when they were off the job.[70] Even this minimal level of interracial interaction was exceptional for the time; Charlie Barnet argued that Helbock "was very liberally minded" about racial "mixing" compared to the management of the Famous Door, another 52nd Street club.[71] Although interaction and influence between black and white musicians was essential to the music and culture of the Onyx Club, the club was very much a white-dominated environment during Prohibition.

The significance of the jam sessions at the Onyx, then, mainly reflected the specific concerns of the white musicians who controlled the club.[72] Although these sessions demonstrated the influence of African American performers, the Onyx circle's attitudes toward informal music making differed from those of many black musicians.[73] While black jazz musicians in this era, like the white musicians at the Onyx, were influenced by what Eric Porter calls "the artistic ethos of Romanticism, including the ideal of not 'selling out,'" for most this notion "existed side by side with the desire to gain remuneration and respectability through popularity."[74] Historian Scott DeVeaux argues that, in contrast to white musicians, who often saw themselves as "romantic outsiders" who resisted the mainstream, black musicians "had little taste for romanticizing poverty, even in the service of art, and were far less inclined to disparage the virtues of a steady wage."[75] As DeVeaux demonstrates, the Rhythm Club, the major site of jamming by black musicians in Harlem in the 1930s, was also a "clearinghouse for employment" where musicians went to line up jobs.[76] While for the white musicians at the Onyx the jam session was defined in contrast to the working world, for African Americans in Harlem the jam session "was both recreational *and* vocational."[77] The Onyx musicians, then, borrowed selectively from their black models, adopting the camaraderie and musical practices of the jam session while downplaying its original relation to professional concerns.

Indeed, the very degree to which the jam session was associated with black male performers may have contributed to its distinction from commerce in the minds of white musicians. As historian David Roediger argues in his analysis of blackface minstrelsy, white working-class men have often associated black identity with liberation from the discipline

of the industrial workplace.[78] Eric Lott points out that minstrel enact-
ments of the anti-industrial pleasures attributed to African Americans
showcased "an attractive masculinity"; "to put on the cultural forms of
'blackness,'" Lott writes, "was to engage in a complex affair of manly
mimicry."[79] This mimicry often reflected a contradictory relationship to
a stereotypical notion of black male sexuality, which minstrel audiences
saw as both frightening and titillating. Although the white musicians
at the Onyx were not engaged in minstrelsy as such, their imitation of
black musical practices and renunciation of formal labor in a setting
dominated by men demonstrates striking similarities between their jam
sessions and earlier minstrel shows.[80] A disturbing incident remembered
by music publisher Sam Weiss, in which white bandleaders Ben Bernie
and Paul Whiteman bet on the size of African American musician Wilbur
Daniels's penis while the Spirits of Rhythm were at the Onyx, suggests
further that minstrel stereotypes of black masculinity and sexuality
played a role at the club.[81] The racial fantasies prevalent at the Onyx
could survive largely intact because of the job segregation still standard
in New York at the time.[82] Because the white musicians of the Onyx did
not often work formally with black musicians, there were not many situations in which they dealt with blacks professionally, and there were thus
few opportunities for white musicians to perceive African Americans as
fellow professionals engaged in a formal system of labor. To play black,
then, both personally and musically, was a way for the musicians at the
Onyx to assume an identity that was both distinctly masculine and free
from labor restraints.[83]

Imitation of black musicians may also, paradoxically, have played a
role in allowing musicians at the Onyx to construct themselves as white.
The Onyx circle comprised members of a variety of European American
groups, some of which had only recently come to be seen as white eth-
nicities rather than as distinct racial categories.[84] A wave of southern and
eastern European immigrants to the United States that peaked between
1890 and 1920 had led to fierce debates over their racial classification.
Italian Americans such as Joe Venuti and Eddie Lang (born Salvatore
Massaro), for example, were widely regarded as what James R. Barrett and
David Roediger call "inbetween people," those who ranked above African
and Asian Americans but below whites in the racial hierarchy.[85] One illustration of this "inbetween" status was the National Origins Quota
system instituted in 1924, which in effect decreed that Italians were
nonwhite with respect to immigration restrictions but were white for
purposes of naturalization.[86] Similarly, Jewish Americans such as Benny

Goodman and Manny Klein were seen as "inconclusively white" by many Americans in the first decades of the twentieth century.[87] Although racialized views of Italian and Jewish Americans were beginning to be effaced in the popular imagination by the 1930s—historian Matthew Frye Jacobson writes that "increasingly in the 1920s and afterward the landscape of American popular culture was peopled simply by blacks and whites"—these groups were only beginning to be seen as unambiguously white during the heyday of the Onyx Club.[88] As early as the 1830s, minstrelsy's ethnically diverse audiences and performers had seen blackface as a way of asserting a "common whiteness"; Roediger argues that "the simple physical disguise—and elaborate cultural disguise—of blacking up served to emphasize that those on stage were really white and that whiteness really mattered."[89] In the era of the Onyx Club, a similar dynamic was perhaps most visible in the 1927 film *The Jazz Singer*, in which the Jewish cantor Jakie Rabinowitz transforms into vaudevillian Jack Robin as "blackface propels him above both his father and African Americans into the American melting pot."[90] Although the musicians at the Onyx were emulating the craft of skilled African American performers rather than enacting the generic racial stereotypes of minstrelsy, their adoption of black musical practices similarly highlighted through contrast their shared whiteness.[91] If the Onyx circle's representations and imitations of African American music were benign in comparison to their blackface precedents, they nonetheless may have served a similar function in allowing musicians to consolidate a white identity.

"Then for the World"　The pivotal role that many members of the Onyx circle went on to play in jazz history was the result of their ambivalence toward the anticommercial attitudes espoused in the club. A realistic assessment of these musicians suggests that market interests always tempered their pursuit of what they deemed uncorrupted music. Although the Onyx Club was to some extent a retreat from the music industry, it was at times also the site of musicians' business activities, such as finding jobs.[92] Sometime relatively soon after its opening, the Onyx itself became a place of employment for at least a few musicians, as Joe Helbock began to hire solo pianists including Tatum, Smith, Bourne, and Sullivan. Industry figures such as "executives" and "arrangers" also were present at the Onyx. Jack Egan asserted that the Onyx was a focal point for discovering new "talent" and that "hot licks thrown off in a careless moment during a jam session would be jotted down on a scrap of paper and a month later come out as the theme of a smash hit song."[93] Paul Douglas's characterization of Onyx Club jam sessions as "music first for the musicians, then for the world" similarly implies that even the most esoteric musical gestures eventually reached a larger public, a process that Douglas himself aided with his radio broadcasts and magazine articles. Moreover, the speakeasy had at least some nonmusician patrons who came to listen, which indicates both that the Onyx was not entirely insular and that musicians were to some extent playing for an audience even in the club.[94] Outside the Onyx, these musicians were also enmeshed in the practices of the commercial music industry. For all its anarchic energy, *Onyx Club Revue* was not truly an effective example of workers' resistance but only a brief, rebellious digression at a session that produced a series of conventional pop records. It is not reasonable to expect that these musicians would have risked lucrative careers for an insider idea of authentic jazz that at first seemed to have little commercial viability outside the confines of the Onyx Club.

Nonetheless, the standards of musical integrity prevalent at the Onyx have since become basic tenets of much jazz criticism.[95] Although the commercial music industry was instrumental in establishing the levels of technical skill that jazz musicians employed at the Onyx and elsewhere, the music of the studios has largely been construed as contrary to the jazz tradition. When Samuel Charters, for example, writes that "musicians like Goodman, [Red] Nichols, and the Dorseys were 'business' musicians more than they were jazz musicians. Music was their profession, and they played the jobs that offered the highest salary," he invokes a conceptual distinction between "business" and "jazz" that these very musicians were involved in creating.[96] If such distinctions were to become commonplace in jazz discourse, they were nonetheless difficult to maintain on 52nd Street, where anticommercial rhetoric and the commercial market coexisted in uneasy proximity. As the first legal jazz clubs appeared on the street, their increasing popularity with the general public forced the Onyx Club circle to confront the world of popular entertainment.

Chapter Two **Let's Have a Jubilee** 52nd Street Goes Commercial

The Onyx Club's status as an exclusive hideaway for musicians was threatened by the repeal of Prohibition in December 1933, which allowed 52nd Street's drinking establishments to come into the open as legally operated clubs and restaurants.[1] During the following two years, the street transformed from a row of furtive speakeasies into a heavily advertised and publicized nightclub district, known for such attractions as the 21 Club's fine cuisine and Leon & Eddie's lively stage revues as well as for improvised jazz. By the end of 1935, there were three major jazz venues on 52nd Street—the Onyx, the Famous Door, and the Hickory House—as well as other clubs, such as Leon & Eddie's, that occasionally featured jazz. Although musicians continued to seek a place on the street to call their own, their attempts at insularity were repeatedly thwarted by the general public's increasing interest in swing music. 52nd Street's new audience was attracted to jazz by many of the same traits that had appealed to the Onyx Club's circle of musicians—the music's tantalizing blurring of racial categories, its seeming resistance to standard rules of decorum, and its ability to enliven contemporary pop tunes with improvisation and swinging rhythm. Moreover, like the musicians, this audience was willing to sit and listen to the music rather than dance.[2] Although this public attention created new opportunities for musicians, who could now earn a living on 52nd Street itself as well as in nearby studios, it also threatened to make the street part of the mainstream entertainment industry that its jazz musicians had originally aspired to resist. The 52nd Street jazz scene had come to an ironic juncture at which musical practices initially inspired by anticommercial attitudes were themselves becoming marketable commodities. The growing popularity of jazz on 52nd Street was one catalyst of the national craze for swing that began around 1935, which exposed a mass audience to the image of "hot" musicians who seemed to express themselves with an abandon that transcended conventional norms of musical performance. On New Year's Day 1936, *Variety* reported that "West 52d street, New York, is the capital of the swing world."[3]

This chapter tells the stories of several musicians who helped bring public attention to 52nd Street between 1934 and 1936. First, I address the Spirits of Rhythm, the first African American group to appear on the street, and their manager, white singer and promoter Red McKenzie. The relationship between the band and their manager exemplifies the uneasy racial dynamic prevalent on the street, where white musicians and audiences demonstrated respect for the talents of black musicians but also continued to uphold stereotypes of black spontaneity and irrationality. Next, I turn to Louis Prima and Wingy Manone, two charismatic Italian American trumpeters whose perceived transgressions of conventional racial boundaries, as well as their infectious blend of New Orleans jazz and contemporary popular music, attracted large audiences to the Famous Door and the Hickory House. Finally, I discuss trombonist Mike Riley and trumpeter Ed Farley, white musicians whose combination of jazz and comedy brought them national fame and demonstrated that the irreverent anticommercialism of 52nd Street's musicians' circle could readily become the basis of commercially successful entertainment. As these performers drew ever-larger crowds to 52nd Street, they popularized not only improvised jazz but also the notions of natural black musicianship and anticommercial integrity that had motivated the street's first musicians. Moreover, the musicians discussed in this chapter helped to create a public conception of 52nd Street as a uniquely vibrant site of spontaneous musical performances, interracial interaction, and uninhibited personal expression, an image that continued to inform 52nd Street's audiences and performers throughout the street's tenure as a center for jazz.

"Guitar, Suitcase, and 3 Tipples": The Spirits of Rhythm and Red McKenzie

Although in its early years the 52nd Street jazz scene was dominated by white performers, the first jazz group that could be openly marketed on the street was comprised of black musicians. Sometime in the fall of 1933, Joe Helbock hired the first ensemble to perform for pay at the Onyx: the Spirits of Rhythm, a quintet of African American musicians managed by white singer and promoter Red McKenzie. The Spirits of Rhythm employed a novel combination of instruments including a guitar (played by Teddy Bunn); three tiples, or small lutes with five courses of two strings each (played by Wilbur Daniels, Douglas Daniels, and Leo Watson); and a suitcase brushed with whisk brooms (played by Virgil Scoggins). They had begun working as a quartet in St. Louis in 1927 and had already attracted some attention for their appearances with white bandleader Ben Bernie, during which they were billed as the Sepia Nephews. McKenzie was a well-known figure in the white musicians' fraternity who had been involved in the world of popular music for almost ten years by 1933. After rising to prominence in the 1920s as a member of the Mound City Blue Blowers, a "novelty" group in which he played a comb and tissue paper, McKenzie had gone on to organize jazz record dates in which prominent musicians participated. The Spirits of Rhythm, along with intermission act Art Tatum, remained on the bill when Joe Helbock opened the legitimate Onyx at 72 West 52nd Street in February 1934.[4]

The Spirits of Rhythm's lively performances were well suited for the Onyx Club, where white musicians, as we have seen, connected black music with ideals of spontaneity and anticommercialism. Recordings that the Spirits made between September and December 1933, around the time that they were getting started at the Onyx, include interpretations of pop standards such as *Nobody's Sweetheart* and *I Got Rhythm* in which the group balances sophisticated vocal arrangements with energetic improvisation and showcases the distinctive light timbre of the guitar and tiples.[5] In each recording, the musicians establish a swinging four-beat rhythm through strums on the tiples and guitar, the light beat of Scoggins's whisk brooms, and the walking bass lines of Wilson Myers, who eventually became the sixth Spirit.[6] The typical features of the Spirits' style are in evidence in their October 24, 1933 recording of *I Got Rhythm*. After a fourteen-bar introduction during which a solo tiple states the A section of Gershwin's melody and establishes the key of A major, the first chorus features one of the Daniels brothers singing the melody while the other singers back him up with a scatted riff, or short repeated melody, during the A section and softly hummed chords during the bridge.[7] The second chorus features a tiple solo, likely by Douglas Daniels, the most notable feature of which is a quotation from the 1926 pop song *Horses,* a snippet famously associated with the words "crazy over horses" that features a repeated octave leap on the tonic.[8] The third chorus consists of a scat vocal by Leo Watson, whose warm timbre and brassy articulation suggest the sound of a trombone. The fourth chorus is a guitar solo by Teddy Bunn, whose bluesy style features bent strings and frequently plays on the relationship between the minor and major third degree of the scale. In the fifth and final chorus, Bunn's guitar solo continues for the first sixteen bars, punctuated by a sung riff. During the bridge, Daniels enters to sing the melody while the other Spirits hum in the background. In the final eight bars, Bunn's solo returns, and the performance slows for a final phrase sung in harmony by the group. Other recordings made by the Spirits of Rhythm in late 1933 feature a similar blend of swinging rhythm, skillful vocal harmonies, and improvised scat, tiple, and guitar solos.

Although these recordings were made in a studio rather than at the Onyx, it seems likely that the group's blend of improvisatory creativity and precisely arranged vocal harmonies was heard at the club as well. The band's tiny tiples and Virgil Scoggins's use of a suitcase instead of a drum kit gave their performances an informal appearance, as if the musicians could be making this music in the course of their everyday activities. This was a perception perhaps encouraged by the band's very name, which seems to reinforce racial stereotypes by locating rhythm as an essential, transcendent property of the musicians. Leo Watson's adept scat singing attracted particular attention in the jazz press. *Metronome* (actually referring to Teddy Bunn, but almost certainly meaning Watson) reported that he "gives a clever vocal imitation of the trombone and also spices his vocals with such as 'Flang, flang, a doodle, prrr a dacky, dacky and tee oo, di da da, gaw gaw gaw,' etc." Other critics cited Watson's tendency to free-associate, incorporating quotes from other songs and verbal phrases related in startling ways to the song on which he was improvising.[9]

At the Onyx, the group's musical strengths were complemented by the dynamic and humorous stage presence of Watson, whose manic performances led one writer to remember him as "one of the most amazing characters you've ever heard." Watson's tendency to "jump up almost any old time and shout strange riffs, holding his Ukelele [i.e., tiple] as if it were a trombone" drew particular attention from several commentators. Teddy Bunn also remembered engaging in physical feats while performing, such as "throwing my guitar up in the air and bringing it back and playing." These humorous stunts were complemented by the group's irreverent approach toward its repertoire. Jazz critic Otis Ferguson wrote in a 1941 profile that Bunn and Watson "collaborate in burlesquing all but the song out of music" and that "they sing a few blues in a straight way, but most of the numbers they kid." [10]

The obvious spontaneity and supposed irrationality of Watson's musical style and comic persona sometimes led white observers to resort to racist language in describing him. Ferguson, for example, ostensibly complimented Watson's "furious ape approach," while writer Carlton Brown claimed in 1944 that Watson "looked like Gargantua and sang like an inspired and articulate gorilla who had been reared in a musical atmosphere." These impressions are informed both by minstrel stereotypes of instinctive black creativity and by an element of fear and repulsion, evident in the descriptions of Watson as a menacing gorilla. This offensive imagery can be traced back to the early 1900s, when racist tracts such as Charles Carroll's *The Negro a Beast* (1900) "describ[ed] the Negro as literally an ape rather than a human being" and linked this idea to fears of miscegenation and what was believed to be an uncontrollable, violent black sexuality; this notion remained current throughout the early part of the century through depictions of bestial blacks like those in D. W. Griffith's 1915 film *The Birth of a Nation*. A less direct but even more spectacular dramatization of such fears, the spectacle of the rampaging King Kong abducting a white woman as he wreaks havoc on midtown Manhattan, first terrified and titillated moviegoers in 1933, the same year in which the Spirits of Rhythm first appeared at the Onyx. The incident, cited in chapter 1, in which white musicians speculated about the size of Wilbur Daniels's penis indicates that images of excessive black sexuality informed the group's reception in the club itself as well as in print. Although the Spirits' white reviewers largely viewed themselves as racial liberals who did not subscribe consciously to racist dogma, they were nonetheless affected by the derogatory images of blacks that entered into everyday discourse at this time. [11]

On the other hand, white musicians and critics sometimes made a point of describing the Spirits of Rhythm as talented individuals, not simply as representatives of a racial type. While *Down Beat*'s description of Virgil Scoggins—"You should see that boy do his stuff with those whiskbrooms. Phew, does he swish those gadgets"—is condescending in its tone, it is also sincere in its praise of Scoggins's ability. Similarly, the aforementioned *Metronome* review may emphasize the perceived irrationality of Watson's scat syllables, but it also acknowledges his "clever" mimicry of trombone style and notes that "the Spirits make their own arrangements," which implies an awareness that the group's performances were not simply spontaneous outpourings. Other reviews predictably

emphasized the group's rhythmic style, again in ways that seem to com-
bine racial stereotypes with genuine respect. White lyricist and Onyx
customer Johnny Mercer remembered that the Spirits of Rhythm had a
musical influence on him and composer Bernie Hanighen: "The middle
part of 'My Old Man' [by Mercer and Hanighen] is written around a riff
developed by the Spirits of Rhythm. . . . I think Bernie built 'Man' on Leo
Watson's style of singing. The words just went along." The sheet music
for *My Old Man* includes a composed scat break ("With a flanky danky
doodle and a umgaga") that seems to mimic Watson's style. The Spirits of
Rhythm's recording of *My Old Man,* made on December 6, 1933, includes
a reference to the Onyx Club (a substitution for the better-known Cotton
Club, to which the sheet music refers), as well as an original scat break
by Watson in place of Mercer and Hanighen's composed version. White
musicians' and critics' response to the Spirits of Rhythm was a double-
edged one that allowed them to indulge in liberating and titillating stereotypes of blackness while also genuinely respecting and learning from
the group's musicianship.[12]

At the Onyx, this complex racial dynamic was epitomized by the relationship between the Spirits of Rhythm and their manager Red McKenzie.
McKenzie appears to have held an ambivalent view of African American
musicians that pitted a romantic image of black creativity against racist condescension. A 1933 *Metronome* article quotes McKenzie describing
a conversion experience when he heard black musicians in New Orleans
in the 1920s: "Those jigahoos in New Orleans had something—I mean, a
different something about the way they played, and I hustled my lean
saddle ass to all those joints down there to get the swing of it. I'd fool
round with a comb a little, and the blues those spades put in my ear was
great stuff for it. I learned to play 'em all on a comb, and the first thing
I knew I was liking blues more than the horses." Here, McKenzie tells a
kind of origin myth that links his music to the authenticity of black New
Orleans while he simultaneously distances himself from his black role
models with slurs like "jigahoo" and "spade." Other accounts of McKenzie
create a similarly contradictory picture. White clarinetist Mezz Mezzrow,
who himself aspired to adopt an African American identity, wrote that
McKenzie "g[ave] you kind of a Southern-gangster impression because
he tried to use Negro colloquialisms," but Mezzrow also claimed that
McKenzie "just wasn't steeped in the real colored man's [musical] idiom,
like some of us had started out to be." Although McKenzie's involvement
in early interracial recording sessions suggests a willingness to work

with African Americans, his comments quoted here suggest that he may have had mixed feelings about his black collaborators.[13]

There are hints that McKenzie's conflicted attitudes about race had an impact on the Spirits of Rhythm. In 1977, Spirits guitarist Teddy Bunn told interviewer Chuck Rosenberg that McKenzie was "all right with us," but Bunn added that "we could tell, you know, about him being prejudiced, he was, from that town he was from. St. Louis, you know. . . . That's a very prejudiced town, because I worked there too, with the Spirits." Although Bunn's comments are vague, perhaps because he was reluctant to discuss racial issues with a white interviewer, he seems to suggest that even if McKenzie was not explicitly racist, his prejudices were nonetheless apparent to the group. Bunn explained that the Spirits responded stoically to McKenzie's "attitude": "Well, we done our sessions, you know, and got it over with, and that was it." Despite Bunn's casual dismissal of McKenzie, it is clear that the latter's professional clout, as a well-known promoter within the white jazz world, greatly outweighed that of the Spirits of Rhythm. For example, a laudatory 1934 *Metronome* profile of McKenzie struck a note of paternalist condescension toward the Spirits, explaining that "at the present time [McKenzie] is bending his every effort to train and assist the famous Nephews, a quintet of colored boys just chuck full of rhythm, appearing nightly at the Onyx Club."[14]

This "assistance" at times involved McKenzie performing with the Spirits of Rhythm. Pianist Ram Ramirez later remembered that McKenzie sang with the group at the Onyx, although most sources do not mention this. They did, however, collaborate in the recording studio, and a group of four sides recorded on September 11, 1934, in which the Spirits of Rhythm back up McKenzie's lead vocals, provide an intriguing glimpse into the relationship between the band and their manager. On most of the recordings, including *'Way Down Yonder in New Orleans* and *I've Got the World on a String,* McKenzie simply takes the place of lead singer Doug Daniels on the first chorus, stating the melody in a fairly straightforward way but also taking some liberties with time and phrasing. In the background, the Spirits of Rhythm hum in harmony. At first, the recordings seem to feature a white star supported unobtrusively by black subordinates. After McKenzie's vocal choruses, however, tiple, guitar and scat solos showcase the creativity of the Spirits of Rhythm. While the improvised ingenuity of these solos is impressive, the solos might also have reinforced conventional notions of black musicianship for some listeners through the juxtaposition of McKenzie's mastery of the composed melody and the Spirits' spontaneity. During *From Monday On,* however, this dynamic is subverted in a striking way. After singing the first chorus straight, McKenzie returns in the third to perform an improvised scat solo. Because this solo occupies exactly the same position in the performance that Leo Watson's scatting usually does, and because McKenzie rarely scatted on record, it seems clear that he is taking this opportunity to imitate Watson. By implicitly acknowledging Watson as a skilled performer worthy of emulation, McKenzie takes on a subservient role, openly learning from the very musicians whom he supposedly "train[ed] and assist[ed]." This series of recordings demonstrates that the balance of power among these musicians could take contradictory forms simultaneously: although McKenzie was the superior of the Spirits of Rhythm in professional terms, he also could become their student in musical matters.[15]

The blend of high-spirited comedy and swinging music that the Spirits of Rhythm brought to the Onyx attracted great popular attention, as, to a lesser extent, did their intermission act, Art Tatum. Tatum, whose virtuosic performances do not appear to have involved comedy or extramusical showmanship, presented a very different figure than the Spirits' ebullient Leo Watson, and the two brought different audiences to the club. Sam Weiss told Arnold Shaw that "because they were such good entertainers, the Spirits attracted the squares. . . . The musicians and jazz critics came to hear Art Tatum. The Spirits were a noisy bunch like the crowds they drew. Tatum had to be heard." This split was perhaps not as well defined as Weiss suggests—musicians and critics, as we have seen, sometimes demonstrated respect for the musicianship of the Spirits of Rhythm as well as that of Tatum. It is significant, nonetheless, that the Spirits of Rhythm were the first group to draw "squares" to the Onyx. For the first time, the Onyx began to seem inhospitable to the white musicians' circle that had first patronized it. Bandleader Lennie Hayton remembered that the atmosphere changed after "the Onyx moved downstairs [i.e., to the legal club at 72 West 52nd Street] and brought in the Spirits of Rhythm. By the time we got to the club after our radio shows, the Spirits had the place jammed. Even if you got in, it was no place to unwind and relax." Violinist Harry Bluestone gave a similar account: "It was a hangup . . . to get a table and, sometimes, just to get in." As Arnold Shaw points out, in late 1934 and early 1935, white studio musicians began to gather at other clubs, such as the Jam Club on 48th Street and the Casino Deluxe at 35 West 52nd, in the hope of finding a new place to play and relax. This conflict between "square" members of the general public and the insular group of musicians who frequented the Onyx was to become increasingly tense by the end of 1935 as the club became more and more popular.[16]

"What's on Your Mind There, Creole?" Louis Prima, Wingy Manone, and the Famous Door

In the meantime, however, musicians reacted to the influx of "squares" at the Onyx by founding another club of their own: the Famous Door. Unlike the Onyx, the Famous Door was originally owned and operated by musicians. A group of white studio musicians led by Lennie Hayton and his manager Jack Colt took up a collection in order to start a club, and they bought out the lease of the Casino Deluxe, a club briefly located at 35 West 52nd Street in early 1935.[17] On February 28, 1935, the night before the Famous Door opened, the Onyx Club burned to the ground.[18] The Famous Door thus inherited the Onyx's status as the only jazz club on the block beginning March 1, and the Onyx's clientele of musicians gravitated to it; soon after the new club's opening, *Down Beat* reported that "since the burning of the Onyx Club, the Famous Door is now one of the favorite spots of the musicians about town." [19]

The musicians' interest in the Famous Door was due in part to its featured performer: as *Down Beat* mentioned, "the band in this new spot is Louis Prima, a swing combination." [20] Although trumpeter and singer Prima is best known today for the rollicking fusion of rock 'n' roll, jazz, and comedy that made him a staple of the Las Vegas lounge scene in the late 1950s, he began his career immersed in the New Orleans jazz tradition that fascinated 52nd Street's original community of musicians. Born in New Orleans in 1910, Prima worked professionally there for several years before moving to New York in 1934 at the request of "sweet" bandleader Guy Lombardo; shortly thereafter, he was hired to work at the Famous Door.[21] In many ways, Prima's performances perpetuated the ideas of authentic jazz that had been prevalent at the Onyx Club. His music placed heavy emphasis on improvisation, spontaneity, and imitation of African American musical practices. In his persona as well as in his music, he evoked a tantalizing sense of racial hybridity. Furthermore, his status as featured performer at an exclusive musicians' club appeared to set Prima apart from run-of-the-mill commercial entertainment. Nonetheless, Prima became a commercial success, demonstrating that the racial fantasies and freewheeling musical style prized within 52nd Street's musicians' circle could also attract a mass audience.

The music that Prima played at the Famous Door, with a quintet consisting of his own trumpet along with clarinet, piano, bass, and guitar, combined the Tin Pan Alley songs of the day with traits of the traditional jazz associated with his hometown. Recordings made between September 1934 and July 1935 feature a septet or sextet (billed as "Louis Prima and His New Orleans Gang") playing mainly thirty-two-bar popular tunes in a form that jazz historian Richard Sudhalter describes as "more or less straightforward melody chorus, Prima vocal . . . , solos by a sideman or two, then the leader's trumpet back for the big finale." While the opening chorus is sometimes played homophonically (in other words, with all of the melodic instruments moving together in the same rhythm) by trumpet, clarinet, and (when present) trombone, the "big finale" is often jammed polyphonically in New Orleans style. Prima's vocal choruses often involve scat improvisation, and his fellow instrumental soloists include clarinetist Pee Wee Russell and guitarist Garry McAdams from the Famous Door quintet as well as guests such as tenor saxophonist Eddie Miller. The rhythm section (supplemented with a drummer for the recordings) plays mostly in a swinging four-beat style. The minimal arrangements include some devices associated with New Orleans jazz, such as stop time, in which the band plays only on selected beats, leaving spaces for the soloist to fill (as during Prima's trumpet solo on *In a Little Gypsy Tea Room.*) On the other hand, the band also uses techniques associated with contemporary big-band jazz, such as repeated riffs (as in the final eight bars of the last chorus of *Swing Me with Rhythm.*) This hybrid style, which employed elements of New Orleans performance practice in interpretations of popular melodies, soon became dominant among white bands on 52nd Street.[22]

The most significant influence on Prima, both in musical style and in stage presence, was Louis Armstrong. Prima claimed later in his career that "from the first time I heard Armstrong I felt such a close understanding of his phrasing, his handling of a tune, that it was impossible for me to do some tunes without being like him." Prima's debt to Armstrong is most evident in his raspy singing, in which he emphasizes musical qualities of timbre, pitch, and rhythm over enunciation of the words and freely mixes sung text with nonlexical scat syllables. Armstrong himself said in 1935, "I don't know Prima . . . but his voice on phonograph records tells you that he's a mighty sweet boy," which may have been Armstrong's sly, signifying way of praising his own vocal style by ostensibly commending Prima's imitation. Prima's trumpet style, with its virtuosic emphasis on high notes and flashy gestures such as glissandi, or sliding between pitches (as during his solo on *Let's Have a Jubilee*) also owed much to Armstrong's influence. As an example, we can compare Prima's

1935 recording of *Chinatown, My Chinatown* with Armstrong's 1931 version. Like Armstrong, Prima plays the tune in a fast two-beat rhythm. In his sung choruses, Prima's voice recalls the timbre of Armstrong's; moreover, Prima employs a scat phrase that Armstrong plays during his trumpet solo on the earlier recording. Most strikingly, Prima borrows one of the most dramatic gestures of Armstrong's version—both musicians end the penultimate chorus of the recording by sustaining the fifth degree of the scale in the high register of the trumpet. This recording can be heard as a kind of tribute to Prima's primary influence.[23]

Prima's debt to Armstrong was noted widely at the time. French musician Léon Vauchant reported in the fall of 1935 that "Louis Prima, a trumpeter from New Orleans, who imitates Louis Armstrong" was playing at the Famous Door. During a 1935 broadcast of his popular radio show, Rudy Vallee described Armstrong as the originator of swing and then referred to Prima as one of his disciples. Artie Shapiro, who played bass on a Prima recording session in 1934 and saw him perform at the Famous Door, recalled in 2002 that Prima "reminded me of Louis [Armstrong]. . . . He had the same way about him that Louis did. And he sounded like him." Shapiro's comments suggest that Armstrong's influence on Prima was not limited to musical style but rather pervaded his physical manner as well; this is also suggested by *Down Beat*'s 1936 claim that "to the crowd, Prima is the second edition of Louis Armstrong as far as showmanship is concerned." A 1937 film of Prima performing *Chinatown, My Chinatown* reveals an ebullient, energetic stage presence that is reminiscent of that of Armstrong. If Prima was indeed imitating Armstrong physically as well as musically, this suggests that his stage persona depended on an enactment of black identity that was personal as well as musical.[24]

The cross-racial imitation evident in Prima's impersonation of Armstrong is also apparent in Prima's recording of his own theme song, *Let's Have a Jubilee*, which draws on an array of conventional images of black musicality. After a polyphonic chorus in the band's typical New Orleans–influenced style, Prima sings the song's verse, in which he expresses an optimistic view of life through references to the natural environment ("a new day is in the sky," "come on and greet that morning sun.") The band sings "Hallelujah!" as a repeated refrain. The folksy text and ecstatic refrain seem to refer to familiar stereotypes of African American religious traditions, of the sort dramatized in such popular fictions as King Vidor's 1929 film *Hallelujah!* and Marc Connelly's play *The Green Pastures*, which premiered in 1930. Prima then sings a chorus, inviting listeners to join with him in celebrating the jubilee. A repeated two-bar vamp follows during which Prima calls out each band member by name to play a four-bar solo. These introductions can be traced to Armstrong's influence—in particular, to the Hot Five record *Gut Bucket Blues* (1925), in which Armstrong introduces each musician in turn and also famously asserts, "Everybody from New Orleans can really do that thing!" Some of the nicknames that Prima applies to his white bandmates allude to New Orleans as a site of origins or to racial stereotypes. He refers to clarinetist Sidney Arodin, a native of Westwego, Louisiana, as "Bayou Pon Pon Arodin," citing the name of a traditional Cajun song. More disturbingly, Prima calls pianist Claude Thornhill "Baboon-Face" and trombonist Georg Brunis "Liver-Lip," both names that may apply minstrel depictions of African Americans to these white musicians. To Arodin, he asks, "What's on your mind there, Creole?" using a term that simultaneously evokes associations of New Orleans, African Americans, and hybrid black-white identities like that assumed by Prima. Prima may also have been making a specific reference to Arodin, who was, according to Richard Sudhalter, often rumored to be a " 'Creole of color,' passing for white." The next chorus features a Prima trumpet solo in his Armstrong-derived style. Finally, a brief quotation from *I've Been Working on the Railroad* leads into a short coda. This quotation seems completely incongruous unless it is explained as a racial signifier—with its references to "strumming on the old banjo," this tune alludes to the minstrel tradition already evoked by Prima. *Let's Have a Jubilee* is thus a potpourri of ideas about blackness, referencing New Orleans jazz, folk religion, the virtuosity of Louis Armstrong, minstrel stereotypes, and the hybrid racial identities associated with Creole New Orleans all in one brief performance.[25]

This complex array of signifiers of racial authenticity is further complicated by the fact that, as we have seen, Italian Americans such as Prima were still perceived as racially indeterminate by many Americans in the 1930s. It is perhaps not surprising that many of those who saw and heard Prima at the Famous Door and elsewhere thought of him as at least partially black. Indeed, before he was hired by the Famous Door, Prima had been rejected by Leon & Eddie's, a 52nd Street club not generally associated with jazz or black performers, because of such an assessment. Prima's biographer Garry Boulard explains that in 1934 the club's co-owner, Eddie Davis, was "highly receptive to [Guy] Lombardo's favorable reviews of Prima" and "was ready to hire Louis. But when he met the musician he was startled—Prima is a Negro, Davis thought. That misconception abruptly ended any possibility of Prima performing at Leon and Eddie's." British jazz critic Leonard Feather writes that in the mid-1930s, "because of Louis Prima's apparently swarthy complexion in photographs we had seen, and because of such spoken remarks on his records as 'What's on your mind, Creole?,' it had been widely assumed in England that he was black." In the late 1930s, black audiences at Harlem's Apollo Theatre had a similar impression. Sammy Davis Jr., who performed with Prima at the Apollo, recalled that "half the people who came to the theatre thought Prima was black anyway. Mixed. So he was a big favorite." Even those who viewed Prima himself as white often heard his music as black. *Billboard,* for example, in an article crediting Prima's Famous Door performances with starting a "vogue" for "jam bands," claimed that "the music of a jam band is the music of a hot Negro orchestra made more compact, even hotter . . . That may explain why people like it—because it is savagely rhythmic, almost primitive in its qualities."[26]

It is not clear what Prima thought about the racial confusion that surrounded him. Feather recalls that when he met Prima in 1936, the trumpeter made it plain that he was not black and added, "'hell . . . I've never even *used* any coloured musicians.' From his tone of voice it was clear that he never intended to." Feather's account suggests that Prima may have been motivated by racist attitudes to distance himself from blackness. Garry Boulard, in contrast, quotes Prima's warm reminiscence of the racially integrated New Orleans neighborhood where he grew up and claims that Prima flouted segregation law by allowing black musicians to sit in with his band in New Orleans in the early 1930s. At around the same time, Prima's New Orleans stage act included an intentionally provocative comedy bit in which black dancer Earl Palmer played his son.[27] After arriving in New York, Prima continued to evoke ideas of racial mixture with such songs as *Basin Street Blues,* in which he describes Basin Street in New Orleans as "the street where all the boys dark and light all meet."[28] Prima's fealty to Armstrong and his adoption of a range of black musical practices further suggest that he was comfortable taking on aspects of a perceived black identity, as part of what critic Thomas Ferraro terms "a tradition of Italian musicians crossing the [racial] line for the pleasure of the music itself."[29] It is likely, then, that Prima was ambivalent about his stage persona, sometimes embracing his in-between status as an apparent Creole and sometimes insisting on the privileges of whiteness.

Prima's alluring but indeterminate relationship to blackness extended to the entire genre of music with which he was associated, which was becoming known generically as "Dixieland." The jazz press, which cast Prima as the leader of a "Dixieland" revival in 1935, drew attention to his

New Orleans birthplace in discussing him and his music, while touching obliquely on racial issues. *Metronome* answered its own question, "Is Dixieland Stuff Coming Back?" in the affirmative, suggesting that as the economy improved, the public would gravitate toward the "torrid" tempos and "livelier pace" of Dixieland. The writer pointed out that "Prima and his piano player, Frank Pinero had [*sic*] from that town where jazz was born, N'Orleans," and argued, in a bit of a stretch, that "the instrumentation of the Original Dixieland Jazz Band was almost the same as Prima's crew excepting La Rocca the leader, who played cornet instead of trumpet, with drums instead of bass fiddle, and trombone instead of guitar." *Metronome* described the Dixieland revival both as a commercial novelty and as part of an authentic past. In a similar article, *Down Beat*'s Lathrop Mack likewise connected Prima, as well as trumpeter Wingy Manone, to the legacy of the Original Dixieland Jazz Band, pointing to their shared New Orleans origin and also to the fact that Manone and Prima, like the ODJB's LaRocca, were Italians. Both Mack and *Metronome*'s anonymous reporter made reference to race in describing the origins of Dixieland style. Mack claimed that "these two boys [i.e., Prima and Manone] have recaptured, with their small orchestras, the 'Afric Cadences' and 'Barnyard Arepeggoways' with which the Original Dixieland Jazz Band took New York by storm in 1917." *Metronome,* after erroneously asserting that Manone's band consisted of "all colored boys, and hot," added offhandedly "of course, when you get into the colored bands you find Dixieland stuff almost exclusively." The same author's description of Prima seems to invoke racialized images of ecstatic performance: "When Prima gets going, he is something to watch. Tilting his trumpet sharply upward, he closes his eyes, puffs out his cheeks, and lets go with that old Gabriel stuff to a fare thee well." Although Prima only drew on certain aspects of traditional New Orleans jazz rather than emulating the style absolutely, his music was received as the authentic original, complete with its racial significations.[30]

At the Famous Door, Prima's dynamic showmanship and swinging, improvisatory music attracted other musicians almost immediately. The legendary story of the club's opening night tells of owner Jack Colt sinking into despair over the initial lack of business, only to revive when the club filled up after midnight; Robert Sylvester explains that Colt "had opened a night club for musicians and forgotten that musicians don't go anywhere until after midnight—unless they're hired to go somewhere." Contemporaneous reports suggest that this clientele remained loyal to Prima and the Famous, Door for some time. *Down Beat* reported in its April–May 1935 issue that "since the burning of the Onyx Club, the Famous Door is now one of the favorite spots of the musicians around town." A French reporter wrote later in the year that "all the hot musicians foregather there." *Metronome* claimed that "the place became famous for its jam sessions" while Prima was playing there, and *Down Beat* stated that the sessions were led by Manny Klein, a familiar figure from the Onyx. For a time, the Famous Door appeared to be the logical successor to the Onyx Club for New York's exclusive fraternity of white professional musicians.[31]

Prima's "hot" music and charismatic presence, however, soon began to draw an enthusiastic public to the club, just as the Spirits of Rhythm had at the Onyx. By June 1935, the jazz and entertainment press began to take notice of the changing audience at the Famous Door. In July, Abel Green wrote in *Variety* that the Famous Door had "now become one of the 'must' spots in the nocturnal tourism for natives and visitors." According to Green, young people formed much of the crowd: "the kids come in just to sit around and gasp at Prima's torrid trumpeting and grow zestful with the ultra-modernistic rhythmpation this unique quin[t]et gives out. Considering that the kids have no place to dance, taking their appreciation of the hotcha music in sittin' down fashion, that's something to wonder about." In a June 1935 article in which he reviewed Prima's performances at the Famous Door, jazz critic and promoter John Hammond made unfavorable mention of the presence of wealthy people at the club, writing scornfully that "there are several spots being regularly patronized by a curious mixture of Broadway and Park Avenue nitwits, who come primarily for the purpose of hearing the best of the musicians gather in jam sessions after finishing work . . . this art is acquiring something of a snob appeal." In the same issue of *Down Beat,* Lathrop Mack used similar language in complaining that, as his article headline stated, "Park Ave. Nit-Wits Spoil Jam Nights at 'The Door.'" Mack claimed that while "for three months [the Famous Door] never failed to supply a swell 'jam' on Wednesday nights," things had changed: "But now the public has caught on. Every columnist in the city plugs the spot, and the musicians are saying that the management 'got snooty' with them. So they are looking for somewhere else to go. Jewels and gardenias are the decorations at 'the door' now, instead of hot o[b]bligatos."[32]

As Mack's reference to "jewels and gardenias" suggests, women were a highly visible part of Prima's new audience. Although, by the end of the 1930s, women regularly patronized 52nd Street, their presence in a club previously dominated by male musicians was still noteworthy in 1935.

Male commentators later suggested that women were attracted to the Famous Door mainly by Prima's sexy persona and ecstatic performances. Sam Weiss insisted, "don't minimize [Prima's] appeal to the dames. Somehow the word got around that he was rather well fortified, and there were a lot of tables just bulging with females. . . . When he shouted, 'Let's have a jubilee,' . . . a lot of those sex-starved dames would practically have an orgasm. I think they thought he was shouting, 'Let's have an orgy,' in that hoarse, horny voice of his." Eddie Davis, who sang down the block at Leon & Eddie's, remembered that "you could hear them breathing all the way down The Street!" The leering sexism of these accounts, whose narrators fantasize about impressionable "dames" who are unable to control their physical desires, suggests that the values of the bachelor subculture influenced some musicians' views of Prima's audience. Nonetheless, Weiss and Davis usefully draw attention to the sexual aspects of Prima's appeal. Weiss's mention of Prima's "well fortified" anatomy recalls his phallic reference to Wilbur Daniels of the Spirits of Rhythm; this suggests that stereotypes of black sexuality might have applied to the Italian American Prima as well as to African American musicians. Garry Boulard suggests that "the women who packed the tiny Famous Door . . . were . . . interested in this wavy-haired creature up from the Deep South who looked and sounded like a black man, and danced that way too."[33] Prima's blurring of the line between whiteness and blackness may have allowed audiences to safely indulge a fascination with black sexuality while watching an ostensibly "white" performer.

Whatever the nature of Prima's appeal, nonmusicians continued to come to the Famous Door to see and hear him, and their presence began to outweigh that of the musicians who had founded the club. *Variety* reported in July that the "kids" who flocked to the Famous Door displayed "an appreciation seemingly parring and betimes eclipsing the professional enthusing from the radio-musiker bunch, which has taken to regard The Famous Door as its 'clubhouse.'" The public adulation bestowed upon Prima seems to have grated on both writers in the jazz press and his fellow musicians. John Hammond wrote disparagingly in June that "Louis Prima's, at the Famous Door, is perhaps the most popular [small band in New York], but it fails to give me the slightest semblance of a boot. Louis is a good trumpeter, but he persists in playing identical solos night after night, and indulges in certain tricks which grow a bit tiresome after awhile." Although Hammond's criticism was aimed at Prima's trumpet style, it also appears to have been a reaction to what Hammond perceived as his undeserved popularity. Garry Boulard writes that trombonist

Georg Brunis, who worked with Prima's group during his Famous Door stay, eventually quit because he was both "disgusted by Prima's on-stage mannerisms" and angry about not sharing top billing with Prima. This story suggests that Brunis may have been conflicted about Prima's commercial success, both envying it and disparaging the stage antics that helped Prima achieve it. Although, according to Arnold Shaw, Thursday night jam sessions were instituted as "a desperate attempt to save the Door for the musicians and for jamming," public interest continued to overwhelm the musicians. In July 1935, *Down Beat*'s Lathrop Mack wrote that "Prima . . . had the musicians congregating at the Famous Door until the delighted public crowded them out." [34]

Mack went on to suggest that white trumpeter Joseph Matthews "Wingy" Manone, who like Prima was credited as a major figure in the nascent Dixieland revival, was replacing Prima as the musicians' favorite. [35] Manone, who was born in New Orleans in 1900, had an easily romanticized past that made him an ideal candidate for their adulation. The trumpeter, whose nickname derived from the fact that he had lost his right arm in a streetcar accident as a child, began performing on riverboats as a teenager and had played in venues from New York to Chicago to California by the early 1930s; a 1935 profile even claimed that he "once acted as referee in a Chicago gang war." [36] *Down Beat* paid tribute to his experience by suggesting that, along with Georg Brunis, Manone was "the last of the old hot men." [37] By 1935, Manone was notable among 52nd Street's musicians as an especially avid jam session participant. An article by the pseudonymous "Old Viper" in the April 1935 issue of *Hot News and Rhythm Record Review* reports that "my last jam session was at Wingy Mannone's place" (it is not clear which place is meant here) and describes Manone's enthusiasm: "Wingy, the inimitable, cornered us and said, 'I'm got me a five-piece band around the corner. Come with me, send you man! . . . Well, childer [sic], we went, and Wingy kept his promise." [38] Manone also led more formally organized bands at short-lived clubs such as the Casino Deluxe, the club that briefly preceded the Famous Door at 35 West 52nd. [39] By the summer of 1935, he was performing at Adrian Rollini's Tap Room on West 48th Street for an audience of "swing men and hot fans" who had been "crowded out at the Famous Door" and who often took part in jam sessions. [40] In August, Manone was hired to play at the Hickory House, a steakhouse at 144 West 52nd Street between Sixth and Seventh avenues whose owner, John Popkin, had decided to begin featuring jazz. [41] *Down Beat* reported the change of venue in a "flash bulletin": "Wingy Mannone opens at the Hickory House August 6th with a four piece combo which will play on a raised platform inside a Circular Bar."[42] This marked the beginning of almost a solid year of working on 52nd Street for Manone, who appeared regularly at both the Hickory House and the Famous Door between August 1935 and June 1936.[43]

Manone's music was similar to Prima's. Recordings that Manone made during his initial tenure on 52nd Street demonstrate a fusion of hot improvisation and contemporary pop music. The performances typically emphasize improvised solos played by Manone and clarinetist Joe Marsala as well as several guest stars (trombonist Jack Teagarden, for example, plays on an October 8 session). The rhythm section plays mostly in a swinging four-beat style but sometimes in two. The band often plays in New Orleans–style polyphony, although they occasionally simulate this effect by including a clarinet solo on top of a homophonic texture in the other horns (as in the last chorus of *I've Got a Feelin' You're Foolin'.*) As a singer, Manone, although not as directly imitative as Prima, also reflects Armstrong's influence in his rhythmic freedom and willingness to depart from the composed melody. Manone's group at the Hickory House was a quartet, comprising his trumpet and Marsala's clarinet backed by Carmen Mastren's guitar and Sid Weiss's bass, in contrast to the six- to eight-piece bands featured on his records. His live performances, however, were similarly improvisatory and energetic. Jazz critic Leonard Feather reported in *Swing Music* that Manone was even more "unselfconscious and informal" at the Hickory House than on record and claimed that "he can play the blues for half-an-hour without a stop, and, if you have any feeling at all for real jazz, will not bore you." *Variety*'s Abel Green wrote that in Manone's group "no piano is needed, for Frankie Signorelli, or some other great jazz pianist, is just as apt to wander in and sit in, making corn on the ivories, just for his own amusement. This informality of showmanship and musicianly cooperation is something to marvel at."[44]

Like Prima, Manone quickly became popular on 52nd Street; Feather explained that "all around the crowded Hickory House" Manone's music "was 'getting' musicians, showfolk, [and] laymen all the same way." The initial source of his popularity was a hit record, *The Isle of Capri,* in which Manone lampooned a romantic Xavier Cugat song with a revised, comical set of lyrics describing a musician stranded on an island. Manone's irreverent treatment of the ostensibly romantic song attracted favorable attention in the jazz press: reviewer Warren Scholl noted favorably that "they murder, crucify and hack these hackneyed numbers in a thoroughly pleasing manner," while Manone claimed proudly that his mother told him, "Son, the way you brutalized that number is a shame." As in *Onyx Club Revue*, jazz here appeared to be an assault against inauthentic sentimentality, a perception that Manone linked to African American models when he explained that the Spirits of Rhythm provided the inspiration for his version. In addition to receiving composer royalties for his version of *Isle of Capri*, Manone was achieving great success at the Hickory House in 1935: *Down Beat* reported in September that he and his band had the "crowd under their spell" and in October that "Wingy Mannone's torrid trumpeting has brought so many shekels into the coffers of the Hickory House that he has been given a new contract for 8 weeks at twice the salary for which he was originally engaged."[45]

Manone's popularity, like Prima's, was linked to his ability to perform a black identity while still remaining acceptably "white." This was an ambiguity that Manone exploited in recordings such as *House Rent Party Day*, in which he describes a party including "brown-skin shebas by the dozen" and simulates a craps game in a stereotypical black dialect. (Prima had already recorded the same tune a few months before Manone.) The confusion over Manone's identity, as we have seen, led *Metronome* to claim that his band was "colored." The complex tangle of race, musical style, and sexuality that went into Manone's reception is perhaps best illustrated, however, by a 1935 *Down Beat* report subtitled "Wingy Mannone Will Wed Iowa Farm Beauty Who Bet He Wasn't Colored." The text stated, "Connie Rosenfeld, the lady in question, left Des Moines and the farm for Atlantic City, having won a beauty contest, and dropped in at the Hickory House, N.Y. on her way back to settle a bet. Coming from a family of record fans, Connie had taken her sister up on the statement that Wingy played the 'Isle of Capri' so well he must be colored. She not only won the bet but also the man. That was a month ago, and now Wingy is planning on featuring his wife-to-be on vocals."[46] The tabloid style of this story makes it difficult to take seriously, but it also exemplifies the sensational, sexually titillating atmosphere that surrounded Manone's racially fraught persona. Rosenfeld, initially attracted to Manone by his ambiguous racial identity, could enter into a relationship with him when his blackness turned out to be just an act; she planned, however, to become a member of Manone's band, which implies that she herself may have had an interest in assuming a racially indeterminate role. In the end, although Manone was unambiguously "white" enough to settle a bet, his performances alluringly exceeded the supposedly definite boundaries of fixed racial categories.

"The Music Goes 'Round and Around": Riley and Farley and Their Onyx Club Boys   In the early to mid-1930s, musicians on 52nd Street generally espoused a conception of authentic jazz in which improvised music, spontaneous personal behavior, masculine self-reliance, and emulation of black musicians were all seen as related forms of resistance to the world of commercial entertainment. Whenever the general public began to take an interest in their private institutions, musicians reacted by setting up new ones—founding the Famous Door after the Spirits of Rhythm became popular at the Onyx, then growing restless when Louis Prima similarly brought public attention to the Famous Door. By 1935, the values of the exclusive musicians' circle coexisted uneasily on 52nd Street with the more conventional tastes of a wider audience seeking novelty and excitement. This uneasy truce was sorely tested by the brief vogue of Mike Riley and Ed Farley, musicians who openly courted this wider audience with comedy routines as well as with their music. Although humorous, irreverent behavior, as we have seen, was normally celebrated by 52nd Street's musicians' fraternity, the vast commercial success achieved by Riley and Farley demonstrated that transgressive displays of spontaneous self-expression could easily become commodified slapstick. This threatening realization led some of 52nd Street's musicians to reject Riley and Farley's clowning in order to assert their own distance from mainstream entertainment.

The rise to fame of Riley and Farley began in the summer of 1935 at the Onyx Club, which had been rebuilt following the fire that had gutted it in February. Red McKenzie opened there on July 23, 1935, with a group of somewhere between five and seven instrumentalists, including guitarist Eddie Condon, trombonist Riley, and trumpeter Farley.[47] In a report on the opening, *Down Beat* asserted that the Onyx was now even "more of a musicians['] hangout than before."[48] Studio recordings made under the name "Red McKenzie and His Rhythm Kings" in July and August 1935 include Tin Pan Alley pop tunes such as *Let's Swing It* and *Double Trouble,* with McKenzie's singing set against improvised instrumental solos and polyphonic ensembles derived from traditional New Orleans jazz; this was in essence the style already associated with successful 52nd Street performers Prima and Manone. At the Onyx, the band revived the tradition of late-night jam sessions at which long-standing patrons such as Bud Freeman, Tommy Dorsey, and Artie Schutt sat in.[49] The Onyx appeared at first to have recovered its original status as a haven for spontaneous, casual hot jazz played by a close-knit group of musicians.

By October, under unknown circumstances, the group had come under the leadership of Riley and Farley. Although they continued to play mainly in the "Dixieland" style featured on the McKenzie recordings, they also drew on an eclectic mix of influences, as an NBC radio broadcast from October 20, 1935 demonstrates.[50] The band, which comprises seven instrumentalists as well as guest singer Ella Logan, begins its fourteen-minute set with a novelty song, *The Music Goes 'Round and Around,* that features Riley's comic singing. The second number, *Livin' in a Great Big Way,* begins and ends with choruses of polyphonic improvisation in the New Orleans idiom, albeit in a four-beat rhythm rather than the two-beat associated with New Orleans. The second and third choruses, a clarinet and trombone solo, respectively, are backed by riffs in the other horns; the syncopated riff played by the trumpet and trombone during the clarinet solo evokes Duke Ellington's *It Don't Mean a Thing If It Ain't Got That Swing.* Like Prima and Manone, Riley and Farley were modifying and modernizing the New Orleans tradition rather than imitating it precisely. The third tune is a contemporaneously published pop ballad, *Loafin' Time,* in which Scottish singer Logan is backed by a "sweet" arrangement underpinned by Farley's muted trumpet playing and Slats Long's understated clarinet.[51] The following number, *Jazz Me Blues,* is a relatively faithful rendition of a New Orleans classic played largely polyphonically and including traditional breaks, in which the band drops out briefly to showcase a soloist. Another surprising juxtaposition follows as Riley and Farley play a version of Duke Ellington's *Mood Indigo* that emphasizes the wah-wah trumpet and trombone effects associated with Ellington's "jungle style" and includes an unusual vocal chorus by Riley in which he employs a yodeling falsetto. Finally, the band closes with a fast polyphonic version of the Scottish folk song *Oh, Dear, What Can the Matter Be* during which Logan sings a complex scat phrase likely derived from Louis Armstrong's style. In all, this performance shows that Riley and Farley were influenced by a broad range of African American musical practices, from New Orleans to Ellington to Armstrong.

The values of spontaneity and self-expression represented musically in the jam sessions at the Onyx and in Riley and Farley's performances were mirrored in the clowning and slapstick humor for which the group also was becoming known. In discussing the band's opening, *Down Beat* reported that "McKenzie's is more or less one of those acrobatic type of orchestras; as Red says—'anything to entertain the boys.'" In October 1935, after Riley and Farley had replaced McKenzie as the band's leaders, music critic George Simon praised Riley in *Metronome* for his "A-1 clowning." By November, profiles of the band had begun to focus as much on their broad physical comedy as on their music. *Down Beat* mentioned that "clothes ripping" and egg throwing were part of Riley and Farley's show, and it also described an incident in which a member of the Rudy Vallee band arose from the audience and got into the act by slapping Riley across the face with a beefsteak. At the same time, however, critics continued to praise Riley and Farley as musicians. In the same review in which he complimented the duo's comedy skills, George Simon drew attention to the authenticity of their music, calling the band's performances "plenty of the real dixieland stuff . . . unadulterated." Writing in 1939, Wilder Hobson recalled Riley's skill as both a musician and a comedian: "I remember Mike Riley playing fiendishly eclectic trombone solos in which everybody else's style came in for a few bars, and right in the middle he would suddenly yell 'Hello, Joe!' at an imaginary friend in the back of the house." Musicians who played with Riley similarly commended his musicianship as well as his comedy. Bassist Artie Shapiro, who jammed with Riley on 52nd Street in the 1930s, insisted that "he was a good player!" Bassist Bill Crow, who worked as a drummer and vocalist with Riley in the 1950s, remembered that while Riley "was used to that kind of knockabout vaudeville humor," he was also "a Dixieland hard-drivin' trombone player" with "absolutely no nuances of subtlety at all." Although Crow performed with Riley years after his 52nd Street stardom, his appraisal of Riley's combination of vaudeville comedy and straightforward improvisation recalls that made by critics in the 1930s.[52]

The initial reception of Riley and Farley indicates that a dichotomy between vaudeville comedy and authentic jazz, commonly made today in criticism of figures such as Louis Armstrong, was not yet dominant among white musicians and critics on 52nd Street in 1935. Rather, both throwing eggs and playing improvised trombone solos were viewed favorably as irreverent breaches of convention. As we have seen, other white musicians, such as Wingy Manone, similarly combined jazz with comedy and were nonetheless popular with their fellow musicians on 52nd Street. In late 1935, the comic antics of Riley and Farley were just one facet of a stage show in which music and other forms of entertainment played connected roles.

The proper ratio of comedy to jazz, however, was by no means clear or uncontroversial at the time, as is best demonstrated by turmoil within the band itself—by November both Eddie Condon and Red McKenzie had left.

Condon remembers scornfully in his autobiography that "during rehears-als [Riley and Farley] had conducted themselves as musicians; an audience transformed them into clowns. They poured water over each other, scuf-fled, mugged, and did everything but play music." When Riley and Farley began hitting each other with pies every night, the sardonic Condon nick-named them "Lemon Meringue" and "Mince," respectively. After he re-peatedly protested Riley and Farley's behavior by leaving the bandstand, Condon was fired from the group. McKenzie left sometime afterward, and by March 1936 he and Condon were performing with a different band at the Famous Door.[53] Condon's emphasis on the role of the audience in cor-rupting Riley and Farley suggests the threat that public attention posed to his standard of authentic jazz. A mainstream audience was unaware of the jazz traditions that Condon aspired to emulate. They also represented the commercial interests that the Onyx Club's white musicians purported to resist. If Riley and Farley's clowning, as such, was not seen as problem-atic, it nonetheless was beginning to attract an audience that had the po-tential to undermine the Onyx Club's status as a musicians' club. Condon's rejection of Riley and Farley reflected attitudes that would soon become apparent in other musicians of the Onyx Club circle.

The turning point in Riley and Farley's careers came near the end of 1935, when they began to attract attention for one of their featured numbers at the Onyx, the supposedly original tune *The Music Goes 'Round and Around*. Although the actual circumstances of the song's composition were shrouded in mystery and eventually sparked a lawsuit, an apocry-phal story of its origin was widely reported in the months to follow.[54] Supposedly, a drunken patron at the Onyx came up to Riley and asked him how his flugelhorn worked.[55] Riley's response, "I blow through here, the music goes round and around, and it comes out here," facetiously traced the music through the crooks of his horn. This phrase was elabo-rated into a routine that he and Farley performed both at the Onyx and on their Decca recording of the song, made on September 26, 1935, and released under the name "Mike Riley & Eddie Farley and Their Onyx Club Boys."[56] The band's performance on the recording is typical of their New Orleans–influenced brand of jazz, with Farley's straight statement of the melody on his trumpet and clarinetist Slats Long's tendency to play consonant harmony a third above the melody ensuring that the tune is still approachable for listeners unaccustomed to the style. The most no-table feature of the recording, however, is the interaction between Riley, who clowns around as sings about his horn, and Farley, who plays the "straight man" by feigning exasperation with Riley. Their infectious and seemingly spontaneous good humor had a strong effect on audiences, as can be heard during their performance of *The Music Goes 'Round and Around* on Rudy Vallee's *Fleischmann's Yeast Hour,* an NBC radio show, on November 21, 1935.[57] After a mock argument between Riley and Farley sets the stage, Riley "explains" how his horn works, and then asks the audience to join in with him on the chorus, which they do enthusiastically. Later, the audience can be heard laughing with delight at the shouts of "Whoo! Whoo!" that Riley and Farley interpolate into the tune. Riley and Farley's combination of comedy and jazz clearly had popular appeal beyond the confines of the Onyx Club.

By January 1936, *The Music Goes 'Round and Around* was the biggest hit song in the United States, and Riley and Farley were national stars with a one-year Decca recording contract; in February, they traveled to Hollywood to appear in a movie that had been renamed after their hit.[58] The song became so popular and ubiquitous that historians Barry Ulanov and David Stowe both credit it with launching the swing era.[59] Frank Norris, writing in the *New Republic* in January 1936, claimed that 45,000 copies of the sheet music of *The Music Goes 'Round and Around* had sold in three weeks, that "a hat, a dress, [and] a sofa had been named after it," and that "if one failed to hear it in English as it was played over the radio once every five minutes, there was still a good chance of catching it broadcast in Yiddish, Danish, Japanese, Irish brogue or pig Latin."[60] Feature writers in the mainstream press tried valiantly to explain how this seemingly inconsequential ditty and its madcap creators could have captured the heart of the nation. Some discussions focused on the music, introducing curious readers to a newfangled genre of popular music known as "swing" and sometimes crediting its development to African American musicians such as Louis Armstrong.[61] Still others emphasized the unfettered performances of Riley and Farley and the circumstances of their song's creation in what *Time* termed "a small dive called the Onyx Club in Manhattan's iniquitous West 52nd Street."[62] In short, the popular press began to focus, if only superficially, on the very things that had drawn musicians to Riley and Farley's performances—their role in the vanguard of a novel and racially hybrid musical style and the spontaneity of their comedy and personal behavior.

As we have seen, a mass audience for "hot jazz" posed a threat to the musicians of the Onyx Club circle. The widespread appreciation of Riley and Farley by an audience with neither an insider's knowledge of jazz nor an inclination against commercialism led to fears that the exclusive atmosphere of the Onyx might once again be diluted by "squares." In the

December 1935–January 1936 issue of *Down Beat,* reporter Jack Egan captured the new atmosphere in an article tellingly entitled "Outside 'Ikkies' Try Squeezing In to Hear Big Noise." After rather defensively claiming that the Onyx is "still the music makers' rendezvous," Egan wrote that the club was "gayer now than ever with plenty of outsiders, ikkies as we call them, squeezing into the picture to see what the noise is all about . . . Outstanding event of the month at the spot was the distribution of membership pins to the Farley-Riley Round and Around Club." [63] With their Round and Around Club, Riley and Farley were creating an overtly artificial sense of belonging, one to which anyone with a membership pin was entitled. Musicians, who formerly had occupied an insider status at the club, were in danger of being crowded out by the so-called ikkies whom Riley and Farley attracted with their antics. Riley and Farley's act, which had seemed to provide a liberating alternative to commercialism, had itself become a highly successful commodity.

This development alienated the duo from their original audience of musicians, to whom Riley and Farley appealed for forgiveness after their popular appeal began to wane. [64] A *Down Beat* article from August 1936 suggests that many musicians had followed Eddie Condon's lead in rejecting Riley and Farley. Somewhat poignantly, the chastened Farley answered his accusers with a promise to return to "jamming," presumably in the African American tradition prized at the Onyx. Farley protested that "jam music wasn't worth a penny" without "showmanship" and explained that he and Riley had only engaged in slapstick to draw in customers for their music, with no intention of "reaching such gigantic proportions." After their movie flopped, Farley complained, it became fashionable for "the boys [in other words, other musicians] . . . to exhibit their witticisms by cracking about our work." In what sounds like an attempt to put himself and Riley back into the good graces of musicians, Farley promised "you can bet we're glad to jam again for the cats. We put on a good show before and I think we can do it again if people will stop using disparaging remarks as a form of humor." [65] Although Riley and Farley both went on to have viable careers as bandleaders, they never again achieved either the popular success of *The Music Goes 'Round and Around* or their status as authentic insiders within the jazz community. Bill Crow remembers that, years later, Riley bitterly defended his choice to work as a comedian rather than in the rarified world of jazz: " 'You gotta do comedy if you want to make money,' [Riley] told me one night on the bandstand. 'Listen, this is a high F!' He jammed his horn to his mouth and played a loud one. 'You think anybody out there gives a damn?' " [66]

The brief vogue of Riley and Farley in 1935 and 1936 highlighted the tensions surrounding commercialism that informed 52nd Street's first musicians. As hot jazz became increasingly popular with a mass audience, it ran the risk of being assimilated into the commercial marketplace that it ostensibly resisted. To maintain the perceived barrier between their music and the market, 52nd Street's musicians began to draw distinctions between authentic jazz as a musical form and the other forms of performance, such as Riley and Farley's vaudeville comedy, that so often accompanied it. This dichotomy was neatly summed up years later by Artie Shapiro, who remembered that other musicians "took [Riley] for what he was doing . . . he had a pop record, you know, a hit record, and he was milking it for all he could, and he was more or less a showman . . . he was concentrating on the show-biz part."[67] This turn away from showy performance styles was not unique to white jazz musicians at this time—as Scott DeVeaux demonstrates in *The Birth of Bebop*, some African American musicians, such as Coleman Hawkins, also rejected vaudeville comedy and minstrel stereotypes in the 1930s in favor of the dignified stance of the concert artist.[68] Both examples suggest that a view of jazz as an autonomous high art with values distinct from those of "entertainment," often considered an innovation of bebop musicians in the 1940s, was becoming current as early as the mid-1930s.[69] As we shall see, musicians and audiences continued to grapple with this distinction throughout the history of 52nd Street's jazz scene.

Even as 52nd Street began to attract a large audience of nonmusicians, the legacy of musicians' clubs such as the Onyx and the Famous Door continued to have an impact on the street's culture and reputation. From the mid-1930s on, hopeful young white musicians from across the United States came to New York knowing that "The Street" was the place where they could test their mettle and attempt to gain admission to an elite musicians' group. I close this chapter with the account of one such musician, drummer Johnny Blowers, who learned to play jazz by listening to the records of members of the original Onyx Club circle. Blowers arrived in New York City on September 7, 1937, and went to 52nd Street "two or three days after [he] was in New York and got settled."

I didn't know anything about New York, and I didn't know anyone, so, really, it was going to be very difficult as far as jazz music is concerned, because— it's not that New York is cruel or anything, but they had to know you. You had to have some kind of a reputation so that they would know how you played. Because that's what I did—I went over to 52nd Street, I went to the Hickory

House . . . and tried to get to talk to the leaders, different ones, to see if I could just sit in. And I knew all of the music, because I've been a musician all of my life. I came from a professional family. My dad played drums and my mother played piano. And of course I listened to much jazz in my hometown of Spartanburg, South Carolina. . . . I listened to records that were [by] Red Nichols and the Five Pennies, and dates that Benny Goodman was on with groups, and Tommy Dorsey, and Jimmy Dorsey, and all these different guys. This is before they became leaders, way back in the twenties. So I would listen to all these records . . . and I knew 'em, backwards and forwards. I didn't need any music, or anything. But you see, they didn't know me. And—Wingy Manone, if you've read about that name, he was a trumpet player. And I remember very well, he was at the Hickory House, and he was nice enough, but he said "No, uh-uh, I can't take a chance. You might mess up." And I said, "No, I won't," but that wasn't good enough. So then, you go on up, you go east on 52nd Street, you cross Sixth Avenue, and that's where you started with the clubs . . . people would come in to the street about nine o'clock at night, and it ran till four o'clock in the morning. So here I was, eating my heart listening to these guys and hearing them play, and wondering how on earth I'm ever going to—how are you going to break into this, because that's not easy.[70]

After initially scuffling around New York, Blowers was taken under the wing of the ubiquitous Red McKenzie, who assured him "you'll work. Just keep playing like you're playing." McKenzie helped Blowers to find jobs first at Nick's in Greenwich Village and later with trumpeter Bunny Berigan's big band. Now, Blowers could return to the site of his initial rejection as a respected figure in the jazz world: "Every time we came in town, off of a tour, I would go to . . . 52nd Street, Hickory House, 'cause everybody knew me then. And I didn't go to sit in, but I went to listen. 'Cause I didn't have to sit in, I was working all the time."[71]

If 52nd Street represented opportunity and fellowship for white musicians such as Blowers in the 1930s, it offered different challenges and possibilities for the first African American musicians to perform there. It is these musicians to whom we now turn.

Chapter Three **Here Comes the Man with the Jive Stuff Smith**

The first African American musicians to perform on 52nd Street confronted the notions of racial identity and artistic integrity already held by their white predecessors on the street. As we have seen, these ideas centered on an association between authentic jazz and a vision of black identity linked to anticommercial values, irreverent personal behavior, and an improvisatory, "hot" musical style. Although such conceptions were informed in part by interactions among black and white musicians, whites and blacks occupied asymmetrical positions within the developing image of jazz on 52nd Street. For white musicians, playing jazz was a way to temporarily adopt an ostensibly black persona that provided an invigorating sense of freedom from conventional musical and economic restrictions. African American musicians, in contrast, were assumed to have permanent and innate black identities within which jazz performance itself was rooted. For black musicians, then, the vision of jazz developed in the early days of 52nd Street was not transformative; rather, it involved an attempt by whites to define the essence of a supposedly static black identity. Faced with ideas of authentic jazz that presumed to explain their authentic selves, African American musicians on 52nd Street in the 1930s found various ways to push the boundaries of authenticity, sometimes adopting the standards upheld by 52nd Street's white musicians and sometimes rejecting or subverting them for their own purposes.

The next two chapters examine two of the most popular and visible African American groups on 52nd Street in the 1930s, groups whose conceptions of jazz appeared to be diametrically opposed. The violinist Stuff Smith, whose band opened at the Onyx Club in 1936, drew a large, interracial audience with a blend of broad comedy, Harlem jive, and swinging improvised jazz. Smith's musical style and stage presence both conformed to aspects of the stereotype of the carefree, spontaneous black performer and presented a newly assertive image of black identity that reflected political and cultural developments in Harlem. In contrast, the John Kirby Sextet and singer Maxine Sullivan, who succeeded Smith at the Onyx in 1937, downplayed traditional markers of racial identity. Instead, they emphasized a restrained, tightly arranged musical style that seemed to contradict stereotypes of wild, abandoned black music and to derive as much from European "classical" and folk idioms as from conventional notions of the jazz tradition. Both groups thus pointed to alternative visions of racial authenticity, Smith showcasing an affirmative, self-confident black identity and Kirby and Sullivan demonstrating that African American musicians need not be restricted to those musical forms and practices that normally were ascribed to blacks. The popular success of both groups meant that the images of authenticity that they presented had an impact on a large and racially diverse audience. Both groups were particularly successful in drawing African American musicians and audience members to 52nd Street, which allowed an increasingly wide range of perspectives to influence the ideas about race and commerce current on the street. The examples of Smith, Kirby, and Sullivan indicate that, despite the continued power and tenacity of previously held standards of racial and musical authenticity, African American musicians often were able to negotiate standards of their own that altered dominant perceptions.

"Screwy Ideas and Fake Fingering": Stuff Smith at the Onyx Club   Although 52nd Street's jazz scene had been sparked by white musicians' interest in emulating African American music, black musicians themselves were largely marginal figures on the street in 1935 and early 1936. As the headlining act at a 52nd Street club, the Spirits of Rhythm proved to be the exception rather than the rule, and those African American performers who followed them on the street often served as "relief" (intermission) acts for white stars. Pianist Teddy Wilson, for example, was the "relief artist" for Wingy Manone at the Famous Door at the end of 1935. *Variety* reporter Abel Green made a clumsy joke linking the two musicians' professional relationship to Italy's recent invasion of Ethiopia,

revealing an uneasiness in the face of interracial contact even as he affected a tone of nonchalance: "any Italo-Ethiopian political complications go by the boards when [pianist Frank] Signorelli and Mannone get together with Wilson. For that matter, so far as the swing addicts are concerned Mussolini and Selassie don't mean a thing when the boys and girls talk swing."[1] Most black musicians had less success than Wilson in attracting a following on 52nd Street. In September 1935, for example, singer Billie Holiday appeared briefly at the Famous Door but was rejected by the "Park Avenue crowd" and fired after four nights.[2] Other now-celebrated black performers, such as trumpeter Roy Eldridge, also appeared on 52nd Street in 1935 but failed to attract the widespread adulation visited on white performers such as Louis Prima or Riley and Farley.[3] Although the white founders of the 52nd Street jazz scene, as we have seen, upheld African American performers as the bearers of an authentic jazz tradition, black musicians nonetheless struggled to find a foothold on the street.

Violinist Le Roy Gordon "Stuff" Smith, the first African American musician to become a major popular success while on 52nd Street, demonstrated that 52nd Street's black musicians could maintain some control over representations of black identity even as they accommodated the expectations of 52nd Street's musicians and audiences. Smith's band got its start in Buffalo, New York, in the early 1930s. Its most prominent members, Smith, trumpeter Jonah Jones, and drummer Cozy Cole, had each spent years honing their skills in big bands, and their early careers exemplify the broad range of performing experiences that many musicians, white and black, brought to 52nd Street. Smith, born in Portsmouth, Ohio, in 1909, had been a professional violinist from around the age of seventeen, starting as a member of the Aunt Jemima Revue band.[4] His most significant engagement before the Onyx Club had been with Alphonso Trent, leader of a well-regarded territory band that Smith joined in 1927. Trent's band was based in Dallas and Cincinnati but traveled throughout the United States in the late 1920s.[5] During a stand in Buffalo, Smith married a local woman named Marion Harris, and after the birth of their son Jack he quit the Trent band in 1930 to move to Buffalo permanently.[6] By 1931 or 1932, he had organized a seven-piece band to play at a local club called Little Harlem.[7] Jones, who grew up in Louisville, Kentucky, came to Buffalo to play at the Vendome Hotel with guitarist Luke Stewart and later became a member of Jimmie Lunceford's band, which was then based in Buffalo.[8] Concerned because the twenty dollars a week he received from Lunceford barely covered his rent, Jones joined

Smith's band at Little Harlem sometime around 1933 at an improved weekly salary of thirty-five dollars.[9] By 1934, Smith expanded the band to include twelve musicians; this unit played first at the Vendome Hotel and then on an ill-fated tour of eastern theaters that ended when the band broke with Smith and was taken over by Louis Armstrong's estranged wife Lil Armstrong.[10] With Armstrong, Jones was featured as "King Louis the Second" on such Louis Armstrong specialties as *Ding Dong Daddy from Dumas* and *Big Butter and Egg Man*.[11] In 1935, Jones rejoined Smith, who had assembled a new group (expanded to a sextet with Jones's arrival) to play at the Silver Grill, a "white club" in the "colored neighborhood, a Harlem neighborhood in Buffalo."[12] Around this time, Smith and Jones played in jam sessions with drummer Cozy Cole, who was playing in Buffalo with a band led by singer Willie Bryant. Although Cole later joined Smith's band on 52nd Street, he did not play with them professionally in Buffalo.[13]

During their time in Buffalo, Smith and his band established the musical style and stage presence for which they were to become known at the Onyx Club. Their performances were notable for long improvised solos in which the musicians inspired each other to ever-greater intensity. In a 1999 interview, Jones remembered playing with Smith at Little Harlem: "We had a ball there, ya know. We'd get in there and we'd blow and blow and blow and Stuff would [Jonah shows moving a bow on violin with his hand] heavy and I got so I could take ten choruses and stuff. They'd holler, one more Jonah, ya know, and swing again, ya know and I'd take 12 choruses. Young, I had big chops, chops were strong. He would be playing behind me like a reed section, cha-cha-cha-da-cha-cha . . ." *Down Beat* reporter Jack Kassiner, who saw the band at the Silver Grill, wrote in 1936 that "it is not uncommon for Stuff and his boys to play six or more choruses of a jam tune, all of them different in melodic, rhythmic and harmonic structure. His crazy whole-tone scales and interpolation of symphonic licks are uncanny." Another *Down Beat* report referred to rumors about "a young colored fiddle player in some Buffalo dive, and the way he carries on with the bow": "One jag that was in here, says he played 17 choruses one night on Honeysuckle Rose, and every chorus was different. The consensus of opinion is that he has more screwy ideas and fake fingering, and hot licks in one minute than all the rest of the jigs in the business."[14] These accounts suggest that both the band members and their audience enjoyed the relentless ingenuity of these long improvisations, which white reporters associated with both professional and technical skill and a supposedly "uncanny" black improvisatory genius.

The band's musical abandon was mirrored in its unfettered approach to stage performance. Jonah Jones recalled a typical night at the Silver Grill:

[The audience] would be dancing . . . when Stuff was there and he go around to me and say, hey Jonah, I feel like a little snort. . . . Don't you feel like you could have one. We'd be on the bandstand playing . . . Stuff would leave the door and go back to the . . . bar and come back to the . . . bandstand and he'd have a tray with six glasses on it and half a bottle of whiskey and people would be still standing there waiting for us, the dancing people and we'd pour out ½ glasses to drink and they're still standing there. When are they going to play? Nobody said nothing, ya know, and we're drinking this whiskey, you know and then finally [sings] a-di-di-di-do-di-da-di-di and everybody started dancing again.[15]

White audiences no doubt received such a display in various ways, with some perhaps viewing it as merely a funny piece of stage business and others as confirmation of racist stereotypes about the irresponsibility and dissipation of blacks. It is likely that some perceived a connection between the band's behavior and the style of their music, with improprieties such as stopping in the middle of a set for a drink seen as analogous to such irreverent musical practices as repeatedly changing the structure of a tune or incorporating "symphonic licks" into a jazz performance. As we have seen, white musicians on 52nd Street made such an association among spontaneous personal behavior, improvisatory music, and a supposedly authentic black identity.

It is not surprising, then, that the Onyx Club settled on Smith's band as a replacement for Riley and Farley, who left New York in January 1936 to begin their short-lived Hollywood careers.[16] Jonah Jones recalled that bandleader Ben Bernie and his saxophonist Dick Stabile, white musicians who regularly came to see the Smith band at the Silver Grill when they were in Buffalo, suggested that the band come to the Onyx Club and brought an agent from New York (possibly booker Charles Green or Onyx owner Joe Helbock himself) to listen to them. After Smith decided to take the job at the Onyx, the owner of the Silver Grill offered to double the salaries of Jones and the rest of the band if they stayed on. Jones agreed to the arrangement, and Smith went to New York and assembled a new band for rehearsals. Two weeks before the opening, Helbock found out about Smith's new musicians and insisted on having the group from Buffalo instead. After further negotiations, Jones and the four other musicians in the sextet (Raymond Smith, piano; Bobby Bennett, guitar; Mack Walker, bass; John Washington, drums) joined Smith in New York in time for their opening on February 3 or 4, 1936.[17]

Reports of Smith's opening night at the Onyx indicate that, now that Riley and Farley had left the Onyx Club, musicians hoped to once again revive its status as an exclusive hangout. In a 1936 essay describing the opening, Jack Egan explained that "to make sure the public wouldn't take the opening into their own hands, Joe [Helbock] reserved every table in the room for musicians and ruled admission by invitation only."[18] The audience included the Casa Loma Orchestra, a popular big band, and their wives, along with many other musicians; in a *Down Beat* report, Egan listed over twenty, all of whom were white. This list included some of the Onyx's original patrons, such as Dick McDonough, Carl Kress, and Manny Klein.[19] Egan claimed that the band was "somewhat scared by the celebrities they faced"; years later, Jones remembered that it was the first time that he had seen an audience wearing tuxedos in a jazz club.[20] Despite perhaps feeling somewhat out of their element, the band was an immediate success with the musicians who attended the opening at the Onyx. "Those who were in the audience that night really had a clambake," wrote Egan. "Those who weren't missed one of the greatest receptions ever given any band on its New York debut. America's ace bandsmen and bandleaders screamed with delight at the antics of 'Stuff' and Jonah. They banged their feet and stood up and cheered for Smith's fiddle playing and Jonah's trumpet blasting to say nothing of the uncanny work of the four rhythm beaters. 'Stuff' was amazed no end at it all. But the amazement of the audience had it all over Smithie's feelings."[21]

In a pattern that must have seemed disappointingly familiar to those musicians who still hoped to keep the Onyx for themselves, Smith began to attract a popular following almost as soon as he opened at the club, and he began a rise to fame that in many ways paralleled that of his predecessors Riley and Farley. On February 23, the band appeared on a radio show hosted by popular bandleader Paul Whiteman. During the broadcast, Whiteman evoked the atmosphere of the Onyx Club with a brief orchestral performance of *The Music Goes 'Round and Around* and plugged the club to his radio audience as a "hotbed of hot music" where "all the musicians in town tak[e] a busman's holiday" after work.[22] Smith also appeared on Rudy Vallee's radio program on April 23. *Down Beat* reported in the same month that although "Very Few Spots Are Doing Business in New York," as the piece was headlined, "the Onyx continues to pack 'em in at least once during every evening."[23] On May 24, Smith appeared along with sixteen other bands in a sold-out swing concert put on by Onyx owner Helbock at New York's Imperial Theatre.[24] By July 1936, the band had begun to broadcast from the Onyx Club itself over station WHN. Scrapbooks maintained by teenage jazz fan Robert Inman in the 1930s, which include set lists from the band's July 24 and July 31 broadcasts, indicate that the band's repertoire included *I'se a Muggin'* and *You'se a Viper* as well as versions of *Mary Had a Little Lamb* and *Mendelssohn's Swing Song* (an allusion to the composer's well-known *Spring Song,* op. 62, no. 6.)[25] In October 1936, *Down Beat* reported that Smith had been signed for another six months at the Onyx beginning August 3 and that he was expected to break the attendance record established by Riley and Farley during the Christmas season of 1935. The writer went on to say that "the Onyx is again sporting two heavy ropes to keep out the overflow, almost every night, so that gives you a rough idea of just how successful a musicians' rendezvous can become."[26] That Smith jealously guarded his success is made apparent in an October 1936 report about an up-and-coming singer who worked briefly with the group: "Billie Holiday lasted a week at the Onyx Club, where she scored a deserved hit with the patrons. Stuff Smith, alas, objected to her presence, refused to allow her encores, and finally blew up when a New York columnist raved about her. Joe Helbock regretfully had to let her go the day before the column appeared."[27] After this incident, Smith continued a successful run at the Onyx, remaining the headliner at the club when Helbock moved it down the street from number 72 to number 62 in March 1937.[28] When Smith finally left the Onyx in May 1937, after over a year at the club, it was for the same reason that Riley and Farley had left before: he had been offered a part in a Hollywood movie.[29] In Smith's case, the movie was *52nd Street,* a United Artists release that purported to tell the true story of the increasingly famous nightclub district.[30] The widespread attention devoted to Smith made him a major figure in the increasing fame and popularity of 52nd Street.

The musicians of 52nd Street seem to have responded to Smith's popularity with less rancor than they did in the case of Riley and Farley. In his March 1936 review of the Smith band, Jack Egan indicated that the attitudes of musicians were in a stage of transition. Egan wrote that at the Onyx "there's been the collegiate influence, led by Pete MacDonald and his Princetonians—and Doris Ramage, the blonde eyeful he travels around with. At first the musicians sort of resented the collegians invading their favorite haunts, but lately they've been taking things more lightly, coming around to the realization that it's the collegiate crowd that makes—or breaks—a dance band. If you think not just look up a few of the many examples all around you."[31] Egan suggests here that musicians' change of heart toward this faction of the popular audience was based overtly on a calculated appraisal of potential market value, a stance that seems to contradict the professed anticommercialism of these musicians. It appears that as swing music, in general, and 52nd Street, in particular, became popular with the general public, musicians gradually began to believe that they could play in an authentic style while still attracting a commercial audience. Moreover, Smith had claims to the authentic jazz tradition that Riley and Farley did not; he was black, and his comical stage presence was both linked to an improvisatory musical style and drawn from a distinctly African American tradition. A closer look at the close connection between Smith's musical style and his lively, humorous stage persona helps explain why the Onyx Club's demanding musicians' circle would have enjoyed his performances despite their apparent concessions to a popular audience.

"Variety Is the Keynote": Smith in Performance　Prominently featured in Smith's live performances at the Onyx were his and Jonah Jones's skill as improvisers and the band's powerful sense of swing. Jack Egan, describing the band's opening at the Onyx, praised Smith for playing "swing fiddle—but hot" and Jones for "blow[ing] plenty of horn." Accounts of the band's performances at the Onyx indicate that, as in Buffalo, Jones and Smith took lengthy solos that pushed the boundaries of their considerable stamina and creativity. Cultural critic Gilbert Seldes, describing Smith's Onyx Club performances in November 1936, expressed amazement at the band's ability to "rise step by step in speed and tone, repeating some thirty or forty bars of music until it seemed impossible to listen to it any longer. Yet that was only the beginning, and it was after the music had reached apparently its extreme limits that the really expert work began and the effects were multiplied by geometric progression." Smith remembered that "we had an arrangement on 'Stomping At The Savoy' that would last half an hour and we used to play it all the time."[32] Jones recalled that "it was nothing for us to play one number for forty-five minutes or an hour," and that "many a night I sat up there and played 25 choruses, you know, and he's just hollering for more. Stuff's hollering for more."[33] This kind of mutual support is audible in a radio broadcast from February 1936, during which a member of the band interjects "Swing, Stuff!" and other encouragements during Smith's solo on *Ding*

Dong Daddy from Dumas and the entire group yells "higher!" as Jones plays an ascending chromatic passage in the high register of the trumpet.[34] The spontaneity apparent in the band's solos was paralleled in Smith's approach to repertoire and arranging. Jones remembered that because Smith "never knew how to read music" he had no notated arrangements but rather taught each musician his part by playing it on the violin.[35] This lack of reliance on a written "book" enabled the band to keep its arrangements flexible and encouraged its members to take risks. For example, Smith, who "could hear a number once on the radio" and memorize it, once made the band stop talking at a party to listen to a broadcast of *Embraceable You,* and then announced that "tonight when we go to work, we're going to play that." Despite the band's protests ("Everybody said, no Stuff, we don't know that now. We forgot it. We listened to other stuff"), Smith forged ahead with the tune during their set at the Onyx, prompting more cautious members of the band to argue that "we shouldn't be practicing here."[36] Drummer LeRoy Battle, who played with Smith several years later at 52nd Street's Downbeat Club, similarly recalled that Smith had a flexible approach to performance. "[Smith] was very antsy, you know what I mean? Yeah, very antsy. You couldn't tell what he was going to do next. He would change his mind—'Let's do it this way—no, never mind'—we rehearsed it like that, and then the night that we would perform, he'd do it another way. . . . So you had to stay on your toes."[37] The band's emphasis on improvisation and spontaneity endeared the group to the white musicians' circle at the Onyx Club, who, as we have seen, upheld these values as the essence of jazz.

Although the time constraints of the 78 rpm records made by the band in 1936 and 1937 precluded the extended improvisations and formal flexibility featured at the Onyx, the recordings reveal other aspects of Smith's style. The band's recorded repertoire consists mainly of popular tunes in the standard AABA form, such as *Robins and Roses* and *I Don't Want to Make History,* with such occasional exceptions as the original composition *I'se a Muggin',* based on a repeated riff, and Raymond Scott's *Twilight in Turkey,* a programmatic instrumental with a comparatively complex structure.[38] On most of the recordings, Smith sings a chorus, drawing on the rhythmic freedom and scat interjections popularized by Louis Armstrong but using a lighter, less gravelly timbre. Both Smith and Jonah Jones often take instrumental solos of a chorus or more. Their hard-driving styles complement one another. Jones, who sometimes uses a mute for a growling effect, employs bluesy bent notes and flashy glissandi. Smith often accompanies Jones's solos with harmonized figures intended to emulate the interaction between sections in a big band; Smith later claimed that he approached the violin as though "the E and the A [strings] were the brass and the D and the G the reeds."[39] In a 1937 interview, Smith explained that "when I play under my trumpet-man Jonah . . . I play lots of double stops and use all the fifths I can wherever they'll fit in."[40] In his own solos, Smith often used only "the last six or eight inches of his bow" to achieve what he called "my equivalent of a horn player's breath control."[41] His style employs virtuosic sequences and arpeggios as well as an unpredictable approach to harmony that sometimes results in dissonances surprising for jazz of the mid-1930s. Trumpeter Herman Autrey, who played with Smith in 1942, remembered his exceptional harmonic abilities: "And I used to get such a kick out of Stuff, because Stuff would be playing . . . dah, dum, dumdle, dum . . . you said to Stuff, go up to minor, and he would. . . . I mean he was just capable and able to do it, where a lot of guys would have to stop and think."[42] At the Onyx, Smith's powerful violin sound was probably enhanced eventually by his innovative use of electric amplification.[43] Another prominent feature of Smith's recordings is the aggressive four-beat swing established by the four-piece rhythm section, which benefited after March 1936 from the presence of skilled drummer Cozy Cole.[44] Jack Egan wrote that "the rhythm 'sends' the entire audience [at the Onyx] all night long." Jones recalled that the band would get into "what we used to call a 'groove,' where everybody felt the same thing. Cozy will tell you that. We'd get into that thing and play an hour, and it was no pressure, no strain. It just flowed, and we didn't get tired, because everyone was swinging. . . . What we had was a tempo and a groove." Drummer Cliff Leeman, who heard the band at the Onyx in 1936, claimed that they were the "swingingest, damnest band I heard, and the walls almost came down with the pulsing beat." Like many other musicians, Leeman had special praise for Cole's press roll, which he said "got the whole place rocking."[45] It is clear that Smith's appeal for musicians at the Onyx Club was due in large part to the band's musical skill and creativity.

On the other hand, the band's comical stage presence also attracted the Onyx Club audience. Jack Egan drew attention to Smith's sartorial trademark, a battered silk top hat, and called Jones "a terrific showman."[46] Some of the band's appeal derived from its members' physical ebullience while playing. Danish record producer Timme Rosenkrantz, for example, described Smith as a "little, nimble fellow, who jumps and dances and almost stands on his head as he plays," and a 1937 *March of Time* newsreel filmed at the Onyx shows the band members bouncing up and down and smiling broadly as they play.[47] A photo of the group taken at the Onyx in March 1937 by jazz photographer Charles Peterson shows them snapping their fingers and clapping, while a 1936 publicity shot captures Smith dancing.[48] Much of the band's performance style, however, involved calculated comedy bits rather than simply high spirits. As Jones remembered, "we did a lot of novelty stuff [at the Onyx] along with the playing, although we hadn't done so much before. We got such a good response with one novelty number that we made up another. We'd make 'em up on the bandstand, and clown around."[49] "Novelties" presented by the group included their trademark funny hats—in addition to Smith's top hat, Jones wore a derby, while the *March of Time* newsreel shows Cozy Cole and guitarist Bobby Bennett wearing bizarre hats with long phallic appendages.[50] Smith recalled in 1965 that Cole sometimes wore a straw hat with a "little light" attached that "would flicker as he shook his head."[51] Smith and the band also told funny stories and one-liners. LeRoy Battle remembered that once when Smith invited him to announce for the band, Battle ended a set with "next set, stick around. Next set we're going to play some numbers we know."[52] Smith himself told a jive version of the story of Adam and Eve in which Adam gets high by smoking the grass he finds in the "God-damn of E-damn."[53] Perhaps the most striking aspect of the band's stage presence was the unpredictable, irreverent behavior of Smith, whom bassist Al Hall later remembered as a "pixie."[54] Rosenkrantz wrote that "all of a sudden, while his band was playing, he would disappear, and you might find him in either the men's or the ladies' room, playing a pretty solo for the local authority, or he might go to the bar and quench his thirst with a quantity of firewater." On another occasion, he might "stop in the middle of a solo when a young and beautiful woman entered the room and point out to the audience the woman's anatomical qualities, which remarks sometimes registered unfavorably with her escort. But that didn't stop Stuff."[55] In short, as a 1936 review put it, Smith and the band "k[ept] the customers much amused with all sorts of screwy antics" as well as with their music.[56]

To describe Smith's performances in terms of music on the one hand and comedy on the other, however, obscures the degree to which these seemingly distinct elements of performance were perceived as related parts of a coherent whole. Jonah Jones later claimed that at the Onyx "it wasn't like a show or nothing. We just played," which suggests that he might have viewed the band's well-documented theatricality as an aspect of musical practice rather than as a separate form of performance. George Simon, in a May 1936 review, argued that "Stuff Smith is just what's needed around town in the way of swinging jam outfits, for Smith and his boys not only swing out, but they swing out with a sense of humor, as well. . . . Smith and his boys prove that you can really swing out and still have plenty of wacky fun at the same time—for which the sextet is to be highly commended!" A combination of musicianship and comic skill was especially apparent in what Jack Egan called Smith's "special novelty arrangements." Egan reported, for example, that "it takes the boys a half hour to play '[The Music Goes] Round and Around' the number starting as a bolero and including a corn chorus on fiddle, an exhibition in shim sham, truckin' and imitations of Joe Louis and Max Baer doing the latter plus ten choruses on the trumpet."[57]

The complex tangle of musical practices and racial signifiers described here illustrates the inadequacy of a conventional formalist approach to music analysis in addressing Smith's performances. To understand why this performance appealed to its audience, we need to situate it within both the specific context of the 52nd Street entertainment district and broader trends in contemporary African American performance. Smith's version of *The Music Goes 'Round and Around* was on one level probably a parody of his predecessors at the Onyx Club, Riley and Farley. By interpreting Riley and Farley's hit song in a number of musical styles, from bolero to "corn," Smith both demonstrated his own mastery of the material and poked fun at the ubiquity of *The Music Goes 'Round and Around.* Jones's "ten choruses on the trumpet" showcased his fertile musical imagination for a predominantly white audience who expected such abilities of black performers. The group's dancing similarly showed off its members' virtuosity in an idiom that was specifically associated with African American performers. The Shim Sham was a four-part routine, first popularized at Connie's Inn in Harlem in 1931, that was designed to fit over one chorus of a thirty-two-bar tune. Truckin', which seems to have been a regular feature of Smith's performances, was a dance in which certain typical gestures—"the shoulders are often hunched up, one above the other, the hips sway . . . and the feet execute a variety of shuffles while the index finger of one hand wiggles shoulder-high at the sky"—were combined with individual improvisations.[58] In the performance discussed by Egan, truckin' was tied to a contemporaneous event in the world of sports: on September 24, 1935, "Brown Bomber" Joe Louis had knocked out white boxer Max Baer in the fourth round in front of a large crowd at Yankee Stadium.[59] Although Egan's review is not specific about the band's "imitations," it is likely that the performance celebrated Louis's triumph, for "to Harlemites" such as the Smith band "in the middle and late thirties, Joe Louis was easily the most heroic figure in America."[60] Smith's version of *The Music Goes 'Round* thus combined music, comedy, and topical references into a multifaceted, unpredictable whole. Smith himself explained in 1939 that "I try to give the public a combination of entertainment, comedy, novelty and swing. Variety is the keynote."[61] The complexity of the band's performances calls for an analytic strategy that addresses the roles of comedy and racial signification as well as musical sound.

"I'se a Muggin'": Jazz and Humor   Such a strategy can be derived from theoretical work on the function and mechanics of humor and from the history of African American humor in particular. An assessment of the significance of humor in Smith's performances helps explain why Smith's audience at the Onyx Club received him favorably despite his emphasis on comedy. Although, as we have seen, the white musicians of the Onyx began to draw an increasingly rigid line between authentic jazz and inauthentic "show business" after Riley and Farley's mixture of slapstick and jazz became commercially successful, this distinction was by no means fixed or universally accepted when Smith arrived at the Onyx. Smith differed from Riley and Farley in several significant ways. He was African American; he was undeniably a superlative improviser with remarkable imagination and technique; and his performances seem to have stressed musical virtuosity at least as much as comic antics. Moreover, Smith's songs and stage patter were rooted in the idiom of jive, which was associated with African Americans in Harlem and thus was part of the milieu that the Onyx Club's musicians saw as central to jazz. All of these factors would have predisposed the Onyx Club circle to view him as an authentic jazz musician. Perhaps most significantly, Smith's comedy shared structural and technical features with his musical style and thus could be seen as an essential counterpart to that style rather than as a distraction from it.[62] In examining the role of humor in Smith's performances, then, we can also shed light on his musical style.

Although scholars have debated the role of humor in Western concert music since the early 1800s, discussions of humor are rare in the literature on jazz.[63] This oversight often stems from honorable intentions: scholars dedicated to defending jazz as a high art have been wary of any approach that might seem to link it to the less prestigious world of popular entertainment. The formalist methods, derived from the study of Western concert music, that are often used to study jazz serve to demonstrate the music's legitimacy and complexity but offer little room for apparently extramusical considerations such as humor. In recent years, the

most promising approach to the conjunction of jazz and humor has involved literary critic Henry Louis Gates's notion of Signifyin(g), an African
American rhetorical strategy involving imitation and (often ironic) revi-
sion. The application of this idea in jazz scholarship has yielded fruit-
ful results, such as Ingrid Monson's nuanced discussion of the racial and
musical ironies in John Coltrane's *My Favorite Things* or Samuel Floyd's
interpretation of Louis Armstrong's improvisations as "Signifyin(g) revi-
sions" of older melodies.[64] Many of Smith's comic performances, particularly those that comment critically on minstrel stereotypes, can be read
persuasively through the ironic lens of Signifyin(g). Signifyin(g) is a useful analytical tool both because it situates jazz squarely within African
American culture and because it allows us to see connections among
a variety of expressive practices, from speech to music to literature to
dance.

If the Signifyin(g) trope's broad applicability accounts for its useful-
ness in a variety of contexts, however, it sometimes makes Signifyin(g)
appear to be a monolithic, essentialist category that lacks specificity. As
Guthrie Ramsey and Ronald Radano have each recently argued, analyses
based on Signifyin(g) need to be situated in specific historical and social
contexts in order to be effective.[65] Such an approach reveals that the notion of Signifyin(g) is more applicable to some aspects of humor than to
others. While Signifyin(g) works well to explain parody and other forms
of humor that are explicitly intertextual or revisionist, it is harder to see
how it operates in those forms of humor that do not make direct reference
to other texts. While acknowledging the continued value of Signifyin(g)
as a method of understanding jazz, we might also usefully explore new
approaches to the interrelationship of jazz and humor. In particular, we
need to address this relationship in a way that enables close readings of
individual performances as well as broader analysis of cultural and historical issues.

In analyzing Smith's performances, I draw on a theory of humor pro-
posed by film theorist Jerry Palmer. Because it is derived from analysis
of film and television, Palmer's approach provides a way to situate jazz
within wider trends in popular entertainment. Moreover, it enables close
readings of music that are not limited to conventional harmonic analysis
but that also do not exclude it altogether. Palmer argues that a "gag" (as
the term is used in reference to silent film) results from two elements.
The first is a peripeteia, or "the construction of a shock or surprise"; in
a verbal joke, this is the effect created by the punch line. The second
is a situation that is seen as simultaneously implausible and plausible

but in which implausibility outweighs plausibility. Palmer refers to the combination of these two components as the "logic of the absurd." As an example, he cites a somewhat tasteless slapstick gag, from a film by Smith's contemporaries Laurel and Hardy, in which a police officer is crushed by an elevator and emerges as a dwarf. The element of shock certainly applies here: the survival of the officer is a surprise constructed by the preceding narrative, which does not prepare the viewer for such a radical departure from realism. The second element comes into play because this extraordinary event can be interpreted in two contradictory ways. The first "tells us that what we see on the screen is intensely implausible": although it is commonly known that being crushed by an elevator is fatal, the officer survives. The second "line of reasoning," in contrast, "tells us that the event does in fact have a measure of plausibility": objects that are crushed generally become smaller, which is precisely what happens to the officer. Although both of these arguments vie for supremacy as the viewer perceives the gag, the first "is clearly a much stronger line of argument than the second, as it has the not inconsiderable merit of being true to the world as we know it on the basis of everyday life," while the second "is clearly only tenable on the basis of a piece of false reasoning" (i.e., "the assumption that what is true of inorganic or non-animate forms of being can be unproblematically transposed to the realm of the animate"). Palmer argues that the structure of the logic of the absurd is what defines comedy, and he asserts moreover that "this structure is nowhere to be found except in the fundamental forms of comedy."[66]

Here, I extend Palmer's argument to demonstrate that the structures he describes also are integral to music, which, like comedy, relies on surprise and various forms of what might be termed "plausibility" to create meaning. A useful example of this homology between comedy and music is Smith's biggest popular success, his composition *I'se a Muggin'*. In his review of the band's opening at the Onyx, Jack Egan reported that "the big feature is their own 'I'se a Muggin' which [publisher] Santly bought up before the band was in town a week."[67] On February 11, only a week after the Onyx opening, the band went into the Brunswick studios to record the tune, which *Down Beat*'s record reviewer described as a "natural."[68] By April, Egan wrote that "'I'se a Muggin'" [is] gaining in popularity at a terrific rate around town," and Rudy Vallee claimed on his radio show that *I'se a Muggin'* had become "one of the most popular pastimes since they stopped blowin' in here and pushing the first valve down."[69] Other bands, both black and white, rushed to record their own versions of the tune.[70]

I'se a Muggin' was significant in that it represented Smith to a general audience as well as to other musicians.

An initial hearing of Smith's double-sided record of *I'se a Muggin'* might suggest that the band's musical performance was merely a backdrop for their manic verbal comedy. Although the performance follows a straightforward verse-chorus form, it is unusual in that both the verses and the chorus are harmonized with the same chord progression: a two-bar vamp—the chord changes are essentially I–vi–ii–V—that repeats throughout with only occasional variation.[71] The eight-bar chorus comprises three iterations of the song's title, sung to a catchy riff by Smith and followed by a second riff scatted by the band; after three times through this back-and-forth pattern, Smith and the band join together to sing a two-bar scat phrase that appears to borrow its off-kilter, syncopated rhythm from Duke Ellington's *It Don't Mean a Thing.* Each verse begins with a few lines sung solo by Smith but quickly turns into a repetitive, bantering call-and-response between Smith and the rest of the band. The first verse, for example, starts with Smith singing, "Every night upon the stand / You hear the boys holler"—and the rest of the band finishes the rhyme: "Jam, jam!" Thereafter, Smith and the band sing lines back and forth: "Where, where? / Over there! / Over there? / Yes, over there!" and so on. In the second verse, Smith invites the band to "Come on down, gates, and swing with me / Come on down, let's drink some tea," a reference to marijuana. These lines are followed by another call-and-response section in which Smith and the band sing short phrases dealing with "tea" and "the mighty mezz," a reference to the marijuana peddled in Harlem by clarinetist Mezz Mezzrow.[72] Smith begins the third verse by singing, "I went down to the railroad station"; the call-and-response that follows discusses his attempts to call a redcap at the station. This evolves into a fast three-way sung exchange between Smith, Jones, and a third musician (possibly guitarist Bobby Bennett), in which each plays a different color "cap" and shifts responsibility to the next; for example: "Who me, sir?" "Yes, you, sir!" "Not me, sir." "Then who, sir?" "The blue cap, sir!"[73] As this banter continues, Jones appears to become confused by the rapid round-and-round of the exchange and proceeds to do all three parts by himself: "Who me, sir—yes, you, sir—not me, sir—then who, sir—ah, the red cap, sir—who me, sir—yes, you, sir—not me, sir—then who, sir—ah, the red cap, sir—who me, sir—yes, you, sir—not me, sir—then who, sir—ah, the black cap, sir!" As the record ends, Smith cajoles listeners to "turn us [i.e., the record] over" to hear part 2 of *I'se a Muggin',* which I will discuss shortly. The overall effect of the record is of a flamboyant verbal virtuosity that accelerates into chaos as the short phrases skillfully bandied about by Smith and the band devolve into Jones's comical outburst.

If both the musical performance and the verbal comedy of *I'se a Muggin'* are viewed in terms of Palmer's "logic of the absurd," it becomes clear that the music is an integrated part of a comic whole rather than an unrelated support. Both the music and the comic exchanges derive their effect from relentless repetition that frustrates forward motion. As we have seen, every time that Smith begins a verse, he is almost immediately interrupted by the others in the band, who engage him in a repetitive and ultimately pointless exchange from which he is extricated only by the arrival of the chorus. This pattern neatly illustrates Palmer's model of comedy. We are surprised by the band's interruption of Smith just as he seems to be settling into the verse. The interruption is plausible inasmuch as interruption is a common feature of verbal communication, but it is implausible in that it stalls the normal flow of a musical performance. This implausibility is emphasized by the contrast between Smith, who sings his text in a pitched and thus conventionally "musical" way, and the other musicians, who shout their text. In the verses of *I'se a Muggin'*, the "logic of the absurd" thus privileges disruption and disturbance over linear flow. This imbalance is mirrored in the tune's most fundamental structure, the two-bar vamp. Although the swing and conviction of the band's performance, as well as the vamp's conventional chord changes, demonstrate the basic "plausibility" of the vamp, its constant cycling is both surprising and implausible in the context of 1930s pop music, which generally relied on harmonic and formal change (as, for example, in the B section, or *bridge,* of a standard AABA form) to generate forward motion. Although this vamp may not be heard as inherently "comic," it creates a tension between plausibility and implausibility that parallels that of the overtly comic aspects of the performance. Finally, we can speculate that, in performance, *I'se a Muggin'* was accompanied by physical comedy that similarly explored this tension.[74] Jones's apparent mental breakdown, during which he takes on the role of several characters, could easily have been dramatized with manic gestures that would have been plausible given his supposed confusion but implausibly frenzied in the context of a staged performance. It is worth noting that in the vocabulary of Harlem jive, *muggin'* could refer both to music ("improvising an introduction or background, during which the musicians get the feel of their instruments and their colleagues") and to physical gestures ("making faces, making love.")[75] This parallel suggests that physical

Figure 1. Excerpt from "novelty" version of *The Sheik of Araby* performed by Stuff Smith, ca. 1946. Transcribed from LeRoy Battle, interview by the author, May 23, 2002. Mr. Battle sang this excerpt unaccompanied; I have transcribed and harmonized it in B-flat major, the key of the original piano-and-vocal score of *The Sheik of Araby* (Harry B. Smith, Francis Wheeler, and Ted Snyder, *The Sheik of Araby* [New York: Mills Music, 1921]). Unbracketed text represents Smith's singing of the song's original text, while bracketed portions represent newly added text sung by the band.

comedy, like verbal comedy, had perceived connections to musical practice among some black musicians.

Another example of a structural homology between comedy and music is a risqué "novelty number" that LeRoy Battle performed during his stint with Smith. Battle remembered that Smith would "do a take-off on . . . *The Sheik of Araby*," transcribed in figure 1.[76]

In the figure, the unbracketed text represents Smith's singing of the original text of this 1920s standard, while the text in parentheses is a newly added rejoinder sung after each line by the band. The new text, which would certainly have been surprising to audiences familiar with the song, fulfills the first condition of the logic of the absurd, and it also creates a conflict between plausibility and implausibility. Its implausibility derives from the contrast between the new text's seemingly inappropriate sexual candor and the euphemistic language of the original, as well as from the way in which it alters, or perhaps simply makes unexpectedly explicit, the meaning of the original song. The new text's plausibility, in contrast, is due to the fact that the phrase "with no clothes on" consistently makes literal sense in context. This plausibility is accentuated by the way in which the meaning of "with no clothes on" changes according to context even as the phrase itself remains the same—for example, in its third iteration, it seems to describe the unsuspecting object of the sheik's desire, while in the fourth it appears to refer to the sheik himself. The notion that an unchanging text can take on different meanings in various contexts is paralleled in the melody of *The Sheik of Araby*. The melody revolves around the pitch G—three of the four phrases represented in this transcription end on this pitch—but the function of G is variable depending on the accompanying harmony. For example, the first phrase begins with G as the sixth of a B-flat major chord and ends with G as the fifth of a C minor seventh. Like the repeated line of text, this repeated pitch thus alters in significance depending on context. By reinforcing and prolonging the last pitch of each phrase, the new line of music and text draws attention to this dynamic. As in *I'se a Muggin'*, the comic, "novelty" aspects of this performance are thus consistent with its musical structure.

Although Smith clearly intended his reworking of *The Sheik of Araby* to be humorous, the model of comedy that I have sketched out also can be applied to those of Smith's performances that more closely conform to conventional notions of jazz. One example is an eight-bar violin solo, transcribed in figure 2, that concludes the third chorus of *Onyx Club Spree*, recorded in 1937.[77]

This solo comprises two contrasting sections: an unusual five-bar passage that seems to disregard the underlying harmony, and a three-bar conclusion that returns to a clear F major tonality. Readers versed in conventional formal analysis of jazz might reasonably view the opening passage as an experiment in extended harmony. For example, the repeated G in bar 1 could be heard as the ninth in an F^{maj9}, while the last four eighth notes in bar 1 might be outlining a D^{7b9}. Alternately, the passage could be heard as polytonal, with bar 1 in G minor or possibly C minor against the underlying F major. Neither of these approaches, however, seems to explain the passage adequately. What a transcription does not reveal is Smith's somewhat wooden and nonchalant articulation and phrasing in the first five bars, which suggests whimsical noodling rather than intense harmonic exploration. Moreover, the ascending and descending sequence in bars 4 and 5, although it might at first appear to be an avant-garde employment of fifth-based harmony, is more easily explained as a gesture based on the physical properties of the violin, played by moving from the first position to the open string on the second, third, and fourth strings of the instrument.

Rather than apply a standard analysis of harmonic procedures, then, a more valuable analytic strategy might involve viewing the passage

Figure 2. Violin solo, last eight bars of third chorus, Stuff Smith and His Onyx Club Boys, *Onyx Club Spree,* matrix 62175-A, Decca 1279, recorded May 4, 1937, New York, reissued on Jazz Archives CD 108.

through the lens of the "logic of the absurd" and its contrast of plausibility and implausibility. The opening of Smith's solo contains this contrast internally. The passage is surprising after the more conservative eight-bar piano solo by Clyde Hart that precedes it. Although the passage seems harmonically implausible—it sounds as if Smith is hearing a different chord progression than we are—Smith's unconcerned, offhand execution makes it sound as though *he* is convinced of its plausibility. On a wider level, the structure of the entire solo embodies the contradiction between plausibility and implausibility. Smith's implausible opening passage is made to sound plausible in retrospect when he links it to a more conventional gesture in F major. At the same time, however, this conclusion makes the opening seem even more implausible, because if Smith is capable of playing conventionally, there seems to be no reason that he should not have been doing so all along.[78] This brief solo suggests that the structure of comedy was not simply a musical trick employed to accompany "novelty songs" but also informed Smith's style as an improvising soloist.

"A Man from Way Uptown": Jive, Stereotypes, and Subversion Although the "logic of the absurd" is a useful tool in close analysis of the mechanics of Smith's music, it tells us little about the challenges Smith faced as a black musician performing for a predominantly white audience. In the mid-1930s, African American entertainers, although still encumbered by the racist traditions of minstrelsy, were beginning to find ways of subverting minstrel stereotypes to project a more affirmative version of black identity. Those black comedians who, like Smith, performed for white audiences were to some extent obliged to embody derogatory images of blackness in order to survive commercially. Such images were epitomized by the performances of the film actor Stepin Fetchit (Lincoln Perry), whose "slow-moving, dim-witted coon" persona peaked in popularity in 1934 and 1935.[79] At the same time, the hugely popular radio show *Amos 'n' Andy,* followed nightly by an estimated forty million listeners in 1935, featured white actors' portrayals of "standard Negro stereotypes [such as] naïveté, imprudence, venality, and ignorance."[80] In New York, these stereotypes were countered by the vibrant reality of 1930s Harlem, where "black men and women from all walks of life had been politicized and sometimes even radicalized by Depression-era political organizing."[81] Black resentment of poverty and racial discrimination reached a boiling point on March 19, 1935, when rumors that a white store guard had beaten a black child to death for stealing a penknife led to rioting on 125th Street.[82] Apollo Theatre emcee Ralph Cooper later argued that "the so-called riots helped end the grand illusion that Harlem was full of happy-go-lucky blacks too busy singin' and dancin' and struttin' to want a slice of the American pie."[83] In addition, more conventional, if less visible, political movements, such as a "Don't Buy Where You Can't Work" boycott campaign against discrimination in hiring, sought to improve economic and social conditions for African Americans in Harlem.[84] As cultural historian Mel Watkins demonstrates, black comedians of the 1930s "began reflecting the black community's more assertive mood" in such venues as Harlem's Apollo Theatre, which opened in 1934.[85] Here, the largely black audience, "many of whom presumably had taken part in the riot of 1935 . . . began demanding less veiled expression of actual black resentments regarding the larger society."[86] This demand was met by such comedians as Moms Mabley, who mixed sexual double entendres with satire of white racism, and Pigmeat Markham, whose celebrated "Here Come de Judge" routine lampooned the irrationality of the criminal justice system.[87] Although such performances did not entirely escape the minstrel legacy—for example, most Apollo comics in the 1930s still wore blackface—they reworked the conventions of this legacy to create stage comedy that spoke to and about black audiences.[88] When Smith arrived in New York in 1936, then, he entered a city in which black performers were employing a range of comic stances, from stereotypically servile to aggressively satiric, for a variety of audiences.

Smith's performances reflected the gamut of contemporary African American comedy, sometimes appearing to conform to minstrel stereotypes and sometimes celebrating the culture of Harlem while lampooning his audience. Playing for a white audience at the Onyx Club, Smith was obligated to represent certain stereotypical notions of black authenticity even as he slyly undermined them. An example of this strategy is part 2 of *I'se a Muggin'*, in which Smith, speaking over the same vamp used in part 1, invites the audience to join in a counting game. In a performance on Paul Whiteman's *Musical Varieties* radio show, broadcast February 23, 1936, Smith refers to this section as "the difficulty part of the piece" and explains that it involves counting from "numerality 1 to numerality 80."[89] Smith's vocabulary here, which appears to strive for loftiness but only succeeds in sounding foolish, recalls the introduction to the studio recording, in which Smith and Jones argue over whether to use the words *cipher* or *naught* in their counting before finally settling on *zero*. Such verbal comedy can be traced back to the "stump speech" of the minstrel theater, in which, through the pompous but nonsensical rhetoric of the blackface speaker, "blacks' ability to understand or interpret sophisticated ideas [was] ridiculed and mocked."[90] Whiteman seems to reinforce this interpretation with an intentional malapropism of his own when he explains that Smith will "ask [. . .] the class to swing out with a little alge-bree-ay." Smith's performance thus appears at first to perpetuate traditional, derogatory images of blackness.

This stance changes, however, once Smith explains the rules of the counting game, in which the band and audience count upward from one, but replace any number that contains seven or is a multiple of seven with "uh-uh" and any number ending in zero with "woof-woof." (For example, the numbers twenty through twenty-nine are rendered as "woof-woof, uh-uh, 22, 23, 24, 25, 26, uh-uh, uh-uh, 29.") As they continue to play the *I'se a Muggin'* vamp, Smith and the band begin counting in rhythm, with a new number beginning on the first beat of each measure. Despite the seeming simplicity of the rules, this is a tricky game, which involves keeping track simultaneously of two ten-measure cycles (numbers ending in zero and seven) and a seven-measure cycle (multiples of seven). Smith and the band perform the game flawlessly at a brisk tempo. As two radio broadcasts from early 1936 indicate, their audiences often were not so skilled. During both the Whiteman show mentioned earlier and a Rudy Vallee broadcast of April 23, the audience laughs during the counting game but does not seem to count along, catching on only during the range from seventy to seventy-nine, which the band chants as "uh-1! uh-2!" and so on.[91] Although the audience's laughter cannot be interpreted conclusively, it seems likely that it was in part an amused but chagrined reaction to its defeat in the face of an intellectual and performative challenge. Here, Smith and the band demonstrated their superiority over the audience on two fronts at once. The first is musical: by reciting numbers precisely in time, the band managed to make the game swing. Second, and most significantly, the band was demonstrating intellectual and mathematical abilities beyond those of the audience, whose members were unable to keep up with the counting game. As Mel Watkins points out, even to address a white audience directly was a risky gesture for black comedians until the 1950s: "a black performer who demanded a personal response would have transgressed a boundary by suggesting an equality intolerable to most non-blacks."[92] By not only addressing the members of the white audience but beating them publicly at an intellectual task, Smith and the band appear to be reclaiming this performance from the racial stereotypes with which it began, instead making it a sly display of their own intelligence.

In addition to such subtle subversions of older stereotypes of African American performers, Smith's performances manifested a newer and more aggressive sensibility, exemplified in the group's use of Harlem jive. The word *jive* is most commonly understood today to refer to the speech of jazz musicians, particularly African Americans, during the 1930s and 1940s, but in its heyday it meant "all things to all men," as *New York Amsterdam News* reporter Dan Burley pointed out in 1944.[93] *Jive* could refer to jazz music itself—for example, a 1937 article in the journal *American Speech* suggests that it is synonymous with *ride,* defined (albeit incomprehensibly) as "the quality of intrinsic rhythmicity characterizing the melodic pattern of a lick."[94] The word could signify insincerity or deceit, particularly when used for comic effect or in a seduction ("I'm jiving a chick").[95] It could be a sly euphemism for marijuana, as in Smith's own composition *Here Comes the Man with the Jive,* suggesting its close connection to the culture of "tea-pads" and drug peddling in Harlem.[96] In his *Original Handbook of Harlem Jive* (1944), Dan Burley's broad definition of *jive* includes "anything that is tangible, that which is intangible and pertains to a manner of living and thinking."[97] For some African Americans, *jive* seems to have represented what cultural critic Raymond Williams calls a "structure of feeling," one that drew music, speech, comedy, drugs, and other aspects of everyday life, "tangible" or "intangible," into a language of social transgression and racial affirmation.[98]

Although the urban sensibility represented by jive already had been dramatized in black theaters like the Apollo, it was a relative novelty for white audiences on 52nd Street.[99] The Smith band, fascinated by the atmosphere and culture of Harlem, brought this sensibility to the Onyx Club by employing jive vocabulary, making frequent reference to Harlem drug culture, and more generally embodying the cunning, self-confident attitude associated with jive. [100] Examples include two of Smith's original compositions, *Here Comes the Man with the Jive* and *You'se a Viper*. In the former, Smith sings that "there's a man from way uptown / Who'll take away your blues / And any time the man comes 'round / the vipers spread the news."[101] *Viper* was Harlem slang for a pot smoker.[102] Smith then takes on the role of marijuana dealer, singing, "I'm the jive jive man / I'm the jive jive man / I've got my jive right in my hand." *You'se a Viper*, sung by Jones, focuses on the viper rather than the dealer. Its first chorus begins, "Dreamed about a reefer five foot long / The mighty mezz, but not too strong / You'll get high, but not for long / 'Cause you'se a viper."[103] In later verses, Jones emphasizes details of the viper's life that would have struck a chord with those familiar with them. For example, he says that the viper likes to "truck into the candy store." Trumpeter Harry Edison, discussing this song, pointed to the well-known fact that "you'd have a sweet taste after you smoked the joint. You want something sweet, you know."[104] Some of Smith's jive routines took on more fanciful themes. An example is the Garden of Eden story already mentioned, which used jive anachronistically for comic effect—Adam climbs "Mount Mary's-y'-Mama," and Eve's first words to Adam are "Get up, you square! I'm going to put your boots on and lace them way up to your gills."[105] In these and other examples, jive played an integral part in the Smith band's comic style at the Onyx Club.

Black musicians who present jive to white audiences sometimes are disparaged or dismissed in jazz historiography; for example, David Stowe writes that Cab Calloway "tamed his own jive talk through commercialization." Such criticism is founded in a belief, dating back to the swing era itself, that jive was a language of authentic resistance to mainstream white culture and that attempts to market it to that mainstream were a form of selling out. Dan Burley, for example, argued in 1944 that jive "is a medium of escape, a safety valve for people pressed up against the wall for centuries, deprived of the advantages of complete social, economic, moral and intellectual freedom." Mezz Mezzrow and Bernard Wolfe wrote a few years later that "jive is a private affair, a secret inner-circle code cooked up partly to mystify the outsiders, while it brings those in the know closer together because they alone have the key to the puzzle." More recently, Burton W. Peretti has asserted that "jive gained its form and content—and its insular function" from a "black linguistic tradition" of "deception, opposite meanings, protective exaggeration, and veiling slang."[106]

While these commentaries outline one meaning of jive, they run the risk of reducing jive to a function of an essentialist vision of black identity. First, it should be noted that jive was not an insider language for African Americans in general, or even for most blacks in Harlem— the tea-pad culture that supported jive was only one part of a rich tapestry of religious, political, commercial, and artistic concerns described in such works as Claude McKay's *Harlem: Negro Metropolis* (1940). Peretti makes this point, albeit with somewhat loaded language, when he argues that, rather than jazz musicians, "it was the less-musical, less-successful, less-integrated urban blacks who brought jive to its fruition in the late thirties." The African Americans who created and popularized jive were resisting other segments of the black community as much as they were resisting hegemonic white culture. Second, to reduce jive to a defensive reaction against a white mainstream masks the vibrant, optimistic creativity that produced it. As Burley argued, "everyone knows that life isn't half as thrilling, as exciting, or as picturesque as it should be. Jive undertakes to remedy that situation with language that makes up for the dullness of mere existence." This suggests that jive was as much an affirmative reflection of changing values within black communities as it was a protective response to white encroachment.[107]

Rather than view Smith's jive as an authentically black form corrupted through presentation to whites at the Onyx Club, then, we should see it as one part of a complex web of social interactions between blacks and whites. At the Onyx, such interracial exchanges involved multiple interpretations of both the language and attitude of jive and the musical practices of jazz. In Smith's performances, jive and jazz were related parts of a compelling stage presentation in which jazz improvisation expressed the sensibility of jive even as jive itself drew both its playfulness and its power from the broader context of the music. Both verbally and musically, Smith countered images of black irrationality and simplicity by demonstrating the complexity and sophistication of African American urban culture. If at some times the conventional ideas about black performers already prevalent on 52nd Street compelled Smith to enact racial stereotypes, at other times he was able to work within these restrictions to show his audience a creative, self-confident image of black identity.

"The Onyx Fairly Jumps": Sitting in with Stuff This audience initially consisted largely of white musicians, whose interest in Smith led to musical and social exchanges that continued to make influence across racial lines an important part of 52nd Street's culture. The improvisational flexibility of Smith's music inspired many musicians to sit in with the band at the Onyx Club. Cozy Cole recalled that Smith held visiting musicians to a high standard. "Like with Stuff Smith . . . we were playing at the Onyx Club and guys used to come in and want to sit in and Stuff would tell them right quick, 'no, don't jump up on this bandstand if you can't play.' You know, cause we're liable to play anything. Don't jump up here if you can't play and swing, don't come up here."[108] Joe Venuti, who as the most acclaimed violinist in 1920s jazz had been an early influence on Smith, was one musician frightened by Smith's prowess.[109] Jonah Jones remembered that when Venuti came to the Onyx,

Stuff would announce him. And now ladies and gentlemen we have the greatest violin player in the world and if y'all give a great hand, he'll come in and sit in with us . . . and [Venuti]'d turn his back. Wouldn't even look up at us. . . . He wouldn't even think about coming up there, ya know, 'cause Stuff . . . was something else. . . . So after the set was over, I went downstairs to the table with him and said, yeah man, why didn't you come up there and sit in with us, ya know and blow a few notes? He said, uhuh. He said, when I sit there and listen to that guy . . . as great as he's playing now, if I take my violin out of the case and get up there with him, he's going to change into a cage of apes. I fell down laughing.[110]

Despite Smith's ability to intimidate would-be sitters-in, many musicians regularly got up on the stand to play with him and the band. Cole remembered that musicians who sat in included Artie Dollinger, Bernie Privin, Jack Teagarden, Jimmy and Tommy Dorsey, Artie Shaw, Benny Goodman, Chris Griffin, Ziggy Elman, Allen Reuss, and Lou McGarity, several of whom had been associated with the Onyx Club since its speakeasy days.[111] More surprisingly, Smith remembered that classical violinists Fritz Kreisler and Jascha Heifetz sometimes sat in on piano and traded tips about violin technique.[112] Jones recalled that he and Pee Wee Hunt, a trombonist in the Casa Loma Orchestra, sometimes "would do a little . . . jive number, just spontaneously," and also remembered that Johnny Mercer sometimes sang with the band.[113] Jam sessions begun at the Onyx Club would often continue after hours at the uptown apartment of Timme Rosenkrantz, which Smith remembered as "the best joint to go to after the Onyx closed. . . . All the musicians used to say, Let's go to Timme's. . . . And then about twenty of us would go. . . . And we used to drink Pernod and drink, er, other things. And eat. And Inez [Cavanaugh, a singer and Rosenkrantz's companion] would fix us some spaghetti and hamburgers. And Timme would be back there recording."[114] The casual music making described here recalls the jam sessions at the original Onyx Club; in the earlier sessions, however, black musicians rarely played such a significant role. Interracial interactions such as these were still relatively rare in the jazz world; for example, Benny Goodman's hiring of black pianist Teddy Wilson, often seen as a milestone in jazz history, took place in 1935, only a year before Smith opened at the Onyx.

In some cases, such musical interactions led to personal relationships that extended beyond the bounds of the jam session. Jonah Jones, for example, formed a close friendship with white trumpeter Bunny Berigan. Jones remembered one incident in which the two friends shared a joke.

Bunny would come down to the Onyx and stand there outside the door and wait until I get my break and we'd go out to 6th Avenue together and he'd say [Jonah shows smoking a joint] [h]ere's some new stuff Jonah, try this. We go walking down 6th Avenue . . . and then a policeman was coming towards us with a stick and I don't think he knew what it was in them days because when he was coming towards us . . . Bunny said, let's make him contact high. I say, what do you mean. He say, you get a mouthful, I get a mouthful and when he gets up on us . . . let's let him walk between us and blow it in his nose. . . . I said, yeah . . . and when he walked up on us, we blow [blows] right in his nose and we was laughing and he was looking back at us with his stick. . . . So, Bunny say, he's contact high and don't know it and [laughs] we're laughing our butt off too and he never said nothing about [it], you know.[115]

Jones recalled that such evenings often would end with him and Berigan going to Harlem at four in the morning and jamming and drinking for hours on end, until "finally, he'd go home with me and my wife would be up at that time. . . . We lived on 158th Street then. Washington Heights they called it. And my wife put us both to bed. Ya know, 'cause then she called up his wife, he was living on Long Island, and say, both of them just come in here and both of 'em drunk and I put 'em to bed. . . . Sometimes, he'd stay there all the time, ya know, for the whole night or something. We were so close."[116] Similarly, white drummer Cliff Leeman began a long-term friendship with Cozy Cole after first seeing the Smith band at the Onyx.[117] Although close relationships like these did not necessarily undermine white musicians' misconceptions about African Americans, they may have led them to begin to base their ideas of racial identity on real musicians rather than an anonymous stereotype.

The Smith band also began to attract African American musicians to 52nd Street as customers. Some black patrons were perhaps drawn by coverage of Smith in black newspapers such as the *New York Amsterdam News*.[118] Bassist Leonard Gaskin, who later worked with Smith, remembered that his first trip to 52nd Street was inspired by the hope of hearing the violinist.

There were a number of groups [on 52nd Street], but this particular group was headed by Stuff Smith, violinist, and he had a bunch of fellows, and they had a little hit called *I'se a Muggin'*. And of course I was . . . about fifteen years old, and I had a mentor, more or less, who was two years my senior, who lived on my street in Brooklyn, and he was . . . studying bass, and he was on the hockey team, and he was a good student . . . and he says "You have to listen to this." And we went together down to 52nd Street, and of course, we couldn't go in, we were too young, so we stood [outside]—many times I went to 52nd Street in the early days and I . . . either didn't have the money, or I wasn't able to go in because of many things, money, youth, understanding— all the bewilderment that goes with youth . . . so that would be about my first encounter [with 52nd Street].[119]

That Gaskin's inability to enter the club was due to his age or lack of money, rather than racial discrimination, is supported by an interview with bassist Milt Hinton in which he remembers that in 1936 and 1937, 52nd Street's clubs were attended by both "blacks and whites. They were small clubs, and they were just jammed . . . out-of-towners mainly, with blacks." Hinton cites Smith specifically as one of the musicians whom he would go to hear. Another African American musician who heard Smith at the Onyx was vibraphonist Lionel Hampton, who wrote in the *Baltimore Afro-American* in 1938, "I went by to see Stuff Smith and his boys one night last week and the cats are really in their old Fifty-second Street groove. The Onyx fairly jumps. You can't get near the door, front or back, and everybody's either happy or drunk."[120] Accounts of Onyx jam sessions including such luminaries as Fats Waller and Cab Calloway suggest that some black musicians were encouraged to drop in and join Smith on stage.[121] By 1938, in a review of Smith, *Variety* claimed that "from an academic viewpoint, the Onyx anew brings up the observation that swing is perhaps the greatest common denominator for equalizing the races. There's no color line with the alligators, and in truth the topmost killer-dillers are from Harlem, transplanted to the 52d street environment. And perhaps the most appreciative audience constitutes the professional musicians as a class."[122] Black musicians continued to attend Smith's performances on 52nd Street into the 1940s. Bassist Carline Ray, who heard Smith on the street in the mid-1940s, recalled that she "was just mesmerized by him. . . . He had a wonderful sense of humor, he had such facility on his instrument . . . I had never heard anybody play jazz on a violin before that, so . . . he really got my attention."[123]

Although one might speculate that African American musicians' conceptions of authentic jazz differed drastically from those of the Onyx Club's original clientele of white musicians, many black musicians held values similar to those of their predecessors on 52nd Street. Leonard Gaskin, for example, asserted that "when I first saw [Smith] . . . he was a showman. There's a difference between show and music, a musician and an entertainer. They're two different things."[124] Just as Smith did in his performances, other African American musicians and audience members engaged existing ideas about jazz in a variety of ways, sometimes resisting them and at other times perpetuating them. Although black audience members and musicians had a profound impact on conceptions of jazz on 52nd Street, then, their influence cannot be reduced to a monolithic "black perspective." As Smith's successors at the Onyx Club would demonstrate, the range of what could be considered authentic black music was becoming increasingly broad on 52nd Street in the mid-1930s.

Chapter Four **A Little Law and Order in My Music**
The John Kirby Sextet and Maxine Sullivan

During Stuff Smith's tenure at the Onyx Club from February 1936 to May 1937, West 52nd Street's reputation for lively nightlife and energetic small-group jazz flourished. Such long-standing clubs as the Hickory House and the Onyx competed with more ephemeral and obscure venues such as Tillie's Kitchen, Caliente, and Through the Looking Glass.[1] Several musicians, including Smith, Wingy Manone, and Red McKenzie, appeared frequently on 52nd Street, while many others had brief stints there. As the street's jazz scene evolved, the racial disparities that had characterized it from the beginning persisted. While Smith was immensely popular at the Onyx, his success did not inspire the street's other clubs to feature African Americans as headlining performers. Instead, such black musicians as pianist Teddy Wilson, singer Baby White, and vocal group The Three Peppers continued to appear mainly in secondary roles as "supporting" or "relief" acts.[2] In 1936 and 1937, 52nd Street's clubs were still dominated by white musicians such as Manone who infused contemporary popular music with the improvisatory energy of New Orleans jazz. As we have seen, these musicians helped perpetuate and popularize an image of jazz and its African American creators as spontaneous, uninhibited, and informal.

Smith's successors at the Onyx, a group led by bassist John Kirby and featuring the singer Maxine Sullivan, presented a striking alternative to this conventional notion of black musicianship. When Kirby's band began its engagement at the club in 1937, it played in an improvisatory swing style reminiscent of Smith's, but by 1938 it began to employ complex arrangements and a novel repertoire that comprised swing versions of European "classics" and folk songs. This new style placed the group at the center of a vogue for "swinging the classics" that swept popular music in the late 1930s. As cultural historian David Stowe points out, this trend can be interpreted in two seemingly contradictory ways. On the one hand, it was an attempt to gain "cultural legitimacy" for swing by linking it to great works of high art, while on the other hand, it was an attack on the notion of high art itself, a subversive practice that "tweak[ed] the notion of an autonomous tradition of art music that existed apart from and above the commercial market of popular taste."[3] For African American musicians such as Kirby and Sullivan, this contradiction was inevitably bound to ideas of race. By demonstrating their mastery of music in the European canon, these musicians asserted their own sophistication as serious artists and demonstrated that African American performers need not be bound to a restrictive standard of racial authenticity. Ironically, however, this stance sometimes served to accentuate racial difference in the minds of their audiences by juxtaposing the band's black identities against what appeared to be "white" musical material. In negotiating their complex relationship to race and artistry, then, Sullivan and the Kirby group paradoxically both invoked a standard of artistic freedom that transcended race and represented a black identity that was new on 52nd Street.[4]

The Onyx Hop: John Kirby and the Spirits of Rhythm   In May 1937, *Down Beat* announced that Smith planned to leave New York around May 15 and that his place at the Onyx probably would be taken by a small group led by bassist John Kirby. The group, which had been "rehearsing . . . around town for several weeks," comprised Kirby, clarinetist Buster Bailey, alto saxophonist Pete Brown, pianist Don Frye, drummer Freddie Moore, "and [guitarist] Teddy Bunn and Leo Watson of The Six Spirits of Rhythm." Although this article is not clear about Watson's role, in June the magazine reported that he was the drummer (presumably replacing Moore, who is not mentioned.)[5] All of these musicians were New York professionals of long standing: Kirby and Bailey had each spent years in Fletcher Henderson's band, while Brown, Frye, and Moore had performed as a trio.[6] The leadership of the group appears to have remained uncertain for some time. Although the May announcement claimed that Kirby was the leader, the June report credited leadership to Watson, and a July advertisement referred to the group in cumbersome fashion as "John

Kirby with Leo and His Spirits of Rhythm featuring Buster Bailey and Frank Newton" (the latter had by this time joined the band on trumpet).[7] Maxine Sullivan, who began singing with the group during the summer of 1937, remembered that the band was led by Newton.[8]

The casual organization of the band was paralleled at first by a loose, improvisatory approach to performance. Photographs of this early version of the Kirby band reveal an irreverent, flamboyant stage presence probably modeled after that of both the original Spirits of Rhythm, two of whom were in the group, and Stuff Smith, who was quite literally looking over their shoulders (an enlarged photograph of the Smith band was mounted behind the bandstand at the Onyx Club).[9] Pictures of the Kirby group taken sometime between May and September 1937 show them wearing funny hats such as crowns and pith helmets, which, as we have seen, was a sartorial trademark of the Smith band. In one of these photographs, Teddy Bunn perches precariously on top of the piano as Don Frye smiles up at him.[10] A photograph taken on September 9, 1937, shows Watson standing on a chair and grinning at the camera, while Bailey does what looks like a dance step and Brown pretends to pout.[11] These images demonstrate a comical, physically ebullient performance style reminiscent of those of Smith and the Spirits.

A series of 1937 recordings including several members of the band and released under the name "Frankie Newton and His Uptown Serenaders" also demonstrate a spontaneous musical style that likely informed performances at the Onyx.[12] The recorded performances comprise popular tunes played mainly in a swinging four-beat rhythm. The minimal arrangements often begin with a statement of the melody played either homophonically by trumpet, saxophones, and clarinet (as in *Please Don't Talk About Me When I'm Gone*) or by a soloist backed by sustained harmonies played by the other horns (as in *There's No Two Ways About It*.)[13] After this, the focus of most of the instrumental performances is improvisation, as soloists in succession play over simple riffs or sustained chords that could have been devised on the spot as part of a "head arrangement."[14] In a 1983 interview, drummer Freddie Moore suggested that, at the Onyx, the band combined this improvisatory style with more structured arrangements. Moore remembered that the band "had to do a lot of rehearsing" and that they used sheet music in rehearsal, although not during the actual performance; moreover, Kirby did not allow other musicians to sit in with the group because they would interfere with the arrangements.[15] On the other hand, Moore recalled that "the sidemen mostly ran that band," which suggests that Kirby's control was not total, and talked about the diverse range of styles with which he accompanied the various soloists in the group.[16] It appears that the group, while making use of relatively complicated arrangements, continued to emphasize virtuosic improvisation as had the Smith band.

Perhaps the most revealing of the Kirby band's early recordings in regard to its stage presence is *The Onyx Hop*, which refers directly to the Onyx Club and its reputation for rowdy revelry.[17] Although the performance begins with a tricky riff and includes improvised solos, its centerpiece is a vocal duet in which Newton and Brown half sing and half speak in a discordant style that evokes the slurred voices of drunks:

Come with me and smoke some tea and I shall carry on
Look out, fellow, let me pass—I shan't be out here long
Love my wife—but what has that got to do with this song?
She stayed out one hour over time—I stayed out all night long

Newton and Brown go on to describe a trip to the Onyx Club in which the narrator gets drunk on Scotch and fails to make it home. With its references to smoking tea, *The Onyx Hop* carries on the tradition of jive marijuana songs established at the Onyx by Smith and associated with black Harlem, and its celebration of all-night entertainment over domestic responsibility would have appealed both to the Onyx's long-standing clientele of musicians, who prided themselves on their hard drinking and disregard for conventional decorum, and to those members of the general public attracted by this lively and slightly scandalous atmosphere.

Indeed, in August 1937, *Down Beat* said of the Onyx that "you'll see everybody there from swing-mad debbies to [critic and record producer] John Hammond[,] and [bandleader] Ina Ray Hutton never misses a night when she is in town," which suggests that Kirby, like Smith, managed to appeal to a broader audience without alienating members of the music industry.[18] In particular, Kirby continued to attract the college-age crowd that had supported Smith. Herb Shultz, who first came to 52nd Street as "an 18-year old college freshman, who quickly learned it took only an hour and ten minutes to get from Princeton, N.J. to the Onyx," remembers his first trip to the Onyx in rhapsodic terms:

As I entered this most famous of the jazz clubs for the first time—I can feel the excitement still—Buster Bailey was standing forward on the little bandstand, chin down, blowing a long, limpid clarinet solo of great beauty. The tune was 'Who's Sorry Now.' Bailey's style was as familiar to me as—say—the words of the Lord's Prayer, from having listened endlessly to records he had made with Bessie Smith and with the Fletcher Henderson band. But, in contrast to the impersonal adventures of record-listening, it was an almost shattering experience simultaneously to *see* and *hear* this veteran jazz craftsman playing his lovely, effortless-sounding stuff, standing there *plain* (as the poet would say) at the dim far end of the long, narrow, silver-and-blue colored nightclub.[19]

Shultz went on to experience "an endless panorama of sights" including "Pete Brown, the huge, magnificent 'jump' saxophonist, deftly fingering his alto horn at the Onyx as though it were a little child's toy" and "the hunch of Frankie Newton's shoulders as he leaned forward into one of his blasting trumpet solos."[20] Teenage jazz fan Robert Inman and his friends were excited by an opportunity to meet members of the band.

I remember Frankie Newton. . . . He was out at the Onyx. . . . We went in and between sets, us kids were looking for autographs, so we finally found our way out the back, kind of a dumpy backyard, you know. It wasn't a yard, it was just . . . buildings all around. So Frankie Newton, and, oh, a couple of other musicians were there, and we talked with them. You know, they were nice to us kids. I mean [laughs], we were very young . . . but . . . we got all their autographs.[21]

These accounts suggest that audiences were attracted both by the group's improvised music and by the opportunity for direct contact with musicians whom they admired. The intimacy of 52nd Street's small clubs enabled personal interactions between white fans and black musicians that were unusual for the time.

Critics and reporters, while they generally joined these young fans in praising the Kirby band's musicianship, expressed mixed feelings about the group's stage presence. In a May 1937 report on the band, *Down Beat* asserted that "[Brown] and Buster [Bailey] team together admirably and the rest of the band rocks quite nicely when not indulging in the kind of jive that the customers yell for." Although the many possible meanings of *jive* make it difficult to interpret this statement with any certainty, the reporter seems to imply that the band sometimes pandered to its audience, either by altering its musical style or by de-emphasizing music in favor of staging. In the following issue of *Down Beat*, John Hammond was more precise in his complaints, targeting Leo Watson as a detriment to the band's musical integrity. Hammond wrote that "Leo, who has been playing drums for only two or three months[,] gets in everybody's way, and the result is wry expressions on the faces of the swell soloists and very little kick for the listener." Hammond went on to suggest that Joe Helbock replace Watson with a skilled drummer such as Sid Catlett and "give Leo a baton" so that he could serve as a conductor rather than as an instrumentalist. He concluded in terms that make clear his perception of a distinction between popular entertainment and genuine jazz: "Leo is a great showman and entertainer, but he has no business impeding the music of such masters as Buster Bailey and John Kirby."[22]

Critics were not, however, unanimous in rejecting the band's clowning. In the August–September 1937 issue of the French journal *Jazz Hot*, Helen Oakley published a detailed analysis of the band's performances in which she hailed them as an example of authentic, noncommercial jazz.[23] Oakley claimed that "the comedy provided by the band is really funny," and she implied that in her opinion it did not detract from its music, which, she said, "to lovers of real Jazz . . . is almost unbelievable." Moreover, the band's antics do not seem to have represented an undesirable courting of the general audience to Oakley. She wrote that "out of the welter of commercial music to which we have grown so accustomed during the past few years, there emerged, miraculously enough, this little band to warm the hearts of those who take their music seriously," and she argued that "there are no commercial bring-downs whatsoever" in the band's performances. These reviews indicate that, in 1937, the Kirby band had become the subject of unresolved debates about the role of entertainment and commercialism in jazz.

"Scotch and Tom-Toms": Maxine Sullivan   These debates, however, paled in comparison to the controversy that arose around the band's new singer, Maxine Sullivan. Sullivan, who grew up as Marietta Williams in Homestead, Pennsylvania, just outside of Pittsburgh, began her singing career around 1936 at an "after-hours spot" in Pittsburgh with the unlikely name "The Benjamin Harrison Literary Club," where, she recalled years later, she "worked from two o'clock until *unconscious*."[24] In June 1937, she decided to try her luck in New York after bandleader Ina Ray Hutton invited Sullivan to look her up. She and her pianist, Jenny Dillard, caught the Sunday train to New York; Sullivan remembered that "I didn't tell anybody I was going and figured that if nothing happened, I'd be back to work on Monday night."[25] Sullivan found Gladys Mosier, Hutton's pianist, who introduced her to pianist and arranger Claude Thornhill, who was in turn "sufficiently impressed so that I signed a contract with Thornhill and Mosier. Funny thing was that they took me to the Onyx on a Wednesday night to audition. . . . Two nights later, I began working as the relief act. You see, it did happen overnight! But I was frankly too inexperienced to know what a fantastic thing had happened."[26] Sullivan, accompanied only by Dillard's piano, began to attract attention for her unusual repertoire, which included a swing setting of Joyce Kilmer's poem *Trees* ("Only God can make a little ol' tree") that had been her featured number in Pittsburgh.[27] At Thornhill's suggestion, she began to add swing versions of Scottish ballads, such as *Annie Laurie* and *Loch Lomond,* to her performances. In August, claiming in a headline that "She's So Good Ethel Waters Listens," *Down Beat* reported that "the latest sensation at the Onyx Club in New York is Maxine Williams (Sullivan) who, without moving a muscle, swings (believe it or not) such items as 'Trees' and 'Annie Laurie' until everyone in the house yells and pounds the tables for more."[28] Soon thereafter, Sullivan was promoted from intermission singer to vocalist with the Kirby band, and Thornhill wrote arrangements for her and the group.[29] By the end of 1937, *Down Beat*'s Jack Egan informed readers that "Maxine Sullivan, who went into the Onyx several months ago as relief singer, is now the featured attraction there—and knockin' em dead."[30]

Sullivan's version of *Loch Lomond,* arranged by Thornhill, drew particular attention, both at the Onyx and through her popular recording, made August 6, 1937, and released on the Vocalion label.[31] The personnel on the recording include Frankie Newton (trumpet), Buster Bailey (clarinet), Pete Brown (alto sax), and John Kirby (bass), all from the Onyx Club group, as well as drummer O'Neill Spencer, who replaced Leo Watson at the Onyx around this time; the band is expanded to a septet with the addition of two white musicians, tenor saxophonist Babe Russin and pianist Thornhill. Thornhill's arrangement begins with a repeated open fifth that imitates the sound of bagpipes, over which Sullivan sings the song's well-known, eight-bar refrain (which begins "You take the high road and I'll take the low road . . ."). From then on, each section of the performance features subtly different textures and instrumentation. Sullivan sings a verse (the first of these begins "By yon bonnie banks . . .") as Thornhill plays fills behind her on piano and the horns play sustained chords; next, she sings a refrain while Bailey solos on clarinet; after a modulation down a whole step, trumpeter Newton and tenor saxophonist Russin each take improvised solos over the chord changes of the refrain, with different accompaniment styles in the band for each: Newton is backed by a homophonic figure played by the wind instruments, while drummer

Spencer accentuates the offbeats during Russin's solo. The bagpipe effect returns for a two-bar interlude after these solos. After another verse sung by Sullivan, the final refrain features a complex rhythmic structure, including four bars of half time and a repetition in the fourth line of text. These formal alterations make the last refrain sixteen bars long, exactly twice the length of all the previous refrains; but the disjointed effect produced by the changes of rhythm make this difficult to perceive. In short, Thornhill's arrangement of Loch Lomond, while it is unobtrusive and serves primarily to support Sullivan's cool, subtle singing style, is nonetheless an overt display of compositional sophistication and wit that plays on an intriguing combination of swing style and Scottish melody.

In steering Sullivan toward "folk" tunes such as Loch Lomond, Thornhill was not rejecting commercialism; rather, he was actively seeking an individual niche for her in a market already glutted with popular singers. As Sullivan later argued, "when I came to New York—let's face it, you had a whole lot of singers here already. I think Claude was sort of wise to select these things like 'Loch Lomond' and 'Annie Laurie' [to] at least make it a little different from just an average vocalist in front of the band."[32] Sullivan claimed that Tommy Dorsey's 1937 hit record Song of India, an adaptation of a Rimsky-Korsakov composition, showed Thornhill that there was an audience for "classics and folk songs which could be adapted to a swing beat" and that moreover "the adaptors of classics had a good idea because those classics were in the public domain, but the adaptor collected composer's royalties."[33] Thornhill maintained tight control over his new "discovery," in terms of both music and marketing. Sullivan recalled that he and Gladys Mosier had a five-year contract with her and Dillard in which each received a quarter of the total earnings and that Thornhill, an inexperienced agent, was determined to make the most of the arrangement: "I suppose he felt he had something here, had a little gem here and he didn't want anybody to cut in. . . . Claude not being of the business nature, he probably felt that at any minute [he] was going to lose this thing[,] which eventually he did, because the whole situation was bigger than Claude could handle."[34] Although Sullivan pointed to the sophistication of Thornhill's music as evidence that "Claude was definitely not trying to be commercial," she also remembered that "Claude used to come and sit outside the club on the curb and cry while the crowd was coming in. He was quite happy about that," which hardly seems like the behavior of a person immune to the allure of commercial success.[35] Indeed, the jazz press generally made favorable note of Thornhill's contribution to Sullivan's popularity, praising Sullivan's white "discoverer" as highly as they did the singer herself. Critic George Simon, for example, wrote in *Metronome* that "Claude Thornhill, to whom all sorts of credit is due, took care of the discovering aspect some months back, and since then has done a great job not only of managing her, but of supplying her with some of his own really magnificent arrangements."[36] As in the case of Stuff Smith, the jazz press did not necessarily view Thornhill's and Sullivan's open attempts to attract a mass audience as antithetical to authentic jazz.

Sullivan's mannered performances and quiet vocal style were a notable departure from the extroverted comedy and flashy improvisation that had been successfully showcased at the Onyx Club by such African American musicians as the Spirits of Rhythm and Stuff Smith. Nonetheless, she was received positively by both white and black audiences throughout the fall and winter of 1937 into 1938. In October 1937, John Hammond of *Down Beat* reported that Sullivan's records of *Annie Laurie, Blue Skies,* and *Loch Lomond* were "instantaneous hits." In December, Sullivan was praised by the nightclub reporter of the *New York Times,* who said that she had "captured the attention of the searchers for the different" by swinging Scottish songs, albeit "without offending any Scotchman's sensibilities." In January 1938, George Simon of *Metronome* declared Sullivan "The Individual Toast of 1937," claiming that she "has a sense of phrasing, of inflection, and of timing that no other singer, whom this reviewer has ever heard, possesses." A January 22 article in the *Amsterdam News,* New York's leading black newspaper, reveals that Sullivan was well received in her Harlem debut at the Apollo Theatre.[37] These complimentary reviews generally emphasized the cool, collected quality of Sullivan's voice and manner and contrasted her calm performances with the more common image of swing music as noisy and energetic. The *Amsterdam News,* for example, reported that "since the opening show [at the Apollo] last Friday she has been sending audiences home still in a dreamy haze as they've succumbed and fallen under her spell."[38] Simon praised Sullivan's "wonderful taste: her gracious manner, her warm smile, her cleanly appearance, her manner of speech" and the "soothing, syrupy quality of her voice," all of which were "thrilling everyone, including obstreperous drunks, into a state of complete complacency within the walls of the otherwise rocking Onyx Club."[39] These favorable appraisals demonstrate that Sullivan's departure from standard conceptions of black musicianship did not at first alienate either general audiences or critics.

Sullivan's deviation from norms of racial authenticity may have been acceptable to audiences because it was countered by conformity to conventional ideas about gender. As we have seen, the idea of authentic jazz that developed in the early days of the 52nd Street jazz scene associated heated improvisation, irreverent behavior, and anticommercialism with a distinctly masculine identity. As a woman, Sullivan may not have been expected to adhere to these standards as closely as was a male performer such as Stuff Smith. Moreover, Sullivan was to some extent received as an object of sexual desire by white critics; for example, George Simon referred to one of her recordings as "mellow and bed-roomy" and another as a "real, slow, beautiful seducer."[40] Sullivan's placid voice and mild demeanor might have positioned her appealingly in the view of critics as an object to be admired rather than as a creative artist. As a singer, Sullivan also did not risk challenging the swing-era taboo against female instrumentalists, who, as Sherrie Tucker explains, were often seen as "freaks" attempting to take on an unsuitably masculine role.[41] It is possible that Sullivan's performances, although they challenged racial and stylistic boundaries, were nonetheless initially well regarded because they were seen as appropriately feminine.

Moreover, many of those who bought Sullivan's first records or heard her early radio appearances may not have known that she was black. This was a misperception encouraged by Claude Thornhill, who took care at first to mask Sullivan's racial identity, perhaps in an attempt to make record buyers think that her swing versions of Scottish songs were in fact performed by a Scottish singer. Sullivan remembered that "in the beginning when I was at the Onyx Club [Thornhill] was very adam[a]nt about photographs being taken of me . . . he didn't want anybody to realize at the time that I was black."[42] In a 1978 interview, Sullivan recalled that Thornhill suggested her stage name around the time that *Loch Lomond* was recorded: "When the record was made, Thornhill said: 'Marietta, for this record, let's change your name to something Scotch or Irish-sounding . . . like, say, Maxine Sullivan.'"[43] According to another account, Thornhill suggested the change so that Sullivan would not be confused with African American singer Midge Williams, which might also indicate that he was trying to keep listeners from perceiving Sullivan as black.[44] Such strategies were not entirely successful. As early as September 1937, for example, during an appearance on the NBC radio show *Town Hall Tonight,* Sullivan was introduced as a "colored girl who's going to sing a Scotch song," and her swing version of *Loch Lomond,* backed by a full orchestra, was contrasted with that of a male (and presumably white) chorus whose stiff rendition represented "the way *Loch Lomond* used to be sung."[45] Nonetheless, in an era when African

American performers were generally expected to record only blues or hard-driving swing, Thornhill may have hoped to stave off a commercially risky controversy by at least downplaying Sullivan's race if not disguising it completely.[46]

It soon became apparent, however, that it was precisely the contrast between Sullivan's black identity and her Scottish repertoire that fascinated her audience and that the controversy that arose around her was in fact a valuable marketing tool rather than a liability. Sullivan's notoriety began on March 8, 1938, when Leo Fitzpatrick, a Detroit radio executive, cut her off the air in the midst of *Loch Lomond,* as she later remembered, "because he said it was sacrilegious to swing a traditional song."[47] The event led to increased public awareness of Sullivan; she recalled that "when I did 'Loch Lomond' on the air and it was cut off with the station manager in Detroit, then it really became controversial and sort of a national type phenomenon."[48] Sullivan's performances and media coverage now began to intentionally fan the flames of the debate by drawing attention to the unusual juxtaposition of a black singer and a Scottish song. Robert Inman, who saw Sullivan sing at the Onyx Club on March 19, writes that she performed in "a black dress with Scotch plaids." On March 24, Sullivan and the Kirby band appeared on Rudy Vallee's NBC radio show. Vallee, implying that he was taking a risk by allowing Sullivan to appear, announced that although Sullivan "started all the arguments about doing folk songs in swing tempo," she would perform *Loch Lomond,* "let the chips fall where they may." The *New York Journal-American* reported on March 26 that "the Onyx Club, where the vogue for swinging Scotch ballads got its first impetus, does not intend to yield without a battle to that Detroit station which recently banned them from the air. . . . Starting next Tuesday, weekly 'Scotch Nights' will be held at the popular sepian hot spot, on which Maxine Sullivan will sing her full complement of Scottish folk tunes." An April profile of Sullivan in *Stage* drew on racial stereotypes of hot drumming to characterize Sullivan in a succinct headline: "Scotch and Tom-Toms."[49] The Scottish pop singer Ella Logan, who had often performed with Riley and Farley during their vogue, garnered some publicity by claiming that Sullivan had stolen the idea of swinging Scottish songs from her. A photograph of Logan made the front page of April's *Down Beat* under the headline "Maxine Copied Me!" and Sullivan remembered that Logan "appeared one night" at the Onyx "with a bunch of Scotsmen . . . picketing . . . because I was doing 'Loch Lomond.' "[50] Seemingly overnight, Sullivan had become a central figure in a national discussion of racial and musical authenticity. The debate reached such a fervid pitch that first lady Eleanor Roosevelt weighed in, counseling Sullivan that "you cannot please everyone all the time."[51]

Sullivan's studio recording of *Loch Lomond* illustrates the ways in which her music contradicted conventional racial and stylistic categories. Although the group that recorded *Loch Lomond* included white musicians Babe Russin and Claude Thornhill, live performances and public perception of the song generally involved Sullivan and the Kirby band, all African Americans. It is striking, then, that the performers seem largely to reject the so-called "hot rhythms" and fervid improvisation so often ascribed to black musicians. Although the performance does involve improvised solos, the emphasis is on Thornhill's clever arrangement and on Sullivan's statement of the melody, and although the band and singer swing impeccably, they do so in a quiet, understated way. While Sullivan is making reference to a notion of folk authenticity, her chosen folk are those of Scotland, not of the black South. This choice provided an ironic counterpoint to those white musicians on 52nd Street, such as Louis Prima, who tried to claim a vision of the black folk heritage as their own. It also suggested that black musicians deserved to be seen as *conscious* artists with the ability to adapt any material to their own purpose, rather than as *natural* artists who were supposedly limited by their own racial proclivities. That Sullivan was drawing large crowds to the Onyx Club indicates that many white listeners were intrigued by her subversion of traditional racial and musical standards. On the other hand, the outrage among more conservative members of the public regarding these black musicians' treatment of an ostensibly white song demonstrates that deviations from restrictive standards of racial propriety could inspire real animosity.[52]

Although public interest in Sullivan was rooted in a fascination with racial difference, Sullivan herself soon began to downplay the significance of race, defending her style with reference to the supposedly universal prerogatives of the artist or the calculated decisions of the popular entertainer. In the wake of the controversy over *Loch Lomond,* Sullivan tried to reconcile the conflict by defending the artistry and sophistication of her "folk" repertoire, which by mid-1938 had expanded to encompass *Darling Nellie Gray,* the Russian *Ochi Chornia* (recorded as *Dark Eyes*) and even *My Yiddisher Momma.*[53] Critic Leonard Feather reported in May that "Maxine, with the assurance and poise so characteristic of her, is quite satisfied that she has 'done no harm' to the numbers by singing them the way she does . . . for her idea was to interpret their beauty rather than to desecrate them, as any but a prejudiced listener must realise." He wrote that Sullivan asserted, "I don't understand why people should see anything wrong in broadening the scope of your style by using every type of material," and Feather claimed that she was writing an article arguing that "there is too much swing music which is based simply on the mad desire to swing, at the expense of refinement and technique."[54] In September 1938, Sullivan defended her adaptations on commercial rather than artistic grounds, stating that "I've found that different audiences like different styles of singing, and I try to appeal to all types, observing my audience, and singing in the manner which I think appeals to most of them. At the Onyx in New York, I was called upon for more jiving than at Phil Selznick's in Los Angeles."[55] In public statements such as these, Sullivan seems to have been de-emphasizing the striking contrast between a black singer and a European folk repertoire that had caught the public's attention, justifying herself instead in terms of "refinement" and professionalism, categories associated by many white audiences at the time with the standards of European concert music rather than with black performers.

That this stance was not always successful given the racial climate of the 1930s is made apparent by Sullivan's role in the 1939 film *St. Louis Blues,* a film that she later claimed "left much to be desired."[56] Its plot centers on a showboat that runs aground in a small southern town and is forced to recruit local talent. Sullivan recalled, "of course, they discovered me outside of my cabin washing clothes and singing the 'St. Louis Blues,'" and added sardonically, "I think this is when the NAACP decided that there weren't going to be no more stereotypes for Blacks in movies."[57] Indeed, racial stereotypes are central to both the film as a whole and Sullivan's role in particular. In one telling exchange, the showboat's captain, played by the white actor Lloyd Nolan, tries to convince Ida, played by Sullivan, that she should perform *Ochi Chornia* on stage:

CAPTAIN: "Don't you see—everybody expects a colored girl to sing a plantation song—so that isn't good showmanship any more! But when you go out there and sing a Russian song . . ."
IDA: "Well, ain't it agin the law, Captain Dave?"
CAPTAIN: "Oh, no, of course not!"
IDA: "Have they got colored people in Russia?"
CAPTAIN: "Have they—well, sure, millions of them! Didn't you ever hear of the Black Sea?"[58]

The fictional captain succinctly lays out the nature of the real-life Sullivan's popular appeal—it is "good showmanship" for an African

American singer to do a Russian song—in terms that she herself might have accepted in a less degrading context. For example, Sullivan responded to Ella Logan's claims of priority in swinging Scottish songs with, "I always say that there was nothing unusual about a Scots girl singing a Scot song, but when I did it . . ."[59] The exchange in the film, however, is intended to poke fun at Ida's presumed stupidity and backwardness, evidenced both by her fear that singing a Russian song would be against the law and by her ignorance of Russia itself. Here, the emphasis on racial difference in Sullivan's music is employed to reinforce a notion of racial inferiority, and the innocence and naïveté of Sullivan's character Ida precludes any appreciation of her as a mature, serious artist. Moreover, the exchange suggests that the white captain, rather than Sullivan's character, is the arbiter who decides whether crossing racial boundaries is acceptable. Sullivan remembered that she chafed against her stereotypical role: "So I got into sort of a hassle with the director because he came to me and said that . . . I wasn't giving enough of the dialect—the Southern dialect. So I got a little annoyed. I mean, I could've hammed it up a little bit, but . . . I said 'Look, it doesn't make any sense for me to be talking a dialect one minute and singing Ochi Chornia in Russian the next minute.' "[60]

This incident displays the degree to which Sullivan had come to reject any emphasis on racial difference or authenticity in her public image. Although Sullivan rightly saw herself as a sophisticated performer making conscious choices about style and repertoire, the dominant stereotype of the authentic black performer was of an unconscious, natural creator lacking in discipline and rationality. Whereas Stuff Smith took on aspects of this stereotype, working from within it to project a more affirmative vision of black musicianship, Sullivan hoped to step outside of it altogether. Nonetheless, as an African American performer, Sullivan suggested new possibilities for other black musicians even as she resisted racial categorization. Although her experience indicates that it was not entirely possible for African American musicians to escape the boundaries of dominant racial ideologies, either in Hollywood or on 52nd Street, it also demonstrates that these performers had the capacity to stretch those boundaries and fashion an alternative version of black identity.

"Refined and Subtle": The John Kirby Sextet   Sullivan's success with a repertoire drawn from European traditions and a relatively restrained approach to performance appears to have had an effect on Kirby's band, which went from a largely improvisational style to one that emphasized tight arrangements and European "classical" themes. Gradual changes in the personnel of the band between fall 1937 and spring 1938 signaled this shift. Drummer Leo Watson was replaced sometime around August or September 1937 by O'Neill Spencer, who had spent five years with the Mills Blue Rhythm Band, a big band in the style of Cab Calloway's.[61] Watson's former bandmate in the Spirits of Rhythm, guitarist Teddy Bunn, also appears to have left the group around this time.[62] Frankie Newton also left in September, amid rumors of a love triangle involving him, Kirby, and Sullivan (who married Kirby on March 12, 1938).[63] Newton's replacement was the twenty-year-old Charlie Shavers, who also had played briefly with the Mills Blue Rhythm Band. The next set of changes occurred in March 1938, when pianist Don Frye was replaced by Billy Kyle, another Mills Blue Rhythm Band alumnus, and alto saxophonist Pete Brown was replaced by Russell Procope, who had played with a variety of musicians including Jelly Roll Morton and Fletcher Henderson. The resulting group, a sextet consisting of Buster Bailey (clarinet), Kirby (bass), Kyle (piano), Procope (alto sax), Shavers (trumpet), and Spencer (drums), was to remain intact until 1941. Throughout this period, the band performed frequently on 52nd Street, mainly at the Onyx Club but also at the Famous Door and the Hickory House. During their tenure on the street, these musicians developed a distinctive, precisely arranged style of small-band swing.

Although all of the aforementioned changes of personnel were no doubt the result of various professional and personal concerns, as in the rumored love triangle, they also marked a shift in the group's musical character, from a "jamming band" of musicians known best as creative improvisers to an ensemble of "disciplined" players able to read complicated scores as well as play off-the-cuff solos.[64] While Leo Watson, as we have seen, was criticized for his rudimentary drumming, O'Neill Spencer was a talented percussionist widely admired by other musicians for his work with brushes, his ability to play effective double time, and his skill with tympani, vibraphone, and chimes.[65] Similarly, Charlie Shavers was a virtuosic trumpeter (Gunther Schuller credits him with "virtually flawless technique") who also formalized many of the band's complex arrangements.[66] Russell Procope recalled that although many of the sextet's arrangements were originated by the group during casual rehearsals, Shavers and Billy Kyle "wrote out eventually a whole lot of the arrangements we used."[67] Sullivan remembered that while "Kirby took care of mostly the band business . . . it was actually . . . Charlie Shavers and Billy

Kyle who were responsible for the musical ideas."[68] Procope claimed that his own entry into the group stemmed from Kirby's desire for a saxophonist with advanced technical skills. One night, Procope said,

I went in the Onyx Club and talked to Kirby, you know, not actually looking for a job, you know. I wanted to hear his band because they used to broadcast and I used to hear him on the radio, so I wanted to see it. . . . So Kirby said to me—Maxine is getting ready to go on, so he said "Why don't you come on and play Maxine's music." . . . it was all right with Pete [Brown]. You know, in those days you'd sit in. So I was just sitting in. So he loaned me his horn and I played the set with Maxine and it went over pretty big, you know. So Kirby, he hired me on the spot right then. . . . I don't know whether Pete was leaving [already] or not. But I do know that Kirby was looking for someone to play Maxine's music, and all due respect to everybody, when they were recording Maxine they had to get an outside alto player to play the music.[69]

Although Procope was incorrect on this last point—through February 1938, Brown played on all of the recordings for which the Kirby group accompanied Sullivan—it is significant that he remembered Brown's inability to accompany Sullivan as the reason for his replacement. Procope elaborated that although Brown was "really doing what he was doing, as far as playing jazz was concerned" and "was a tremendous performer," nevertheless "I don't suppose he could make the adjustment to playing . . . Maxine's type of music. . . . She . . . had a goodly amount of song arrangements and they were well-made, real beautiful arrangements, and they were music. They weren't just thrown together. They weren't out and out—you know, out and out stomp-down, drag out blues and jazz and that sort of thing. They were arranged, and if you listen to her records you can tell that in a moment."[70] Procope invokes a conceptual distinction between "thrown together" performances and "music," a distinction that privileges carefully written arrangements over spontaneous improvisation.

A similar standard of value pervades the sextet's extensive body of recordings, which, although they often feature improvised solos, center instead on complex arrangements of a diverse range of music. The group's recorded repertoire between 1938 and 1942 can for the most part be grouped into three categories. In the first category are relatively straightforward swing performances of recent pop tunes (such as *It's Only a Paper Moon*), older standards (such as *St. Louis Blues* and *I Love You Truly*), and original compositions by Kirby or Charlie Shavers, often based on riffs (such as Shavers's *It Feels So Good* and Kirby and Shavers's *Fifi's Rhapsody*.)[71] Although these performances sometimes involve the standard string-of-solos form associated with a "jamming band," as in *Little Brown Jug* or *Coquette*, they also highlight "homophonic block-chordal, close-harmony ensembles" usually arranged by Shavers.[72] As Gunther Schuller points out, Shavers's approach to arranging suggested an alternative to the two textures that dominated jazz at the time: New Orleans polyphony and the call-and-response style associated with big bands.[73]

The second category in the sextet's recorded repertoire comprises swing arrangements of "classical" themes, reminiscent of Thornhill's writing for Sullivan. These performances, sometimes arranged by composer Lou Singer, typically include fairly literal readings of the original themes in swing rhythm, interspersed with improvised solos over the chord changes of the piece; examples include Donizetti's *Sextet from "Lucia"* and *Bounce of the Sugar Plum Fairy*, an adaptation of Tchaikovsky.[74] As Sullivan later pointed out, the sextet's traditional and classical repertoire was particularly practical during 1940 and 1941, when a radio network ban on ASCAP tunes led other musicians to follow Kirby's lead by turning to tunes in the public domain.[75] The group also explored more recent concert music with Thomas Griselle's *Nocturne*, published in 1929, and British folk music with Shavers's arrangement of *Drink to Me Only with Thine Eyes*.[76]

The third category comprises what might be called program music—arrangements in which novel harmonies and tone colors are matched to descriptive titles. In *Dawn on the Desert* and *On a Little Street in Singapore*, the band evokes an exotic Orientalist atmosphere through the combination of an unusual melodic mode and a repeated figure in the bass and drums. Another example, Singer's *Bugler's Dilemma*, features Shavers imitating the sound of a bugle in a harmonically complex arrangement. Schuller notes the influence on the sextet of the Raymond Scott Quintette, which had become successful in the mid-1930s with such playful "travelogues" as *Twilight in Turkey* and *Egyptian Barn Dance*.[77] Biographer Alan Williams suggests that Kirby was inspired by the work of black British composer and bandleader Reginald Foresythe, with whom Kirby recorded *Dodging a Divorce* and *The Melancholy Clown* in 1935.[78] All three categories showcased the band's considerable technical prowess and their tight ensemble playing.

The carefully arranged, dynamically restrained, classically influenced music performed by the Kirby Sextet was a novelty on 52nd Street; on its surface, it had little in common with the "Dixieland" idiom popularized

by Prima and Manone or the energetic, spontaneous swing of the original Spirits of Rhythm. Although Stuff Smith occasionally made reference
to the classical tradition with such material as *Mendelssohn's Swing Song,*
the loose, improvisatory style of his group contrasted with the sextet's
tight arrangements. The closest precedent to Kirby's band on 52nd Street
was white xylophonist Red Norvo's sextet, which had appeared at the Famous Door and Hickory House between September 1935 and February
1936.[79] Norvo turned away from the loose, largely improvised Dixieland
music common on 52nd Street. Instead, he and arranger Eddie Sauter devised a more experimental approach to small-group jazz in which improvisation was complemented by textural variety, unusual forms, and innovative orchestration.[80] In reviewing Norvo's band, critics emphasized
the taste and elegance of its arrangements rather than the fiery improvisation associated with such performers as Prima and Manone. *Metronome*'s George Simon, for example, described Norvo's music in February
1936 as "a refined and subtle type of swing . . . that's truly magnificent." [81]
Such reactions suggest that for many observers, Norvo seemed to offer
an intriguing alternative to the dominant view of jazz as wild, unruly
improvisation.

Although similar rhetoric was often used to describe the Kirby Sextet's music, some reviewers continued to view the group through the lens
of racial stereotypes. Examples include a November 1937 photo caption
in *Down Beat,* which reads "Some of the finest black cats in the business,
the Spirits of Rhythm carry on their super-jive in New York's 'rhythm
ravine' on 52nd Street at Ol' Man Helbock's Onyx Club—Yais, Yais!" The
condescending use of dialect and reference to "jive" invoke a clichéd image of happy-go-lucky, energetic black performers. In October 1938, an
article by the Andrews Sisters delineating "three kinds of swing" classi-
fied Kirby's band as "'jam' style," in contrast to "for the crowd" style, in
which musicians cater to watchers rather than dancers, and "lifty" style,
played comparatively quietly for dancing.[82] Although the authors do not
define these nebulous categories in racial terms, their emphasis on the
improvisatory character of "jam" style suggests that they associated the
Kirby Sextet with long-established conceptions of black musical practice.
In 1939, a cartoon map of 52nd Street that ran for several months in the
magazine *Swing: The Guide to Modern Music* illustrated a listing for Kirby's
band at the Onyx Club with a picture of a black trumpeter and clarinetist
in loud suits and with offensive simian features; across the street, a literally "long-haired" violinist scowls at them and says "Terrible! Tch! Tch!"
implying a perceived difference between Kirby's style and the norms of

"classical" performance.[83] These examples suggest that the Kirby Sextet, despite its novel approach to jazz, was nonetheless viewed in terms of traditional conceptions of African American music.

More common, however, were discussions of the group's refinement and high musical standards, often defined in the terms of the Western concert tradition. Jack Gould of the *New York Times,* for example, pointed out that Buster Bailey had apprenticed both in the Fletcher Henderson band and with a classical instructor, and Gould argued that this "double training accounts for a rare combination of a clean virtuosity and a fertile hot style." Gould also bestowed "laurels to Mr. Kirby for using his double bass as a tonal, not a battery, instrument. (Mr. Kirby has been seen to tune up before he plays.)" A 1940 record review in *Down Beat* made the racial implications of such depictions explicit, claiming that "if Charlie Barnet has the most negroid of all ofay [white] bands, then Kirby's is easily the whitest of all Negro outfits. Its precision is amazing."[84] The band's refutation of the common understanding of jazz as cacophony led many commentators to describe its music as "subdued" or "subtle swing," a view reflected in the title of its CBS radio show, *Flow Gently, Sweet Rhythm,* which went on the air in 1940.[85] Another *New York Times* review exaggerated the band's subdued qualities to the point of parody: "On the orchestra stand [at the Onyx], John Kirby and his orchestra are still doing spooky things with tunes, rousing themselves from their hypnosis on occasion to deliver some heretical transcriptions of the Mother Goose rhymes."[86] On yet another occasion, the same paper favorably contrasted the "rich content" of Kirby's and Count Basie's music to the "musical diatribe against more rigid forms" supposedly performed by Louis Prima.[87] The mainstream press appears to have seen the Kirby Sextet as a positive, civilizing influence on a supposedly chaotic jazz tradition.

Public pronouncements by the members of the band indicate that they saw their own music in much the same light. In 1939, Kirby explained that "I believe that jazz, to be good, should be restrained and organized.... For that reason I don't believe in out and out jamming.... if a band these days ever expects to gain any recognition, it must be on something more than its ability to 'get off.' With that idea as my basic thought, the boys and I realize that the only way we can gain distinction apart from our ability to improvise, is to develop a distinguishing ensemble style, and to prove by arrangements and our ability to execute them that the band is musicianly and versatile."[88] Kirby suggests that the band's arranged, "subdued" style, like that of Maxine Sullivan, was rooted in an unabashed desire for commercial success. Billy Kyle made similar comments in a 1940 profile, saying that "I prefer this type of small band to the jam combinations, and I don't generally like jamming at all; I prefer a little law and order in my music." [89] Kirby also makes reference to a highbrow conception of "taste" in his discussion of "swinging the classics": "I believe that symphonic pieces and the classics can be handled by a jazz combination in such a way that serious music lovers won't throw up their hands in despair, crying 'sacrilege!' . . . With a combination like the one we have, we can give tasteful treatment to all these classical things, but with a big orthodox swing band it would be hard to avoid the hackneyed and, to me, not very tasteful *swinging* of the classics that some big bands do." [90] Like Sullivan, Kirby and the sextet appear to have downplayed ideas of racial authenticity in order to assert their legitimacy as artists in the terms of the European tradition.

One effect of the Kirby Sextet's challenge to conventional ideas about jazz is that the group has become a footnote in standard jazz histories, discussed in terms of its difference from the mainstream, if at all. Gunther Schuller, for example, in a disparaging survey of the sextet, argues that its music "can in balance barely be considered in the realm of jazz." [91] Schuller condemns the group for emphasizing arranged ensemble work rather than improvised solos; for example, he asserts that Buster Bailey's "work always smacked of being worked-out, slightly mechanical, and devoid of the spontaneity one associates with major jazz figures." [92] He argues that the group's use of classical themes as part of a "basic conception of an eminently polite music that would not offend genteel tastes and ears" led the group into "effeteness" and a "stifling artificiality." [93] Moreover, Schuller claims that the Kirby Sextet adopted this style not for artistic reasons but rather in a shameless attempt to attract an audience of "carousing 52nd Street tourists" whose bad taste led them to enjoy "musical excursions" that "can hardly be taken seriously by an even mildly discriminating listener." [94] Schuller's implicit model of authentic jazz involves several criteria that, as we have seen, were commonly upheld on 52nd Street itself: improvisation, spontaneity, and an unwillingness to sell out to the commercial mainstream. By these standards, the Kirby Sextet's music strikes him as a middlebrow dilution of both jazz and classical music.

Viewed within the history of racial representation and musical style on 52nd Street, however, the Kirby Sextet represented a courageous and innovative attempt to resist limiting, one-dimensional views of jazz and of African American musicianship more generally. In an era when black musicians were fighting racial discrimination in the world of European concert music, the sextet's arrangements and choice of material enabled the group's members to demonstrate that they possessed the technical skills and musical erudition necessary to perform music of a tradition often seen as more refined and sophisticated than jazz.[95] As the sextet gained popularity on 52nd Street, it demonstrated to a large and diverse audience that black musicians were capable of "musicianly and versatile" performances that involved ingenious arrangements and disciplined ensembles as well as inspired improvisation.

This audience was, on 52nd Street, a now-familiar mix of professional musicians and members of the public in search of the latest trend. Musicians in the audience included Benny Goodman, who wrote in his 1939 autobiography that he picked up Shavers's composition *Undecided* for his band after seeing Kirby at the Famous Door. Russell Procope remembered that radio arrangers sometimes brought new charts to the club for the band to sight-read. The 1939 cartoon map of 52nd Street mentioned earlier describes the Onyx as a place "Where Radio Artists Are Entertained by Their Entertainers," which suggests that the Onyx might have marketed itself as a place where the celebrities of the music world could be sighted. The general audiences attracted by such advertising probably had varying degrees of interest in swing music. In 1938, the *New York Times* reported that "at the Onyx Club John Kirby and his boys . . . are rejoicing the hearts of swing connoisseurs," which indicates that the audience might have been knowledgeable about jazz. On the other hand, a 1941 profile of Don Frye claimed that in the late 1930s "the night club public began to discover jazz . . . and to filter in to the Onyx, filling the air with their curious high voiced chatter."[96] The suggestion that the audience talked over the music and the condescension given to the audience by a writer who obviously considered himself a hip insider imply that the audience members were not jazz aficionados. Other contemporary sources indicate that wealthy members of "society" and theater crowds from Broadway formed a substantial portion of the band's audience on 52nd Street.[97] Overall, the band seems to have been a commercial success; Al Casey, who played guitar with Fats Waller at 52nd Street's Yacht Club in late 1938, recalled that the Kirby band had a bigger "name" than Waller, who was already a famous entertainer.[98]

Kirby also resembled Smith in that his audience included other African American musicians, whose high regard for the sextet indicates that they were not offended by its divergence from popular conceptions of "hot" black music. Bassist Leonard Gaskin claimed that "everybody was" influenced by the Kirby group at the time.[99] Smith and his band, although their musical style was very different from that of Kirby, were vocal in their praise of the group. In 1965, Smith described Russell Procope as a "swinging little cat" and Charlie Shavers as a "good arranger" who was "real fast on his horn." [100] In another interview, Cozy Cole said, "I often think about the ingredients I'd like to have in a small group. Some of that John Kirby co-ordination, because Charlie Shavers, Russell Procope and Buster Bailey were *together*." [101] Jonah Jones singled out Bailey for praise: "Fastness, getting over your horn, meant something then. Buster was *fast*, and a good musician." [102] Gaskin, who worked with Charlie Shavers after the latter left the Kirby band, asserted that Shavers "was one of the most gifted trumpet players that existed during that period . . . he was a heck of an innovator and could play beautiful ballads and beautiful music." Gaskin also recalled that, when he was a teenager, meeting O'Neill Spencer inspired him to pursue a music career: "He was much older, but through my friend who lived in his building, we used to talk, and he'd tell of his experiences—and that whet my appetite, you know." [103] Drummer LeRoy Battle, who admired the Kirby band's "smooth sound," also learned from Spencer: "O'Neill, I talked with him, and he said, 'What you want to do, Roy, is get yourself a wooden shell, you know, on the bass drum.' He said, 'Don't put the mother-of-pearl on it, because that deadens the sound,' see. Little things like that, you see, when I was coming up." [104] These examples suggest that many African American musicians at the time were quite willing to accept the Kirby Sextet despite its deviations from musical norms often associated with black musicians. By challenging these standards, the sextet demonstrated that it was possible for African American musicians to resist restrictive notions of authentic jazz while still pursuing successful careers.

The influence of the Kirby Sextet was especially apparent in the bebop style that appeared in the 1940s. Jazz critic Leonard Feather wrote that "harmonically and melodically" the sextet "was amazingly precocious; in fact, the first number the group ever recorded, Billy Kyle's *From A Flat to C* in October, 1938, was based on the cycle of fifths, a harmonic device that was vaunted a decade later by boppers as if it had just been discovered." [105] The fast, rhythmically complex unison lines in such Kirby Sextet arrangements as *Sweet Georgia Brown* and *Opus 5* presage the intricate "heads" performed by Dizzy Gillespie and Charlie Parker only a few years later.[106] Gillespie worked with Shavers as early as 1936 and in 1944 briefly filled in for Shavers in a late version of the Kirby Sextet.[107] Gillespie's biographer Alyn Shipton argues that "the tight ensemble playing and overall approach to small-group playing developed by Kirby played a role in

Dizzy's thinking during the formative stages of bebop."[108] Gillespie, in turn, pointed out that the style of bop pianist Bud Powell was rooted in that of Billy Kyle.[109] Pioneering bop drummer Max Roach remembered O'Neill Spencer as one of his early role models.[110] Beyond their influence on the sound of bebop, the members of the Kirby Sextet in their understated insistence on representing themselves as refined, sophisticated musicians foreshadowed bop musicians' more overt rejection of popular entertainment, a subject to which we will return in chapter 7.

For black musicians such as Stuff Smith, Maxine Sullivan, and John Kirby, the ideas about jazz that were promoted on 52nd Street represented attempts to classify not only their musical style but also their very identities as African Americans. In response to notions of racial and musical authenticity that had existed on the street before their arrival, these musicians took varying stances; Smith proudly asserted a distinctly black identity, while Kirby and Sullivan downplayed stereotypical racial expectations in order to demonstrate that black musicians need not be constrained by them. None of these performers, however, could entirely transcend the long history of racial representation that informed the 52nd Street jazz scene. Rather, as we have seen, they were part of a conversation in which a diverse array of musicians, critics, audience members, and promoters with varying levels of power negotiated to determine the meaning of authentic jazz. By the peak of the swing era, as 52nd Street became a major popular spectacle, this conversation grew to an uproar.

Chapter Five **Swingin' Down That Lane** 52nd Street at the Height of the Swing Era

From the mid-1930s to the early 1940s, as a popular enthusiasm for swing music swept the United States, 52nd Street brimmed with a profusion of performers and clubs. One of the street's first historians, Charles Edward Smith, wrote in 1962 that "looking back on The Street as it was in the 1930's, trying to see which men were in what clubs and which clubs were at what addresses, was rather like trying to establish a sequence in the colorful, shifting patterns of a kaleidoscope."[1] In its depictions of "Swing Street," the contemporary press described musical abundance and social revelry that verged on pandemonium. A 1939 cartoon map of the street, for example, depicts a carnivalesque street scene including a wealthy drunk with a top hat and cane, scantily clad chorus girls, and sunbathers and sign painters, as well as classical and jazz musicians.[2] A fanciful magazine illustration from 1940 shows a merrily drinking couple sliding down 52nd Street on a trail of musical notes; having passed a series of clubs, restaurants, and shops, drawn at bizarre angles, they splash into a large martini glass.[3] Photographer Charles Peterson, perhaps trying to simulate the giddy perspective of club-hoppers like these, employed multiple exposures to create a dizzying montage of 52nd Street's neon signs in 1936.[4] A more prosaic but equally compelling set of images was created by the New York City Department of Taxes, which photographed every building in the city's five boroughs between 1939 and 1941. The "tax photos" for the blocks of 52nd Street between Fifth and Seventh avenues reveal that, in addition to a wide variety of nightclubs, this short stretch included French, Swiss, and Russian restaurants, a beauty salon, a fur store, book and record shops, a tailor, a violin maker, a department store, a drugstore, and even an auto repair shop.⁵ These images vividly demonstrate that the 52nd Street jazz scene was just one part of a larger commercial culture.

In the midst of all of this activity, the street showcased many of the key innovators of the style now known as small-group swing. By the end of 1938, African American musicians were frequently headlining acts at 52nd Street's clubs, and such exceptional performers as pianist Art Tatum, trumpeter Roy Eldridge, tenor saxophonist Coleman Hawkins, and singer Billie Holiday appeared with small ensembles of four to nine musicians, in which rhythm sections comprising piano, bass, drums, and sometimes guitar backed various combinations of trumpet, trombone, clarinet, or saxophone. Such musicians forged a style in which virtuosic solo improvisation, rather than arranged ensembles or polyphonic jamming, was central. White musicians such as Bud Freeman and clarinetist Joe Marsala continued to be popular attractions on 52nd Street, where they played in a manner that fused the collective improvisation, two-beat rhythms, and repertoire of earlier Chicago and New Orleans jazz with the virtuosic solos and four-beat swing of the new small-group style. White and black musicians also blurred conventional racial boundaries as they informally sat in with one another's bands and occasionally even played together in formally organized groups. While we celebrate many of 52nd Street's musicians today as inspired artists who created many of the great masterworks of the canon of recorded jazz, during their time on 52nd Street they were hardworking professionals attempting to negotiate a balance between their goals and desires as musicians and the more pragmatic concerns raised by the world of commercial entertainment in which they made their living.

Swing-era 52nd Street was informed by two trends that were both contradictory and intertwined: (1) the increasing consolidation and commodification of swing as an industry and (2) a continued fascination among musicians and audiences with jazz as a symbol of authentic self-expression. As we have seen, the tension between these two factors had animated 52nd Street's jazz scene from its beginnings at the Onyx Club, where musicians made business connections and honed their professional skills even as they ostensibly rejected the world of show business and mass entertainment. Recent historians of the swing era indicate that a similar opposition informed the wider jazz world, which encompassed both the conformist dictates of an increasingly powerful music industry and creative resistance to that industry's standards by musicians and audiences. As David Stowe points out, American popular music in the 1930s and 1940s was dominated increasingly by a small number of powerful record companies, radio networks, and booking offices, in what he calls "the incorporation of swing."[6] At the same time, however, Stowe reveals that swing's perceived status as an expression of New Deal populism and egalitarianism led it to have a democratizing effect on the very mass culture industry that seemed to control it.[7] Lewis Erenberg offers a somewhat utopian view of swing as a "national youth culture that transcended class, ethnicity, and race," in which participants were active seekers of swing's progressive potential rather than "passive receivers of musical products."[8] Kenneth J. Bindas takes a similar position, arguing that "swing was a consumable product, but the generational attitude— the swing way of being—that went along with the music was not for sale."[9] These scholars suggest that the culture of the swing era should be viewed as part of a dialogic process in which the tastes and values of swing's audience were as significant as the aims of the industries that marketed and sold swing.

These affirmative visions of the swing era contrast with that espoused by influential contemporary observer Theodor Adorno, whose critical theory is characterized by "his belief that the culture of the masses was a wholly synthetic concoction cynically imposed on them from above."[10] In his 1938 article "On the Fetish Character in Music and the Regression of Listening," Adorno argued that "music for entertainment," rather than liberating its listeners and performers, "seems to complement the reduction of people to silence, the dying out of speech as expression, the inability to communicate at all."[11] Although such music may appear to be linked to individuality and rebellion, Adorno claims that this appearance is illusory and indeed only serves to reinforce dominant ideologies, as "isolated moments of enjoyment . . . in the service of [commercial] success . . . renounce that insubordinate character which was theirs."[12] He is particularly disparaging of the young swing fans known as "jitterbugs," whom he views with characteristic acerbity as "types rise[n] up from the masses of the retarded who differentiate themselves by pseudo-activity and nevertheless make the regression more strikingly visible."[13] As Catherine Gunther Kodat puts it, "the 'ambivalent use' of jazz music on popular radio and in European dance halls led Adorno to conclude that the music expressed less a reality of social opposition than its never-to-be-fulfilled dream."[14] Although Adorno often has been criticized for his limited knowledge of jazz or accused of "racism or anti-American elitism," Kodat points out that his work represents a valuable attempt to situate jazz within a wider culture industry to which the "historical re-alities" of the music are less important than its "ideological uses." [15]

Of particular relevance to the culture of the swing era is Adorno's belief that "the culture industry employed a pseudo-aura to give the effect of individuality to what in fact were totally standardized commodities." [16] Adorno addresses this idea with some specificity in relation to 1930s jazz audiences, arguing, for example, that "the term jitterbugs . . . is hammered into them by the entrepreneurs to make them think that they are on the inside." [17] Those listeners who style themselves as aficiona-dos he sees as particularly deluded, in that their chosen field of personal expertise is force-fed to them by mass marketing; he writes that "the jazz enthusiast . . . legitimizes himself by having knowledge about what is in any case inescapable." [18] In perhaps the most succinct statement of his position, Adorno asserts that "to make oneself a jazz expert or hang over the radio all day, one must have much free time and little freedom." [19]

Although 52nd Street's musicians and audiences were not as lacking in agency as Adorno might argue, neither were they successful in tran-scending the boundaries of commercial hegemony or racial ideology. At first glance, it might appear that various aspects of swing-era 52nd Street can be grouped into two categories that reflect their relation to the com-mercial marketplace. On the one hand, some features of 52nd Street were unabashedly linked to the entertainment industry, such as the increas-ing prominence of big bands, live radio broadcasts, large musical revues, and elaborately decorated clubs, all designed to attract a wide audience. On the other hand, some activities on the street, such as improvised jam sessions and "hot" record collecting, were thought to resist commerce in favor of individual freedom and what Erenberg calls "the democratiza-tion of cultural connoisseurship." [20] Although this binary division pro-vides valuable insight into contemporaneous perceptions of 52nd Street, the reality was a good deal more complicated, with musical and social practices that seemed to belong in one category often finding their way into the other. Even the most ostensibly commercial 52nd Street swing could be marketed as the unmediated expression of individual musicians or of innate racial characteristics. If swing in general was seen as an au-thentic subculture by many of its devotees, 52nd Street was publicized as a less diluted section of this culture that made other swing venues look commercial by comparison. Moreover, those aspects of 52nd Street that were supposedly anticommercial were quickly subsumed by commercial structures; informal jamming was presented for a paying public, and "hot" records were sold in shops on the street. Therefore, 52nd Street was not divided neatly between authentic and commercial activities; rather, ideas of authenticity infiltrated commerce and vice versa. In this regard, the street was a particularly lively example of larger trends in the culture of swing, which, as Stowe demonstrates, was "the popular music of most of the 1930s and 1940s, and therefore the first music to be acted upon by a new kind of culture industry," but was also "a particular *kind* of popular music, one that marked the media through which it gained its mass appeal." [21]

In this chapter and the next, I step back to take a broader look at 52nd Street during the swing era, examining first the street's increasingly visible role as a kind of "public figure" in popular conceptions of swing and then the ramifications of this new role for conceptions of racial identity on the street. Chapter 5 addresses the role of 52nd Street within the larger entertainment industry, discussing the wide array of performances and clubs on the street, how the street was publicized through mass media, and how its musicians and audiences negotiated conflicting standards of commercial success and authentic expression. Chapter 6 explores the racial significance of these conflicting standards by addressing black pianist and bandleader Count Basie, white clarinetist Joe Marsala, and the interracial groups that became increasingly common on the street. In short, I aim to unravel the paradox of how 52nd Street's anticommercial ethos was commodified during the swing era even as musicians and audiences continued to employ notions of anticommercial authenticity to resist the mainstream of mass culture.

"Gayety and Night Life": 52nd Street and the Entertainment Industry   By the late 1930s, the mass media had spread 52nd Street's reputation for lively jazz and entertainment far beyond its borders. In 1937, for example, the United Artists film *52nd Street* purported to tell the story of the street's transformation from a staid block of brownstones into what one reviewer called "the center of New York's gayety and night life." [22] The movie's title song extolled the joys of "swifty, nifty Fifty-Second Street," claiming that visitors can "find romance / In a dozen or more ways" as they "toast the town in champagne / And go swingin' down that lane." [23] (In 1936, Sammy Cahn and Saul Chaplin's song *Fifty-Second Street* had described the street in similarly glowing terms as "a world that's set apart" and as "a place where the swing cats meet.")[24] In response to the film, the November 29, 1937, issue of *Life* included a spread of thirty-nine captioned photographs that covered the entire length of 52nd Street, from tenements near the East River to the "dock of the Italian line" on the Hudson. Entertainment options depicted on the blocks between Fifth and Seventh avenues comprised saxophonist Pete Brown "of the street's hottest band" (i.e., John Kirby's) at the Onyx, comic Pat Harrington at Club 18, singer Eddie Davis at Leon & Eddie's, and "floor-show girl" Estelle Kier of the Club 52nd Street.[25]

Although the film received only mixed reviews during its theatrical run, 52nd Street was promoted in more broadly influential ways throughout the swing era. Beginning around 1936, radio wires in 52nd Street clubs allowed bands to broadcast directly from the street, sometimes over national networks such as NBC and CBS.[26] In December 1938, for example, four bands broadcast from four 52nd Street clubs: Jimmie Lunceford on the Mutual Broadcasting System from the Band Box; Joe Marsala on WMCA from the Hickory House; Red Norvo and Mildred Bailey on CBS from the Famous Door; and Mike Riley on NBC from the Troc.[27] These broadcasts made a point of plugging individual clubs and the street in general. For example, the NBC announcer for a 1940 broadcast of trombonist Will Bradley's band informed listeners that the show was coming from a "gay spot on Swing Alley: The Famous Door, wide open on 52nd Street in New York City."[28] The musicians of 52nd Street also gained public attention through studio recordings issued both by the three major companies—Victor, Decca, and Columbia (CBS after 1938)—and by smaller specialist labels such as Commodore.[29] In April and May 1939, for example, the street's performers included the big band of Woody Herman, then recording for Decca, at the Famous Door; trumpeter Hot Lips Page, who recorded for Bluebird (a subsidiary of Victor) in 1938 and for Decca in 1940, at the Onyx; clarinetist Joe Marsala, who recorded for Vocalion (owned by CBS) in 1938 and for the independent General label in 1940, at the Hickory House; and singer Lee Wiley, who recorded in 1939 and 1940 for the independent Liberty Music Shop label, at the Onyx.[30] Moreover, a wide range of publications covered the street regularly, including music-business periodicals such as *Down Beat* and *Metronome,* fan magazines such as *Swing,* daily newspapers such as the *New York Times* and *New York Post,* and sometimes African American papers such as the *Pittsburgh Courier* and the *New York Amsterdam News.* In only a few years, 52nd Street had gone from an esoteric musicians' haunt to a nationally recognized center for swing music.

Tourists lured to the street in the late 1930s by all of this publicity could choose from an extraordinary assortment of clubs and performers. At its pcak in late 1938 and early 1939, 52nd Street hosted as many as ten jazz clubs at once, a surge in activity fueled in part by speculations that the New York World's Fair would attract out-of-town visitors with money to spend.[31] A *Down Beat* report by the Andrews Sisters gives a sense of the rich array of talent on the street in December 1938.

52nd Street is preparing for the World's Fair with eight name bands in the radius of 200 yards,—Eddie DeLange at the Band Box, who will be followed in two weeks by Jimmy Lunceford; Roy Eldridge who replaced Count Basie at the Famous Door and is to be followed by Red Norvo and Mildred Bailey and John Kirby; Joe Marsala pleasing the Hickory House customers; Pee Wee Russell with his own band at the Little Club; Mike (Music Goes 'Round) Riley will open at the New Troc; Mammy's Chicken Farm keeps Bob Howard and his newly formed orchestra; at the Yacht Club, Thomas 'Fats' Waller continues to attract the swing fans.[32]

This remarkable list comprises only those clubs that were known for presenting jazz. In December 1938, other venues on the street included Club 18, where a raucous group of comedians poked fun at patrons; Leon & Eddie's, which featured the bawdy songs of Eddie Davis as well as such attractions as a glass tank in which women performed tricks; and Tony's, where singer and pianist Spivy entertained the sophisticated writers of the Algonquin Round Table.[33] Unusual attractions continued to flourish throughout the swing era; in 1941, for example, Club Waikiki opened with a show featuring the "genuine Hula dance" as performed by "beautiful Eurasians."[34] Although such clubs as these seemed on the surface to have little in common with the Onyx or the Famous Door, they often had connections to the street's jazz scene. Club 18, for example, had opened as a jazz club featuring trumpeter Bunny Berigan and later switched to comedy to revive business.[35] The Band Box, which showcased jazz bands such as Jimmie Lunceford's in 1938 and 1939, was managed by Club 18's Jack White.[36] According to *Swing,* Leon & Eddie's hosted jam sessions in 1939.[37] Club Waikiki reportedly expressed an interest in hiring John Kirby in 1941.[38] Moreover, its "mistress of ceremonies," Ruth Sato, was, *Down Beat* explained, a "hep cat" who collected records, knew "members of the Basie, Ellington, Goodman and Lunceford bands," and dated bandleader Eddie DeLange; she also wrote a gossip column that appeared in *Swing.*[39] The jazz clubs of 52nd Street, while they were often touted as alternatives to the larger world of popular entertainment, were in fact intimately linked to the street's more overtly commercial attractions.

This connection was manifested in an increasing attention to presentation and staging in 52nd Street's jazz clubs. Although those clubs that presented improvised jazz did not aspire to the elegance of the 21 Club restaurant at 21 West 52nd Street, renowned for its high prices and exclusivity, or to the flamboyance of Leon & Eddie's, with its elaborate floor shows, they did make direct efforts to appeal to patrons. Some clubs adopted a theme that informed their decor. The Yacht Club, for example, "was decorated like a pleasure yacht, and the ceiling represented a night sky ablaze with stars."[40] In January 1938, it became the "Hawaiian Yacht Club," featuring the incongruous combination of New Orleans trumpeter Sharkey Bonano alternating with "a Hawaiian trio and a couple of hula dancers."[41] (*Down Beat* complained that the Hawaiian group was "a bringdown to the jamsters."[42]) Kelly's Stable, which moved from 51st to 52nd Street in 1940, sought to create a "bucolic atmosphere" with sawdust on the floor and carriage lamps next to the stage.[43] Clubs sometimes enhanced performances with special lighting effects. At Maxine Sullivan's Onyx Club performances in March 1938, for example, "the only light in the club was a spotlight on Sullivan with her black dress with Scotch plaids."[44] Clubs also competed for customers by attempting to fit as many performers as possible into the night's entertainment. Malcolm Johnson of the *New York Sun* wrote in 1938 that "there seems to be a suicidal race in progress in West Fifty-second street, or Swing Alley, to see who can squeeze the biggest show into the smallest night club. Right now the Onyx Club, which calls itself the Cradle of Swing, is leading by two acts." At the Onyx, Johnson reported, one could "listen successively to a Dixieland Band, led by [trombonist] Jack Jenn[e]y, hear the Merry Macs, the sensational . . . radio, vocal swing quartet; a very funny Negro clown band; duet work by Carl Kress's guitar and Jack Connors's vibraphone, and a couple of other instrumental acts."[45] Perhaps the most surprising development was that some clubs, despite their small size, began to create spaces in which patrons could dance, apparently starting with the Onyx in July 1937.[46] The Troc, located at 53 West 52nd from 1938 to 1940, followed suit, as did the Famous Door.[47]

Creative attempts to attract an audience were necessary on a street where clubs were lucky to break even. Business was often good on 52nd Street, with contemporaneous reports mentioning at times that the street was "choked most of the night with taxi cabs" or that a new band "broke all records at the spot on opening night."[48] Successful clubs of long standing such as the Hickory House, which stayed in business until 1968, or Jimmy Ryan's, which operated from 1940 to 1962 at its 53

West 52nd Street location, were, however, the exception rather than the rule. A number of short-lived clubs came and went on 52nd Street during the late thirties and early forties. The Band Box, for example, opened in November 1938 at 20 West 52nd only to close around April 1939. The Troc, which also opened in November 1938, was closed by mid-1940.[49] Business difficulties often resulted from a simple inability to appeal to customers. *Down Beat* reported in September 1939, under the heading "52nd Street Dead," that Count Basie was currently "the only notable draw" on 52nd Street.[50] In December of the same year, the magazine asserted that "business is so sad" for Jimmy Mundy's band at the Onyx "that there's a danger the club may fold," which indeed it did at the end of the month.[51] Even those clubs that were heavily patronized, however, could find it difficult to make ends meet. As Malcolm Johnson argued in his discussion of 52nd Street's increasingly large revues, "where this contest ['to see who can squeeze the biggest show into the smallest night club'] will end probably is in the Federal Court under section 77-B of the bankruptcy law. Not that business is not good on 52nd Street and not that the customers don't like the relatively big shows they are getting. The trouble is that there simply isn't enough room in most of the places for enough customers to make them pay."[52] Federal indictments for tax evasion were issued to some 52nd Street clubs and restaurants, including the Famous Door in 1939, which suggests that club owners were sometimes tempted to turn to illegal means to make a profit.[53] Although 52nd Street's clubs were overtly commercial, their position within the entertainment industry was a precarious one.

"No Real Bread": Musicians at Work   The economic risks faced by club owners also confronted 52nd Street's performers. For many musicians, as bassist Milt Hinton recalled, the 52nd Street experience involved "scuffing from one job to another" for low pay and with little job security.[54] Although musicians occasionally secured long-term employment at one club—for example, Joe Marsala played regularly at the Hickory House between 1937 and 1947—most were only able to line up temporary work on 52nd Street, as elsewhere in New York.[55] Drummer Johnny Blowers, who played on 52nd Street in 1941 and 1942, remembered that "the bands would go in [to a club] for two weeks, three weeks, four weeks . . ." As John Hammond later noted, musicians generally were paid the minimum scale mandated by the American Federation of Musicians, which allowed the small clubs to limit expenses. Side musicians were especially likely to be paid the minimum. Bassist Irv Manning, for example, re-membered that he was paid scale while performing with Joe Marsala at the Hickory House in 1940. Even well-known stars, however, sometimes received low wages. A booking agent for Fats Waller complained regard-ing a 1938 engagement at the Yacht Club that "Waller's salary at the Club, that is the minimum, will mean very little to our overhead." Milt Hinton asserted that "52nd Street didn't pay no bread, you know" and that musicians there "weren't in the mainstream of money making"; rather, big-band musicians "were the guys that were making the bread." In some instances, due to slow business at a club or to the dishonesty of its management, musicians did not even receive the minimum. In December 1938, for example, *Down Beat* reported that "Pee Wee Russell had a promising group which included Max Kaminsky and Joe Bushkin, but he worked under a handicap at the Little Club [at 72 West 52nd]. Main trouble, it is alleged, was the lack of proper pay-offs, which is not at all inspiring to good swing. After three weeks the band exited." Musicians in such circumstances could turn to AFM Local 802 for support. The closing of the Onyx Club in December 1939 was precipitated "when two pickets paced up and down outside the history-making 'cradle of swing' with placards denouncing the Club as unfair to members of the Musi-cians' Union," both because the club had failed to pay union members adequately and because it was currently featuring Kenny Watts and his Kilowatts, "a non-union combination." In September 1940, the union picketed the Swing Club at 35 West 52nd, and in October the Famous Door appeared on the "Unfair List of Local 802." Although their recourse to the union could be helpful, it is clear that performing on 52nd Street could be a difficult way for musicians to make a living.[56]

African American performers encountered additional obstacles in midtown Manhattan, where many felt unwelcome or exploited. Billie Holiday, referring to "52nd Street in the late thirties and early forties," as-serted that "you can be up to your boobies in white satin, with gardenias in your hair and no sugar cane for miles, but you can still be working on a plantation." Holiday charged that white performers initially were given preference by club owners, who cynically changed their attitude when "they found they could make money off Negro artists and they couldn't afford their old prejudices."[57] As we have seen, most of the street's per-formers were indeed white in the earliest days of 52nd Street, where Holi-day first performed in 1935.[58] Although, by the height of the swing era, the numbers of black and white musicians on 52nd Street were in approx-imate parity, white musicians sometimes appear to have benefited from preferential hiring; for example, most of the big bands that performed on the street were white. Moreover, black musicians encountered difficulties with the white audiences on whom their commercial success on 52nd Street depended. Fats Waller's son Maurice writes of a particularly "ugly incident" that "marred [Waller's] engagement at the Yacht Club" in 1938. Waller and his brother Larry were smoking a cigarette outside the club when "two white couples came out of the club and the women approached Dad for his autograph. Their dates didn't approve and began cursing the women and Dad with equal fervor." When Larry Waller tried to prevent the men from striking the women, one of the men drew a gun and shot him in the leg. "Infuriated, [Fats Waller] charged the man with the pistol and proceeded to beat him unconscious. . . . The incident was kept out of the newspapers because the people involved wanted neither a court appearance nor the attendant publicity."[59]

Most of the racial tension on the street manifested itself in ways that were less violent but no less real, such as the evocation of racist stereotypes for the amusement of white audiences. Between 1937 and 1940, for example, 60 West 52nd Street was the home of Mammy's Chicken Farm, a club whose name calls to mind patronizing images of southern blacks. Black musicians might also have been aware of the degrading entertainment offered at Club 18, where white comedians harassed a "Negro attendant" named "One-Round Jackson" by breaking crackers over him, playing tic-tac-toe on his head, and "rough[ing] him up" in a football skit.[60] Although black musicians saw 52nd Street as a valuable professional opportunity, they did not necessarily view it as a place to spend their free time, as some white musicians did. Milt Gabler, who hired African American musicians for public jam sessions at Jimmy Ryan's beginning in 1941, recalled that "the problem was to get blacks—musicians included—to bring their wives downtown. They weren't used to socializing outside of Harlem."[61] Although African American performers were an increasingly visible presence on 52nd Street during the swing era, the street continued to be dominated by whites, and black musicians faced social as well as economic challenges.

Although 52nd Street was a hard place to make a living, it offered some advantages for musicians. Many of those who endured the precarious livelihood offered by 52nd Street did so in the hope that the street would become a springboard to greater commercial success; as *Swing* put it, 52nd Street could be a "bandmaker."[62] This was especially true for white big bands, which could develop a reputation on 52nd Street before moving on to more lucrative engagements at hotels and ballrooms or to national tours. Although African American bands had more limited commercial prospects, some, such as Count Basie's, also benefited from exposure on 52nd Street.[63] The view of 52nd Street as a stepping-stone to future success was symbolized visually in a 1939 advertisement for saxophonist Charlie Barnet, in which a series of labeled stairs representing Barnet's progress over the course of the year begins at the bottom with "Jan.–Feb. At the Famous Door New York," and moves upward through March performances at the Paramount Theatre, recording sessions in April, a "coast-to-coast road tour" in May, and a New Jersey engagement in June and July, until a final step is topped by a crown and the slogan "The New King of the Saxophone."[64] Bandleader Woody Herman also profited from appearances at the Famous Door in 1939. According to *Swing*, "after several years of knocking around in second-rate spots and ballrooms," Herman "became the talk of the city in a week" after he began playing at the club, and "his booking agency, which had spotted the band in the Door, found itself almost swamped by competitive agencies who sought to steal the band from them." Thereafter, Herman had appeared at the Meadowbrook Club in New Jersey, was broadcasting over "major networks," and was about to sign a recording contract.[65] Herman recalled years later that "the Door gave you exposure and publicity," but "no real bread."[66] Bandleaders' willingness to postpone "real bread" in the short run in the hopes of long-term profit was often discussed in explicitly commercial terms. Bandleader Teddy Powell, explaining to an interviewer why he "decide[d] to invest so much money and tr[ied] to fight such a hazardous battle" in bringing his band into the Famous Door in 1939, responded in the language of the calculating entrepreneur rather than that of the idealistic artist: " 'Because if you click,' said Teddy, 'you can gross from $500,000 to $750,000 a year and about forty percent of that is profit. That's what the top bands earn, bands like Artie Shaw's and Benny Goodman's and Tommy Dorsey's. If you can reach even the second flight—where Gene Krupa and Jimmy Dorsey and some of the others are—you'll gross over $200,000 a year at the same margin of profit. And that ain't exactly hay!' "[67] Powell's comments indicate that he saw 52nd Street as just one part of a larger entertainment industry.

On the other hand, some musicians chose to play on 52nd Street precisely because it still seemed to offer an alternative to the world of commercial swing. This reasoning seems to have been most common among white musicians, who were the immediate heirs of the equation of authentic jazz and anticommercialism that had informed 52nd Street's musicians throughout the 1930s. Bassist Artie Shapiro, for example, turned down a better-paying job with a big band (also on 52nd Street) in order to remain with a smaller, more improvisational ensemble: "There was a point there where . . . Charlie Barnet . . . was also on 52nd Street, up the street there, and he wanted me—I did work with them for a couple weeks, okay, and the job paid a little better than the one that . . . I was doing before that. But I didn't care for that in a jazz sense so much—it was good, but it wasn't what I liked. And I went back to the Hickory House [with] Eddie Condon and Joe Marsala and Marty Marsala—I preferred that for less money . . . it was more of a jazz group." Other musicians remembered that the owners of the clubs were enthusiastic about jazz or at least did not try to impose their musical standards on their employees. Johnny Blowers recalled that "the guys, the men that owned the clubs knew as much about jazz as the guys that played jazz. In other words, they knew the good jazz musicians, and they were very friendly with the jazz musicians, and they were very honest with all the musicians. . . . The Street was a fabulous place." Irv Manning said that the management of the Hickory House "never said one word boo to us. No . . . everybody was happy and business was good. When business is good, the boss doesn't bother you."[68] This suggests that musicians had to balance their personal notions of authentic jazz against commercial appeal, attracting an audience in order to earn the right to be left alone by their employers. Even those musicians who enjoyed 52nd Street's apparent freedom from commerce, then, were still deeply involved in and influenced by the economics of the street.

"Ickies and Hepcats": The Audience   The audience for jazz on 52nd Street in the late 1930s and early 1940s consisted largely of young white men and women from the middle and sometimes upper classes. Although African American musicians sometimes attended 52nd Street's clubs, black nonmusicians were present only in small numbers. Artie Shapiro remembered that at the Hickory House, black audience members were "kind of rare," although it was not the club's policy to exclude them. Irv Manning claimed that there were no blacks in the audience at the Hickory House, although they were sometimes present at other clubs. African American musicians had similar impressions. Pianist Sammy Price remembered in 1980 that "as late as the thirties" there were "some spots" on 52nd Street that did not welcome blacks. Guitarist Al Casey stated that, although some patrons came from Harlem to hear Fats Waller, the Yacht Club audience was mostly white.[69] Even as African

American performers became an increasing presence on 52nd Street, its audiences remained mainly white.

Despite their racial homogeneity, the patrons of 52nd Street's clubs were otherwise a varied group with diverse interests in jazz. Professional musicians and music-industry figures continued to be a visible contingent on the street, which they patronized long after its venues abandoned any pretense of being exclusive musicians' clubs. During the early years of the swing era, musicians continued to treat the clubs as informal gathering places. In 1937, for example, Jack Egan of *Down Beat* reported in March that Tommy Dorsey had brought five dozen eggs from his farm to sell to patrons of the Onyx and in July that pianist Roy Bargy had held his wedding reception there. Egan reported in December of the same year that "the Onyx further emphasizes the fact that it is the musicians' hangout by hiring a musician as doorman. Chap's name is Joe Cosco and he plays bass fiddle."[70] In addition to musicians, music-industry professionals also were prevalent in 52nd Street's audiences, which suggests that the street was still a place where insiders could conduct casual business. A front-page photograph of Benny Goodman in the October 1, 1939, issue of *Down Beat* shows him seated at the Famous Door with Willard Alexander, who was "in charge of the band division of William Morris agency and former guiding hand of Goodman's band." Al Casey remembered that "song pluggers" would bring new tunes to Fats Waller at the Yacht Club to see if he would perform them: "Oh, they'd come in. And they'd have the lead sheets. . . . And they'd give them to us and hope that we'd do them—half the time we didn't."[71] Although the pluggers' activities were not limited to 52nd Street, they likely saw the street as a relatively relaxed environment where performers could reasonably be expected to experiment with new material in front of an audience. Some of the atmosphere of the original Onyx Club, where musicians combined business and pleasure in a private setting, persisted on 52nd Street during the swing era.

In striking contrast to the old atmosphere, however, was a new emphasis on celebrity and publicity. By the late 1930s and early 1940s, musicians had begun to visit 52nd Street in overt attempts to garner press coverage. The music press often described musicians attending one another's performances on 52nd Street, sometimes with candid photographs similar to coverage of movie stars at a film premiere. An example is the aforementioned *Down Beat* photo of Benny Goodman, which depicts him watching from a table at the Famous Door as Teddy Powell debuts his band. The caption gossips that "the girl at Benny's table is Eunice

Healy, the dancer, who is slated to marry Benny very soon" (a false prediction, as it turned out).[72] Such coverage would have benefited both Powell, who gained cachet through the attendance of such a famous figure as Goodman, and Goodman himself, whose status as a popular icon depended upon his remaining in the public eye. Although black musicians did not receive this type of star coverage as often, their attendance at 52nd Street clubs was sometimes noted. When Coleman Hawkins came back to the United States after five years in Europe, his return celebration on July 31, 1939, included a stop at the Famous Door to hear Count Basie. Here, according to reporter Ed Harris, Hawkins joined a party that comprised a remarkable array of African American performers: "[Ella] Fitzgerald, [Jimmie] Lunceford, Billie Holiday, Charlie Shavers, Russell Procope, Satch Crawford, Jean Walker, Norma McCoy, Buster Bailey, Taps Miller, Hawkins, myself and several whose names I can't recall."[73] These musicians' attendance on 52nd Street, like that of white musicians, could have been inspired both by collegiality toward fellow performers and by a desire for press coverage.

As they became public figures, jazz musicians on 52nd Street often found themselves in the company of nonmusician celebrities known for their roles in the film industry or high society. Although the fame of these patrons means that their representation in the press disproportionately reflected their actual presence in the clubs, they are nonetheless a significant marker of the degree to which 52nd Street had become a part of the glamorous "café society" that was widely covered in the news media.[74] Movie stars' visits to 52nd Street were widely reported by the press. Teenage actor Jackie Cooper, for example, who according to *Down Beat* was "known to musicians as an up-and-coming drummer," sat in with Louis Prima at the Famous Door in 1938.[75] Dorothy Lamour, known as the "Sarong Girl" for her roles in such exotic productions as *The Jungle Princess* (1936), reportedly began a romance with bandleader Charlie Barnet after "Charlie invited Lamour to the Onyx Club."[76] In addition to reporting on performers such as these, *Swing* covered the doings of New York's wealthy set in an unusual section called "Swing and Society Make the Rounds." In a typical column, reporter Pauline Williams gossiped that Maxine Sullivan's return to the Onyx in 1939 would "be welcome news to Sylvia White, the Warren Pershings, Esme O'Brien, Peggy Mabon and scores of others who are mad about Maxine's singing" and explained that Mr. Hobart Crook Durham "goes in for soft drinks at Mammy's Chicken Farm."[77]

It is likely that many of these celebrities and socialites saw 52nd Street as a place to go "slumming" in the same way that they might have viewed

Harlem in the 1920s, ironically helping to increase the street's snob appeal with their presence even as they enjoyed its unpretentious atmosphere. 52nd Street's jazz clubs were relatively spartan and unassuming compared to both the chic East Side spots attended by the wealthy and the enormous palaces that catered to the Broadway crowd.[78] Some of the street's white clubbers sought out patronizing relationships with African American performers. In a 1938 profile of the black novelty act "Dr. Sausage and His Five Pork Chops," then appearing at the Onyx, Dr. Sausage's brother Chick Morrison complains that "these Society cats is always inviting Sausage over to their tables for champagne parties down at the club, and that cat don't drink."[79] On the other hand, because 52nd Street also housed establishments such as the 21 Club and Tony's, which had a reputation for sophistication, the society crowd may, to some extent, have viewed 52nd Street as a seat of refinement rather than as an exotic retreat like Harlem. Moreover, the tone of a given club could change over time depending on who was performing. Al Casey recalled that when the Fats Waller band began its engagement at the Yacht Club in 1938, "it was more elite" than other 52nd Street clubs. "The clientele was more elite. But they took to us! . . . But we started drawing people from up the street who knew who we were, and that helped the crowd. . . . The clientele was a bit different. Until we went in there. Then we drew people from the real joints."[80]

Most of the customers of 52nd Street's "real joints" were neither noted musicians nor wealthy celebrities; rather, they were young white men and women with varying degrees of interest in jazz. For many, attending 52nd Street's clubs was simply a fun, voguish activity that formed part of the national obsession with swing music. Such patrons gained most of their knowledge of swing from mainstream media and were not particularly concerned with the music's history or with seeking out obscure musicians or styles. Critic Wilder Hobson condescendingly suggested in 1939 that the 52nd Street audience saw jazz as just one of a number of fashionable fads, with young attendees "just so squirmingly eager to hear 'Wingy' Mannone or 'Stuff' Smith or go skiing or sit up and see the sunrise or whatever People Were Doing."[81] Although the cramped dimensions of 52nd Street's clubs hindered the exuberant, athletic dancing characteristic of "jitterbugs" in large dance halls, young audience members found other ways to express themselves.[82] At the Hickory House in 1937, for example, listeners at the bar "madly hammer[ed] the time with spoons, glasses or hands" as Joe Marsala's band performed, and "one entranced girl wearing a dress made entirely of leather danced about

among the tables all by herself." [83] As David Stowe points out, it is difficult to generalize about swing's young enthusiasts: "to those with a firsthand knowledge of swing subculture, it was clear that jitterbugs were
a more variegated group than they appeared to appalled outsiders." [84]
The jazz press in this period, however, was beginning to draw a distinction between those swing fans whom they accused of ignorance and bad
taste and those who supposedly demonstrated a genuine appreciation of
and respect for the music. In 1940, for example, critic Leonard Feather
contrasted "ickies" (a disparaging term for jitterbugs) with "hepcats" in
criticizing Stuff Smith's recent performances on 52nd Street: "Stuff has
been tickling the ickies and horrifying the hepcats with his unrighteous
jive at the Hickory House—all comedy and very little music." [85] Feather
implied that "hepcats" had a sincere interest in music, which he felt that
Smith had lately been neglecting, while "ickies" were easily seduced by
theatrics.

Feather's musically astute "hepcats" were part of a larger movement
of jazz devotees in the late 1930s and early 1940s, those who claimed to
reject the commercial trappings of the swing era in a search for authentic jazz. As Scott DeVeaux points out, this search often began, ironically,
with commodities: "most jazz enthusiasts initially approached the music as collectors of commercially available recordings, quickly learning
to distinguish between fodder for the masses and the 'real jazz,' known
only to cognoscenti." [86] As the numbers of these enthusiasts increased,
such organizations as the United Hot Clubs of America and the Hot Record Society, which reissued and commissioned recordings, and such
publications as *Jazz Information* and *H.R.S. Society Rag* developed to cater
to them. [87] To many of these collectors, defending the "real jazz" involved
an "insistence on the superiority of the unadulterated sounds of New Orleans and Chicago jazz." [88] As we have seen, the first white musicians on
52nd Street similarly valorized these styles, both because their improvisatory freedom was a means of resisting the commercial popular music
of the radio studios and for their supposed connection to an authentic
black identity. "Hot collectors" likewise viewed earlier jazz as anticommercial, as the "preindustrial musical products of organic communities" such as, supposedly, those of southern blacks. [89] As record collectors
sought out authentic jazz performances in New York, they gravitated to
"secret, subterranean places" free of "the glare of publicity." [90] Although
52nd Street featured improvisatory music influenced by the classic jazz
of New Orleans and Chicago, its increasing connection to the world of
show business and celebrity made it seem like a dilution of "real jazz"

to some aficionados. DeVeaux writes that "even the conversion of 52nd Street speakeasies like the Onyx Club into nightclubs after the repeal of Prohibition did not satisfy the true jazz fan's desire for an unmediated artistic experience, free from the trappings of commercial culture."[91] Nonetheless, the street continued to attract such connoisseurs, although they were sometimes critical of the music performed there.

As with jitterbugs, it is difficult to generalize about 52nd Street's "hot jazz" enthusiasts, who had varying levels of interest in the music. Although the jazz press tended to cast these two factions as polar opposites, it is likely that many listeners could have been seen as part of either camp depending on the context. Nonetheless, certain features were common among the enthusiasts. The great majority of hot jazz aficionados were white men, and many were alumni or students of prestigious universities.[92] Such students formed a significant portion of the audience on 52nd Street, which was easily accessible from Columbia, Yale, and Princeton, among other institutions. Robert Inman, who visited 52nd Street in 1938, writes that "it was very crowded; particularly with semi-drunk, singing, college kids who had rented a hotel room for the weekend," and recalled in an interview that the drunken singing included school songs of Yale and Dartmouth.[93] Although not all of these students are likely to have been serious jazz fans, at least some probably were. Another characteristic of hot jazz aficionados was their attitude of rapt attention, noted by many musicians who played on the street in this period. As DeVeaux argues, discriminating jazz connoisseurs approached the music as a high art: "If the general public tended to treat jazz as entertainment, the true believers accorded it respect in the only way they knew: a painfully self-conscious aping of established concert etiquette." Al Casey remembered that the Yacht Club audience "would listen" to Fats Waller's band, " 'cause I guess they were comparing us to the bands that usually worked there." Johnny Blowers claimed that in 1941 and 1942 audiences "just wanted to watch and listen." Inman said that "it was dead silence" in the clubs "when a singer or an individual came on" and that it was "fairly quiet in the jam sessions and that kind of thing. . . . they were quiet at the few tables they had, but at the bar was a little noisier."[94] If not everyone in 52nd Street's audiences was hushed and intently focused on the music, that such behavior was at least unexceptional indicates that an attitude of thoughtful connoisseurship was becoming common on 52nd Street by the end of the swing era.

In addition to the clubs, 52nd Street housed another institution of importance to "serious" jazz buffs: the Commodore Music Shop, owned and operated by Milt Gabler. Gabler opened his first record store in 1926 on East 42nd Street, where he eventually "built a small but loyal clientele for the retail and resale of obscure (and expensive) jazz recordings."[95] In 1935, Gabler became a "chief organizer" of the United Hot Clubs of America in an effort to promote record sales, making him an important figure in the nascent hot jazz movement.[96] By 1938, he remembered, he was "doing such a terrific mail-order business that I was able to afford a second store."[97] He decided upon 46 West 52nd Street as the location for a branch shop in order "to be right where it was then happening."[98] The new store ran from September 1938 until October 1941, when Gabler moved his entire operation back to 42nd Street.[99] Although other midtown music stores, such as G. Schirmer at 3 East 43rd Street and Liberty Music Shop at 50th Street and Madison Avenue, sold jazz records, the Commodore Music Shop became known as a mecca for collectors in search of both records and lively conversation about New Orleans and Chicago jazz.[100] Gabler recalled that "we became a congregating place for jazz musicians and fans" and that "when any of the European jazz critics came to this country . . . they inevitably found their way to the Commodore."[101] Bud Freeman remembered inviting Lester Young to the store to hear Freeman's new record of *Three Little Words* (recorded for the Commodore label in 1938.)[102] In 1940, reporter Bob Bach described the store as "the home of the hot discographers, where at any hour of the day or night you can find a small group of ardent jazz fans ever-eager to argue with you over the respective merits of Joe Oliver and Louie [Armstrong] or Bix [Beiderbecke] and [Frank] Tesch[emacher]."[103]

Debates of this sort also were prevalent in *Jazz Information,* the first issue of which "was written, mimeographed and mailed late one night" in September 1939 "in the back room of the 52nd Street Commodore Music Shop."[104] The magazine, which ran sporadically until November 1941, had two "point[s] of policy": "to confine its activities to *hot jazz*" and "to be non-commercial." As a "non-commercial" publication, *Jazz Information* proclaimed that it "made no appeal to jitterbugs; J.I.'s readers had to be hot fans, collectors, and the few musicians who really care about jazz."[105] Although, after the first issue, the editors of *Jazz Information* began to use a professional printer and to run the magazine out of their homes, it continued to advertise Commodore Records and the Commodore Music Shop, report on 52nd Street's clubs and musicians, and more generally reflect the anticommercial ethos of the Commodore and its clientele.[106]

The dispute described earlier by Bob Bach, which pits a famous African American duo against a famous white one, suggests that the significance of race in the creation of jazz was commonly debated at the Commodore. In a fanciful 1940 burlesque on jazz critics and collectors published in *Jazz Information,* writer Fred R. Miller satirically depicted a discussion at "Milt Gabler's 52nd Street wax emporium": "I said, 'There're some white musicians and white records.' He didn't think so. 'A white record,' he said, 'is like a gag. You hear it once and enjoy it, but it hasn't any kick the second time and the third time it bores you stiff.' " [107] If 52nd Street's hot jazz enthusiasts often upheld black jazz performers as more authentic than white ones, they also were not shy about criticizing those black musicians who failed to adhere to a strict notion of authenticity. In their polemical fervor, *Jazz Information*'s white columnists sometimes attacked 52nd Street's black musicians for perceived breaches of taste and tradition. A 1940 review, for example, panned a record by Dr. Sausage and His Five Pork Chops as "trashy jive music by the 52nd Street kazoo jump band," while a Buster Bailey record was accused of possessing "the earmarks of the John Kirby music; half-jazz, half-classical, and not much either way." [108] In another attack on Kirby, the magazine asserted that "with [its] badly digested classicisms . . . John Kirby's band forfeits the right to be considered seriously as jazz or as anything else." [109] Like the Commodore Music Shop, *Jazz Information* looked to many white jazz aficionados like a keeper of the flame of authentic jazz in the face of the increasing commercialization and commodification of both jazz in general and 52nd Street in particular.

This appearance, however, was somewhat deceptive. The Commodore Music Shop was, after all, a shop, which existed primarily to make a profit. While the collegial atmosphere that Gabler fostered there may have made the store seem more like a friendly social club than a place of business, it also helped Gabler sell records. Robert Inman recalled that Gabler would sometimes employ overt, conventional sales gimmicks; for example, on "Saturday afternoon he'd have a radio show with contestants, and if you won the contest you might get three or four records [laughs]— 78s." [110] Moreover, Gabler was also in the business of record production— the Commodore record label was established in 1938, the same year that the 52nd Street store opened—and the store enabled him to market his own product. By his own account, Gabler's marketing was not especially successful. In a biographical sketch written in the 1970s, he claimed that in 1939 and 1940 "the store on 52nd Street is a bomb retailwise. . . . People do not want to carry around breakable and bulky 78 rpm's when club jumping and most days we give struggling musicians more from our till than we take in selling records." [111] Nonetheless, Gabler's store inspired competition: Rabson's Music Shop opened at 111 West 52nd in early 1940 with its own "record head," Henry Principi, and began to issue its own jazz records on the Music Box label.[112] Despite its association with hot jazz, the Commodore shop did not limit its inventory to this style. A 1941 list of best-selling records in New York music shops reveals that Commodore's most popular five items comprised two records by the Glenn Miller Orchestra, one each by the swing bands of Artie Shaw and Will Bradley, and one by cabaret singer Hildegarde. This list is more or less the same as those given for other record stores, such as G. Schirmer, that did not claim to specialize in hot jazz.[113] Realistically, then, Gabler was not opposed to commerce—rather, he hoped to make an esoteric form of music commercially viable without corrupting it.

The editors of *Jazz Information* were certainly aware that Commodore was a commercial enterprise, because they frequently ran ads for the shop and for the Commodore record label.[114] Moreover, their own attitude toward commerce was more ambiguous than some of the magazine's more heated columns might suggest. In declaring *Jazz Information* a "non-commercial" publication, they took pains to point out that "J.I.'s non-commercialism was journalistic, not musical. The term 'non-commercial' as a musical criterion is confusing and rather foolish, and we have tried to avoid it." [115] The magazine sometimes reported unapologetically on major events in the swing world, such as personnel changes in the bands of Glenn Miller and Benny Goodman, and occasionally gave positive reviews to such mainstream bandleaders as Gene Krupa and Jimmy Dorsey. A funny, acerbic 1940 letter to the editor reveals, however, that sporadic displays of open-mindedness were not consolation enough for those readers put off by *Jazz Information*'s purism. Reader C. Miller asks,

Who the hell do you guys think you are anyway? Where do you get off to say a record is commercial just because it doesn't happen to be made by a bunch of riverboat stevedores who play in some cat house where all the keys on the piano are busted but one, and everybody is starving to death and the only kitty in the place has been eaten up long ago, claws and all, but everybody is sensitive and authentic and unusual and inviolate and restrained and subdued and everything but commercial. God no, not that.[116]

After some more ranting, Miller goes on to say,

I realize I've been writing like a wise guy and getting a little too smart even for myself, but I feel that you fellows might put the soft pedal on your vitriolic (and often un-constructive) criticism of bands that know which side their bread is buttered on. Please excuse me for getting porky. I love you all.[117]

Like so many aspects of 52nd Street's music and culture, the relationship of the Commodore Music Shop, *Jazz Information,* and their customers and readers to the commercial music industry was more complex than it seemed on the surface, involving dissent and debate as well as rigid dogmatism. As musicians, both black and white, strove to appeal to the diverse tastes of 52nd Street's patrons while maintaining a sense of their own artistic integrity, they were forced into a tricky balancing act among competing ideas about musical style, commercial success, and racial identity.

Chapter Six **Making It into the Big Time** Count Basie, Joe Marsala, and "Mixed" Bands

On July 11, 1938, the first big band to play on 52nd Street opened at the Famous Door. The band, a group of African American musicians led by pianist Count Basie, had come from Kansas City to New York in 1936 at the urging of critic and promoter John Hammond and had already attracted attention during engagements at larger, more traditional big-band venues such as the Roseland Ballroom, the Apollo Theatre, and the Savoy Ballroom. According to Basie, however, the band's gig at the Famous Door "turned out to be our biggest break." [1] For the next four months, the patrons of the packed club, as well as a national radio audience, marveled at the powerful four-beat swing produced by the band's rhythm section, Basie's spare piano style, and what writer Ralph Ellison later called "that great freedom within discipline" that allowed the group to highlight the creativity of soloists such as Lester Young and Herschel Evans.[2] Meanwhile, a block away at the Hickory House, white clarinetist Joe Marsala led a smaller group, usually comprising seven or eight musicians and known for a freewheeling brand of jazz with roots in New Orleans and Chicago. Marsala's popularity along 52nd Street won him unusually steady employment in a market where rapid turnover was the rule—as he later pointed out, his band was "in and out of the Hickory House for the best part of ten years" from 1937 on.[3] Despite his musical talent, however, Marsala never became a national icon of swing like Basie, and he drew his audience primarily from 52nd Street's core of discriminating jazz devotees.

A comparison of Basie and Marsala shows that the tension between commercial standardization and spontaneous individual expression that pervaded 52nd Street during the swing era was inevitably played out in racial terms. While each musician walked a line between the formal conventions of show business and the informal camaraderie of the jam session, each had his own approach to stage presence and musical style. Basie presented his hard-swinging, improvisatory music in a sleek, streamlined package, with a professional image that showcased precision and resisted racial stereotypes of reckless abandon. Critic Gerald Early's evocative description of Basie's music as "the mighty burning of the unassuming" suggests both its driving intensity and the self-possession and poise with which Basie performed.[4] Marsala, in contrast, capitalized on the mystique of unrestrained, impulsive "hot jazz" that continued to inspire many of 52nd Street's white musicians and patrons. He also, however, drew on aspects of mainstream swing that helped make his music approachable for a larger audience. Both thus epitomized larger trends on 52nd Street, where many black performers sought to undermine conventional notions of natural, spontaneous black musicianship even as white musicians aspired to embody such notions in their own performances. At the same time, however, Basie's and Marsala's involvement in interracial music making helped blur racial boundaries in ways that increasingly informed the street's culture during the swing era.

"Just Play Out": Count Basie at the Famous Door While Basie's engagement at the Famous Door was a commercial success, it was initially a gamble for both the band and the club. The band was managed by Willard Alexander of the Music Corporation of America (MCA), the most powerful booking agency for big bands.[5] Alexander, concerned that Basie had yet to gain widespread popularity in New York, hit on the strategy of booking the band into a 52nd Street club. As Alexander later admitted, the idea seemed "crazy. The clubs couldn't accommodate a big band on their stands, and they were so small, fourteen men would blow the walls out." Although he was able to convince the owners of the Famous Door of the merits of Basie's music, "the hangup . . . was the club's lack of air conditioning. With difficulty, they could seat sixty people. But can you imagine what it would have been like without air conditioning in New York's summer heat and humidity?"[6] The problem was solved when either MCA or Hammond (each later took credit) advanced the Famous Door a loan to cover the cost of an air conditioner in exchange for hiring Basie.[7] The *New York Times* cited "the uncontradicted report that the Music Corporation of America, reputed to be the largest band agency in the country, invested in the Famous Door for the sole purpose of affording a showcase and radio outlet for Count Basie."[8] Basie's appearance at the Famous Door thus involved a consolidation of commercial forces—including a nightclub, a booking agency, and an influential critic and promoter—typical of the swing era.

Basie's performances similarly conformed to many conventions of swing-era entertainment. His band, which included African American singers Jimmy Rushing and Helen Humes, was only one part of a larger revue that comprised Jerry Kruger, a white female singer and master of ceremonies; tap dancer Jerry Wither; and Shavo Sherman, who did "mimicry of Durante, Ted Lewis and Hugh Herbert."[9] The management of the club exacerbated the already cramped conditions by adding a small dance floor for patrons.[10] Most significantly, Alexander arranged radio broadcasts from the club over the CBS network. Basie asserted that "that was the very best thing that could happen for the band, because we had excellent airtime, and that was when radio was it."[11] In September 1938, for example, Basie broadcast four nights a week over CBS starting between 11:00 p.m. and 12:30 a.m.[12] His network affiliation enabled Basie to reach a national audience. He recalled in his autobiography that "those jitney cab drivers out in Chicago used to run up and down South Parkway digging us on their radios . . . and when we got back out there, they used to tell us about it," and he remembered his excitement that "with those broadcasts going out over a coast-to-coast hookup, we could finally really begin to feel that we were making it into the big time."[13] This national exposure came at a cost to the club's patrons. MCA employee Irving Lazar remembered that "because Basie didn't want to hold back—it would have ruined his sound over the air—the entire audience had to get up and stand outside the club for the thirty minutes [of the broadcast]. Since it was summertime, it was no real problem. But that was the procedure throughout the engagement. Come broadcast time and the audience was asked to nurse their drinks on the sidewalk."[14]

This anecdote demonstrates that the Famous Door, while catering to the needs of a major radio network, also maintained some of the casual atmosphere for which 52nd Street was known. It was unusual for a nightclub to expect audiences to squeeze into a cramped room only to be cast back into the street for a half hour. The obvious impracticality of using such a large band in such a small space suggests that the owners of the Famous Door rightly surmised that their patrons would be willing to endure overcrowding and inconvenience in order to hear Basie. Early reports describe Basie's audience as "knowing jitterbugs" or "swing connoisseurs"; Willard Alexander remembered that at the time of the opening, Basie "was not too well known, except among *aficionados* who dug Kansas City swing."[15] Although Basie eventually attracted a mass audience, his initial following on 52nd Street was among the subset of hot jazz fans who saw the street's music as an alternative to mainstream popular music. Moreover, musicians continued to drop in at the Famous Door, sometimes sitting in with the band. *Swing* reported that "sitting in at odd times" during the opening were Benny Carter, Jack Teagarden, Fletcher Henderson, Joe Marsala, Lionel Hampton, Teddy Wilson, and Clarence Profit. In August, the *New York Daily Mirror* claimed that "in addition to playing to standing room only every evening, the Count of Swing has made every band leader in town a regular patron of the Famous Door"; examples included Paul Whiteman, Benny Goodman, Raymond Scott, Gene Krupa, and Duke Ellington. Although such events as a "Bon Voyage Party" thrown for Goodman on July 12 and advertised in the *New York Times* created welcome publicity, they also suggested that these bandleaders continued to think of the Famous Door as a "musicians' club" despite Basie's mass popularity.[16]

The mix of rigorous professionalism and relaxed informality that characterized the band's engagement at the Famous Door was reflected in its sound, which balanced an immaculate, seemingly automatic level of rhythmic precision with highly individualized displays of self-expression. Cultural historian Joel Dinerstein argues that big bands in the 1930s were "icon[s] of humanized machine aesthetics" that reflected the energy and organization of an increasingly industrial society while simultaneously affirming "human agency . . . against a forbidding ground of overmechanization."[17] Dinerstein cites Basie's band as purveyors of a *"soulful* metronomic swing groove" that swung flawlessly without being "mechanically perfect."[18] This groove was sustained by Basie's "All-American Rhythm Section," comprising Basie (piano), Freddie Green (guitar), Jo Jones (drums), and Walter Page (bass), which was renowned for its light but relentless swing.[19] Moreover, the band's style was characterized by riffs in the brass and saxophone sections that created rhythmic momentum through repetition. A performance of *Jumpin' at the Woodside* broadcast from the Famous Door on July 23, 1938, continually renews its rhythmic intensity as the two sections play a changing series of complementary riffs.[20] Although these riffs, like the swing of the rhythm section, were undoubtedly "soulful" in their emotional appeal and their ability to inspire dancers and other listeners, the seamless blending and precision of the musicians effaced individuality, making the band seem at times like an anonymous collective or, as Dinerstein puts it, "a model of corporate organization." [21] In this respect, Basie's style can be seen as the sonic counterpart of the totalizing systems and practices of the commercial music industry.

On the other hand, the band's performances also highlighted improvisation and spontaneity, values central to the notion of authentic self-expression that animated the 52nd Street scene. Trombonist Eddie Bert, who as a teenager was invited to the band's daytime rehearsals at the Famous Door, remembered that "that was a loose band. It was like a small band, but it was a big band. Mostly head arrangements." [22] An alternate reading of the version of *Jumpin' at the Woodside* cited earlier suggests that the constantly shifting riffs signified fertile creativity rather than robotic perfection; the band's powers of imagination allow them to extend the performance for almost seven minutes, over twice the time available to them in their studio recording of the tune. [23] A report from August 1938 reveals that the band sometimes played at even greater length: "The band is at its best when it uses a skeleton arrangement and improvises as the spirit moves the men. They have been known to play a single tune for a half-hour at a time, with brilliant solos and ensemble work piling up to achieve effects unheard of in most other bands." [24] A group of gifted soloists, including tenor saxophonists Lester Young and Herschel Evans, trumpeters Harry "Sweets" Edison and Buck Clayton, and trombonist Dicky Wells, were crucial to the sound of the Basie band. Dinerstein argues that "the musical tension between Basie's soloists and the rhythm section publicly displayed a ritual fight between the needs of the individual and the needs of the group." [25] The most dramatic example of such interaction in *Jumpin' at the Woodside* appears at the end of the performance, when Evans plays an extended clarinet solo that soars freely over the band's tightly executed riffs. Although a similar dynamic was characteristic of many big bands during the swing era, it assumed special significance within the context of 52nd Street, where friction between musical self-expression and commercial standardization was particularly concentrated and visible.

By bringing a big band to 52nd Street, Basie challenged racial conventions as well as musical ones. As John Hammond remembered, "outside Harlem, there were still few places where a Negro band could play in New York" in 1938. [26] In reviewing Basie's opening at the Famous Door, Jack Gould of the *New York Times* mentioned that black musicians did not have the option of "obtain[ing] bookings in the Grade A hotels or the cabarets not expressly of Harlem flavor." [27] Basie's booking at the Famous Door thus undermined racial standards that had prevented many African American big bands from working in midtown Manhattan. Moreover, the socially conscious Hammond insisted that he be "permitted to bring Negro friends into the club to hear Basie," as a result of which "the Jim Crow pattern of the Famous Door was broken, at least for the time of Basie's stay." [28] Although, as we have seen, black patrons were not unprecedented on 52nd Street, their presence was still unusual in a midtown club. Interracial mingling in the audience was paralleled onstage. White musicians who sat in with Basie included Jack Teagarden and Joe Marsala as well as trumpeter Harry James, who played with the band on its July 23 radio broadcast. *Down Beat* reported in August that "the ace number in the show is Jerry Kreuger, white singer, who sends the band every night"; while this could mean simply that the band enjoyed Kruger's singing, it might also suggest that they accompanied her, which would mean that interracial performance was a regular part of the show.[29] Although such collaboration did not represent a radical departure from 52nd Street's unofficial policy of racially segregated bands, it did help expand the boundaries of interracial performance on the street.

The Basie band resisted certain racial stereotypes while inevitably being received in terms of others. Critics applauded what they saw as the controlled, mannered qualities of the band, which supposedly distinguished them from most black entertainers. In his review, Jack Gould complained that "both to his and music's loss, the Negro has been asked to behave like a freak when entertaining a white audience; to put on stupid little hats and imitate a shagging inmate of Bellevue's psychopathic ward." Basie, in contrast, "minimizes exhibitionism and allows his men to just play out, in itself a departure." [30] Gould's claim is supported by the band's July 23, 1938, broadcast, in which the only gesture toward boisterous comedy is Harry Edison enthusiastically shouting "Count Basie!" in what Basie called a "high, keen voice . . . like a girl." [31] Gould also praised the band's "quiet and relaxed execution of the hot ditties" and "the absence of the do-or-die tenseness commonly associated with Negro bands," while a reporter for the *New York Herald-Tribune* credited them with "eschewing the more frenetic aspects of jitterbug music." [32] On the other hand, Basie's music was often seen as the product of a rhythmic genius supposedly innate to black musicians. Gould claimed that "the Negro musician" has an "inherent sense of rhythm." [33] The *Herald-Tribune* asserted that the Basie band "offers rhythmic variations which only a Negro orchestra could furnish." [34] Basie's music, like that of many of 52nd Street's African American musicians, was seen through multiple lenses by white reviewers, as the result of both unconscious racial tendencies and conscious control and restraint.

"Whatever You Had, You Used": Joe Marsala at the Hickory House   Although Basie's performances at the Famous Door were unusual in some ways, his big band nonetheless performed in the most popular and iconic musical style of the era. White clarinetist Joe Marsala, in contrast, led small ensembles that attempted to preserve the New Orleans and Chicago-style jazz that had dominated 52nd Street in its earliest days as a jazz district. Marsala, a native of Chicago who had worked with New Orleans trumpeter Wingy Manone as early as 1929, had a background that gave him a direct claim to the brand of authenticity associated with these early jazz styles. While he made efforts to distinguish his music from conventional big-band swing, Marsala, who performed frequently at the Hickory House between 1937 and 1947, also managed to attract an audience by integrating the musical practices of swing and older jazz.

Marsala's uneasy relationship to mainstream swing was typical of 52nd Street's white musicians in this period. Most continued to employ the polyphonic textures characteristic of New Orleans and Chicago style and emphasized spontaneous improvisation over careful arrangement. Wingy Manone and Louis Prima, who were instrumental in introducing this style to 52nd Street's audiences, continued to appear on the street throughout the late 1930s and early 1940s.[35] New Orleans trumpeter Sharkey Bonano (billed as "Sharkey Bananas") appeared at the Hawaiian Yacht Club in January 1938, with what one reviewer called "a band that's as typically Dixie in its swing rhythms and heat as corn liquor."[36] Recorded evidence demonstrates, however, that much supposed "Dixieland" actually combined traits of New Orleans jazz with those of up-to-date swing. Take, for example, a 1938 recording of *Love Is Just Around the Corner* by Eddie Condon and His Windy City Seven, an all-star group comprised largely of musicians who performed on 52nd Street in the late 1930s, such as tenor saxophonist Bud Freeman, clarinetist Pee Wee Russell, and bassist Artie Shapiro.[37] Its first chorus shows all the hallmarks of Dixieland, including a two-beat bass line and four-part polyphony played by cornet, clarinet, tenor sax, and trombone. Although the polyphonic, improvisatory style derives from New Orleans, the tune itself is not a folk standard: rather, it is a conventional thirty-two-bar pop song, composed by professional songwriters Leo Robin and Lew Gensler, that had been introduced only a few years before by Bing Crosby in the 1934 film *Here Is My Heart.*[38]

While the performance may be willfully old-fashioned, the material is not. Moreover, the cornet, tenor sax, and trombone can be heard playing repetitive riffs behind Russell's clarinet solo on the second and third choruses of the tune—this technique derives more from the style of arranged big bands than from New Orleans. This recording reveals that these musicians were absorbing and employing aspects of contemporary musical practice even as they clung to the principles of older jazz, a strategy that had the advantage of making their music more accessible to the wide public who enjoyed 1930s swing.

Marsala's early experiences on 52nd Street in 1936 and 1937 may have shown him the potential of a musical style that could appeal to a broad audience while retaining the authentic flavor of older jazz. Before he led his own band at the Hickory House, Marsala worked there in 1936 as part of Wingy Manone's group.[39] Manone, as we have seen, achieved commercial success with a mixture of hot New Orleans–style improvisation, popular tunes, and a comical stage persona. When Manone left New York in the summer of 1936 for a vaudeville tour, Marsala and Eddie Condon took over his group at the Hickory House for about a month, during which African American trumpeter Red Allen very briefly worked with them in what was probably the first racially "mixed" band to appear on 52nd Street.[40] Marsala's next appearance on the street was at the Yacht Club with Red McKenzie during the fall of 1936; he then appeared at a club at 54 West 52nd named after McKenzie.[41] In January 1937, *Metronome* reported that "a band of Chicagoans" including Marsala and Condon was playing at McKenzie's.[42] In the same issue, however, critic George T. Simon claimed that "on 52nd Street there's a night club that's already folded, or is just about to fold." Although Simon discreetly avoided naming the club, he explained that "leading musicians in the Chicago school of hot have dropped in there regularly enough" and that "this club has had by far the best swing jam on the street," which suggests that the club was almost certainly McKenzie's. Simon blamed the collapse of McKenzie's not on the commercial potential of "swing," which "on that street is commercial in any form." Rather, "the trouble with this club . . . has been that the musicians and owners have formed their own small clique, have catered only to themselves, and just haven't given a tinker's damn what was happening to the casual customer." The insider musicians' club atmosphere formerly associated with such clubs as the Onyx was alienating rather than attracting McKenzie's patrons. Simon concluded by arguing that unless this clique starts to respect its audience, it "might just as well resign [itself] to jamming in somebody's home: the effect in toto would be the same, and the boys would save an awful lot of dough!"[43] His experiences with Manone and at McKenzie's must have made Marsala aware of both the viability of combining improvised jazz with accessible entertainment and the commercial risks involved in failing to appeal directly to an audience.

Marsala's studio recordings from 1937 and 1938 demonstrate an interest in reconciling Chicago jazz with commercial swing by either combining or juxtaposing them. The eight-piece band's first session, on April 21, 1937, as Joe Marsala's Chicagoans, produced four versions of jazz standards of the 1910s and 1920s, including *Clarinet Marmalade,* composed by Larry Shields of the Original Dixieland Jazz Band, and Jelly Roll Morton's *Wolverine Blues.*[44] Although these performances show some fidelity to their original interpreters with polyphony, breaks for soloists, and mainly two-beat rhythms, they also incorporate more contemporary practices. For example, the Chicagoans' version of *Clarinet Marmalade* includes a sequence of four eight-bar solos by harp, violin, piano, and clarinet, in contrast to the Original Dixieland Jazz Band's 1918 recording, in which soloists play only brief breaks.[45] The tune's two-beat feeling is somewhat ambiguous, as bassist Artie Shapiro occasionally slips into four-beat lines characteristic of 1930s swing rather than earlier jazz. Perhaps the most striking departure from tradition is the presence of harpist Adele Girard (Marsala's wife), whose arpeggiated lines stand out from the rest of the group. In all, these recordings are reminiscent of Prima's and Manone's in their assimilation of older and newer styles of jazz.

In their next recording session, however, the group eschewed overt references to early jazz, drawing instead on an eclectic range of contemporary swing styles. The March 16, 1938, recordings include Leonard Feather's thirty-two-bar pop tune *Mighty Like the Blues,* featuring the muted trumpet of Marsala's brother Marty and a crooning vocal by guitarist Jack LeMaire (Condon had left the band in July 1937.)[46] This was followed by *Woo-Woo,* a novelty number in which the band shouts "Woo woo woo woo woo!" at the end of each phrase. *Woo-Woo* concludes with two choruses of solos in four-beat rhythm, distributed among clarinet, trumpet, and piano; LeMaire sings a scat line in the style of Leo Watson during the last bridge. A third recording, *Hot String Beans,* begins with a repeated two-bar bass figure over which Marty Marsala growls on trumpet and Joe Marsala plays a bluesy line emphasizing the flatted fifth degree of the scale, creating an exotic effect reminiscent of the Orientalist "travelogues" of the John Kirby group. The body of the performance is a slow twelve-bar blues that includes arranged homophonic lines as well as improvised solos. The final recording of the session, *Jim Jam Stomp,* is another blues, played at a furious tempo and featuring the band's new drummer, Buddy Rich, who recalled that he got the job after playing this very tune at a jam session with the band.[47] After one chorus of polyphony, the arrangement consists of a string of solos capped by three choruses of riffs over which Marsala improvises. In contrast to the 1937 session, this set of performances show-cases practices popular among mainstream swing audiences while largely ignoring obvious signifiers of New Orleans and Chicago jazz.

The band's live shows at the Hickory House were similarly eclectic. Robert Inman's scrapbooks, which include set lists for Marsala broadcasts from the Hickory House in 1937 and 1938, reveal that the band's reper-toire extended from popular songs such as *Christopher Columbus* and *They Can't Take That Away from Me* to the jazz standards *Jazz Me Blues* and *Singin' the Blues,* both associated with legendary trumpeter Bix Beiderbecke.[48] Contemporaneous reviews of the band similarly refer to tunes as wide-ranging as *That's a Plenty,* which had been recorded by the New Orleans Rhythm Kings in 1923, and *Little Sir Echo,* a pop song written by Marsala and sung by Girard.[49] The band's approach to this variety of material was itself diverse. Bassist Irv Manning, who played with Marsala in 1940, recalled that while the group memorized written arrangements for "beautiful tunes like *Someone to Watch Over Me,* featuring the harp," they more often "played go-ahead jazz." Artie Shapiro, Marsala's bassist from 1936 to 1939, remembered that the band played "Dixieland, and there was some Chicago, and there was some popular music too . . ." Typically, Shapiro explained, "there was improvisation within the framework of an arrangement . . . a head arrangement, we never had any music. The guys would take choruses, and then there'd be . . . ensemble playing where everybody was improvising—you know, typical Dixieland type of—where the instruments are just playing against each other, you know." However, the music "wasn't exactly absolute, positive Dixieland." Shapiro, for ex-ample, "didn't like the idea of just playing a simple bass, you know—I'd start moving the bass around and start walking the bass. I was one of the few guys in those [days]—there was a couple of other guys, too, around town—that got away from straight one-three, you know [sings "boom, boom, boom" on scale degrees 1–5–1]. We started walking the bass. And Dixieland really requires just one and—two beats to a bar, you know. So we started playing four-four and we started moving the bass around, which changed it a little bit."[50]

The band complemented its music with an understated stage presence. Shapiro remembered that the extent of the musicians' "show biz" was "a little thing" in which "we had three trumpets going—[two] guys [pianist Joe Bushkin and Shapiro himself] doubled on trumpet. We'd have a riff going at the end of a tune. . . . That was our big act [laughs]."[51] In 1940, *Down Beat* reported that new guitarist Carmen Mastren was scheduled to return to the Hickory House with Marsala, "playing not only guitar but also violin, with comedy impersonations of Stuff Smith and Joe Venuti!"[52] Adele Girard, whose unusual instrument and glamorous appearance often were noted in the press, also captured public attention.[53] In musical style and stage presentation, Marsala both targeted a mass audience and aspired to a standard of authentic jazz that privileged improvisation and downplayed elaborate staging.

Despite his swing-oriented repertoire and occasional theatrics, Marsala appears to have viewed himself as resisting the role of the mainstream entertainer. In a 1937 profile, Marsala denounced arranged music, which he associated with commercial radio: "Mr. Marsala, with a crusading light in his black eyes, complains that radio is killing creative music (meaning 'jam'). The studios don't like to have an orchestra go on the air unless they know just what the performance is going to be. 'Pure' swing, says Mr. Marsala, is all improvisation. Therefore you never hear 'pure' swing on the air."[54] Moreover, Marsala linked his style to that of the greats of the Chicago school rather than to contemporary swing. *Down Beat*, for example, reported in 1938 that Marsala "admires Bud Freeman and Bix and believes that his style was influenced by [Frank] Teschmaker," while pianist Bushkin "aspires to play trumpet like Bix." The same article explains that Marsala "dislikes the new style of swing and the confinement of playing in a large band."[55] Shapiro similarly stated that "my favorite way of playing was the small bands [because of] the freedom in it. . . . You created— whatever you had, you used. . . . [In] big bands, you were reading charts."[56]

While striving toward "freedom" and "pure swing," the band admittedly made concessions to commerce. Manning explained succinctly that Marsala "was quite commercial, as a matter of fact." Shapiro was dissatisfied with Adele Girard's harp playing, which he perceived as a publicity ploy rather than as true jazz: "Actually, I didn't enjoy [playing with her] too much. 'Cause she wasn't—well, she was all right, but she wasn't a jazz, too much of a jazz feeling in there. But I guess it was a good thing from a business standpoint, you know, an attraction." Pianist Joe Bushkin also was unhappy with Girard, as well as with the flashy drumming of Buddy Rich. He remembered that Rich "was a great improvement on [Danny] Alvin's boom-boom-boom bass drum—until he started playing too loud behind my solos. Also, Joe had hired Adele Girard on harp. Sometimes I felt like I needed an ear treatment at Bellevue after work." [57] While these criticisms of Girard may reflect the general disparagement of female instrumentalists by male musicians and critics during the swing era, they also demonstrate ambivalence about her commercial appeal. [58] It is notable, however, that while Shapiro made a distinction between "popular music" on the one hand and "Dixieland" or "Chicago" on the other, and Manning drew similar lines between "commercial" music and "go-ahead jazz," each remembered that the Marsala band played in both styles. [59] Although the band may have aspired to resist blatant appeals to a mass audience, they also accepted the necessity of such strategies.

Although Marsala was not a nationally renowned performer like Benny Goodman or Artie Shaw, he drew some of his audience from the mass culture of swing fandom rather than the small circle of "hot jazz" aficionados. The band's broadcasts over WMCA and the Intercity Network helped make Marsala known to a broader audience, and in January 1938 he even took part in an international broadcast to London. [60] This exposure outside of New York brought him to the attention of listeners such as Patricia Coburn of Chambersburg, Pennsylvania, whose breathless 1939 fan letter to *Swing* exemplifies the fervor of jitterbugs. Coburn explains that "on my first trip to the great city of New York one of my greatest ambitions was to reach the famed Hickory House and hear 'The Idol of the East,' Joe Marsala." Afterward, she felt "obliged to write . . . and recommend him to any genuine 'cats,'" perhaps implying that only those who truly understand and appreciate jazz will enjoy Marsala. The values by which she judges him, however, are those that the subculture of "hot jazz" fans rejected; for example, she praises Marsala's "eagerness to play specialties and comply with numerous requests" as "indicative of first rate showmanship." [61] Coburn's letter suggests that she was the kind of jazz fan criticized by Adorno, one who assumes the stance of an aficionado while appreciating music easily accessible through mass media. In covering Marsala, writers in the mainstream press similarly cast themselves as insiders by playing on stereotypes of swing as unfettered musical anarchy. A reviewer for the *New Yorker,* for example, called the band "maniacal" and complained ironically that it had "no reverence for anything, that's the trouble with these swing orchestras." In the same vein, the *New York Times* described Marsala's playing as "frenetic" and called attention to "Adele Girard playing a harp as no angel ever played it," while the *New York Post* claimed that "every minute's a 'jam session'" at the Hickory House. Reviews of this sort linked Marsala to a trendy notion of wild, abandoned swing rather than to "authentic" Chicago jazz. [62]

Despite the media attention he received, Marsala was better known to 52nd Street's coterie of hot jazz enthusiasts than to the general public. *Swing* reported in March 1940 that Marsala "has never managed to get very far away from 52nd Street, which hasn't helped get his name known around." This small, discerning audience tended to listen intently rather than engage in jitterbug antics. Pianist Art Hodes, who sat in with Marsala shortly after arriving in New York from Chicago in 1938, was astonished by the complete attention that Marsala commanded: "You're up there being looked at and listened to. And no one's dancing. I just couldn't believe this was happening." Artie Shapiro recalled that the audience members "weren't rowdy. . . . They were jazz lovers, they loved it. I think they were really enjoying it." Reviewers who wrote for such listeners often advocated for Marsala's music by placing it in historical context. Bob Bach of *Swing* drew a connection between Marsala and Chicago style, pointing out that Marsala was "a devotee of the Windy City type of jazz." *Down Beat*'s Tom Herrick, describing a typical performance of *That's a Plenty* by the group, proclaimed similarly that "the boys . . . proceed to 'take it out' in true Chicago style, proving conclusively that the Windy City has produced a style which will live long after Capone is gone." Herrick, like Marsala himself, believed that improvisation and self-expression were crucial to jazz, claiming that "a good many [musicians in New York] believe that Joe would ruin his band if he added more men because it is the spontaneity of his arrangements which makes the band so appealing; spontaneity which would be lacking in a larger, more organized group playing written music instead of what they feel." While making gestures to a broader audience, Marsala helped perpetuate the cult of improvisation and spontaneity that had informed 52nd Street from the speakeasy era.[63]

"A Very Free Thing": "Mixed" Performances and Public Jam Sessions
As perhaps the first white bandleader on 52nd Street to hire black musicians, Marsala also played a significant role in challenging the street's racial conventions. Racially "mixed" bands, as they were called, were not yet common in the late 1930s and early 1940s. As Leonard Feather points out, although in recording studios "the appearance of a Negro musician with a white band" was "a commonplace among small jazz combos by 1937," live performances by permanently established mixed bands were much rarer. One milestone was Benny Goodman's celebrated hiring of Teddy Wilson for his trio in 1935; as Feather argues, however, "the

appearance in public of a Negro musician with a white band was thought so radical that Wilson was allowed only to appear as an 'act,' a special adjunct rather than a regular member of the organization." Thereafter, "integration crawled along for almost a decade after Goodman had broken the checkerboard ice." [64] Probably the first mixed band on 52nd Street appeared in July 1936, when Marsala and Condon opened at the Hickory House with a band "featuring—for two nights only—the inspired trumpet playing" of black trumpeter Henry "Red" Allen.[65] Marsala recalled that "when Red had to leave to rejoin the Mills Blue Rhythm Band, we had another colored trumpet player, Otis Johnson." [66] In 1939, 52nd Street's Swing Club featured another interracial group: the Dixie Debs, led by singer Sally Sharron, who had worked formerly with Wingy Manone. *Down Beat* described the Debs as "four copper-colored jazz artists" and claimed that "Sally's the only paleface fronting such a group." [67] Several mixed bands appeared on the street in 1940. In February, white pianist Frank Froeba and black pianist Charlie Bourne formed a piano duo at the Torch Club at 18 West 52nd.[68] In April, a "mixed band in reverse," led by Frankie Newton and "all-Negro except for one man," clarinetist Flip Phillips, appeared at Kelly's Stable. *Down Beat* asserted that this was "the first dual-complexioned group ever formed by a colored maestro." [69] In October, Marsala added African American trumpeter Hot Lips Page to his band at the Hickory House.[70] In December, white pianist Joe Sullivan, who had already assembled an interracial band at Café Society in Greenwich Village in 1939, opened at the Famous Door with a sextet that, except for Sullivan himself, consisted entirely of black musicians.[71] This band remained at the Famous Door until the spring of 1941.[72] Besides these rare interracial bands, most groups on swing-era 52nd Street, as elsewhere, were either entirely white or entirely black.

Informal sitting in, however, often brought white and black musicians together. As we have seen, white musicians often sat in with Stuff Smith in the mid-1930s. Wingy Manone remembered that many musicians, both black and white, sat in during his performances at Kelly's Stable, to the point that his band "only had to play about two hours out of the six. Our friends played the rest of the time." In 1940, *Swing* reported a more spectacular event: "More recently there was the night that practically the whole Goodman band sat in with Count Basie's boys until there were more people on the bandstand than at the tables." While sitting in allowed musicians to forge friendships across racial lines, the ideal of musical communication that transcended race was sometimes countered by misunderstanding or suspicion. Irv Manning, who was raised in

England and had only recently arrived in the United States in 1940, re-called an awkward conversation with Hot Lips Page, who was then sitting in with the Marsala band. Manning's inexperience with American racial politics led him to offend the trumpeter inadvertently. Manning remembered, "[Page] says, 'You're from London,' he says, 'I know you're not prejudiced,' and . . . he said, 'What do you think about this situation with black musicians?' And in all my innocence, I said, 'Well, the only thing I can think of as a solution to that is for black people to start a colony in Africa.' Which he didn't take very well. . . . But I didn't mean it in a prejudicial way, 'cause I'm colorblind, you know. And his face dropped . . ." Despite such occasional friction among musicians, casual interracial performance does not appear to have been notably controversial among 52nd Street's predominantly white audiences. Manning recalled that "there was never any tension" in the audience when he performed with interracial bands.[73]

The practice of sitting in took place largely on the fringes of the commercial swing industry. Sitting in was banned by the American Federation of Musicians, which argued that musicians who engaged in informal public jamming were undermining their fellow professionals by playing for free.[74] Moreover, sitting in could interfere with the smooth flow of a stage performance and with a band's rehearsed routines. Al Casey, for example, remembered that Fats Waller, normally a lover of jam sessions, generally did not let other musicians sit in with his band at the Yacht Club because "Fats had his special things he liked to do, you know." Sitting in also could be difficult for musicians with busy schedules. Artie Shapiro recalled that he "very seldom" sat in at other clubs because "we were on the job all the time. [It gave] me very little chance to do that."[75] Despite its frequency on swing-era 52nd Street, sitting in remained to some extent a marginal activity.

Tensions over anticommercialism became more prominent with the appearance of planned jam sessions advertised to a paying public on 52nd Street. As Scott DeVeaux observes, public jam sessions represented an uneasy compromise between commercial appeal and an ideal of unfettered artistry. Although jazz buffs fetishized the jam session "as an inner sanctum of the jazz world known only to musicians and their close associates," they also had a desire to "share its treasures with the outside world." As a wider audience became aware of jam sessions, however, it ran the risk of undermining the very secrecy and insularity that made the sessions attractive. Jazz connoisseurs thus found themselves in the awkward position of "hop[ing] that they could somehow be absorbed into the jam session scene without distorting it."[76] The core audience for public jam sessions, then, saw a distinction between their own sincere dedication to jazz and the supposedly faddish, frivolous attitude of swing's mass audience. Nonetheless, the market appeal of swing inevitably affected the sessions. DeVeaux argues that "the growing popularity of swing after 1935 made it impossible for the jam session to retain its paradoxical position as a noncommercial sphere for professional musicians."[77] Public jam sessions thus reflected the conflict between anticommercialism and mass appeal that had pervaded 52nd Street from its beginnings as a jazz center.

Public jam sessions on 52nd Street began with Milt Gabler of the Commodore Music Shop. In 1935, Gabler began to stage jam sessions in recording studios with the support of the United Hot Clubs of America.[78] In February 1936, Gabler, along with the ubiquitous John Hammond, organized a session in a room above the Famous Door, featuring the great blues singer Bessie Smith in her only appearance on 52nd Street.[79] The Onyx Club followed shortly thereafter with Sunday night sessions in 1936.[80] In the same year, the Hickory House hosted jam sessions on Sunday afternoons, with the Wingy Manone band welcoming guest musicians to the stand; Joe Marsala took over this function by 1937.[81] As it became clear that such sessions could attract an audience, 52nd Street clubs such as the Swing Club and Leon & Eddie's, neither of which was primarily associated with jazz, got into the act by hosting "all-night jam sessions" in 1939.[82] In January 1940, Kelly's Stable on 51st Street began public jam sessions on Sunday afternoons led by Bud Freeman; then Frankie Newton and Ed Harris took over after the club moved to 137 West 52nd Street in March.[83] In January 1941, a series of Sunday sessions sponsored by Gabler began at Jimmy Ryan's.[84] As Arnold Shaw points out, "jamming was [in the early 1940s] hardly a 52d St. or even New York phenomenon"; clubs from Greenwich Village to Chicago to Larchmont, New York, also hosted public jam sessions at the time.[85] Nonetheless, 52nd Street was unusual in featuring so many sessions in such a concentrated area, particularly in 1940 and 1941, when Kelly's Stable, the Hickory House, and Jimmy Ryan's each held Sunday jam sessions.[86]

These sessions varied in their formality. At the Hickory House, visiting musicians sat in with the house band, normally that of Joe Marsala. Club owner John Popkin remembered a long list of musicians, both black and white, who "dropped in," including Hot Lips Page, Chu Berry, Benny Goodman, and Artie Shaw.[87] Artie Shapiro recalled that "all the guys working the big bands came in . . . Harry James, Ziggy Elman, people like that" as well as Lionel Hampton and Willie "The Lion" Smith.[88] Hickory House sessions were casual. *Variety* reported in 1937 that "visiting musicians bring their instruments and join the band, with or without invitation. There are no arrangements and no written notes."[89] Shapiro remembered that visiting soloists would "just say a tune that they liked to play, and we'd play it. . . . It was a very free thing, which I enjoyed very much."[90] Kelly's Stable structured its jam sessions similarly, with guests sitting in with the house band.[91] Sessions at Jimmy Ryan's, in contrast, employed a shifting lineup of musicians that changed from week to week. For the first session, on January 19, 1941, Gabler brought in a septet comprising mainly members of Eddie Condon's circle of white musicians, such as Pee Wee Russell and Bobby Hackett, as well as black drummer Zutty Singleton; many musicians came to sit in with this group. The next week, however, Gabler changed the format, using two separate bands that took turns playing.[92] Other arrangements were also common. A photograph taken at Ryan's on November 23, 1941, for example, shows twelve musicians playing simultaneously.[93] Moreover, a long line of star soloists vied for position. Art Hodes remembered thinking at a Ryan's session: "All I have to do is wait for Earl Hines to step down, some Sunday, Fats Waller, Jimmy Johnson, and then maybe I'll be next. And then here comes Joe Bushkin, where did he come from?"[94] In February 1941, critic Otis Ferguson described the Ryan's sessions as "pretty much a brawl."[95] Nonetheless, the sessions observed certain conventions of order. Ryan's patron Robert Inman recalled that although up to a dozen musicians might be present, they would not all play at once.[96] Hodes remembered that Eddie Condon sometimes led the band informally by pointing to the next soloist.[97] Gabler told Arnold Shaw that "the closing number was always either 'Bugle Call Rag' or 'The Blues'" and that "every musician who was in the club sat in for that and sometimes for the set leading to it" (this perhaps explains the large ensemble in the aforementioned photograph.)[98] Although public jam sessions all involved a certain amount of preparation and organization, their ambience was markedly more relaxed than that of most big-band performances and even of typical performances in 52nd Street's clubs.

The middling level of planning and structure at 52nd Street's public jam sessions constituted a significant step toward more established interracial performances on 52nd Street. Although the sessions were more formal than mere sitting in, they were still more casual than the permanent "mixed" bands that occasionally appeared on the street. Sessions at the Hickory House, Jimmy Ryan's, and Kelly's Stable each involved both black and white musicians. At the Hickory House, although Marsala's house band was, with occasional exceptions, made up entirely of white musicians, African Americans including Lionel Hampton and Willie "The Lion" Smith played at the jam sessions.[99] *Down Beat* reported in 1940 that at the Kelly's Stable sessions, "mixed artists perform."[100] Contemporaneous sources indicate that the bands assembled by Gabler for the Jimmy Ryan's sessions were sometimes interracial.[101] Charles Peterson's photographs of jam sessions at Ryan's in 1941 reveal a great deal of collaboration among black and white performers; the photograph cited earlier, for instance, shows six black and six white musicians playing together.[102]

Nonetheless, 52nd Street's jam sessions sometimes highlighted racial difference. Gabler recalled that when he put together two bands for the Ryan's sessions, "one consisted of members of the Condon mob" of white musicians while the other "was a Harlem-type band built around Red Allen, Edmond Hall, Ben Webster or Don Byas. These men attracted the great black musicians from uptown."[103] Although in practice the sessions involved an element of cooperation among white and black musicians, in theory they thus seem to have involved separate white and black bands that competed against one another. Arnold Shaw claims that "the two-band format embodied a competitive or 'cutting' element that heightened the excitement of the Ryan's jams."[104] Although 52nd Street's public jam sessions aspired toward racial integration, they never truly transcended notions of race.

White musicians and critics discussed public jam sessions in terms that recall the original Onyx Club, where informality, improvisation, and resistance to commerce all contributed to the mystique of authentic jazz. Critic Bob Bach remarked in 1941 that Kelly's Stable "is the logical successor to the old Onyx Club, 52nd Street's most famous jump joint" because "there's a constant stream of the jazz elite dropping in with their horns to jam."[105] Trumpeter Max Kaminsky recalled the Ryan's sessions as "a kind of oasis for musician and fan alike," employing a metaphor that had been applied to the Onyx by Jack Egan in 1936.[106] As at the Onyx, musicians were playing for one another at public sessions as well as for the paying audience. Art Hodes said of the Ryan's sessions that it was "the big thing, to be heard by your peers. It was so important."[107] According to tenor saxophonist Art Engler, "the courtesy that was shown to each man blowing [at Ryan's] was unbelievable. If you got a groove going, they'd encourage you, 'Take another chorus! Keep going, man!' And they'd start to play little groovy things in back of you to push you on."[108] Engler's description of some of the participants calls to mind the Onyx's clientele of radio musicians tired of playing written arrangements: "Even the guys from schmaltzy Mickey Mouse outfits like Sammy Kaye's band would come in the jam [sic]. They were tired of playing from charts and wanted to be free."[109] Artie Shapiro similarly remembered that musicians who sat in at the Hickory House were often "guys that wanted to get away and play with a small group, you know, just jam, you know. They were playing jazz, they were trying to play jazz. When you play in a big band, you don't get too many chances to just go up and play your own, what you felt like playing, you know. So that's why they came in."[110] The repertoire played at the sessions also seems to have reflected anticommercial sentiments. The climactic performance of *Bugle Call Rag* or a blues at Jimmy Ryan's may have implied the primacy of older jazz forms over current popular tunes. Robert Inman remembered that the Ryan's sessions featured "mostly Dixieland, and blues mixed in."[111] Although these styles were not set in stone—Artie Shapiro claimed that the Hickory House jam sessions did not necessarily rely on traditional New Orleans or Chicago tunes—they were featured often enough to suggest a schism between the jam sessions and the wider world of popular music.[112]

Nonetheless, public jam sessions served an important professional function for musicians. Musicians generally were paid union scale to appear, so the jam sessions were themselves an employment opportunity, albeit "on terms that were guaranteed to make no one rich"; Kaminsky claimed that "you could always count on a five or a ten out of Milt for the Sunday jam sessions" at Ryan's.[113] The personnel of sessions was often advertised in advance, encouraging fans of particular musicians to come and hear them.[114] Moreover, sessions allowed musicians to gain public exposure that could eventually lead to steadier and more lucrative employment. Trombonist Vic Dickenson remembered that jam sessions at Jimmy Ryan's "helped [musicians] to get discovered, you know, just playing there."[115] One musician who was "discovered" at a jam session was drummer Buddy Rich. Artie Shapiro, after hearing the twenty-year-old Rich play in a Brooklyn club, invited him to attend a Sunday jam at the Hickory House, confident that Rich was "going to break it up" with his superior drumming.[116] Rich remembered the ensuing scene in dramatic terms:

I went three Sundays in a row . . . and never got to play. On the fourth Sunday at about five forty-five—the session ended at six—Marsala summoned me. I played 'Jazz Me Blues' . . . and then Marsala said, 'Let's play something up!' In those days I lived up. I started out at a tempo like this—taptaptaptaptaptaptaptap—on a thing called 'Jim Jam Stomp.' People were beginning to leave, but they turned around and started coming back just as if a Hollywood director had given instructions in the finale of some crummy grade B movie. The number broke the place up, and Marsala invited me back to play that night. I called my dad and he guessed it would be okay. I played two sets and Marsala asked me to join the band.[117]

In a similar incident, Marsala invited Zutty Singleton, who had just arrived in New York from Chicago, to drum at a Sunday afternoon session. Singleton's wife Marge recalled that "Zutty's first gig in New York was . . . on a Sunday afternoon, they had jam sessions. [Marsala] wanted Zutty to come and sit in and play. And he paid Zutty thirty-five dollars which was a lot of money for us." [118] This was the first of many 52nd Street engagements for Singleton, including a long run at Jimmy Ryan's beginning in 1941.[119] The professional opportunities created by jamming appear to have led AFM Local 802 to relax its policy toward sitting in. Discussing jamming at the Hickory House, *Down Beat* reported in 1938 that "the New York Union is more or less tolerant of these sessions believing that anything that acts as a stimulus to business in the nite spots should be encouraged and as a result some never to be forgotten sessions have transpired there within the last year." [120] Similarly, Wingy Manone remembered that at Kelly's Stable "the union let us get by with sittin' in." [121] The union, whose goal was to ensure fair treatment of musicians in the commercial marketplace, had no particular stake in encouraging improvisatory self-expression, so its tacit approval of jam sessions indicates that sitting in had become a valuable professional experience as well as a musical and social one.

The popularity of 52nd Street's jam sessions suggests that they drew listeners from beyond the circle of jazz aficionados. John Popkin, owner of the Hickory House, recalled that "the customers would be three-deep around the bar." [122] Artie Shapiro similarly remembered that "the house was packed when they had those sessions," and a 1937 review describes a spillover crowd listening from the sidewalk.[123] The sessions at Jimmy Ryan's were equally popular. Robert Inman recalled that "they had about ten rows of chairs in there, and [listeners would] all go in and try to get a good seat" until the club "filled up." [124] Max Kaminsky writes that at the Ryan's sessions "the fans included specimens of all the varieties— the earnest jazz purist; the jivey hep cat; the intense intellectual; extroverts from the advertising world; Broadway types; sentimental drunks; dedicated drinkers; plain people; and plain characters." [125] While some patrons conformed to the stereotype of the manic jitterbug, symbol of the mass swing craze, others listened carefully in the manner preferred by hot jazz enthusiasts. The Hickory House review quoted earlier mentioned the "hypnotic effect" that the jam session has on listeners and claimed that reactions ranged from "ecstasy to stupefaction." [126] Robert Inman recalled that "it was fairly quiet in the jam sessions" at Jimmy Ryan's. [127] More emphatically, Kaminsky asserted that "there was a moment there, in 1941–42, at the Ryan's sessions, when hot jazz seemed at its purest. Hovering on the edge of public discovery and known only to a few, it was as yet completely unselfconscious and untouched by commercialism or publicity. . . . At Ryan's the music was the thing, and when a musician was building a solo, you never heard a sound from the audience. You could *feel* them listening." Although the diverse audience Kaminsky describes belies his claim that the sessions were still "hovering on the edge of public discovery," he claims that this audience saw itself as part of a "fraternity" of aficionados who could fully appreciate improvised jazz. [128]

Public jam sessions and their audiences represented the intensification of contradictory impulses that had pervaded 52nd Street's jazz scene from its very beginning. The sessions ostensibly epitomized musical freedom and disregard for market concerns, but they also were designed to draw audiences to the street's clubs and to help musicians' professional careers. Although the sessions were supposedly sites of open-minded exchange among black and white musicians, they also exemplified the conflicts over race that affected 52nd Street. And while the audience members might have seen themselves as a fraternity of insiders with unique insight into an esoteric music, their very numbers ironically demonstrated the broad commercial potential of improvised jazz. Such ironies had become the rule on swing-era 52nd Street as musicians and promoters struggled to maintain the street's paradoxical reputation as both an "oasis" for musicians and serious jazz fans and a "bandmaker" that informed and reacted to mass taste. By the mid-1940s, this tangle of conflicting concerns would be complicated further by the arrival of a new generation of African American musicians who asserted their own standards of creativity and artistry in an environment previously dominated by white musicians and audiences.

Montage of 52nd Street signs, ca. 1936. Photograph by Charles Peterson.

Joe Helbock, proprietor of the original Onyx Club, in 1947. Photograph © William P. Gottlieb, www.jazzphotos.com.

Leo Watson at the Onyx Club, January 8, 1938. Photograph by Charles Peterson.

Guitarist Eddie Condon, singer Red McKenzie, and trumpeter Bunny Berigan at the Famous
Door, 1936. Photograph by Charles Peterson.

Trumpeter Louis Prima and drummer Cozy Cole at the Hickory House, ca. 1936. Photograph ©
Frank Driggs Collection.

Trumpeter Wingy Manone, with clarinetist Joe Marsala, guitarist Carmen Mastren, and pianist Conrad Lanoue, at Swing Music Concert sponsored by the Onyx Club at the Imperial Theater, New York, May 24, 1936. Photograph by Charles Peterson.

Trumpeter Ed Farley (left) and trombonist Mike Riley, February 1936. Photograph by Charles Peterson.

Violinist Stuff Smith and trumpeter Jonah Jones parody Riley and Farley, 1936. Photographs by Charles Peterson.

Violinist Stuff Smith and trumpeter Jonah Jones parody Riley and Farley, 1936. Photographs by Charles Peterson.

Stuff Smith and His Onyx Club Boys, 1936. *Left to right:* Violinist Stuff Smith, drummer John Washington, guitarist Bobby Bennett, pianist Raymond Smith, bassist Mack Walker, trumpeter Jonah Jones. Photograph by Charles Peterson.

Stuff Smith at the Onyx Club, April 14, 1938. Musicians, *left to right:* guitarist Carl Kress, violinist Stuff Smith, bassist Wellman Braud, trumpeter Hot Lips Page. In the audience, singer Mildred Bailey and xylophonist Red Norvo sit at the far left, and members of John Kirby's band are at the far right. Photograph by Charles Peterson.

"John Kirby with Leo and His Spirits of Rhythm featuring Buster Bailey and Frank Newton" at the Onyx Club, 1937. Group members are guitarist Teddy Bunn; pianist Don Frye; leader and bassist John Kirby; drummer, trombonist, and vocalist Leo Watson; alto saxophonist Pete Brown; trumpeter Frankie Newton; clarinetist Buster Bailey. Photograph by Charles Peterson.

Trumpeter Charlie Shavers and bassist John Kirby at the Onyx Club, April 7, 1939. Photograph by Charles Peterson.

Maxine Sullivan with the John Kirby Sextet at the Onyx Club, October 20, 1938. *Left to right:* French jazz critic Hugues Panassié (in audience), drummer O'Neill Spencer, alto saxophonist Russell Procope, vocalist Maxine Sullivan, clarinetist Buster Bailey. Photograph by Charles Peterson.

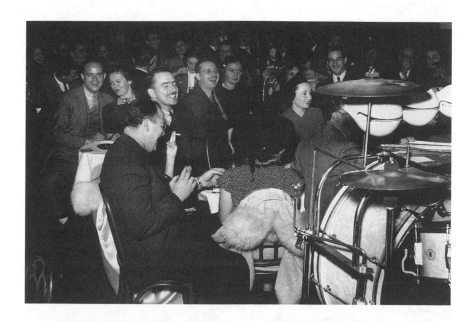

Onyx Club audience at Welcome Home Party for bandleader Glen Gray and his Casa Loma Orchestra, October 10, 1937. (Gray is in the foreground, smiling with his eyes closed.) Photograph by Charles Peterson.

Members of Count Basie's band at the Famous Door, 1938. *Front row, left to right:* tenor saxophonist Herschel Evans, alto saxophonist Earle Warren. *Middle row:* guitarist Freddie Green, trumpeter Buck Clayton. *Back row:* trombonists Benny Morton, Dan Minor, and Dicky Wells. Photograph © Frank Driggs Collection.

Drummer and vibraphonist Lionel Hampton sits in at the Hickory House with the Joe Marsala band, January 1938. *Left to right:* Hampton, trumpeter Marty Marsala, pianist Joe Bushkin (with trumpet), bassist Artie Shapiro, guitarist and violinist Ray Biondi (with trumpet), clarinetist Joe Marsala. Photograph by Charles Peterson. In an interview by the author (March 13, 2002), Shapiro described how for "show biz" effect the band sometimes "had three trumpets going—[two] guys doubled on trumpet."

Sunday afternoon jam session at Jimmy Ryan's, November 23, 1941. *Front row, from left:* tenor saxophonist Franz Jackson, clarinetist Albert Nicholas, trombonist Vic Dickenson. *Middle row:* guitarist Eddie Condon, trombonist Sandy Williams, trumpeter Max Kaminsky, clarinetist Pee Wee Russell, bassist Al Hall. *Back row:* drummer George Wettling, trumpeters Bobby Hackett (seated) and Hot Lips Page (standing), pianist Joe Sullivan. Photograph by Charles Peterson.

Pianists Phil Moore (second from left) and Art Tatum (far right) outside the Downbeat, ca. 1946. Photograph © William P. Gottlieb; www.jazzphotos.com.

Trumpeter and bandleader Dizzy Gillespie at the Downbeat, ca. 1947. Photograph © William P. Gottlieb; www.jazzphotos.com.

Audience at the Downbeat, ca. 1948. Photograph © William P. Gottlieb; www.jazzphotos.com.

Bassist Vivien Garry at Dixon's, ca. May 1947. Photograph © William P. Gottlieb; www.jazzpho-tos.com.

Wilbur (left) and Sidney De Paris outside the Onyx Club, ca. July 1947. Photograph © William P. Gottlieb; www.jazzphotos.com.

Clarinetist Bob Wilber (left) and soprano saxophonist Sidney Bechet (right) at Jimmy Ryan's, ca. June 1947. Photograph © William P. Gottlieb; www.jazzphotos.com.

Trombonist Georg Brunis parades at Jimmy Ryan's, ca. August 1946. *Left to right:* Brunis, probably trumpeter Nick Casti, clarinetist Tony Parenti. Photograph © William P. Gottlieb; www. jazzphotos.com.

View along 52nd Street, facing east from Sixth Avenue, ca. July 1948. Photograph © William P. Gottlieb; www.jazzphotos.com.

Chapter Seven **This Conglomeration of Colors Bebop Comes to Swing Street**

During the fall of 1943, a quintet led by trumpeter John Birks "Dizzy" Gillespie and bassist Oscar Pettiford opened at the Onyx Club, 57 West 52nd Street.[1] Although this opening received only slight attention at the time in the jazz and mainstream press, it has come to be seen as a milestone in jazz history: as Scott DeVeaux writes in *The Birth of Bebop*, "the Gillespie-Pettiford band at the Onyx is generally regarded, with good reason, as the first bop combo to appear in a public venue—'the birth of the bebop era,' as Gillespie has put it."[2] The novel bebop style, forged in afterhours Harlem jam sessions and characterized by a heightened degree of dissonance and chromaticism as well as asymmetrical melodic phrases and polyrhythmic interplay among soloists and rhythm sections, came to be closely associated with 52nd Street in the years ahead.[3] The word *bebop* itself was coined at the Onyx by listeners imitating the scat syllables that Gillespie used to identify his untitled original melodies.[4] Bop innovators such as Gillespie and alto saxophonist Charlie "Bird" Parker became well-known figures on the street in the mid-1940s. A quintet led by Gillespie and featuring Parker performed at the Three Deuces during the spring and summer of 1945, in an engagement that Gillespie later termed "the height of the perfection of our music."[5] From April to July 1946, Gillespie's big band at the Spotlite, which included such pioneering musicians as pianist Thelonious Monk, drummer Kenny Clarke, and bassist Ray Brown, demonstrated that the improvisatory energy of bebop could be adapted to a larger ensemble.[6] By 1947, further appearances on the street by such innovators of bebop, as well as lesser-known bandleaders such as guitarist Bill DeArango and singer Babs Gonzales, had made the very term *52nd Street* synonymous with the bop style.[7] In that year, for example, *Down Beat* described "52nd street jazz as it has developed in the past five years" as "our old friend be-bop," and *Hot Club Magazine,* employing a common variant of the word *bebop,* titled a profile of the street "52nd Re-Bop Street." [8]

Although bebop's brief vogue on 52nd Street in the mid- to late 1940s coincided with, and arguably contributed to, the street's commercial decline as a center for jazz, this period of 52nd Street's history has been the one most discussed by jazz historians, who emphasize the street's fundamental importance in the formation of bebop. As DeVeaux demonstrates, conventional accounts of bebop's development generally rely upon one of two overarching narratives.[9] The first is an evolutionary narrative, grounded in analysis of musical style, that posits bebop as an inevitable link in a progressive chain of jazz idioms extending from turn-of-the-twentieth-century New Orleans to the most avant-garde expressions of the 1960s and beyond. In contrast is a revolutionary narrative, which highlights conflicts over race and commerce in presenting bebop as "a rebellion by black musicians against a white-controlled capitalist hegemony." [10] According to this account, the appearance of bebop marked a crucial moment of social upheaval in which black musicians rejected their restrictive, demeaning roles as popular entertainers catering to the commercial market and instead demanded consideration as serious modern artists. DeVeaux argues that both of these narratives are oversimplifications. By treating the "jazz tradition" as a naturally evolving progression rather than a social construction, the evolutionary narrative masks the long history of conflicts and debates over what constitutes authentic jazz.[11] The revolutionary narrative similarly ignores historical context in proposing a cut-and-dried distinction between bebop and "commercial" music. DeVeaux contends, in contrast, that bebop musicians "saw themselves first and foremost as *professionals*" and that "mass-market capitalism . . . was a system of transactions that defined music as a profession and thereby made their achievements possible." [12] Without denying the role of anticommercial attitudes in the creation of bebop, DeVeaux complicates the revolutionary narrative by compelling us to view bop as part of the music industry as well as a reaction against it.

Even as bebop came to public attention on 52nd Street, competing notions of evolution and revolution informed its reception. Some contemporary musicians, critics, and audience members heard the new music as an evolving variant of the swing music with which they were already familiar. In a letter to the editor of *Down Beat* in July 1944, one of Gillespie's admirers defended the trumpeter's innovations by associating him with an icon of the previous generation: "Anyone who heard Dizzy Gillespie recently at the Onyx club realizes that Dizzy is contributing something new to jazz. In visits there, I noticed that Coleman Hawkins was often present to hear Dizzy blow. Such recognition means Dizzy must be good." [13] In 1945, a writer for the *New York Age* referred to Gillespie, "whose sensational trumpet fills the 52nd Street Three Deuces nightly with swarms of hot jazz fans," as "the 'young Louis Armstrong,'" implying a connection between musicians and styles often thought to be in conflict.[14] Other observers viewed the new style as a revolutionary break with the past. Critic Leonard Feather, in a 1945 article asserting that "there is a revolution taking place in jazz circles," quoted various 52nd Street musicians who viewed Gillespie as avant-garde: " 'Some people say Dizzy stinks,' Ben Webster continued. 'That's because he's beyond their reach. They don't dig him.' And Sammy Price, boogie-woogie pianist, added 'Diz is twenty years ahead of his time.'" [15] In a frequently quoted account of the shock created by bop, drummer Dave Tough described his reaction to the Gillespie-Pettiford quintet at the Onyx: "As we walked in, see, these cats snatched up their horns and blew crazy stuff. One would stop all of a sudden and another would start for no reason at all. We never could tell when a solo was supposed to begin or end. Then they all quit at once and walked off the stand. It scared us." [16] How 52nd Street's musicians and listeners categorized bebop as a musical style was largely a matter of emphasis—while some drew a direct link between bebop and earlier jazz, others felt that the disorienting effect of bebop's "crazy" rhythms and harmonies masked or superseded its relationship to small-group swing.

I argue here that bebop's role in 52nd Street's intertwined traditions of racial representation and anticommercial rhetoric was similarly ambiguous. The revolutionary stance of artistic integrity and racial pride associated with bebop musicians was to some extent an evolution of ideas about black musicianship already current on the street during the swing era. John Kirby, for example, with his carefully arranged, classically oriented repertoire, had suggested that jazz musicians deserved to be regarded as serious artists, while Stuff Smith had demonstrated that self-assured, hip black performers could find a place on 52nd Street. Moreover, despite their seemingly uncompromising approach to their music, bebop musicians, like their predecessors on 52nd Street, were obligated to entertain audiences with humor and other conventionally commercial strategies in order to find work. At the same time, however, 52nd Street underwent some striking changes. Black patrons, black-owned clubs, and casual intermingling among blacks and whites became increasingly prevalent on the street during the mid-1940s, which sometimes led to violence and repression as conservative whites sought to maintain control over the street. In a more subtle but equally revolutionary move, black musicians and audiences subverted notions of black identity that had persisted on 52nd Street since the days of the original Onyx Club. While bebop musicians upheld the value of an anticommercial black music, their resistance to popular taste was grounded in the intellectual prerogatives of artistic modernism rather than a clichéd notion of black musicians as irrational, spontaneous creators. The hipsters who congregated on 52nd Street similarly undermined the image of happy-go-lucky, impulsive black masculinity that had motivated 52nd Street's white founders, replacing it with a far edgier and more aggressive (and worryingly misogynist) masculine ideal. Although bebop and its audience did not eradicate 52nd Street's racial stereotypes or commercial complexities, they presented a powerful challenge to the street's conventions.

"Little Gimmicks": Marketing Bebop   In June 1945, *Metronome* reviewed Dizzy Gillespie's new recording on the independent Guild label of his composition *Groovin' High,* which, the writers explained, was "an original melody that has become a sort of 52nd Street anthem." [17] The recording is a classic of the burgeoning bebop movement, featuring many of the new style's most notable characteristics. Although, as *Metronome* noted, *Groovin' High* is built on the harmonic structure of the 1920 popular song *Whispering,* it seems to owe little to its ancestor, replacing its predictable four-bar phrases with a playful, intricate melody that repeatedly juxtaposes a sparse two bars comprising two widely separated pairs of eighth notes against a convoluted, chromatic two-bar response.[18] This melody, or *head,* is played in unadorned, precise unison by trumpeter Gillespie, alto saxophonist Charlie Parker, and guitarist Remo Palmieri. The three musicians' improvised solos show off their remarkable technical skill and the altered harmonies and complex rhythms that made bebop seem both thrilling and intimidating to audiences in 1945.

In other ways, however, *Groovin' High* may strike a listener well-versed in bebop as uncharacteristic of the style. As bebop historian Thomas Owens notes, "the arrangement is atypically elaborate for bebop performances, with its composed six-measure introduction (most bebop introductions are improvised and run four or eight measures), its modulations (most bebop pieces stay in one key), its choruses of varying lengths, and its dramatic half-speed coda."[19] Rather than simply comprising a string of virtuosic solos, this accessible arrangement serves as a frame for the intricate and potentially unapproachable improvisations that form the core of the performance. The rhythm section, moreover, is rooted in the small-group swing style familiar to 52nd Street audiences by 1945. Pianist Clyde Hart adapts to the innovations of bebop by "comping," or accompanying soloists by interjecting occasional chords, rather than playing the steady left-hand rhythm associated with swing. Drummer Cozy Cole, however, who had played at the Onyx with Stuff Smith almost ten years earlier, keeps time on the hi-hat rather than the ride cymbal favored by bebop drummers. Bassist Slam Stewart accompanies his bowed bass solo with his voice, half singing and half humming an octave above. This distinctive technique had been associated with Stewart since the 1930s, when he had formed the popular duo Slim and Slam with guitarist Slim Gaillard, and it continued to be a feature of Stewart's performances on 52nd Street, where he appeared frequently throughout the 1940s as both a bandleader and a side musician. For all its originality, *Groovin' High* had one foot firmly planted in the established realm of 52nd Street swing.[20]

As *Groovin' High* indicates, in 1945 bebop was only one part of the broader 52nd Street jazz scene rather than an isolated movement of its own. Between 1944 and 1947, 52nd Street was dominated not by the relatively small group of bebop innovators but by better-established musicians who, while they sometimes experimented with aspects of the new style, continued to perform mainly in the small-group swing idiom that had long been associated with the street. Between April and July 1945, for example, as the famous quintet featuring Gillespie and Parker performed at the Three Deuces, other musicians working on the street included Slam Stewart and tenor saxophonist Don Byas (also at the Three Deuces), Art Tatum, Coleman Hawkins, and Billie Holiday (at the Downbeat), Stuff Smith and tenor saxophonist Ben Webster (Onyx), Joe Marsala (Hickory House), and New Orleans–style clarinetist Mezz Mezzrow (Jimmy Ryan's.)[21] Some of 52nd Street's most ubiquitous musicians, such as Hawkins and Webster, had been direct influences on the development of bebop. DeVeaux demonstrates the importance of Hawkins's advanced harmonies and "defiantly modernist stance" to the nascent movement, while pianist and jazz scholar Billy Taylor, who played with Webster at the Three Deuces in 1943, remembered that musicians like Ben Webster and others were actually playing things that were leading the way to what was going to be done by the beboppers . . . and it was already being done to some extent, . . . rhythmically, by people like [drummers] Jo Jones and Kenny Clarke, and so it wasn't a thing where all of a sudden, like many books say, all of a sudden this new thing just. . . . sprung out of nowhere, and it surprised everybody. It grew out of musicians who were already expanding the melodic and harmonic language in their own way.[22]

In turn, both Hawkins and Webster learned from and encouraged the younger musicians whom they had inspired. Hawkins, for example, worked with bebop pioneers including Gillespie and Pettiford on an important 1944 recording session, while Webster hired Parker for his sextet at the Onyx Club in March 1945.[23] Rather than take over 52nd Street, then, bebop musicians gradually worked their way into its clubs, often with the support of their more experienced and better-known elders.

In late 1943, when Gillespie's and Pettiford's quintet made its debut at the Onyx, perhaps the most popular group on the street was the Art Tatum Trio, who anticipated bebop by combining crowd-pleasing humor and novelty with an insistence on being treated as serious artists. The trio, comprising Tatum on piano, Slam Stewart on bass, and Tiny Grimes on guitar, played two extended engagements at the Three Deuces, from August to around December 1943 and again during the summer of 1944.[24] Their opening in 1943 capitalized on a vogue for piano-guitar-bass trios that had been sparked by the Nat King Cole Trio, which showcased swinging, complex interplay among the three instruments as well as the leader's hip, good-humored singing. In the same year, other trios with the same instrumentation were led on 52nd Street by guitarists Al Casey and Leonard Ware as well as pianist Clarence Profit.[25] While such trios mainly worked as "relief acts"—Casey's trio, for example, played "wonderful mood music between shows" at the Onyx in 1944—the Tatum Trio musicians soon became stars in their own right.[26] In January 1944, *Metronome* named the Art Tatum Trio the Act of the Year for 1943.[27] During its 1944 stand at the Three Deuces, the trio was the best-paid group on 52nd Street at a combined salary of $1,000 per week (Gillespie, in contrast, received the union scale of $66 per week at Kelly's Stable in 1943.)[28] Grimes remembered in a 1983 interview that the Three Deuces was "packed every night." [29]

Tatum, who made few overt concessions to commerce and demanded the respect due a concert virtuoso, might have seemed an unlikely candidate for mass popularity. While other African American performers on

52nd Street, such as the John Kirby Sextet, had sought to be respected as artists, Tatum went further than most in the demands that he placed on his audience. His confident, sometimes antagonistic stance was made possible by his remarkable musicianship. In an October 1943 review, Leonard Feather praised Tatum to the point of hyperbole, calling him "beyond doubt the greatest pianist who's ever played jazz" and commending both his remarkable technique and the "magnificent and inspired ideas that this technique enables him to express with such bewildering fluency."[30] On such 1944 trio recordings as *I Got Rhythm* and *I Ain't Got Nobody,* Tatum's fleet piano solos flow seemingly effortlessly at fast tempi; he sometimes interpolates fast runs between phrases of the original melody and sometimes alludes only briefly to the melody before setting off on his own.[31] Although, as Gunther Schuller has noted, Tatum took a more conservative approach to harmony with the trio than as a soloist, avoiding the radical reharmonizations that he often applied to standard tunes, the trio still springs some harmonic surprises, such as a rapid spin around the circle of fifths in *I Got Rhythm.*[32] Recognizing that Tatum's sophisticated, complex music rewarded close listening, the Three Deuces introduced an experimental policy in July 1944 called the "Hour of Silence." *Down Beat* explained: "Idea is to keep the noisier customers quiet for 60 minutes so that rabid fans of Art Tatum can hear the pianist without any clinking glass obbligato." The policy was reportedly unsuccessful, as "many 52d street habitues regard it as their inalienable right to make as much noise as they please and that [*sic*] any musician who's worth his salt will be better for the competition."[33] Tatum, unintimidated by such competition, responded by picking up his microphone and asking the audience, "What do I have to do, perform a major operation to get you to keep quiet?"[34] (Ralph Watkins, owner of Kelly's Stable, remembered less euphemistically that Tatum would shout "Quiet, you motherfuckers!" at noisy patrons.[35]) One of the few extant films made inside a 52nd Street club, a 1943 *March of Time* newsreel featuring the trio at the Three Deuces, suggests that such confrontations may have ended inconclusively. The film shows a well-dressed white audience listening to Tatum; those closest to the band listen attentively as they nod to the beat and tap their hands on the table, but those farther away seem to be talking.[36]

Tatum and his trio likely would not have maintained their popularity if they had not balanced their assertions of artistry with more conventional, accessible forms of entertainment. Feather claimed that "despite his unprepossessing appearance, Art manages to excite the average square audience just as he does musicians. His genius is such that any layman can appreciate him." Grimes, in contrast, recalled that Tatum's genius sometimes hindered his ability to reach the general public: "You know, you can be too good for your own self. To me if Tatum just had a little flash, a little jive, a little whatever. But that wasn't him. He was serious. When he sat down to the piano he played—there was no clownin'. But if he had just had just any little gesture, you might say, that wouldn't have hurt his playing. . . . A little gimmick you might say is the only thing in my eyesight that held him back."[37] Fortunately, Grimes and Stewart supplied the trio with the "little gimmicks" that their leader avoided. Stewart was an exceptional accompanist who has often been praised for his ability to keep pace with Tatum's fast tempi and complicated harmonies, but he drew attention at the Three Deuces mainly for his unusual bowing-and-singing technique.[38] Feather raved that Stewart was "an astonishing bass player who still plays (and simultaneously hums) the most elaborate bowed-bass solos, with a dexterity that would be remarkable enough on a horn, but is almost unbelievable on the bass." Grimes was a less skilled musician who referred to himself with self-deprecating humor as "the low man on the Tatum pole" and remembered that "after we started working I'd go downstairs during every intermission with my guitar and work on whatever song we'd been playing, trying to catch up with them as best I could."[39] Despite his limitations, Grimes found a crowd-pleasing gimmick of his own: introducing humorous, unexpected musical quotations into his solos. On the trio's 1944 recording of *I Would Do Anything For You,* for example, Grimes plays a snippet of Stephen Foster's *Old Folks at Home* during his solo.[40] Although Grimes claimed that his quotations were motivated by friendly competition among the trio, who battled to "see who could think of something that could fit in," his quoting offended some musicians and critics who saw it as a cheap way of grabbing the audience's attention. Feather, for example, complained that "Tiny Grimes is a very talented guitarist, though inclined to use too many quotations from odd sources," while pianist Johnny Guarnieri recalled that "it bugged me that he'd get a bigger rise out of the crowd than anything the great Tatum did." DeVeaux writes more approvingly that Grimes's penchant for quotation "formed a bridge between Tatum's formidable virtuosity and the mass audience."[41] That such a bridge was necessary demonstrates the ambiguous role played by 52nd Street's musicians as bebop appeared on the scene: jazz musicians could reasonably expect their audiences to regard them as something more than mere entertainers, but audiences nonetheless expected to be entertained.

Like Tatum, bebop musicians could to some extent attract an audience with their virtuosity and their reputation as modernists, aided by press coverage that helped create a mystique around bebop. Commentary in the jazz press emphasized the startling technical skill and progressive aspirations of 52nd Street's new generation of musicians. In an August 1945 review of Charlie Parker's quintet at the Three Deuces, for example, Leonard Feather praised the "lightning unison" of the melodies played by Parker and Don Byas, and Feather claimed that Parker "mak[es] every note mean something" despite the speed of his playing. In 1947, *Down Beat* reporter and photographer William Gottlieb "roamed Be-bop Alley, sometimes known as 52nd St." to ask a selection of prominent musicians "what is be-bop?" The answers were all variations on the theme of progress. Trumpeter Howard McGhee explained straightforwardly that "bebop is progressive music. It's the younger generation's idea of the right way to play," while Charlie Parker described bop as "advanced modern music." Arranger and pianist Tadd Dameron argued that bebop "leads the way for new sounds in music" (and added that the style was "highly commercial, too"). In their responses, Dizzy Gillespie and pianist Barbara Carroll both referred to technical advances in phrasing, accenting, and the use of dissonance. Reports on bebop could be condescending at times. In September 1947, for example, *Down Beat* referred to Parker as a "weird wizard" and a "high priest" and described his "other-world look," perhaps alluding generally to primitivist notions of irrational black creativity and more specifically to Parker's reputation for drug abuse. In general, though, the jazz press helped give 52nd Street a reputation for presenting modern, forward-looking music. In November 1947, *Metronome,* looking back a few years, described "The Street" as the place where "Dizzy and Don Byas and Slam and Bird Parker were just beginning to formulate their controversial jazz revolution."[42]

In the mid-1940s, however, bebop was only one of several competing new jazz styles, and the label "modern" could just as easily refer to up-and-coming 52nd Street musicians with only a tangential relationship to bebop.[43] Pianist Erroll Garner, for example, who was frequently featured with Slam Stewart's quartet and his own trio at the Three Deuces in 1945, became one of the most noticed performers on 52nd Street with an original style that critics often likened to the work of European modernist composers. *Down Beat* critic Frank Stacy wrote in February that "for me, Garner's best aspect is his dreamy improvising in what might be called 'modern' moods, smacking of Debussy and others of the French school." In the same month, *Metronome* described Garner's "original keyboard creations" as "a fascinating mixture of Debussy, Ravel, Ellington, and Garner." In October, *Down Beat* claimed that "the harmonic structure" of Garner's *Blues I Can't Forget* "is in the atonal vein employed by contemporary modernists," and suggests that he learned the style from film music, "which draws heavily from the works of modernists."[44] The modern elements of Garner's music, however, differed from those of bebop. While his playing was harmonically complex, he tended to build up dense pastel chords (as in his popular 1945 trio recording of *Laura*) rather than employ the thorny dissonances of bebop, and his approach to rhythm involved "strumming" on the beat with his left hand in the style of a guitar rather than the unpredictable accents played by bebop pianists.[45] Although Garner sometimes worked with bop musicians such as Gillespie and Parker, Gillespie claimed later that "he never played our type of music" (although "we certainly didn't look down on him.")[46] *Modern*, then, as both a stylistic description and a marketing label, was vaguely defined on 52nd Street in 1945.

That bebop came to be regarded as the quintessential modern jazz style on 52nd Street was due largely to Gillespie, the most publicized icon of 52nd Street's "jazz revolution." In an often cited 1946 article that condescendingly linked bebop to "bawdiness" and "narcotics," *Time* described the putative origins of the style: "As such things usually do, it began on Manhattan's 52nd Street. A bandleader named John ('Dizzy') Gillespie, 'looking for a way to emphasize the more beautiful notes in swing,' explained: 'When you hum it, you just naturally say 'bebop, be-de-bop.' " Writers in the jazz press similarly drew attention to the significance of Gillespie's 52nd Street appearances in the creation of bebop, often claiming that listening to the trumpeter's recordings paled in comparison to the experience of seeing him live on the street. A negative *Down Beat* review from 1945, for example, asserts that Gillespie's new record on the Manor label of *Be-Bop* and *Salted [sic] Peanuts* "will undoubtedly give many listeners the wrong impression as to what Dizzy and Charlie Parker and their crew had been putting down on 52nd street." In 1946, critic Mort Schillinger drew on the language of modernism to describe Gillespie's innovations, comparing him to Thomas Wolfe and Picasso and arguing that "the revolution caused by Dizzy's advanced conception was inevitable if Jazz were to keep progressing." Schillinger established 52nd Street as the setting for this revolution, explaining that Gillespie's "opening on 52nd street last summer, with Charlie Parker (alto), and Al Haig (piano), was the clincher that really opened the eyes of the hip elite," and citing a long list of 52nd Street regulars who "picked up on" Gillespie's style, including Hawkins and Webster as well as younger musicians such as Remo Palmieri and tenor saxophonist Dexter Gordon. Even bebop's detractors acknowledged Gillespie's striking influence on the 52nd Street jazz scene. Los Angeles jazz promoter Norman Granz, expressing skepticism about the supposed "renaissance of jazz along 52nd St." in 1945, asserted bluntly that "jazz in New York stinks! Even the drummers on 52nd St. sound like Dizzy Gillespie!"[47] Gillespie attracted attention, then, in part due to his sudden and obvious influence on the sound of 52nd Street jazz.

But Gillespie's visibility on 52nd Street was also the result of his appealing and very marketable reputation as a charming, fashionable hipster. In a 1945 *Esquire* profile of Gillespie, Leonard Feather explained that "along 52nd Street the jazzmen copy not only Dizzy's music, but even his laugh and his odd, half-bent posture and his little goatee which he claims helps keep his lip strong." Schillinger added that "musicians wear the ridiculous little hats that have been around lately because Dizzy wears one" and contended that "surely this *copycatism* accomplishes nothing for the Dizzy fan, but, just as surely, it does Dizzy much harm" by making him appear to be an ephemeral fad rather than a serious musician. Gillespie resented being written off as a mere fashion trend: interviewed by William Gottlieb at the Spotlite in 1946, he explained that his goatee was "strictly utilitarian! Nothing faddish about it," and in his autobiography, he labeled as "lie number one" about bebop the notion that "boppers wore wild clothes and dark glasses at night." Such trademarks, however, brought needed publicity to an unfamiliar, complex new style of jazz. By 1947, Gillespie's manager Billy Shaw was successfully marketing to a wider public those fashion statements that had originally attracted 52nd Street's insiders, constructing what Gillespie's biographer Alyn Shipton calls "a cult of modernism."[48]

As he performed in 52nd Street's clubs, Gillespie reinforced his hip image with his confident, ironic sense of humor. As his nickname suggests, Gillespie had long had a reputation among musicians for irreverent, unpredictable behavior, but he was an inexperienced, awkward bandleader as late as 1945, when his big band toured the South.[49] By 1946, however, when his second big band opened at 52nd Street's Spotlite Club, Gillespie had matured into an assured entertainer. The 1946 film *Jivin' in Be-Bop*, which features Gillespie's big band from the Spotlite, shows Gillespie energetically leading the band as he bounces up and down, bobs his head, and sometimes twirls on one foot; he also cracks corny jokes with hipster emcee Freddie Carter ("In times of trial, what brings us the greatest comfort?" "An acquittal!")[50] Shipton notes that "at the very time his orchestra began to revolutionize big band music, Dizzy's own performances retained much of the elements of black show business that he had experienced during his apprenticeship."[51] Photographs taken by William Gottlieb at the Downbeat in 1947 depict Gillespie engaging in both broad comedy, such as lying on top of the piano, and more subtle wit, such as directing an exaggeratedly romantic gaze at Ella Fitzgerald as she sings.[52] With his genial, relaxed stage persona, Gillespie "put a public face on bebop" that helped the music reach a broader audience.[53]

For all its complexity, Gillespie's music was itself often funny. Billy Taylor, who sat in with Gillespie at the Onyx, remembered that he "was entertaining musically. He wasn't doing some of the things that he later became even more famous for. I mean, Dizzy always was a comedian, so he always would do little jokes, but as soon as he put his horn up to his mouth, he was serious as a heart attack. . . . On one hand he was doing things which were very serious, and he was serious about them. And then in the next tune, he might be doing some nonsensical tune that had funny rhythms with it".[54] While such tunes as *Salt Peanuts* and *Oop Bop Sh'Bam,* in which nonsensical phrases are set to brief, catchy fragments of melody, provide the most obvious examples of Gillespie's musical humor, the entire bebop idiom had the potential to amuse astute listeners. As they juxtaposed unpredictable rhythms and jarring dissonances against familiar chord progressions, Gillespie and other bebop pioneers walked the precarious line between implausibility and plausibility that had made the music of predecessors like Stuff Smith seem pleasingly absurd.[55] The head of *Groovin' High,* for example, builds on the puckish contrast between a simple, consonant gesture—a pair of eighth notes drawn directly from a major triad—and the twisted chromatic phrase that follows. While Gillespie's stage presence signaled that an obscure, dissonant type of jazz could be funny and thus approachable, it was nonetheless the musical language of bebop that made the humor work.

While Gillespie was following in the footsteps of 52nd Street performers such as Stuff Smith in what DeVeaux terms "signifying on the traditional role of the black entertainer," his humor had a barbed edge that brought its assertiveness closer to the surface. In a largely favorable 1947 review of Gillespie's big band, which had played recently at the Downbeat, Barry Ulanov of *Metronome* complained about Gillespie's sarcastic musical quotations, such as "a sour interpolation of *Jingle Bells*" during his "lovely coda to *I Can't Get Started*" that "twists and tears the preceding loveliness to pieces." Although Ulanov liked what he saw as Gillespie's anticommercial (and thus presumably masculine) stance, claiming that "his acrid musical comment" is "generally refreshing, vigorous, in virile contrast to the pantywaist admirers of the lush tune and syrupy treatment who crowd most of the meaning out of jazz," he found Gillespie's irony too caustic to be attractive. According to Ulanov, "Dizzy, like most of his colleagues and imitators, is afraid to commit himself to any musical statement bordering on the exalted; his personal philosophy is a bitter one and that bitterness rips through much of what he does." That Gillespie's mockery of what Ulanov called "the banal prettiness of the popular song melody" could draw attention even within the context of the 52nd Street jazz scene, which had from its beginnings been conceived of as an alternative to mainstream popular music, demonstrates the originality of Gillespie's stance. Rather than veil his sarcasm behind the familiar stereotype of the frivolous black entertainer, Gillespie presented himself as a calculating satirist, one who might make jokes but was nonetheless, as Billy Taylor puts it, "serious as a heart attack" about his music. Barbara Carroll, whose trio worked opposite Gillespie's band at the Downbeat in 1947, recalled that Gillespie "wasn't flamboyant, but he did little cute things, sort of dancing around, you know, things like that to ingratiate him with the audiences—but that did not negate the seriousness of his trumpet playing. He was a very serious trumpet player and a very fabulous one." [56]

A number of less famous musicians on 52nd Street found their own ways of making bebop palatable to a broad audience. Saxophonist Charlie Ventura, who led a big band at the Spotlite from October to December 1946 and smaller combos at the Three Deuces in the spring and fall of 1947, drew on elements of bebop while maintaining an accessible connection to earlier swing. [57] Ventura played with a full tone and wide vibrato more reminiscent of Coleman Hawkins than of bebop, in what Leonard Feather termed a "compromise style." [58] His big band, however, played arrangements by trumpeter Neal Hefti that "gave everything a distinctly Dizzy flavor." [59] In Hefti's arrangement of *How High the Moon*, for example, the trumpet section plays a long unison passage that incorporates the off-kilter rhythms and surprising dissonances of Gillespie's style, and later the sax section quietly plays six bars of *Ornithology*, Benny Harris's bop anthem based on the chord changes of *How High the Moon*.[60] Ventura's audience-friendly brand of bebop made him one of the most popular acts on the street in 1947, when Feather praised him for "bringing business back to 52nd Street." [61] Another act that succeeded in popularizing bebop was Babs' Three Bips and a Bop, who performed at the Onyx in the fall of 1947.[62] The Bips were a piano-bass-guitar trio fronted by the flamboyant singer Babs Gonzales (whose previous adventures had involved a stint as Errol Flynn's turbaned chauffeur under the alias Ram Singh) and including Tadd Dameron on piano.[63] Gonzales recalled that he "formed the Bips because I felt bebop needed a vocal bridge to the people."[64] Such 1947 recordings as *Lop-Pow* and *Dob Bla Bli* demonstrate the hallmarks of the group's style: complex bebop lines scatted in unison, and vocal solos by Gonzales, whose approach updates the scat tradition begun on 52nd Street by Leo Watson.[65] The group's vocal take on instrumental bebop drew favorable attention: Bob Bach, for instance, wrote in *Metronome* that the Bips represented "the natural breakthrough of the Gillespie-Parker musical revolution into the vocal field" and called them "new and original and interesting."[66] While pleasing bebop aficionados with their musicianship, the group also made gestures to a wider audience. *Oop-Pop-A-Da,* for example, includes lyrics describing the song's scat syllables as "something new you can easy do / It's a crazy refrain," in an apparent attempt to encourage wary listeners to try singing along to bebop.[67]

By leavening their musical rigor with commercial savvy, bebop musicians survived on 52nd Street in the same unsteady way that their predecessors had during the swing era, with the jazz press often describing good business on the street between 1944 and 1946 while occasionally warning that disaster was just around the corner (such warnings became more prevalent throughout 1947.)[68] World War II created a larger audience with money to spend on entertainment; *Down Beat* reported in 1944 that "the war with its boom days and overtime payrolls is reviving the jazz interest on 52nd Street."[69] The war, however, also created new restrictions on business. In the spring of 1944, a "cabaret tax" on clubs that featured singing or dancing forced some clubs to limit their offerings to instrumental music.[70] A more serious obstacle arose on February 26, 1945, when a nationwide nightclub curfew went into effect. *Metronome* explained that "all the night clubs in the land would have to close at 12 midnight to save fuel, manpower and transportation," adding that "52nd Street, number one jazz street in America, was clearly doomed to at best very shadowy operation."[71] Some of the street's clubs responded to the loss in revenue by laying off musicians or by starting the night's entertainment as early as seven o'clock, until the curfew was lifted in May "and 52nd Street came to life once more."[72] Recordings continued to promote the street's musicians, with a myriad of independent companies springing up in 1943 and 1944 while members of the American Federation of Musicians were banned from recording with the major labels Columbia and Victor.[73] Many of 52nd Street's musicians recorded frequently for a wide variety of labels. *Metronome* claimed facetiously in 1945 that "tenor man Don Byas of the Three Deuces on 52nd St." was "an exclusive Signature, Continental, National, Keynote, Asch, Jamboree, Commodore, Manor, Savoy, Hargail recording artist."[74] Radio broadcasts also continued to publicize 52nd Street. The most important radio personality on the street was disc jockey and emcee "Symphony Sid" Torin, whose Sunday night broadcasts from the Three Deuces over WHOM were popular with black listeners in Harlem.[75] Such exposure helped bop carve out a commercial niche on 52nd Street. In May 1945, for example, a *Metronome* headline proclaimed that "Dizzy Keeps Street Alive" with his quintet at the Three Deuces.[76] Even as late as September 1947, when 52nd Street was in commercial decline, *Down Beat* reported that Parker (at the Three Deuces) and Gillespie (at the Downbeat) were the two most popular acts on the street.[77]

Although bebop musicians commanded respect for their artistry and intelligence, they did not change the economics of the street's jazz scene or make jazz into an autonomous high art free of the market. While bebop certainly represented a noteworthy shift in musical style on 52nd Street, it looked mainly like business as usual from a commercial standpoint.

"'Zombie' Jive": Race and Resistance

If many of 52nd Street's musicians and audiences, both black and white, heard bop as the sound of revolution, it was in large part because the racial dynamic surrounding the music was increasingly radical by the standards of the 1940s. As De-Veaux points out, the revolutionary narrative of bebop is generally "situated not within but outside the jazz tradition, in the collision between jazz as an artistic endeavor and the social forces of commerce and race." This narrative typically describes bebop as a militant statement of black identity. Amiri Baraka, for example, points to such events as the March on Washington movement of 1941 and the Harlem riot of 1943 to argue that "between the thirties and the end of World War II, there was perhaps as radical a change in the psychological perspective of the Negro American toward America as there was between the Emancipation and 1930." Bebop, with its "willfully harsh, *anti-assimilationist* sound," reflected this new, assertive perspective by rejecting what Baraka sees as the sterility of white, mainstream swing. Bebop was thus revolutionary not only because it broke away from previous jazz styles but also because it reflected black political and social concerns. According to the revolutionary narrative, then, black identity and modernist upheaval were mutually reinforcing in bebop; or, as Ingrid Monson puts it, "the modernism of the beboppers explicitly sought to carve out a new space for a specifically African American creativity." Monson's metaphor takes on special resonance for 52nd Street, which was literally a "new space" for many black musicians and patrons in the mid-1940s. During this time, the increasing presence of African Americans on 52nd Street began to pose a challenge to the street's former status as a white-dominated entertainment district. As black audiences, musicians, and club owners became significant aspects of the street's culture, black identity became something that white performers and patrons had to negotiate in fluid social situations rather than simply view or enact onstage.[78]

"Mixed" bands led by black musicians were one notable development. While during the swing era, 52nd Street's mixed bands typically comprised white musicians and a black guest star, mixed bop groups often included white apprentices grateful to be learning from African American bandleaders. White pianist Al Haig's account of joining Gillespie's band demonstrates the authority that black musicians had begun to wield on 52nd Street. After being astonished by a Gillespie broadcast that he heard in Boston, Haig left for New York on a quest to find the trumpeter. He remembered that "when I got through with my job, I'd immediately run up to Fifty-second Street, looking in every club for Dizzy, to see if I could find him sitting in somewhere."[79] When he finally met his hero, Haig "was very tentative and diffident and scared about actually even talking about music with him, and there was never enough time."[80] One night when Haig was working at the Spotlite with guitarist Tiny Grimes, Gillespie and Charlie Parker terrified the insecure pianist by walking onto the stand and playing with the band. "But what that was in fact was an audition because when I got through—when they got through, they said, 'We're forming a quintet. We'd like to have you.' . . . It was very upsetting. But I said, 'Sure.' They said they'd be in touch, packed up their instruments and went out."[81] Haig eventually joined the quintet for its engagement at the Three Deuces. His experience demonstrates that Gillespie and Parker were confident of their superiority over white musicians of lesser skill and saw it as their prerogative to accept or reject them.

A similar dynamic was common in less formal situations in which white musicians sat in with black groups. White drummer John Robinson described his occasional role in Erroll Garner's band as that of an understudy. "I was sitting in with Erroll Garner and Slam Stewart. Sitting in for Harold West, who was the drummer. . . . I would go in there, play for a set, for no money, and he would get around, go to the White Rose [a popular bar on the corner of 52nd Street and Sixth Avenue], and drink and whoop it up!" Robinson remembered that most black musicians were kind to him despite his inexperience. For example, "Dizzy wanted to play real fast, but the time I sat in with him and Charlie Parker, Charlie knew my ability, and he knew that I couldn't really play that fast, so we played slower, and all of that . . . most of the people that befriended me during those years were black. Harold West, [Art] 'Trappy' Trappier . . . those drummers."[82] Trombonist Frank Rosolino had a similar experience with Parker. "I sat in with Bird and Oscar Pettiford at the Three Deuces. . . . Erroll Garner was working at the Deuces, too, and he said 'Come on, man, come on. Why don't you sit in?' You're scared stiff because it's Bird, but the fact that they let me sit in was a beautiful feeling. They'd always encourage me, which I really appreciated."[83] Black musicians were not always this welcoming to white acolytes, however. Black trumpeter Miles Davis, then in Parker's band, once dissuaded white clarinetist Tony Scott from sitting in by telling him, "Bird don't like no one to play with him"; when Parker later invited Scott to play, it became clear that Davis had in fact been expressing his own opinion.[84] African American bassist John Simmons remembered with condescension white drummer Shelly Manne's attempts to sit in on 52nd Street:

Now he learned how to play drums but he didn't know anything about jazz. . . . Shelly would ask me 'Can I sit in, can I sit in.' And he stayed on this so long, I'd say let the man sit in. All right he'd come on . . . when [drummer Kenny Clarke] was real tired, or he wanted to talk to a girl or . . . something, so Shelly would get on the stand and I'd have to tell him how to cock his cymbals to get the sound that [Count Basie's drummer] Jo Jones got and what cymbal to play behind [tenor saxophonist] Ike Quebec when he played, you know.[85]

Regardless of whether they encouraged white musicians or scorned them, black musicians were asserting a new level of control within 52nd Street's jazz scene.

Another facet of the increasing black presence on the street was the appearance of two black-owned clubs. The first of these was Tondelayo's, which opened around August 1944 at 18 West 52nd and was "named after the black dancer (née Wilhelmina Gray) who fronted the club with money provided by her husband, John Levy," who was also African American.[86] Tondelayo had been performing in New York for some time. In 1937, for example, she appeared at the Ubangi Club in Harlem as a "rhumba and native dancer" in a performance that *Variety* called "the last word in nitery erotica this side of a stag affair."[87] Her stage name evoked both exoticism and miscegenation. It likely derived from Leon Gordon's 1923 play *White Cargo,* in which "Tondeleyo" [*sic*] is a half-French, half-African temptress who seduces a British colonialist in West Africa.[88] White actress Hedy Lamarr reprised the role in a sultry 1942 film version of the play. Publicity for the club capitalized on the image of Tondelayo as sexy and primitive; in January 1945, for example, a photograph in the *New York Daily Mirror,* captioned "Charming Hostess," showed the scantily clad Tondelayo, apparently in the middle of a dance, and pointed out that she "entertains nightly at Tondelayos, her 52nd St. rendezvous." Advertisements for the club in the *New York Amsterdam News* in 1944 featured a drawing of a female dancer wearing a headdress and accompanied by a seated man who is perhaps playing an African drum.[89] Although the mere presence of these advertisements in the black press does not indicate either that African American readers embraced these stereotypes or that they attended Tondelayo's in great numbers, it is clear that the club hoped to attract black patrons. Tondelayo's most significant contribution to the budding bop movement was made in the fall of 1944, when Charlie Parker sat in frequently with Tiny Grimes.[90]

A second black-owned club was the Spotlite at 56 West 52nd, opened in about November 1944 by Clark Monroe.[91] Although Monroe had briefly fronted a band at 52nd Street's Kelly's Stable in the fall of 1943, his impact had been felt mainly in Harlem, where his club Monroe's Uptown House was an important meeting and performing place for young musicians of the bebop movement.[92] Bassist Leonard Gaskin, who played with Monroe at Kelly's Stable and also worked with Charlie Parker at the Spotlite in 1945, argued that Monroe's experience at the Uptown House, where "he had been hiring musicians for a long time," distinguished him from other 52nd Street club owners who were less knowledgeable about music.[93] The Spotlite's most important contribution to bebop came in 1946, when Monroe encouraged Gillespie to expand his small group into a big band.[94] In addition to bop musicians, Monroe also hired such swing-era stars as Billie Holiday, Ben Webster, and Coleman Hawkins.[95] Like Tondelayo's, the Spotlite advertised in the black press, with notices that often made reference to Monroe's race. On January 6, 1945, for example, *The People's Voice,* a paper edited by prominent black politician Adam Clayton Powell Jr., ran two ads for the club; one referred to Monroe as "Harlem's Favorite Host," while the other included a photo of the debonair Monroe with the caption "The Brown Baron."[96] These clear indications of Monroe's racial identity were likely intended to signal that his was a hospitable midtown club for patrons from Harlem.

As we have seen, although African Americans had begun to attend 52nd Street's clubs during the swing era, they were present only in small numbers, and many of the blacks in the audience were musicians. The recollections of 52nd Street's musicians and patrons, both white and black, suggest that a similar dynamic continued into the mid-1940s. White critic and historian Dan Morgenstern, a frequent observer of the 52nd Street scene beginning in 1947, remembered that although the Onyx, for example, "was really pretty black-and-tan," "there were not a lot of black customers in these clubs," and certain clubs "discreetly discouraged African Americans from frequenting" them during busy times of night. White drummer John Robinson said that although the street's clubs welcomed black customers—their philosophy was "if you have the green, you're welcome een"—only a "smattering" of blacks attended. African American guitarist Lawrence Lucie remembered that the 52nd Street audience comprised "all nationalities," including blacks from Harlem. Other black musicians, however, recalled a less diverse crowd at the clubs. African American bassist Carline Ray, who frequently attended 52nd Street clubs in the mid-1940s, asserted that "there were a lot of white folks down there" and speculated that "maybe any of the black people that might have been in the audiences might have been other musicians."[97] Black drummer LeRoy Battle, who played on the street in 1946, agreed that audiences were "mostly white," although "certain artists would draw more black." Billie Holiday, for example, "drew a lot of white, but she drew a lot of black too," and Billy Eckstine would "draw the black ladies" with his suave manner and his provocative blues hit *Jelly, Jelly*.[98] A William Gottlieb photograph of the audience at the Downbeat, taken in 1948, probably reflects the overall demographics of the street—of the twenty-five or so patrons visible, less than a third appear to be African American.[99]

The increasing prominence of blacks in the 52nd Street audience in the mid-1940s was due not as much to their numbers, then, as to the appearance of a flashy, controversial subcultural figure: the hipster. As Monson points out, hipsters were characterized by their "goatee, beret, glasses, and zoot suit," heroin use, a slang vocabulary associated with bebop, "and, of course, the music itself."[100] As we have seen, the most publicized sartorial symbol of hip among the bop pioneers on 52nd Street was Dizzy Gillespie. Not long after bebop's appearance on 52nd Street, hipsters became a recognized part of the scene. In October 1944, for example, *Jazz Record* mentioned a recent storm that "blew 52nd Street's hip children off to bed—peg pants and all." [101] By this time, hipster culture was being commodified on the street by white pianist and singer Harry "The Hipster" Gibson, who appeared at the Three Deuces, the Downbeat, and the Spotlite at various times during 1944.[102] Gibson both spoofed and celebrated the hipster drug and fashion culture with such tunes as *Handsome Harry the Hipster* and the infamous *Who Put the Benzedrine in Mrs. Murphy's Ovaltine?*[103] By 1946, *Down Beat* reporter Tom Piper expressed concern that hipsters, or as he called them, "zombies," were taking over the street. In an article entitled "Zombies Put Kiss of Death on 52nd St. Jazz," Piper complained that hipsters "come with their zoot suits, long haircuts, reefers and 'zombie' jive to night spots that feature top jazz talent. Soon they become the 'atmosphere' that pervades the spots." Eventually, according to Piper, zombies drove away the rest of the audience. "As soon as they start hanging around certain clubs, the decent citizenry avoid the spots like the plague." [104]

Why were the "decent citizenry" so upset? Although Piper was quick to deny any racial prejudice, pointing out that "Zombies are composed of all colors," Monson suggests that the very term *zombie,* with its allusions to stereotypical images of voodoo, carries racial significance.[105] On one level, hipsters were part of a long tradition of bringing black subcultural style to 52nd Street, one that extended back at least to Stuff Smith and his jive. Unlike Smith, however, many black hipsters were in the audience, sharing social space with whites, rather than performing onstage. Some hipsters were visibly involved in criminal activities that alarmed more conservative audience members. Miles Davis recalled that 52nd Street "attracted hustlers and fast-living pimps with plenty of whores, hipsters, and drug dealers." [106] Although the "reefers" that disturbed Piper were nothing new on the street, harder drugs like heroin represented a troubling new trend, of which Charlie Parker was probably the most notorious symbol. One night at the Three Deuces, Gillespie, furious to discover Parker shooting up heroin in the bathroom, surprised the audience by accidentally saying "That motherfucker is shooting dope in there" in front of a live microphone.[107] Malcolm X remembered snorting cocaine in the Onyx Club's bathroom during his days as hustler Detroit Red.[108] Some of the street's hipsters made their living as pimps. A 52nd Street "night-lifer" interviewed by the *New York Amsterdam News* in 1944 assertively boasted, "Grin and bear it, buddy—yes—I am a pimp. Where there are fine young things, you'll always find me." [109] Even more troubling than drugs and prostitution to many whites, however, was black hipsters' insistence on the right to socialize with white women. As another hipster told the *Amsterdam News:*

"I work in the garment center. The ofay [white] boys always been telling me to bring them up to Harlem to meet some fine colored gals. I used to tell them to take me down in the Village to meet some fine ofay gals. This made them sore. Now—since I've gotten a foothold in 52nd Street, I tell them to come up here and let me introduce them to some ofay gals. This burns them up and boy do I get a kick out of strutting in and out of these joints with a righteous blond." The boy grinned.[110]

Although musical collaboration among whites and blacks was becoming commonplace on 52nd Street, interracial sexual relationships still had the power to shock.

The threat posed by 52nd Street's hipsters derived from the way in which they exaggerated primitivist stereotypes about black masculinity until they became confrontational and intimidating rather than merely titillating. Although, as we have seen, 52nd Street's jazz scene was founded by white musicians who valorized black men for their supposed virility and contempt for convention, it was a different matter when blacks themselves began to enact these values aggressively on the street. That hipsters' authority was so often measured in terms of their power with women sheds a troubling light on the misogynist underpinnings of hipness, which, as Monson argues, has always been a notion "weighted in gender as well as race." As Robin D. G. Kelley argues, for many hipsters, "white women, like virtually all women (save one's mama), were merely property to be possessed, sported, used and tossed out."[111] The hipsters' sexism was, of course, simply a more open version of attitudes already prevalent in the 52nd Street scene, which continued to be male-dominated both onstage and in the audience into the bebop era; the Gottlieb photo cited earlier, for example, shows only two women amid a large group of men in the Downbeat's audience. By challenging the dominance of 52nd Street's established white bachelor subculture and demonstrating authority over white women, however, hipsters intentionally crossed a line that made the street's old guard uncomfortable.

Hipsters' ostentatious displays of masculinity ran the risk of perpetuating stereotypes about black sexuality, in what Monson terms "the bald equation of the primitive with sex, and sex with the music and body of the black male jazz musician."[112] It should be noted, then, that not all blacks on 52nd Street during the bebop era were hipsters and that not all hipsters were black. Black musicians such as Gillespie and Parker embraced only certain aspects of hip style and were offended by caricatured portrayals of themselves in the press.[113] Many of the most prominent hipsters on 52nd Street were white. Street regular Teddy Reig, for example, who was white, was a self-proclaimed "hustler" who initially earned his club-going money with schemes such as selling worn-out records that had been doctored with shoe polish to look brand new. In 1945, he became a producer for the independent record label Savoy, where he organized recording sessions for such 52nd Street figures as Charlie Parker, Miles Davis, and Don Byas.[114] Although "zombies" were stereotypically African American, the reality was more complicated.

Moreover, a new trend of women instrumentalists on the street undermined the notion of women as mere accessories to hip men. At a time when jazz critics and audiences often disparaged female singers, virtuosic instrumentalists presented a different kind of challenge to sexist assumptions. Many of these performers led trios, including bassist and singer Vivien Garry, featured at Kelly's Stable in 1945 and at several other clubs in 1947; guitarist Mary Osborne, at Kelly's Stable in 1946 and the Hickory House in 1948; pianist Barbara Carroll, at the Downbeat in 1947; and pianist, vibraphonist, and singer Dardanelle, at Dixon's and the Hickory House in 1947.[115] While all of these musicians were white, African American women instrumentalists, such as pianist Dorothy Donegan, also appeared occasionally on the street during this era.[116] As Sherrie Tucker has shown, women musicians often were treated as glamorous sex objects rather than serious musicians during the swing era, and such attitudes persisted into the 1940s on 52nd Street.[117] *Down Beat,* for example, made a point of describing Garry as "lush-figured" and claimed condescendingly that "her intonation is far better than most gals achieve on the instrument," while Dardanelle's trio was said to do "mighty well" "for its size, weight, and sex."[118] At the same time, however, the obvious talent of these musicians led reviewers to grant them respect. Garry's trio, for example, was praised for its "solid musicianship" and "brilliant ideas," while Garry reportedly sang "not unlike a hip 52nd street character," which suggests that men did not have a monopoly on hipness.[119] *Down Beat* similarly applauded Carroll not only for her modern music, calling her "something of an ultimate in this matter of absorbing be-bop," but for her hip, relaxed demeanor: "she manages to sit there so cool-like, letting the Dizzy stuff gush out in an endless, continuous stream."[120] Carroll herself remembered that "you were discriminated against strictly because you were a female, as happened with many other areas, other professions. . . . With jazz, once you established the fact that you could play then you were accepted." [121]

While whites like Reig and Carroll found a place in the hip culture of 52nd Street, others reacted violently to hipsters and the street's new racial climate.[122] The usual culprits in these accounts are southern servicemen shocked by what they saw as the excessive license and arrogance of blacks. Slam Stewart recalled one of the tactics that sailors used to pick a fight.

I did notice that some of the sailors would . . . seem to resent a musician, even standing at the bar drinking, you know, standing right next to him, you know. I saw one incident where one of the musicians, maybe one of the servicemen said something to one of the musicians. There was an argument . . . and the musician had a drink in front of him and [the sailor] took his hand and hit his drink over the bar. . . . I've seen a lot of scuffles happen that way. . . . that was the tension during the war years, you know.[123]

Other incidents were even more dramatic. Gillespie, for example, remembered an episode in which "three cracker sailors" saw him and Oscar Pettiford on the sidewalk talking to Madame Bricktop (Ada Smith), a light-skinned, red-haired African American singer and entertainer. The sailors attacked the two men, exclaiming, "What you niggers doing with this white woman!" and Gillespie saved himself only by using his trumpet as a weapon and holing up on the catwalk at the end of a subway platform.[124] John Simmons recalled a street brawl that "was like D-Day. Everyone emerged into the streets fighting. At the same time. Out of all of the clubs. Don Byas . . . hit somebody in the mouth with his horn; Benny Harris broke his trumpet across somebody's head." On another occasion, Simmons foiled a group of threatening white southern soldiers by walking into the White Rose bar, which was well known for racial intermingling; when the soldiers "looked in there and saw all this conglomeration of colors and ethnic groups, I invited them and said come on in. (Laughter). They walked out." [125] These anecdotes, recalled years after the fact, have begun to acquire the status of legend, and it is fair to point out that not every white southerner who came to 52nd Street was bent on racially motivated violence.[126] Contemporaneous reports make it clear, however, that violence was a reality on the street. *Down Beat*, for example, perhaps describing the fight remembered by Simmons, reported in June 1944 on a "recent mixed brawl" on 52nd Street. "Some sailors resenting the presence of Negroes in night clubs took it in their own hands to establish white supremacy along swing lane, but the fast arrival of police nipped that plan in the bud. More than a dozen sailors and jazz musicians were involved in the fracas." In August, under the headline "Racial Hatred Rears Ugly Mug in Music," *Down Beat* stated that "a number of brief skirmishes have been quelled along 52nd street recently, and police are on duty in the area in extra force to prevent further troubles." [127]

Whether the authorities prevented trouble on 52nd Street or contributed to it, however, was a matter of debate. Some police officers appear to have been sincerely concerned about preventing racist violence. John Robinson fondly remembered a certain "cop on the beat on 52nd Street, his name was Mac, and he didn't take no shit from nobody . . . if there was any friction between black and white, he'd straighten it out." Other officers, however, could be violent themselves. Teddy Reig recalled one such incident: "The cops that worked around 52nd Street had a bar where they got free food and drinks. The cops that went on at midnight were really crocked by 4 a.m. One of these guys was standing in the shadows one night and when I walked by he called me a 'nigger lover.' I said, 'Why don't you come into the light and say that?' He did, and I knocked him cold, took his club away from him, and dared him to make a move. . . . I got arrested, and everybody from the Street came to court." [128]

Racist repression sometimes was the result of official policy rather than the whims of individual police officers. As David Stowe points out, "the most publicized of these crackdowns occurred in July 1944," when "after weeks of pressure on the White Rose's manager to exclude blacks, the bar was charged with solicitation involving a white prostitute and black pimp." Journalists Ed Sullivan and Walter Winchell aided the attack with inflammatory columns on racial mixing at the bar. Eventually, "with scores of uniformed police patrolling the block, the manager consented to close at midnight and to allow a policeman to be posted inside during business hours." [129] The jazz press, which generally took a liberal stance on racial integration, blamed the police and white racists for 52nd Street's troubles but also reproached the street's criminal element and lax sexual mores. *Metronome,* accusing "white troublemakers who may well produce a race riot," claimed that "democracy is having difficulties along 52nd Street" but argued that "the situation is admittedly not helped by the fact that there is a lunatic fringe of pimps, prostitutes, and tea-peddlers, both white and colored, who can be found hanging around the musicians and who are too often encouraged by them." *Down Beat,* in an article entitled "Vagrant Chicks Blamed in Part for Racial Row," reported that White Rose owner Abe Turkewitz "pinned the blame for the racial brawls that took place in his bar, as well as in neighboring clubs, on the number of young girls, both white and colored, who have been hanging around musicians." [130] A more major event occurred in November 1945, when "all entertainment" was banned for several nights at the Three Deuces, Spotlite, Downbeat, and Onyx clubs "on a police order charging that the clubs were rendezvous for persons engaging in the narcotics and marijuana traffic." [131] *Down Beat* reported that "many musicians and club operators felt that the real issue involved was a racial one, centering mainly around the considerable mixed trade patronizing the Alley [52nd Street] spots." [132] The *New York Amsterdam News* agreed, although it suggested that the police were also cracking down on gays and lesbians (described mockingly as "switchy-twitchy men and manly appearing women.")[133] Miles Davis, who was working with Charlie Parker at the Spotlite before the ban, expressed a similar view in his autobiography, recalling that "the police shut down the Spotlite and some of the other clubs on 52nd for some bullshit about drugs and phony liquor licenses. But the real reason I think they shut it down for a couple of weeks was because they didn't like all them niggers coming downtown. They didn't like all them black men being with all them rich, fine white women." [134] Yet another incident suggests that racial tension was not limited to those clubs that featured bebop. In his 1946 article on "zombies," Tom Piper complained that "one of the most famous institutions in jazz had to be discontinued. Milt Gabler's Jimmy Ryan Sunday Afternoon Sessions were actually cancelled because they drew a young audience and the police did not want them mingling with the Zombies." [135]

Although battles over musical style might have seemed trivial compared to the literal battles over race being waged on 52nd Street, music reflected and symbolized the turmoil of the street. Bop, beyond being an unusual and complex new idiom, was the music most closely associated with hipsters and with 52nd Street's changing racial climate. Whether it was exhilarating or disturbing depended in part on listeners' views of this new climate and of black musicians' place within it. While bebop musicians and their advocates sought a place in the vanguard, their adversaries fought to perpetuate musical practices and racial conceptions that harked back to the very beginnings of the street's jazz scene.

Chapter Eight **Apples and Oranges** 52nd Street and the Jazz War

As bebop became a significant presence in 52nd Street's jazz scene, the new style's legitimacy there and in the world of jazz at large was under constant attack. The appearance of bebop was the major event in the most celebrated conflict over musical style in the history of jazz, a battle among self-consciously progressive adherents of bebop, advocates of mainstream swing, and Dixieland partisans, whom their opponents derisively dubbed "moldy figs." As historian Bernard Gendron demonstrates, this "jazz war" had its roots in the late 1930s, when "hot jazz" aficionados such as those discussed in chapter 5 began to uphold the New Orleans style as an antidote to what they saw as the excessive commercialism of the swing industry.[1] Beginning in 1942, swing-oriented publications such as *Metronome* repeatedly attacked "the exclusionary purism and incessant carping of the revivalists," who "counterattacked with charges of crass commercialism, faddism and Eurocentrism."[2]

These warring parties appeared at first to hold irreconcilable beliefs. Followers of the New Orleans style, as we have seen, valued music that seemed to resist commercial forces, evoked the sounds of a bygone era, and purportedly was rooted in emotion and spontaneity rather than calculated technique. Swing supporters, in contrast, embraced the commercial market, celebrated the notion of musical progress, and praised the technical advances that swing musicians supposedly had made over their New Orleans forebears.[3] In the second stage of this battle, however, swing and New Orleans partisans united against a common enemy: bebop. Around 1946, as bebop became emblematic of modernism in jazz, Gendron observes, "swing music suddenly found itself relegated to the company of New Orleans jazz, on the side of the traditional and the tried-and-true," and advocates of both styles joined in accusing bop of "inaccessibility," "elitism," and "avant-garde posturing."[4] Although these two stages are often discussed as if they were separate conflicts, Gendron demonstrates that they were so closely related that "many contemporaries failed to distinguish between them."[5] By the late 1940s, the jazz press began to suggest that Dixieland revivalists and bop fans were "natural and unrelenting opponents," although Gendron argues that in fact those in the Dixieland camp had "already spent most of their animus against swing."[6] Although in retrospect this "war" sometimes looks like trivial bickering or simply a means of stirring up publicity, it had serious ramifications for how we think about and discuss jazz. Gendron illustrates that as disparate groups clashed, they "collectively and unwittingly" advanced shared beliefs about the terms in which jazz should be discussed and in the process "had a formative and enduring impact on the way in which jazz history got constructed and jazz as an art form got legitimated."[7] In a related argument, Scott DeVeaux demonstrates that the common notion of a "jazz tradition" that encompasses an evolving chain of styles was forged in the aftermath of this jazz war as revivalists and beboppers sought to reconcile their differences, with each realizing that "it proved as much in the interests of the modernists to have their music legitimated as the latest phase of a (now) long and distinguished tradition, as it was in the interests of the proponents of earlier jazz styles (whether New Orleans jazz or swing) not to be swept aside as merely antiquarian."[8] In the end, then, this conflict actually brought the combatants closer together, with various styles of jazz newly conceptualized as different stages of the same music.

Historians often depict 52nd Street as the front line of the jazz war. Samuel Charters, for example, writes that "most of this" battle "was taking place against the new background of the Fifty-second Street jazz clubs."[9] In reality, however, the war was much more heated in the press than on the street itself. Bebop audiences and musicians and their New Orleans–style counterparts on 52nd Street often simply ignored each other while pursuing their own interests. Nonetheless, the concerns that informed the war affected jazz and its reception in the street's clubs. Central to these concerns was the status of jazz as an art: was it a folk art that reflected the essence of a long-standing tradition or a progressive modern art constantly spurred along by individual invention? This question was tied to competing perceptions of the role of black musicians.

While the idea persisted on 52nd Street that authentic jazz was the product of untutored, spontaneous black performers, bebop was associated with African American musicians who insisted on being recognized as serious, self-aware artists. Bebop's rise to prominence was a challenge not only to earlier styles of jazz but also to the ideas of racial authenticity that had informed 52nd Street's jazz scene from its beginnings at the old Onyx Club. Nonetheless, these older styles and their practitioners were to some extent reconciled with bebop as collaboration among 52nd Street's musicians helped create the idea of an inclusive, coherent jazz tradition.

"52nd St. vs. New Orleans": Dixieland at Jimmy Ryan's   Although musicians and audiences who preferred New Orleans or Chicago jazz continued to support these styles as they had in the swing era, it was clear by the mid-1940s that they were fighting a losing battle on 52nd Street. By this time, New York's Dixieland jazz scene centered on Greenwich Village, at such clubs as Nick's (at 10th Street and Seventh Avenue) and the Stuyvesant Casino (140 Second Avenue, between Eighth and Ninth streets.) Only one 52nd Street club, Jimmy Ryan's at 53 West 52nd, regularly featured older styles, and engagements by Dixieland players at other clubs were often short-lived. In 1946, for example, *Down Beat* reported that "among harder hit spots is the Keyboard [at 54 West 52nd] which recently booked Wild Bill Davison and his jazz crew but was forced to release the dixie trumpeter when the cash register refused to jump in rhythm with the band." [10] By this time, the term *52nd Street* itself had become a kind of shorthand in the traditional jazz press for the supposed pretentiousness of bebop. In June 1944, for example, critic George Avakian credited Chicago pianist Art Hodes with a "great sense of harmony—*jazz* harmony, not something dreamed up to knock out the customers in a 52nd Street jive joint." [11] The next year, Hodes himself, as editor of *Jazz Record,* wrote that his agent had told him about "a certain 52nd Street owner who told me he couldn't use you because you played dixieland and what he wanted was jazz," implying that 52nd Street's clubs were misguided about the true nature of jazz. [12] Critic Frederic Ramsey Jr. asked in 1945, "What is the place of the jazz artist, especially the folk artist who can't or won't conform to slick-paper standards, the Fifty-Second Street canons of performance?" His question suggests that 52nd Street's commercialism had tainted the music presented there. [13] Another critic who associated 52nd Street with inauthentic modern jazz was Rudi Blesh, a staunch defender of the New Orleans tradition. In 1945, Blesh sarcastically commented that a radio broadcast supposedly featuring New Orleans jazz had included "the veteran New Orleans guitarist, Mary Osborne, of North Dakota and Fiftysecond Street," who "entertained on the traditional electric guitar." In a clearer summation of the perceived schism between 52nd Street and traditional jazz, Blesh wrote in 1946 that jazz aficionados "argue like mad about Chicago vs. Re Bop, or 52nd St. vs. New Orleans."[14] For lovers of Dixieland, 52nd Street had become the enemy's territory.

Audiences at Jimmy Ryan's therefore developed a siege mentality, convinced that the club was the only place left on 52nd Street where real jazz still could be heard.[15] During the bebop era, two overlapping images of authentic jazz were prevalent at Ryan's, one involving fidelity to the traditions of black New Orleans and the other the notion of jazz as an informal, good-time music. Although both of these stances had been common from the earliest days of the 52nd Street jazz scene, they now were threatened by the progressive black modernism of bop. Ryan's thus represented a last stand for many of the performance practices and ideas about jazz that had originally informed 52nd Street's musicians and audiences.

Although a predominantly white, male audience was typical of every 52nd Street jazz club, Ryan's attracted an older, more staid crowd than those clubs that featured bebop. White photographer William Gottlieb described the typical Ryan's patron as "older, conservative, white," and white bassist Bill Crow, who visited the club in 1948, said that the audience included "a lot of graduates of Ivy League colleges who had fallen in love with jazz when they were in school, and were now businessmen, and felt comfortable going to these jazz clubs—they liked the liberation of it, and felt that they had a personal connection to it some kind of ways, like following your old sports team, you know." At the same time, a new generation of white collegians was starting to explore hot jazz. White jazz enthusiast Al Vollmer, who was a regular patron at Ryan's beginning around 1947, remembered that "the people that would have been at Ryan's would have been the college kids—the college kids on their vacations would come there."[16] Coverage of the club in small jazz magazines by women reporters such as Mary Beckwith and Peggy Hart indicates that at least some women took an active interest in Dixieland.[17] Vollmer speculated, however, that most women at the club were accompanying male jazz fans, although "maybe some more liberal college girls might [have come] there on their own."[18] Black musicians occasionally dropped in at Ryan's to hear one another play. Crow remembered that trumpeters Hot Lips Page and Bunk Johnson came to the club to hear the De Paris

Brothers.[19] Vollmer recalled, however, that blacks were "uncommon" in the audience, and African American pianist Billy Taylor asserted that few young blacks attended Ryan's. Taylor explained that "there were a lot of young white people who were interested" in early jazz, "and they really helped keep that part of the music alive in many clubs." [20]

Despite its racial uniformity, Ryan's audience encompassed a variety of views on jazz. While some patrons were earnest scholars of jazz history and discography with a reverential attitude toward the music, others simply came to enjoy a convivial atmosphere and energetic performances. Vollmer remembered that "the college kids, they were there, but some of them probably were there because they could take a date there, and it was smart to go, and it was perhaps a little daring to be into jazz, and . . . well, of course, this was shortly after jazz had been America's popular music." A March 1943 profile of the club reported that "the bar is up front, and there is usually a crowd around it, with a lot of talking and noise, so if you really want to hear the music, get a seat at a table as far to the back as possible. Better go on a week-day night, and avoid the Saturday night crowd, which is noisy and very athletic on the two-by-four dance floor." Despite the presence of this raucous faction, consistent coverage of Ryan's in the mid- to late 1940s by small, specialized magazines such as *Jazz Record* and *American Jazz Review* indicates that many serious hot jazz aficionados also patronized the club. Vollmer, for example, had begun collecting jazz records as a teenager in Sweden before moving to the United States in 1947, and he was thrilled to realize that at Ryan's he could speak to musicians such as trombonist Wilbur De Paris about their recording careers.[21]

Such relationships between fans and musicians were facilitated at Ryan's by long-term engagements; as Arnold Shaw points out, "instead of frequently changing his bill, Jimmy [Ryan] held cats over for long periods during which they had the time and freedom to refine their musical ideas." Throughout the mid-1940s, a series of performers, black and white, and almost all with connections to New Orleans or Chicago, appeared at Ryan's for several months each. White pianist Art Hodes, who performed in Chicago for much of the 1920s and 1930s, played at Ryan's from April to December 1944. White clarinetist Mezz Mezzrow, a Chicago native, was featured from January to April 1945. Of the black musicians who performed at the club, perhaps the most notable was clarinetist and soprano saxophonist Sidney Bechet, one of the most famous and influential musicians of the New Orleans tradition, who played at Ryan's throughout 1947. Black pianist Hank Duncan, who had performed with prominent New Orleans trumpeter King Oliver in 1931, appeared with an interracial trio including white clarinetist Sol Yaged and white drummer Danny Alvin from June to November 1945. These and other musicians appealed to an audience that continued to regard New Orleans and Chicago as the wellsprings of jazz.[22]

The most celebrated symbol of authentic New Orleans jazz to appear at Ryan's was African American trumpeter Willie "Bunk" Johnson. Johnson had first come to the attention of New York's community of hot jazz enthusiasts in the late 1930s, when the editors of the important early jazz history *Jazzmen* "discovered" him working on a Louisiana farm.[23] Johnson, who claimed to have taught the young Louis Armstrong how to play trumpet, became a central figure in the book, and his discoverers, after buying him a new pair of dentures that enabled him to play again, arranged recording sessions and performing engagements in San Francisco and New York.[24] Aficionados of New Orleans jazz, as historian James Lincoln Collier puts it, approached Johnson as "a genuine relic of the past, a piece of the true cross." Lewis A. Erenberg argues that Johnson's "resurrection" was "the hot music cult's most notable achievement."[25] As these messianic metaphors suggest, the traditional jazz community hoped that Johnson's 1945 performances at the Stuyvesant Casino would mark the dawn of a new era and reinvigorate the New York jazz scene.[26]

Although Johnson never played a steady engagement at Ryan's, he sometimes performed at the club's jam sessions. One such session, on March 10, 1945, was the subject of an article in *Jazz Record* that demonstrates that Johnson played the role of a historical exhibit for some in the Ryan's audience.[27] Awestruck reporter Lewis Eaton described a personal encounter that he had with Johnson before the performance, claiming that "he is one of the finest gentlemen I've ever met, both in his speech and his manners, and not at all an illiterate black man from Iberia, La., as might be gathered from previous stories." Despite this caveat, Eaton stressed Johnson's working-class background ("He showed me his hands, which are tough and calloused from driving a truck and trailer to make a living"). He also outlined a conversation in which Johnson claimed to have taught a wide range of black New Orleans trumpeters including Armstrong, King Oliver, Freddie Keppard, Tommy Ladnier, and some "N. O. boys who stayed home." Of Johnson's playing, Eaton wrote that on a blues "Bunk really hit his stride. He can really blow the blues down and you have to hear it to appreciate it. Phrases and notes from out of the past in the real New Orleans tradition such as have never been heard in Ryan's or anywhere in N.Y." These comments suggest that Eaton valued Johnson primarily for his direct connection to the supposed folk origins of jazz in New Orleans rather than as an entertainer in the conventional sense. Indeed, although Eaton pointed out that Johnson was a "great showman and scene stealer," he was mainly interested in the historical significance of this fact, such as the possibility that "Louis [Armstrong] might have got his handkerchief tricks from Bunk."[28] In *Down Beat,* critic Ralph Gleason discussed Johnson in similar language, writing that "the biggest thrill I have ever gotten out of jazz, Bunk gave me that afternoon when he stood up on the bandstand, greyhaired, hands gnarled and calloused from rice field labor, and 'drove down the blues.'"[29] By November 1947, Bob Aurthur of *Jazz Record* complained that Johnson was being treated not "as an elderly human being with recognizable human failings" but as a "god," despite the diminution of his talents with age.[30] Aurthur describes a Ryan's session at which Johnson's poor playing disappointed listeners drawn by his reputation. Johnson's deification as a New Orleans icon demonstrates the self-consciously serious attitude of many in Ryan's audience.

In contrast, the De Paris Brothers, trumpeter Sidney and trombonist Wilbur, could be appreciated by patrons who regarded authentic African American jazz as a source of informal fun rather than a weighty art. The De Parises, who hailed from Indiana, had both played professionally since the 1920s, and each had worked with important New Orleans musicians: Sidney with Zutty Singleton, Sidney Bechet, and Jelly Roll Morton, and Wilbur with Louis Armstrong. The brothers played a long run at Ryan's from May 1943 to April 1944 and later became mainstays at the club between 1952 and 1962.[31] Recordings made in 1944 demonstrate that, like many 52nd Street performers associated with New Orleans jazz, the De Paris Brothers adopted certain aspects of older styles while rejecting others. *Change O'Key Boogie,* for example, is a twelve-bar blues that features a front line of clarinet, trumpet, and trombone playing polyphonically for several choruses, all hallmarks of New Orleans style. The performance begins, however, with several choruses of Clyde Hart's boogie-woogie piano, a style that enjoyed mass popularity during the swing era, and it includes four key changes, a gesture not normally associated with New Orleans–style blues. The band's live performances reflected a similar blend of tradition and innovation. To some extent, they strove for a New Orleans sound. Drummer Freddie Moore, who worked with Wilbur De Paris at Ryan's in the early 1950s, remembered that although everybody in the band "got along fine," nevertheless "they let me out because they said they wanted a New Orleans drummer . . . after I left, they got Zutty Singleton." In 1944, however, the *New Yorker* described the band as a "very fine, soft, slow, easy, and hot quintet," with all adjectives except the last distinguishing their music from the conventional image of raucous Dixieland. Moreover, the reviewer explained that "this band also knocks out first-class sambas and rumbas," which hardly conformed to most listeners' notions of authentic New Orleans jazz.[32]

Despite the De Paris Brothers' skill and versatility, many audience members viewed their music simply as a backdrop for boisterous carousing. Although the band played to these expectations to some extent with humorous stage antics, such as Wilbur De Paris blocking the entrance to the women's room with his trombone slide, they also chafed against the limitations of this role. Al Vollmer, who frequently went to hear Wilbur De Paris in the 1950s, remembered that the audience's restrictive expectations affronted the trombonist.

In fact, there was a good bit of sarcasm in his whole presentation, because I think he had a not altogether unfounded [belief] that he was throwing pearls to swine at Ryan's—people came there to carouse and drink and stuff. . . . I mean, I think that he probably as anybody would like it if you asked for his numbers that he had written or something that they had worked out within the band, rather than this naïve and incessant call for *The Saints [Go Marching In]*, you see. I'm sure that as a musician of his knowledge and caliber . . . I can see where he might have been offended by . . . these half-inebriated college kids, you know.[33]

De Paris's subtle sarcasm toward his audience manifested itself in original compositions such as *March of the Charcoal Grays*, so called "because the charcoal gray suit was what every college kid had."[34] Despite such sly attempts to defend his integrity as an artist, De Paris, like Johnson, was impeded by stereotypes of African American creativity and musicianship that predated or ignored the modernist aspirations of bebop.

"Spiritual Sons": Kid Bands at Ryan's   White musicians who performed at Ryan's tended to view jazz through one of the lenses applied to Johnson and the De Paris Brothers, either as a folk art to be emulated as accurately as possible or as an informal, unpretentious form of music. The former position was best represented by the so-called kid bands that appeared at Ryan's, beginning with McKenzie's Candy Kids, who opened there on January 18, 1946.[35] The Candy Kids were a quintet promoted by Red McKenzie, who had been part of the 52nd Street scene as early as 1933, when he managed the Spirits of Rhythm; the name Candy Kids was first used by a McKenzie-led band that recorded in 1924 and 1925.[36] Two of the Candy Kids at Ryan's were seasoned professionals rather than "kids": the elder statesman of the group, forty-three-year-old drummer Danny Alvin, had worked professionally since 1918 with musicians including Wingy Manone and Art Hodes, and twenty-eight-year-old clarinetist Al DeRose had performed with Ina Ray Hutton, Red Norvo, and Joe Marsala before joining the band.[37] The others in the group, however, were less experienced. *American Jazz Review* reported that this was twenty-three-year-old pianist Lou Bredice's "first real jazz job."[38] Although trumpeter Johnny Windhurst had already worked with Sidney Bechet, and trombonist Eddie Hubble with pianist Jess Stacy, they were only nineteen and eighteen, respectively. *American Jazz Review* reported that Hubble was "a member of the Hot Club of Scarsdale," a group of suburban teenagers who "h[e]ld regular sessions every Sunday at various homes, just for the kicks."[39] By December 1946, another young band with connections to the Scarsdale jazz scene was performing at Ryan's: the Wildcats, led by eighteen-year-old clarinetist and saxophonist Bob Wilber. The Wildcats' shifting personnel included Hubble and Windhurst of the Candy Kids as well as sixteen-year-old cornetist Johnny Glasel ("a senior at Scarsdale High"), eighteen-year-old drummer Eddie Phyfe of nearby Larchmont, and twenty-year-old drummer Denny Strong, who with Wilber "started the Hot Club of Scarsdale."[40] Although the band, pointing out that "after all, only a few of them ever went to Scarsdale High," rejected the claim "that their colective [sic] name is . . . 'The Scarsdale High School Dixieland Band,'" their youth and background led at least one critic to compare them to suburban Chicago's Austin High School Gang of the 1920s, which had spawned such notable white musicians as Bud Freeman, Jimmy McPartland, and Frank Teschemacher.[41] Ironically, the Wildcats' parochial, middle-class background, seemingly far from the source of jazz, linked them to a group of musicians celebrated by traditional jazz purists.

The white kid bands self-consciously mimicked the style of black New Orleans musicians. The Candy Kids' repertoire included both New Orleans standards such as *Muskrat Ramble* and Jazz Age pop tunes such as *The Sheik of Araby,* while the Wildcats recorded such numbers as *Willie the Weeper* and *Mabel's Dream,* associated with Louis Armstrong and King Oliver, respectively.[42] The Wildcats' 1947 recording of *Willie the Weeper* demonstrates their fealty to New Orleans tradition.[43] In it, the band employs New Orleans techniques such as polyphony and stop time; Wilber plays clarinet with a wide vibrato clearly derived from the style of Sidney Bechet; and Glasel's use of a cornet rather than the by-then conventional trumpet, as well as his timbre on the instrument, suggest a desire to imitate Louis Armstrong's early style. Reviewers partial to New Orleans and Chicago styles praised the young musicians by comparing them to their musical ancestors. Peggy Hart of *American Jazz Review* wrote in February 1946 that "on fast tunes," trumpeter Johnny Windhurst of the Candy Kids "sounds a bit like Bix [Beiderbecke], which is OK as far as I'm concerned." In 1947, Bob Aurthur of *Jazz Record* claimed that "Wilber has a following that is probably reminiscent of the kids who used to follow Bix." More commonly, however, the members of the kid bands were compared to African American musicians. Reporter Mary Beckwith, for example, wrote that she thought she heard Sidney Bechet's soprano sax as she walked into Ryan's one evening, only to discover Wilber on the bandstand. Hart claimed that pianist Dick Wellstood of the Wildcats "goes to the piano and plays right out of Jelly-Roll [Morton]'s book, in as authentic a New Orleans idiom as will ever be heard." In a review of the Wildcats' recordings, George Avakian compared Wilber to Bechet, Wellstood to stride piano great James P. Johnson, and Glasel to both Louis Armstrong and black Louisiana trumpeter Tommy Ladnier.[44]

Critics less sympathetic to the New Orleans revival turned such comparisons against the group, suggesting that their imitation of older styles betrayed an absence of originality and creativity. *Down Beat* gave the band a condescending review in December 1946, describing them as "a combo that sounded straight off a collection of record collectors' items. The hornman, Johnny Glazel [*sic*], blew a cornet so much like Louis' older recorded stuff that he even played Louis' mistakes. What's more, he sported a handkerchief at all times in his left hand like guess who?" The reporter slyly suggested that, contrary to the band's beliefs, self-expression was incompatible with emulation of their idols: "When the *Beat,* after discussing the Armstrong-Bechet sounds that the band so faithfully reproduced, got around to discussing the band's general style, [bassist Charlie] Traeger blandly revealed, 'We just play the way we feel!' "[45] Although few doubted that the young musicians at Ryan's were skilled mimics of New Orleans style, listeners were divided as to whether such mimicry demonstrated an admirable attention to authenticity or simply a lack of imagination.

Although these young musicians learned much of what they knew about New Orleans jazz from records—*Down Beat* reported that "all the gang started out as record collectors, with most of them New Orleans specialists"—they also actively sought out the living originators of the style.[46] Bob Wilber's playing, for example, was similar to that of Sidney Bechet because Wilber had become not only Bechet's protégé but also his housemate. Wilber recalled that clarinetist Mezz Mezzrow referred him to Bechet, who had opened an informal "school of music at his home in Brooklyn."

> I ended up sort of being his favorite pupil, I guess, and after a couple of months he said, "Well, gee, you're living over there in the Village and it's a long ride in the subway—why don't you move in? I've got an extra room." So I did. I would have been eighteen when I started studying with Sidney and I lived there at the house with him and we would practice with the two horns and study and fool around all day and at night we'd hop on the subway and go over to 52nd Street where he was playing at Jimmy Ryan's and I'd play on the stand with him.[47]

In addition to performing together at the club, Bechet and Wilber recorded together after Bechet generously offered to use the Wildcats as his backing band for a 1947 Columbia session.[48] On *Spreadin' Joy*, Wilber and Bechet play a clarinet duet that highlights their timbral similarity.[49] Bechet remembered that listeners to these records commented that "the two clarinet parts sound more like Sidney Bechet playing a duet with himself than anything on the one-man band record" that Bechet had made in 1941.[50]

The revivalist press was intrigued by the unusual relationship between Wilber, a white suburban teenager, and Bechet, a middle-aged African American who had helped forge the New Orleans jazz tradition. In *Jazz Record*, Al Avakian wrote that Wilber was Bechet's "spiritual son" and asked histrionically, "How did the 'teen-age [sic] son of a Scarsdale businessman and the aging veteran of the high and low roads of jazz ever get together? How did this green, bespectacled high school student learn and absorb the style of one of the creators of jazz in less than two years and to such a point that a standard gag today on hearing Sidney play is: 'Gee, plays just like Bob Wilber, doesn't he?'"[51] That these questions were rooted in a fascination with racial difference becomes apparent later in Avakian's article when Bechet's speech is transcribed in dialect ("Yas, he kept comin' back and he can really blow now. Man, he can blow") that contrasts with Wilber's standard English.[52] Wilber's admiration of and affection for Bechet were undoubtedly sincere; in 1946, he described his mentor as "a thorough, sympathetic, and understanding teacher and a wonderful person." In the same interview, however, Wilber explained that

"I think of jazz as a Negroid music, based up[on] . . . his amazing rhythmic sense, his great sense of humor, and his continual search for freedom," which suggests that he still held a conventionally essentialist view
of black musicianship despite extensive exposure to an idiosyncratic in-
dividualist such as Bechet.[53] In addition to the well-known bond between
Wilber and Bechet, there were several less-publicized mentor-apprentice
relationships between white musicians. *Jazz Record* reported, for example,
that Johnny Windhurst had become trombonist Jack Teagarden's "No. 1
prodigy and protege," while *American Jazz Review* devoted a feature article to fourteen-year-old trombonist Mickey Gravine, explaining that "we
first ran into Mickey when he was playing That's a Plenty along side of
Georg Brunis at Jimmy Ryan's 52nd St. club. George is mighty proud of
his 'protege' and announces Mickey as 'my 14-year old Son.' "[54]

All of this excitement over metaphorical fathers and sons demonstrates how desperate revivalists were to keep New Orleans jazz alive as
its original practitioners passed away and newer styles such as bebop
began to take over the jazz world. Such concerns explain the optimistic, effusive praise that critics lavished on bands such as the Wildcats,
who, while certainly talented and earnest, were at this point unseasoned
adolescents who had yet to prove that they deserved to be crowned the
next Armstrong or Bechet. Critic George Avakian was particularly enthusiastic in asserting that the Wildcats represented the next generation of
authentic jazz. In February 1947, he wrote that "the promise that young
jazz musicians were developing . . . has reached its most important development in the emergence of a closeknit, permanent band which can hold
its own in any league and provides the best music on Sundays at Jimmy
Ryan's." His pointed italics suggest that other young musicians, perhaps
the beboppers, were not truly playing jazz. In June of the same year, in
a review of the Wildcats' records, Avakian proclaimed that "every one of
these kids is fine, and the total effect is the biggest shot in the arm yet
recorded for the future of jazz. With kids like this around, there's hope
for a couple of generations to come." Critic Bob Aurthur commented
similarly in discussing Wilber's inspirational effect on other young musicians: "I think that the people who are worried about replacements for
the present day greats can stop worrying. Reports from all over the country tell us of young bands and of young people who would rather play hot
music than anything else."[55]

Several reports suggested that Bechet himself regarded Wilber in
much the same light. Mary Beckwith argued that "significant of Bob's
worth was the great Sidney Bechet's comment to a concert audience: 'I

hope you like him—he's coming and I'm going.' What Sidney meant, simply enough, is that there'll be someone to take his place when he lays his own horns down for the last time." Art Hodes of *Jazz Record* praised Bechet for having "taken the pains and trouble to see that some youngster carries on the real jazz tradition. Anyone who has heard Bob Wilber play knows that Bechet has done his job well. It remains for Bob to carry on from there. The real jazz will never die as long as master musicians impart their knowledge to willing youngsters." In his autobiography, Wilber takes a similar view of his mentor's aims and implies that the Wildcats took the place of young black musicians who supposedly had abandoned Bechet. "The musical ideals that [Bechet] had stood for all his life were under attack and being ignored by young musicians of his race. Bop was all the rage, and Ryan's was the only traditional-jazz spot left on 52nd Street. Sidney felt all this very acutely, and I think he believed that through this group of young, willing pupils [i.e., the Wildcats] he could perpetuate his musical message." [56]

Although these accounts may describe Bechet's feelings accurately, they also reflect the desire of white traditional jazz enthusiasts to legitimize their pursuits through the authority of a black New Orleans icon. In his autobiography, Bechet does not describe Wilber as the torchbearer for the New Orleans tradition; instead, he tells of Wilber's difficulty in finding a musical voice of his own. Bechet explains that it "is very embarrassing and troublesome to you when you really can't find yourself, you know. [Wilber] would have liked to play Jazz. But he played so close to me that it began to annoy him, because people used to say, 'Oh, that boy, he plays just like Bechet. It's just Bechet playing.'" Bechet suggests that the true spirit of jazz consists not of carrying on a static tradition but of creating something new: "You see, you want something of your own, and it's a pretty tough proposition to get something of your own in America." [57] Contrary to the claims of white critics and musicians, then, Bechet seems to have wished that his protégé speak for himself rather than for the New Orleans tradition.

"See the Pee-Rade": Georg Brunis and Comedy   Ideas of what was acceptable within this tradition, however, varied among white musicians and audiences at Ryan's. While such groups as the Wildcats took a studious approach to re-creating the New Orleans canon, others performed in a casual, comical manner that emphasized relaxed fun over historical accuracy. At the original Onyx Club, as we have seen, informality was seen as a form of resistance to the structured environment of radio studios and the commercial music industry in general. Now, however, a relaxed stage presence was more likely to be viewed as a corrective to the supposed austerity and affectedness of bebop. Comedy and stagecraft, then, persisted as markers of authentic jazz at Ryan's even as many of 52nd Street's younger musicians became increasingly uneasy with roles as popular entertainers.

Probably the most flamboyant entertainer at Ryan's was white trombonist Georg Brunis, whose quintet had a long and successful run at the club from May to December 1946.[58] Brunis's background made him a likely candidate for the canon of authentic jazz upheld at the club. Born in New Orleans in 1902, Brunis was well known among early jazz aficionados as a former member of the New Orleans Rhythm Kings, and he had appeared on 52nd Street as early as 1935, when *Down Beat* referred to him and Wingy Manone as "the last of the old hot men."[59] In his 1946 performances at Ryan's, Brunis balanced Dixieland standards with more experimental fare. *American Jazz Review* explained that "by assuming a 'we're here to please, not to tease' policy, Brunis and his boys have to try anything that is thrown up to them [i.e., requested]."[60] A later report stated that "there isn't a tune written that they won't give a try, hot or sweet, and play well."[61] While Brunis's repertoire included such warhorses as *High Society, Wolverine Blues,* and *Ja-Da,* it also surprisingly encompassed "Chickery-Chick (honest), the rhumba Amor, conga Cacheta, Hey Ba Ba Re Bop (so help us), and, the Tin Roof Blues, complete with the vocal."[62] Brunis's forays into Latin music were merely irrelevant to most contemporary understandings of New Orleans jazz, but his flirtations with popular dance music (*Chickery Chick* was a number one hit for sweet bandleader Sammy Kaye in 1945) and bebop risked offending those listeners who vociferously opposed these styles. Even Brunis's performances of standards were unusual in their brevity. At Brunis's opening performance on May 17, "in the short space of twenty-five minutes, a total of ten numbers (complete) were presented; the first four were played in ten minutes!"[63] While such concision might seem to run counter to a tradition that prized improvisation and spontaneity, the Ryan's audience does not appear to have been put off by Brunis's deviations from convention. *American Jazz Review* praised the band for making even "conga . . . and re-bop . . . come out pretty," and referred to the band's speedy opening set as "something to remember," which was probably meant as a compliment.[64] In June, the magazine reported that "Georg Brunis' fine 'what's coming next?' deluxe band is doing exceptionally well at Jimmy

Ryan's 52nd Street nitery," which suggests that the audience accepted Brunis's irreverence toward tradition in exchange for a less predictable performance.[65]

Even more striking than Brunis's musical style, however, was his broad physical comedy, which recalled the performances of Riley and Farley a decade previous. Brunis had already been clowning on stage for some time; in 1935, for example, *Down Beat* ran a photograph of him playing the trombone with his foot.[66] As Arnold Shaw points out, Brunis developed this and other routines during his long tenure with crowd-pleasing clarinetist Ted Lewis.[67] By 1946, according to Bob Aurthur of *Jazz Record*, "what Georg really wanted was a band and a place to play where the wonderful ham in him could be given full vent."[68] Brunis's comic repertoire by now included imitations of Ted Lewis and Eddie Condon, "hilarious renditions of 'Sister Kate' and 'Ugly Chile,'" and an updated version of the playing-trombone-with-his-foot routine in which he also lay on his back and invited audience members to stand on his stomach ("'But not over a hundred and fifty pounds,' he'd say, 'and no broads with high heels.'")[69] Despite this unusual offer, Brunis's most popular stunt was the parade that he often led through and sometimes beyond the club, recalled here by Ryan's co-owner Matty Walsh.

On certain numbers like "The Saints [Go Marching In]," he'd go parading around the club. Suddenly, he'd stomp outside with Tony Parenti tootling the clarinet behind him, march across the street into the Famous Door or Three Deuces, come marching back and head for the ladies' room. As the audience howled, he'd go parading in and then come out, holding up fingers to indicate the number of women he'd surprised. Of course, as soon as we saw him go marching out of the club, somebody would duck into the ladies' room and clear the place out. The regular visitors to the club knew that there were no women inside. But the occasional customer would laugh himself sick, thinking that Brunis had actually walked in on several unsuspecting women.[70]

Contemporaneous reports support this recollection, although most agree that *High Society* was Brunis's preferred marching tune.[71] In 1946, *American Jazz Review* stated simply that the parade was "really great," while *Jazz Record* reported that "the customers love it."[72] A William Gottlieb photograph taken around August 1946 shows Brunis marching off the stand as what appear to be two sailors seated nearby laugh delightedly.[73] Brunis himself explained that his hamming was calculated to appeal to an audience beyond the coterie of hot jazz aficionados: "as he once explained to a doubting Eddie Condon, 'A lot of guys come in to hear jazz, but how about the poor girls they drag with them?' "[74] When Brunis left Ryan's in December, *Down Beat* claimed that "jazz undergrads and the uninformed, for their part, were more shocked by the absence of Brunis' bouncing personality . . . than they were by the want of his music."[75]

Brunis's theatrics and the audience's approval demonstrate that the Ryan's scene was at times informed by notions of authentic jazz closer to those of the early Onyx Club than to the self-conscious seriousness of many hot jazz revivalists. One such notion, as we have seen, was a perceived link between jazz and an unrestrained white masculinity. The sophomoric, vaguely misogynistic humor of Brunis's parade into the "ladies' room," like his warning to "broads" and his assumption that women might date jazz buffs but were not serious about jazz themselves, demonstrate that the "bachelor subculture" of the old Onyx persisted at Ryan's. Although the parade was a premeditated piece of stage business, its seeming spontaneity and unruliness (several writers pointed out that police on the street opposed it) recalls Riley and Farley's pie-throwing and clothes-ripping antics.[76] Some commentators, however, looked back even farther to find the roots of the parade in old New Orleans. Bob Aurthur argued that "the Pee-rade, by the way, isn't new. It dates back to Georg's first professional jobs as a seven-year old in New Orleans when he advertised prize fights."[77] *American Jazz Review,* while not directly mentioning New Orleans, implied that the parade arose naturally out of the music's original social function: "the boys believe that a parade tune should be paraded to, so they march around the joint."[78] Aurthur wrote that "the kids had picked up Brunis as a substitute for Bunk [Johnson] for their adulation," suggesting that the Ryan's audience was comfortable with Brunis as the representative of a timeless folk tradition.[79] Although a lighthearted comedian such as Brunis might seem to have been an unlikely defender of authentic New Orleans jazz, his acceptance at Ryan's reveals that spontaneous good humor retained its potency as a resistant stance that complemented an iconoclastic, embattled music.

By the mid-1940s, however, the revivalists often saw themselves as resisting 52nd Street itself rather than the larger world of mainstream popular music. Art Hodes, in an August 1946 review of Chicago-style trumpeter Wild Bill Davison at the Keyboard Club, wrote sardonically that "I'd like to know what all the boys on the street think of this foreign invasion. Brunis on one side and Bill on the other. Sacrilege!"[80] Brunis's parade, which brought Dixieland out of the confines of Ryan's into a street purportedly dominated by bebop, at times involved an open assertion of defiance. Drummer Eddie Phyfe remembered that during the summer of 1946 "Georg Brunis took his . . . band and marched across the street playing 'The Saints Go Marching In' to the club where Dizzy was playing one night. Then Dizzy got seventeen guys and marched over to Jimmy Ryan's and played 'Salt Peanuts' or something in the door."[81] This theatrical enactment of the conflict between "moldy figs" and modernists might well have been a publicity stunt by both sides rather than an expression of genuine animosity; a report from around the same time claimed that Gillespie had come to Ryan's to listen to Brunis's band.[82] Nonetheless, this event demonstrates that, at least in the popular imagination, 52nd Street was the site of what *Down Beat* called a "clash of Dixieland and re-bop."[83]

"So Far In, You're Far Out": Musicians and the Jazz War   Although the clash between traditionalists and beboppers was more impassioned in the jazz press than on the street itself, incidents like the battle of the Gillespie and Brunis bands reveal that musicians themselves were to some extent openly involved in this conflict. Gillespie, as the most visible symbol of the bop movement, frequently figured in these battles. In his autobiography, he blamed the jazz war on the inadequacies of older musicians. "The squabble between the boppers and the 'moldy figs' . . . arose because the older musicians insisted on attacking our music and putting it down. Ooooh, they were very much against our music, because it required more than what they were doing. They'd say, 'That music ain't shit, man!' They really did, but then you noticed a few of the older guys started playing our riffs, like Henry 'Red' Allen. The others remained hostile to it."[84] Pianist Johnny Guarnieri had a similar attitude. "Most of us never went to Jimmy Ryan's to listen. The cats there were interlopers who played strictly Dixieland. Today I don't look down on Dixieland the way I did. But to us, jazz was four-beat pulsation and the two-beat thing was old hat. Harmonically, too. We were listening for new sounds and looking for the guys who were coming in with fresh ideas."[85] Leonard Gaskin remembered that 52nd Street musicians who played in opposing styles "did put each other down, more or less," although he thought the disagreements were silly.[86] Dan Morgenstern recalled that the conflict stemmed from social as well as musical considerations. Although "generally speaking, there was quite a bit of interaction" between musicians in various styles, discord arose when older musicians typecast boppers as "junkies" or when boppers attacked the crowd-pleasing manner of their elders:

Among some of the older musicians there was a kind of standoffishness, or—well, the junkies didn't really hang out that much anyway, but there was a definite difference between guys who smoked pot or drank whiskey and the junkies. There was disapproval. It was okay to get high, but the junkie thing was considered by—many of the older musicians thought it was bad for business. And there was also an attitude that the younger musicians would say that . . . we don't want to be entertainers, and the older guys would say, well, we don't want to turn people off by not telling them what tunes we're playing and being more open. So these were generational things.[87]

Beyond occasional open quarrels, personal interactions on 52nd Street between Dixieland and bop musicians often were characterized by apathy or a live-and-let-live attitude. LeRoy Battle recalled that "the beboppers . . . were so wrapped up in themselves" that "they didn't have time to" disparage musicians who played differently. John Robinson, who started his career with a Dixieland band in Atlanta before moving to New York and getting involved with bebop, remembered that the two styles were like "apples and oranges," and that although he rarely attended Jimmy Ryan's, he was not critical of the music played there.[88] Such statements suggest that many musicians did not really view bop and New Orleans as part of the same tradition; to some bop musicians, Dixieland was so foreign that it did not occur to them to criticize it.

Some surprising collaborations, however, indicate that many of 52nd Street's musicians thought otherwise. Stylistic boundaries were sometimes bridged by bop and traditional musicians who simply took the time to listen to one another. Gillespie, for example, went to hear both Brunis at Jimmy Ryan's and Wild Bill Davison at the Keyboard during the summer of 1946.[89] Bob Wilber recalls a telling incident in which Gillespie, rehearsing his big band in a Broadway studio in 1947, dropped in on the Wildcats, who were playing next door. "Eyeing us quizzically, he asked, 'What kinda stuff you guys playin'? Man, that's some crazy shit. You cats are so far in, you're far out!'"[90] Although Gillespie was certainly making fun of the Wildcats, his remarks also imply a grudging respect for the band, perhaps for its dogged tenacity in pursuing a style that, like bebop, was far removed from mainstream taste. Conversely, Wilber took an interest in bebop. He later claimed that although bop and New Orleans "were sort of going in opposite directions and it seemed like all the fans were either going one way or the other and there was no middle ground," he took a different view.

Well, a lot of musicians, including myself, were interested in creative players whether they were playing traditional jazz or the modern jazz of the day. It was all music and we were interested in the creative aspects of it. We used to hang around as kids on 52nd Street in the '40s and we were listening to Sidney Bechet, who would be playing at Jimmy Ryan's, and then we'd go across the street and listen to Charlie Parker and Dizzy Gillespie, who were over at the Deuces . . . I didn't want to get typed as strictly a traditional player.[91]

Wildcats drummer Eddie Phyfe remembered that he had a similar attitude. "There were labels being attached to everybody during that era . . . you know, the 'moldy figs' and the 'sour grapes' and all that nonsense, but they meant absolutely nothing to me. I just played music and most of the people I listened to played anything."[92]

Performers whose music had little in common sometimes formed close friendships. The pioneering African American bop drummer Kenny Clarke remembered that he and white Chicago drummer Dave Tough "were really good friends" who "would always be tramping up and down 52nd Street"; Tough eventually embraced bebop and repudiated Dixieland.[93] Pianist Billy Taylor, who was "excited by the new sounds" of bop on 52nd Street, also remembered his excitement at getting to know the De Paris Brothers.[94]

Wilbur De Paris was a good friend—Wilbur, and his brother Sidney, were good friends of mine. I used to go up there and listen to them, because these were two New Orleans musicians who I liked very much, personally. I didn't know a lot of the older musicians, and these were two . . . who I just took to and who took to me. So I enjoyed them, I would go and talk to them, and both of those guys I found fascinating, because they were both very articulate and they told me things about New Orleans and about other things that I had heard about, but didn't know much about. I asked them a lot of questions. I asked them, you know, "what kind of music did they play when you were a kid?" and all that stuff. . . . This was at the White Rose, or backstage. You know, there was an area where they'd let musicians sit out in the back of the club or something if it wasn't too crowded. And you know, I'd sit out there and talk to them—and everything wasn't a question, these were just men that I respected and that I liked, and they had played with Duke Ellington and

Louis Armstrong, and all these guys, you know. It was an honor to be a young guy who . . . they were comfortable with.[95]

Despite their stylistic differences, Taylor had a clear sense that he and the De Paris Brothers were linked by a common tradition.

In addition to these friendly interactions, unexpected musical crossovers sometimes took place on 52nd Street. Drummer Cliff Leeman, best known in the 1940s for his work with the big bands of Artie Shaw, Charlie Barnet, and Woody Herman, played an unusual engagement at the Famous Door with Ben Webster. Leeman remembered that "the Famous Door wanted to be different from the other clubs on the Street, there was so much bop going on and everything was happening, bop was being flown then . . . so they asked Ben if he wanted to come in with a Dixieland band. I don't think anybody that hears this or any musician was aware of what was happening then. And if they hear this interview, they will certainly get a laugh out of it." [96] Webster assembled a band including Count Basie veterans Buck Clayton (trumpet) and Bennie Morton (trombone); bop pioneer Thelonious Monk was the pianist for one "disaster rehearsal" during which he only deigned to "lean on one elbow and poke a couple of notes." [97] After this inauspicious start, the band opened at the Famous Door with arranged versions of New Orleans standards. "Ben opened with a couple of traditional arrangements. He kind of weakened on the second set, and demanded only an arrangement of 'Muskrat Ramble,' and by the third set, he collected the arrangements and carefully put them under the piano and we never saw them again." [98] Not every attempt at a crossover was unsuccessful, however. Leeman happily remembered performing at Jimmy Ryan's with Sidney Bechet, where the drummer was "lucky to have the ability to go from a Webster oriented group to work with and please a traditional New Orleans legend." [99] Although Leeman's style had been "changing throughout the years to adapt to a more modern technique . . . as the swing era progressed," he modified his playing to suit Bechet: "Of course I did it his way. The ideas of backing Sidney were lots of snare drums, and press rolls, and general New Orleans background. . . . Working with Sidney, to me, became another feather in my cap, and I cherish the memories of working with him, it was a wonderful experience." [100] Although Leeman did not abandon his "modern" pursuits, his respect for Bechet's musicianship led him to bridge the gap with New Orleans jazz.

This kind of mutual respect among 52nd Street's performers was perhaps most apparent at the White Rose bar at the corner of Sixth Avenue, where musicians frequently drank between sets. As we have seen, the White Rose was well known for racial intermingling, and it was also a spot where a wide variety of musicians and fans hung out harmoniously. Critic Leonard Feather, one of the most fervent supporters of bop, thought of Jimmy Ryan's as "foreign territory" and remembered that "the only place where the two worlds met was the White Rose bar." [101] Pianist John Malachi reminisced about meeting his heroes at the White Rose: "Guys would go around there and just drink. And you know, standing next to Art Tatum or whomever, or shaking hands with this one and saying 'Hello' to this one. . . . For a young musician, you really felt like you were into something." [102] Johnny Guarnieri, who rejected Dixieland as "old hat," recalled that "the White Rose bar just around the corner was a neutral meeting ground for all the guys, including those who weren't working. . . . At the White Rose everybody loved everybody, including the Dixieland cats at Jimmy Ryan's. I went there—though I didn't drink—just to be with everybody. It was a wonderful feeling. This was our world and there was love in it." [103]

If 52nd Street was a place where fissures separating competing ideas about race and musical style constantly threatened to erupt, it also supported unusual collaborations between blacks and whites and between bebop and New Orleans musicians. Although such relationships did not heal all of the rifts created by the jazz war, they did suggest to some musicians and listeners that disparate styles formed related parts of a single tradition. Rather than a relentless battle between committed revolutionaries and die-hard reactionaries, the jazz war on 52nd Street involved compromise and consideration as well as disagreement. If the idea of the jazz tradition was the eventual result of consensus among critics, it was also forged by 52nd Street's musicians and audiences in those moments when camaraderie and open-mindedness challenged stylistic and racial difference.

Conclusion **Long May It Be Remembered**

Both contemporaneous observers and subsequent historians saw 1948 as the year when 52nd Street's jazz scene died. Leonard Feather asserted in the April 1948 issue of *Metronome* that, as his headline succinctly put it, "The Street Is Dead." Feather wrote, "Fifty Second Street, unless we are happily mistaken, is on its last legs, and it looks like the end of an era."[1] The cover of the May 1 *New Yorker* was an illustration of the sun setting over 52nd Street.[2] In July, William Gottlieb told *Collier's* readers that "signs of The Street's forthcoming demise are everywhere apparent. . . . One by one, the bright lights are being turned off."[3] By December, a *Down Beat* headline warned, "52nd Street Gasping Last Gasps."[4]

There were several reasons for 52nd Street's decline. Large commercial interests had begun to take over the desirable midtown property. Gottlieb predicted that "by 1950, Rockefeller Center, against which [52nd Street] is timorously snuggled, will have encroached on the southern half of The Street. On the northern half, Lord & Taylor, M-G-M and others will replace the hot trumpets, hot onion soup and hot chorus girls with cold towers of commerce."[5] Feather argued that "lack of talent with sufficient drawing power" as well as "managers and agents who put such a high price on the talent that does have drawing power" were also factors in making the street "moribund."[6] Most commonly, however, observers connected the decline of 52nd Street's jazz scene to its rise as a vice district known for hard drugs and sleazy striptease. The new atmosphere is depicted vividly in *The Strip-Tease Murder Case*, a tawdry 1950 grindhouse movie produced by Arthur Jarwood and Chauncey Olman, each of whom had owned or managed several 52nd Street jazz clubs during the 1940s. The film opens with a montage including murky images of 52nd Street's neon signs, a jazz band inside a club, a drug deal, and a man picking up a woman, over which a hip narrator intones:

This is a story of . . . a street in Manhattan known as Burlesque Boulevard. Now before I bring you up to date on the happenin's of that night, let me tell you a little about the street. Burlesque Boulevard is just a new moniker for a very wise old street. That's right—52nd Street. [At one] time, 52nd Street was known as the Cradle of Swing, for the simple reason that it was well known for giving birth to new ideas in music. As Basin Street in New Orleans, Beale Street in Memphis, and other streets throughout the country where the greatest jazzmen of the times used to congregate. Then the old street changed. Somebody, somewhere, somehow, gave it a new name. They called it Sin Street. Why? Well, if you felt like a bit of misbehavin' was in order, you could latch on to all the needed accessories right on the street. You didn't have a date one night? You merely walked down the street and [whistles] you had a date. You wanted something with more kick than alcohol? Just name it. A little embroidery job with the white stuff? In a flash. And any resemblance to the tea I'm speaking of in Orange Pekoe was strictly accidental. Then the old street became known as Burlesque Boulevard. . . . now, the wise old street is the home of all of New York's burley shows.[7]

Both burlesque and drugs became the targets of legal action. As Feather explained, "the Street's reputation has been blackened by reports of dope raids and arrests, by items in the newspaper columns, and by the associations of some of the musicians."[8] In 1950, three clubs "were under suspension by the State Liquor Authority at the same time" for allowing "indecent performances and exhibitions."[9] Moreover, clubs had increasingly become "clip joints" with what Feather described as "discourteous service and a general how-much-can-we-get-out-of-you-for-how-little attitude towards the customers."[10] In the late 1940s the focus of the midtown jazz scene shifted to such clubs as the Royal Roost (opened about 1945), Bop City (opened 1948), and Birdland (opened 1949), all located on Broadway between 49th and 53rd streets. Although the Hickory House and Jimmy Ryan's continued to offer jazz into the 1960s, 52nd Street's days as a jazz mecca were over.[11]

Even the most astute observer in 1948 might have been skeptical of predictions of the street's demise, however, because images of decline and ruin had already pervaded discussions of 52nd Street for years. As early as 1935, musicians had begun to worry that the presence of a mass audience on the street had destroyed its former status as a musicians' retreat. In 1937, *Down Beat*'s Jack Egan wrote that "Fifty-Second Street is going to the dogs—the latest spot to open on Swing Alley features old time ballads . . . place named Barne's . . . And the payoff is that it's on the site of the old Onyx Club! Sacrilege!" In 1939, the same publication, reporting slow business on the street, stated in a terse heading: "52nd Street Dead." [12] In May 1941, Ruth Sato of *Swing* complained that "every night when we walk to work on 52nd Street we get a sad feeling. . . . Not ONE night club on Swing Street can afford to offer a solid Jazz band to the public." [13] That this claim was published in a month when 52nd Street's array of talent included Billie Holiday, Hot Lips Page, Zutty Singleton, and Stuff Smith suggests that Sato's melancholia was as much part of a long-standing, conventional discourse of decline as it was a reaction to actual conditions. [14] In 1942, reporter Dave Dexter Jr. asserted in a headline that "Swing Street Is Dead" and went on to say, "New York's West 52nd Street is flat on its back. Five and six years ago it blazed with neon light and loud music, played by the greats of American jazz. Today the street is shabby and rundown. . . . [This is a] picture story of the degradation of a thoroughfare once famous, and visited annually by thousands of non–New Yorkers seeking good jazz, excitement and 'atmosphere.'" [15] In 1944, the *New Yorker* reported ironically on the "state of disrepair into which quaint, storied old Fifty-second Street has been allowed to fall." [16] In 1945, Dexter, tacitly acknowledging that the street had not in fact died in 1942, argued in *Metronome* that "West 52nd Street isn't the hip and congenial avenue it once was." *Down Beat* opined in the same year that "part of 52nd street is being razed by housewreckers. And much of the rest is brought down by lack of new talent." [17] The situation looked no better in 1946. *Down Beat* claimed that "these are worrisome days along the street." In the *New Republic,* Charles Miller grumbled that "Fifty-second Street, the stronghold of re-bop, hip characters and the most outrageous clipping I've seen in a long time, is nothing like the Fifty-second Street that once made the word 'jump' mean something." *Hollywood Note* declared that "death, as it must to all things, is coming to Swing Alley." Art Hodes of *Jazz Record* wrote the street's epitaph in his column: "Here's to a street. Long may it be remembered." [18] Taken together, these reports give the paradoxical impression that 52nd Street was in a state of perpetual but never-ending deterioration, with the lamentable decline of one generation becoming the fondly remembered golden age of the next. Although the commentators define the good old days of 52nd Street in various ways, all suggest that the present day is but a pale reflection of past glory.

In short, 52nd Street was viewed across its entire history through a lens of nostalgia. In *The Future of Nostalgia,* cultural critic Svetlana Boym describes this state as "a longing for a home that no longer exists or has never existed." [19] Faced with a modern world that seems to displace individuals and tear apart communities, people who see themselves as oppressed and threatened create an imaginary past to which they long to return. This longing, which denies the realities of historical change and seeks the "creation of a delusionary homeland" where the ruptures of modernity can be healed, Boym terms a "restorative nostalgia." [20] Although nostalgic visions draw their power and appeal from an idealized sense of the past, it is always a past "remade in the image of the present or a desired future." [21] Despite its backward gaze, nostalgia always reflects the concerns of the present.

As much as it celebrated the hip and the new, 52nd Street was also always in the grip of a restorative nostalgia. Its history was marked by a series of attempts to re-create a mythic past that resisted the supposedly artificial, inauthentic present. At the beginning, white musicians who identified modern musicianship with the stifling atmosphere of radio and recording studios sought to enact an image of preindustrial music making that derived from African American models. During the swing era, the object of nostalgia became 52nd Street itself, as public jam sessions tried to evoke the liberating atmosphere of the street's original musicians' clubs during a period of increasing commodification and commercialization. In the 1940s, 52nd Street's nostalgics turned against the street as they aspired to perpetuate an idealized version of New Orleans jazz in the face of musical change and social upheaval. These waves of nostalgia had some positive effects. They encouraged musicians working in idiosyncratic styles to persevere in spite of the indifference or ignorance of the mass audience, and they were grounded in a belief that jazz had the potential to create a supportive, organic community.

Much of 52nd Street's nostalgia, however, reinforced a condescending notion of black musicianship that relegated African American musicians to the role of bearers of racial and musical authenticity. The black musicians of 52nd Street contended with essentialist stereotypes that cast them as paradigms of timeless qualities of spontaneity and natural musicianship rather than as consciously innovative artists. As we have seen, these musicians found creative ways to subvert such stereotypes. Such musicians as Stuff Smith in the 1930s and the bebop musicians of the

1940s asserted the legitimacy of an urban, modern black identity that contradicted the notion of a supposedly unchanging black essence. John Kirby and Maxine Sullivan, in contrast, insisted on being judged on the terms of European concert music and at times attempted to efface racial boundaries altogether. Although such strategies were effective to some degree in undermining nostalgic images of black identity, they could not entirely overcome the racial ideologies that pervaded the street. If 52nd Street's restorative nostalgia helped to create and to preserve jazz, it also perpetuated damaging notions of race.

Today, 52nd Street itself has predictably become the object of nostalgia for wistful jazz lovers who long for the era when its vibrant jazz scene flourished. "Swing Street" is now a symbol of the canon of authentic jazz as well as the archetype of an ideal jazz community, one in which the supposedly universal language of music helped break down racial barriers. There is certainly much to celebrate in the street's history: its moments of interracial interaction and support, the creativity and determination of its musicians, and the resolve often displayed by many of its performers and patrons, both black and white, in resisting racial discrimination remain sources of inspiration and admiration for us today. We should resist the temptation, however, to reduce 52nd Street's story to a utopian vision of racial and musical harmony, or to a morality play in which heroic musicians upheld racial equality and artistic integrity in the face of a racist society and a crass commercial entertainment industry. On 52nd Street, neither racial attitudes nor musical style progressed inexorably toward an inevitable goal but rather were constantly changing in surprising and contradictory ways as musicians and their audiences collaborated and competed to continually redefine the meaning of jazz. In this spirited environment, egregious racial stereotypes coexisted with radical assertions of black identity, and conservative revivalists of traditional jazz walked the street alongside willfully modern hipsters. If 52nd Street's music and culture often led toward new conceptions of race, this was less through moments of dramatic breakthrough than through a long process of negotiation in which racial boundaries were sometimes reinforced, sometimes tested, and sometimes rearranged. There is no simple truth to be heard about jazz and race on 52nd Street. Listening closely, though, reveals that the social significance and cultural resonance of jazz have long been as dynamic, unpredictable, and rich as the music itself.

Appendix **Chronology of 52nd Street Clubs**

The following appendix is organized in two parts: (1) an alphabetical list of 52nd Street's clubs from 1930 to 1950 with their addresses and opening and closing dates, and (2) two time lines that present the same information visually. Whenever possible I have relied upon primary sources in determining dates and addresses. In many cases opening and closing dates were unavailable or had to be extrapolated from vague or contradictory reports; when dates are uncertain I have described my sources and reasoning in the footnotes.

All clubs listed were located on Manhattan's West 52nd Street, with address numbers ranging from 9 through 72 between Fifth and Sixth avenues and from 106 through 150 between Sixth and Seventh; the only exception included here is number 201, which was on the northwest corner of 52nd and Seventh. The list includes only those 52nd Street clubs for which jazz was a primary aspect of their activity. I therefore do not mention clubs that were known mainly for striptease (such as Club Nocturne), for nonjazz cabaret performances (such as Tony's), or for large revues in which jazz was not central (such as Leon & Eddie's.) When a jazz club appears to have switched definitively to a nonjazz policy or vice versa, I make note of this in the alphabetical list, and on the time line I plot only the period during which the club featured jazz. When it is unclear whether or not a club featured jazz, I have made the best judgment possible based on available sources. In ambiguous cases, such as the Famous Door and the Three Deuces, which flipped back and forth from burlesque to jazz during the late 1940s, or the Orchid, where strippers often were accompanied by jazz musicians, I normally have opted to include the clubs and dates in question.

Alphabetical List

Each club name is followed by alternate names or spellings, if any (in parentheses), and the club's address, with "West 52nd Street" abbreviated as "W 52." Roman numerals are used when the same name was used at multiple addresses.

Band Box (Bandbox) 20 W 52
    opened November 9, 1938[1]
    closed ca. April 1939[2]

Cafe Maria 35 W 52
    opened sometime after May 10, 1936[3]
    closed December 1937[4]

Caliente 66 W 52
    opened March 8, 1936[5]
    closed ca. May 1937[6]

Casino Deluxe 35 W 52
    opened in 1934 or 1935[7]
    closed before March 1, 1935[8]

Club 18
    I: 18 W 52, 20 W 52, 131 W 52
    opened at 18 W 52 ca. June 1936[9]
    switched from jazz to comedy ca. August 1936[10]
    moved to 20 W 52 on April 13, 1939[11]
    moved to 131 W 52 ca. 1945[12]
    closed sometime before October 7, 1946[13]

    II: 131 W 52
    opened sometime between May 7, 1947, and May 21, 1947[14]
    closed sometime between July 16, 1947, and August 8, 1947[15]

III: 131 W 52
opened sometime after October 8, 1947[16]
closed sometime before October 22, 1947[17]

Dixon's 131 W 52
opened as a jazz club October 7, 1946[18]
closed sometime between May 7, 1947, and May 21, 1947[19]

Dizzy Club (Lou Richman's Dizzy Club) 64 W 52
opened sometime before March 27, 1937[20]
closed sometime after May 31, 1939[21]

Downbeat 66 W 52
opened May 1944[22]
closed between March 15, 1947, and March 26, 1947[23]
reopened June 1947[24]
closed ca. February 1948[25]

Famous Door
I: 35 W 52
opened March 1, 1935[26]
closed week of May 10, 1936[27]

II: 66 W 52
opened November 30, 1937[28]
closed June 12, 1940[29]
reopened September 25, 1940[30]

III: 201 W 52
moved to this address on October 28, 1943[31]
closed ca. early January 1944[32]

IV: 56 W 52
opened ca. December 1946[33]
closed January 1950[34]

52nd Street Club 66 W 52
opened sometime after May 1937
closed sometime before November 30, 1937[35]

Flamingo 38 W 52
"active in the 1940s": became a striptease club in the 1950s[36]

Bert Frohman's 54 W 52[37]
opened ca. April 1939[38]
closed sometime after June 1939[39]

Hickory House 144 W 52
opened 1933[40]
began to feature jazz August 6, 1935[41]
closed 1968[42]

Jimmy Ryan's 53 W 52
opened September 1940[43]
moved to 154 W 54 in 1962[44]

Kelly's Stable 137 W 52
moved to 137 W 52 from 141 W 51 the first week of March 1940[45]
closed January 6, 1947[46]

Key Club 18 W 52
opened June 1939[47]
closed June or July 1939[48]

Keyboard 54 W 52
opened November 15, 1945[49]
switched to burlesque ca. August 1946[50]

Little Club 72 W 52
opened ca. November 1938[51]
closed during or after May 1939[52]

Mammy's Chicken Farm (Mama's Chicken Shack, Mammy's Chicken Fry,
Mammy's Chicken Koop, Mammy's Chicken Shack) 60 W 52
opened sometime before June 27, 1937[53]
closed sometime after January 20, 1940[54]

McKenzie's (Red McKenzie's) 54 W 52
opened ca. November 1936[55]
closed ca. January 1937[56]

O'Leary's Barn 137 W 52
    opened sometime before May 1939[57]
    closed ca. July 1939[58]

Onyx[59]
    I: 35 W 52
    opened between 1927 and 1930[60]

    II: 72 W 52
    moved to this address February 1934[61]
    closed February 28, 1935[62]
    reopened July 23, 1935[63]

    III: 62 W 52
    moved to this address between March 13 and March 20, 1937[64]
    closed last week of December 1939[65]

    IV: 57 W 52
    opened June 1942[66]
    closed June 1946[67]
    reopened July 1947[68]
    closed December 1948[69]

Orchid (Black Orchid, Orchid Room) 57 W 52
    opened 1949[70]
    closed sometime after 1950[71]

Plantation Club 72 W 52
    opened sometime before June 1, 1943[72]
    closed June 1943[73]

Samoa 62 (or 60?) W 52[74]
    opened ca. 1940 or 1941[75]
    became a striptease club in 1943[76]
    closed ca. late 1950s–1960[77]

Spotlite 56 W 52
    opened ca. November 1944[78]
    closed ca. December 1946[79]

Swing Club 35 W 52
    opened December 1937[80]
    closed sometime after September 13, 1940[81]

Three Deuces 72 W 52[82]
    opened June 1943[83]
    closed August 1953[84]

Through the Looking Glass (Thru the Looking Glass): address unknown[85]
    opened October 10, 1935[86]
    closed sometime after July 1936[87]

Tillie's Kitchen (Tillie's Chicken Shack, Tillie's Restaurant) 106 W 52
    opened fall 1935[88]
    stopped employing musicians ca. June 1936[89]

Tondelayo's 18 W 52
    opened sometime before August 19, 1944[90]
    closed sometime after April 1945[91]

Torch Club 18 W 52
    opened sometime before February 1, 1940[92]
    switched from jazz to comedy in June 1940[93]

Town Casino 9 W 52
    opened ca. October 1933[94]
    closed ca. October 1936[95]

Troc (Trocadero)
    I: 53 W 52
    opened November 1, 1938[96]
    closed sometime between March 1, 1940, and September 1940[97]

    II: 60 W 52
    opened January 29, 1943[98]
    may have closed ca. June 1944[99]

Troubadour 131 W 52
    opened August 8, 1947[100]
    closed September 24, 1947[101]

Two O'Clock Club (Performers and Musicians Guild) 201 W 52
    opened ca. October 1942[102]
    closed spring 1943[103]

Yacht Club (Hawaiian Yacht Club)
    I: 38 W 52
    opened ca. 1933 or 1934[104]

    II: 150 W 52
    moved to this address in early October 1937[105]

    III: 66 W 52
    moved to this address ca. September 1943[106]
    closed May 1944[107]

Graphs

The information in the foregoing list is displayed in the two graphs that follow (figures 3 and 4). Rows refer to street addresses, labeled on the vertical axis at the left, while columns represent dates, labeled on the horizontal axis across the bottom. In order to keep the graph concise and uncluttered, I have opted not to write out precise dates here. Question marks indicate instances in which I have confirmed some definite dates for a club's operation but cannot give a specific opening or closing date. Wavy lines represent instances in which I am less certain about when the club was in operation.

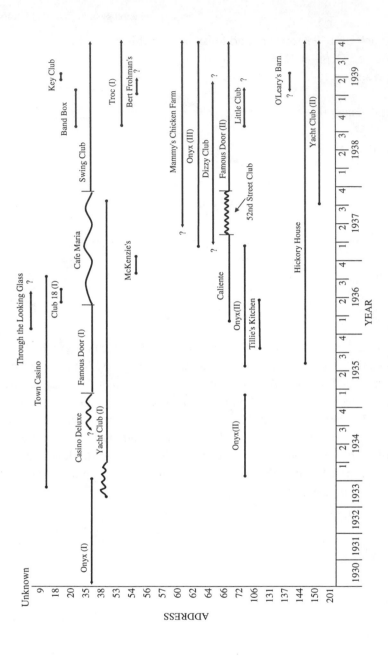

Figure 3. 52nd Street Jazz Clubs, 1930–1939

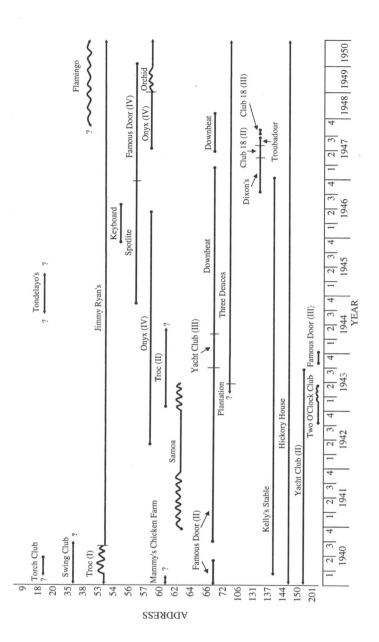

Figure 4. 52nd Street Jazz Clubs, 1940–1950

Notes

Introduction

Epigraph from Robert Sylvester, *Notes of a Guilty Bystander* (Englewood Cliffs, NJ: Prentice-Hall, 1970), 253.

1. Leonard Feather, "New York Roundup: Dizzy Gillespie," *Metronome* 62, no. 7 (July 1946): 20.

2. "Brunis at Ryan's," *American Jazz Review* 2, no. 9 (July 1946): 1.

3. "Jazz Uptown," *American Jazz Review* 2, no. 9 (July 1946): 4.

4. "I Thought I Heard . . . ," *Jazz Record*, no. 46 (July 1946): 2; "New York Night Spots," [*Rhythm?*], July 1946, 31, box 2, folder 2/3, Bob Howard Papers, Manuscripts, Archives and Rare Books Division, Schomburg Center for Research in Black Culture, New York Public Library.

5. Arnold Shaw, *52nd Street: The Street of Jazz* (New York: Da Capo, 1977). Originally published as *The Street That Never Slept: New York's Fabled 52nd Street* (New York: Coward, McCann & Geoghegan, 1971).

6. Shaw, *52nd Street*, x; Ira Gitler, *Swing to Bop: An Oral History of the Transition in Jazz in the 1940s* (New York: Oxford University Press, 1985), 141.

7. Lewis A. Erenberg, *Swingin' the Dream: Big Band Jazz and the Rebirth of American Culture* (Chicago: University of Chicago Press, 1998), 159.

8. David W. Stowe, *Swing Changes: Big-Band Jazz in New Deal America* (Cambridge, MA: Harvard University Press, 1994), 163.

9. Scott DeVeaux, "Constructing the Jazz Tradition: Jazz Historiography," *Black American Literature Forum* 25, no. 3 (1991): 525–60.

10. See, for example, the foundational collection edited by Henry Louis Gates Jr., *"Race," Writing, and Difference* (Chicago: University of Chicago Press, 1986).

11. Ronald Radano and Philip V. Bohlman, "Introduction: Music and Race, Their Past, Their Presence," in *Music and the Racial Imagination,* ed. Radano and Bohlman (Chicago: University of Chicago Press, 2000), 2, 7–8.

12. Ted Gioia, *The Imperfect Art: Reflections on Jazz and Modern Culture* (Stanford, CA: Stanford Alumni Association, 1988), 30–31.

13. Regina Bendix, *In Search of Authenticity: The Formation of Folklore Studies* (Madison: University of Wisconsin Press, 1997), 16. John Gennari and Ted Gioia both have discussed Rousseau's primitivism in connection with early jazz criticism (John Remo Gennari, "Jazz Criticism: Its Development and Ideologies," *Black American Literature Forum* 25, no. 3 [fall 1991]: 466; Gioia, *Imperfect Art,* 21).

14. George M. Fredrickson, *The Black Image in the White Mind: The Debate on Afro-American Character and Destiny, 1817–1914* (New York: Harper & Row, 1971), 101.

15. See Eric Lott, *Love and Theft: Blackface Minstrelsy and the American Working Class* (New York: Oxford University Press, 1993); and David R. Roediger, *The Wages of Whiteness: Race and the Making of the American Working Class* (London: Verso, 1991), each of which I address in more detail in chapter 1.

16. Ronald Radano, "Denoting Difference: The Writing of the Slave Spirituals," *Critical Inquiry* 22, no. 3 (Spring 1996): 511, 526–44; also see Benjamin Filene, *Romancing the Folk: Public Memory & American Roots Music* (Chapel Hill: University of North Carolina Press, 2000), 27–29; Bendix, *In Search of Authenticity,* 91–93.

17. Marianna Torgovnick, *Gone Primitive: Savage Intellects, Modern Lives* (Chicago: University of Chicago Press, 1990), 85–104.

18. Gioia, *Imperfect Art,* 28–31.

19. Filene, *Romancing the Folk,* 52.

20. Ibid., 59.

21. Francis Davis, *The History of the Blues* (New York: Hyperion, 1995), 169.

22. Mel Watkins, *On the Real Side: Laughing, Lying, and Signifying—The Underground Tradition of African-American Humor That Transformed American Culture, from Slavery to Richard Pryor* (New York: Touchstone, 1994), 52.

23. W. E. Burghardt Du Bois, *The Souls of Black Folk* (1903; repr., New York: Signet Classic, 1969), 45.

24. Houston A. Baker Jr., *Modernism and the Harlem Renaissance* (Chicago: University of Chicago Press, 1987), 47–52.

25. Ibid., 80.

26. Alain Locke, *The Negro and His Music* (Washington, DC: Associates in Negro Folk Education, 1936), 72, 130.

27. Burton W. Peretti, *The Creation of Jazz: Music, Race, and Culture in Urban America* (Urbana: University of Illinois Press, Illini Books, 1994), 72.

28. Sociologist Paul Lopes has recently argued similarly that the "jazz art world" should be viewed as a "socially heterogeneous community" whose members "actively transformed the meaning and practice of jazz as they collectively engaged in the production and consumption of this music." Paul Lopes, *The Rise of a Jazz Art World* (Cambridge: Cambridge University Press, 2002), 277.

29. Scott DeVeaux, *The Birth of Bebop: A Social and Musical History* (Berkeley and Los Angeles: University of California Press, 1997), 23.

Chapter One

1. For the Keller recordings, see Brian A. L. Rust, *The Complete Entertainment Discography from the Mid-1890s to 1942*, 2nd ed. (New York: Da Capo, 1989), 444. Klein is quoted in Arnold Shaw, *52nd Street: The Street of Jazz* (New York: Da Capo, 1977), 75. Joe Venuti and Friends, *Onyx Club Revue (No. 1)*, matrix T01253, recorded January 24, 1933, New York, reissued on *The Classic Columbia and Okeh Joe Venuti and Eddie Lang Sessions*, Mosaic CD MD8-213. I thank John Clement and Vincent Pelote of the Institute of Jazz Studies, Rutgers University–Newark for bringing this reissue to my attention.

2. Both whiteness and masculinity have recently become the subjects of growing bodies of jazz scholarship. Most studies of whiteness in jazz, including important essays by Ingrid Monson and Robert K. McMichael, have focused on white hipsters of the bebop era and their successors, with discussions of earlier jazz confined largely to the racial boundary crossing of the colorful clarinetist Mezz Mezzrow. On bebop and later jazz, see Ingrid Monson, "The Problem with White Hipness: Race, Gender and Cultural Conceptions in Jazz Historical Discourse," *Journal of the American Musicological Society* 48, no. 3 (Fall 1995): 396–422; Robert K. McMichael, "'We Insist—Freedom Now!': Black Moral Authority, Jazz, and the Changeable Shape of Whiteness," *American Music* 16, no. 4 (Winter 1998): 375–416; Andrew Ross, "Hip, and the Long Front of Color," in *No Respect: Intellectuals and Popular Culture* (New York: Routledge, 1989), 65–101; Jon Panish, *The Color of Jazz: Race and Representation in Postwar American Culture* (Jackson: University Press of Mississippi, 1997). On Mezzrow, see Gayle Wald, "Mezz Mezzrow and the Voluntary Negro Blues," in *Race and the Subject of Masculinities*, ed. Harry Stecopoulos and Michael Uebel, 116–37 (Durham, NC: Duke University Press, 1997); Monson, "Problem with White Hipness," 402–3; Panish, *Color of Jazz*, 52–55; Scott Saul, *Freedom Is, Freedom Ain't: Jazz and the Making of the Sixties* (Cambridge, MA: Harvard University Press, 2002), 40–55; and Mezzrow's autobiography, which incorporates an essay by coauthor Bernard Wolfe (Milton "Mezz" Mezzrow and Bernard Wolfe, *Really the Blues* [1946; repr., New York: Citadel, 1990]). Other studies of whiteness in jazz discourse include three works by Nicholas M. Evans: *Writing Jazz: Race, Nationalism and Modern Culture in the 1920s* (New York: Garland, 2000); "Jazz, Minstrelsy, and White-American Blues," *Minnesota Review* 47 (Fall 1996): 81–91; and "'Racial Cross-Dressing' in the Jazz Age: Cultural Therapy and Its Discontents in Cabaret Nightlife," in *Hop on Pop: The Politics and Pleasures of Popular Culture*, ed. Henry Jenkins, Tara McPherson, and Jane Shattuc, 388–414 (Durham, NC: Duke University Press, 2002), which examines white appropriations of black culture during the 1920s and involves a brief discussion of some of the musicians whom I address here. Sherrie Tucker sardonically refers to scholarship on masculinity in jazz as "Miles Davis

Studies" due to the abundance of scholarship on the trumpeter's relation to gender issues (Sherrie Tucker, "Big Ears: Listening for Gender in Jazz Studies," *Current Musicology* 71–73 [Spring 2001–Spring 2002]: 389). Studies of Davis include Hazel Carby, *Race Men* (Cambridge, MA: Harvard University Press, 1998), 135–68; Gerald Early, "On Miles Davis, Vince Lombardi, and the Crisis of Masculinity in Mid-Century America," *Daedalus* 131, no. 1 (Winter 2002): 154–59; Farah Jasmine Griffin, "Ladies Sing Miles," in *Miles Davis and American Culture*, ed. Gerald Early (St. Louis: Missouri Historical Society Press, 2001): 180–87; Pearl Cleage, "Mad at Miles," in *Deals with the Devil and Other Reasons to Riot* (New York: Ballantine, 1993), 36–43. Other discussions of masculinity in jazz include David Ake, "Re-Masculating Jazz: Ornette Coleman, 'Lonely Woman,' and the New York Jazz Scene in the Late 1950s," *American Music* 16, no. 1 (Spring 1998): 25–44; Nichole T. Rustin, "Mingus Fingers: Charles Mingus, Black Masculinity, and Postwar Jazz Culture" (PhD diss., New York University, 1999); Monique Guillory, " 'Black Bodies Swingin': Race, Gender, and Jazz," in *Soul: Black Power, Politics, and Pleasure*, ed. Monique Guillory and Richard C. Green, 191–215 (New York: New York University Press, 1998); Krin Gabbard, "Signifyin(g) the Phallus: *Mo' Better Blues* and Representations of the Jazz Trumpet," in *Representing Jazz*, ed. Krin Gabbard, 104–30 (Durham, NC: Duke University Press, 1995); Krin Gabbard, "Louis Armstrong's Life as a Man," *Chronicle of Higher Education*, June 30, 2000, B9–B10; Eric Porter, *What Is This Thing Called Jazz? African American Musicians as Artists, Critics, and Activists* (Berkeley and Los Angeles: University of California Press, 2002), 138–47. The discussions of white masculinity in jazz that are most pertinent to my argument here are Monson, "Problem with White Hipness," and Wald, "Mezz Mezzrow," both of which reflect on the ways in which white men have drawn on perceptions of black music and culture in order to construct a new or heightened sense of masculinity. Here, I follow the lead of these scholars by examining the intersection of race and gender at the Onyx Club. In addressing white musicians of the 1930s, I do not mean to argue that they have been unfairly excluded from the jazz canon or neglected in jazz scholarship, a position taken by Richard M. Sudhalter in *Lost Chords: White Musicians and Their Contributions to Jazz, 1915–1945* (New York: Oxford University Press, 1999), xv–xxii. Rather, it is because these musicians are in fact central to both public perceptions of jazz and most historical narratives of the swing era that it is crucial to understand their relationship to issues of race and gender. In addition to Sudhalter's work, studies that address white musicians of the pre–World War II era include Gunther Schuller, *The Swing Era: The Development of Jazz, 1930–1945* (New York: Oxford University Press, 1989), 3–45, 632–769; Burton W. Peretti, *The Creation of Jazz: Music, Race, and Culture in Urban America* (Urbana: University of Illinois Press, 1992), 76–99; Neil Leonard, *Jazz and the White Americans: The Acceptance of a New Art Form* (Chicago: University of Chicago Press, 1962), 52–72; Dave Oliphant, *The Early Swing Era, 1930 to 1941* (Westport, CT: Greenwood Press, 2002), 97–146, 262–323; William Howland Kenney, *Chicago Jazz: A Cultural History, 1904–1930* (New York: Oxford University Press, 1993), 61–116.

3. Burton W. Peretti argues similarly of white Chicago musicians of the 1920s that "minstrel stereotypes shaped the Chicagoans' perception even as they consciously admired and emulated the black musicians they encountered on the South Side" (Peretti, *Creation of Jazz*, 190). Many of the white musicians to whom Peretti refers later became regular patrons of the Onyx after moving to New York. Peretti's discussion of these musicians generally assumes that their white identities were stable, and it focuses on the degree to which they embraced or misunderstood black music and culture; here, I build on the implications of his work by suggesting that shifting notions of white identity were themselves constituted through such interracial interactions.

4. On the opening date of the Onyx, see note 60 to the appendix. The police commissioner's estimate is cited in John Kobler, *Ardent Spirits: The Rise and Fall of Prohibition* (1973; repr., New York: Da Capo, 1993), 223–24. On Benchley, see Shaw, *52nd Street*, 9; Kobler, *Ardent Spirits*, 225. As of 2007, the 21 Club is still in operation at 21 West 52nd Street; profiles of the club include Marilyn Kaytor, *"21": The Life and Times of New York's Favorite Club* (New York: Viking, 1975); Shaw, *52nd Street*, 23–35; Al Hirschfeld, *Manhattan Oases: New York's 1932 Speak-easies* (New York: E. P. Dutton, 1932), 16–17; *The Iron Gate of Jack & Charlie's '21'* (New York: n.p., 1936). Lloyd Morris writes that the 21 Club had a "dance floor with orchestra" during Prohibition (Lloyd Morris, *Incredible New York: High Life and Low Life from 1850 to 1950* [1951; repr., Syracuse: Syracuse University Press, 1996], 326), but none of the sources cited previously mention this. For the Committee of Fourteen report, see typescript "Night Clubs and Speakeasies Located on Numbered Streets," 41–42, folder "Inv. Reports—Night Clubs on Numbered Streets," box 37, Committee of Fourteen Records, Manuscripts and Archives Division, The New York Public Library, Astor, Lenox, and Tilden Foundations. On the Yacht Club, Shaw, *52nd Street*, 178. On Morgan's club, Shaw, *52nd Street*, 199; Jimmy Durante and Jack Kofoed, *Night Clubs* (New York: Alfred A. Knopf, 1931), 66. Durante and Kofoed write that "Helen Morgan's Summer Home" was "a roof garden, on 52nd St." that opened in spring 1929, and that Morgan "received a padlock and a personal injunction" from the police soon thereafter. I have not determined the exact address of this club. Sylvester's recollections are found in Robert Sylvester, *Notes of a Guilty Bystander* (Englewood Cliffs, NJ: Prentice-Hall, 1970), 244. Sylvester does not cite a source for this information; he began working as a journalist in New York in 1928, so it is possible that he was writing from personal experience (Robert Sylvester, *No Cover Charge: A Backward Look at the Night Clubs* [New York: Dial, 1956], dust jacket). Both Tony's and Leon & Eddie's persisted as legitimate nightclubs after the repeal of Prohibition; here, I cite only sources that refer specifically to the speakeasy era. On Leon & Eddie's, see Louis Sobol, *The Longest Street: A Memoir* (New York: Crown, 1968), 67–68; Shaw, *52nd Street*, 41–43; Maurice Zolotow, "The Night-Club Business," *American Mercury* 55, no. 226 (October 1942): 418. On Tony's, see Hirschfeld, *Manhattan Oases*, 36–37; Shaw, *52nd Street*, 174–75; Bill Gottlieb, "Good-Time Street," *Collier's* 122, no. 1 (July 3, 1948): 25, 48. I have been unable

to locate a reference that explicitly states that Soma sang while standing on his head during Prohibition, although it seems plausible enough; for a photograph of him performing the feat in the 1940s, see Gottlieb, "Good-Time Street," 25.

5. Ric Burns and James Sanders, *New York: An Illustrated History* (New York: Alfred A. Knopf, 1999), 338–39.

6. Ibid., 342; Robert Campbell, *The Golden Years of Broadcasting: A Celebration of the First 50 Years of Radio and TV on NBC* (New York: Rutledge, 1976), 29; Robert Slater, *This . . . Is CBS: A Chronicle of 60 Years* (Englewood Cliffs, NJ: Prentice Hall, 1988), 8, 16–17.

7. Samuel B. Charters and Leonard Kunstadt, *Jazz: A History of the New York Scene* (Garden City, NY: Doubleday, 1962), 185; also see Lewis A. Erenberg, *Steppin' Out: New York Nightlife and the Transformation of American Culture, 1890–1930* (Westport, CT: Greenwood Press, 1981), 241–46.

8. Burns and Sanders, *New York,* 372–82; Eric Homberger, *The Historical Atlas of New York City* (New York: Henry Holt, 1994), 142–43.

9. Wilder Hobson, "Fifty-second Street," in *Jazzmen,* ed. Frederic Ramsey Jr. and Charles Edward Smith (1939; repr., New York: Liveright Editions, 1985), 249–50.

10. Jimmy McPartland, interview by Helen Armstead Johnson, New York, 1972, transcript, 139, National Endowment for the Arts Jazz Oral History Project (hereafter cited as JOHP), Institute of Jazz Studies, Rutgers University–Newark; Eddie Condon with Thomas Sugrue, *We Called It Music: A Generation of Jazz* (1947; repr., New York: Da Capo, 1992), 196–99; Shaw, *52nd Street,* 53; Hoagy Carmichael with Stephen Longstreet, *Sometimes I Wonder: The Story of Hoagy Carmichael* (New York: Farrar, Straus and Giroux, 1965), 206. Carmichael does not name the club here, but his description of a "musicians' speak-easy on Fifty-second Street that was a hangout for us, an upstairs smelly place" certainly refers to the Onyx.

11. This list is compiled from Paul Douglas, "Oh Say Can You Swing," *Stage* 15, no. 7 (April 1938): 38–39; Egan, "Oasis of Swing"; Hobson, "Fifty-second Street," 249–50; Willie the Lion Smith with George Hoefer, *Music on My Mind: The Memoirs of an American Pianist* (Garden City, NY: Doubleday, 1964), 203–4. Arnold Shaw adds pianist Frank Signorelli to the list, although he does not cite a source (Shaw, *52nd Street,* 63). As I address subsequently, pianists Willie "the Lion" Smith and Art Tatum are the only African American musicians not paid a salary by Helbock who are known to have played at the Prohibition-era Onyx (and both of them eventually became paid employees); other black musicians hired to work at the club include the Spirits of Rhythm and Charlie Bourne (Hobson, "Fifty-second Street," 250; Shaw, *52nd Street,* 67).

12. Charters and Kunstadt, *Jazz,* 145–51; on "hot soloists," see Marshall W. Stearns, *The Story of Jazz* (London: Oxford University Press, 1956), 180.

13. Kenney, *Chicago Jazz,* 150–53, 160–61; Charters and Kunstadt, *Jazz,* 159–60.

14. Charters and Kunstadt, *Jazz,* 159–60; David W. Stowe, *Swing Changes: Big-Band Jazz in New Deal America* (Cambridge, MA: Harvard University Press, 1994), 133.

15. Peretti, *Creation of Jazz*, 167.

16. Ibid.

17. Burton Peretti claims that "the radio network jobs were the best paying in the jazz world" (ibid., 162), while Charters says of recording that "the money was very good, better than they could have gotten doing anything else" (Charters and Kunstadt, *Jazz*, 261).

18. Charters and Kunstadt, *Jazz*, 262–63.

19. Shaw, *52nd Street*, 64.

20. Ibid., 59–60; Egan, "Oasis of Swing."

21. Howard Chudacoff, *The Age of the Bachelor: Creating an American Subculture* (Princeton, NJ: Princeton University Press, 1999), 109–14, 224–40; also see Madelon Powers, *Faces Along the Bar: Lore and Order in the Workingman's Saloon, 1870–1920* (Chicago: University of Chicago Press, 1998); Roy Rosenzweig, *Eight Hours for What We Will: Workers and Leisure in an Industrial City, 1870–1920* (Cambridge: Cambridge University Press, 1983), 53–64. In some instances saloons were important gathering places for gay men, and by 1930 many speakeasies in New York, particularly in Greenwich Village and Harlem, catered to a gay clientele (Chudacoff, *Age of the Bachelor*, 114–15; George Chauncey, *Gay New York: Gender, Urban Culture, and the Making of the Gay Male World, 1890–1940* [New York: Basic Books, 1994], 227–67). Although I have found no evidence of an open gay presence at the Onyx, this could be a result of underreporting; as Burton Peretti points out, "homosexuality . . . is almost never mentioned in early or recent jazz narratives," although it appears in "the most candid sources" (Peretti, *Creation of Jazz*, 125). Nonetheless, Peretti argues that "early jazz players certainly did *not* foster a notable oasis of experimentation and tolerance [toward gays] in modern urban America, as the ranks of art-music composers and other occupations did at this time" (ibid., 126).

22. Profiles of Helbock include Douglas, "Oh Say Can You Swing"; Egan, "Oasis of Swing"; George Hoefer, "Father of the Street: Onyx Days Recalled," *Down Beat's Music '66: 11th Yearbook,* special edition, *Down Beat* 33 (1966): 90–96, 107–9; Shaw, *52nd Street*, 52–58; Herb Shultz, "The Life and Death of Jazz Street" (typescript, in the collection of the author, n.d.), 7–10. I thank Herb Shultz for providing me with a copy of the latter source. Helbock's central role in establishing 52nd Street as a center for jazz music has often been noted: Douglas writes that "Joe Helbock had more to do with swing music, as it flourishes today, than all the short-haired Toscaninis put together" ("Oh Say Can You Swing," 38), while Hoefer refers to him as the "Father of the Street."

23. Douglas, "Oh Say Can You Swing," 38.

24. Chudacoff, *Age of the Bachelor.*

25. Powers, *Faces Along the Bar,* 46.

26. Ibid., 30–32; also see Kathy Peiss, *Cheap Amusements: Working Women and Leisure in Turn-of-the-Century New York* (Philadelphia: Temple University Press, 1986), 27–28.

27. Frank Victor, "Who's Who among Guitarists: This Time It's Carl Kress," *Metronome* 49, no. 10 (October 1933): 32.

28. Douglas, "Oh Say Can You Swing," 39.

29. Manny Klein, interview by Bruce Talbot, Los Angeles, October 9, 1992, cassette recording, tape 1, side 1, JOHP (but note that this interview is housed at the National Museum of American History, Smithsonian Institution, Washington, DC, rather than at the Institute of Jazz Studies.)

30. Shaw, *52nd Street,* 76.

31. David Montgomery, *Workers' Control in America: Studies in the History of Work, Technology, and Labor Struggles* (Cambridge: Cambridge University Press, 1979), 26.

32. Ibid., 14.

33. Ibid., 114.

34. Ibid., 98, 116.

35. Michael Denning, *The Cultural Front: The Laboring of American Culture in the Twentieth Century* (London: Verso, 1996), 42.

36. C. Wright Mills, "The Cultural Apparatus," in *Power, Politics and People: The Collected Essays of C. Wright Mills,* ed. Irving Louis Horowitz (New York: Ballantine, 1963), 418–19, quoted in Denning, *Cultural Front,* 49.

37. See, for example, Robin D. G. Kelley, "Without a Song: New York Musicians Strike Out against Technology," in *Three Strikes: Miners, Musicians, Salesgirls, and the Fighting Spirit of Labor's Last Century,* by Howard Zinn, Dana Frank, and Robin D. G. Kelley, 119–55 (Boston: Beacon, 2001), which addresses Local 802's 1936 picketing campaign against movie theaters.

38. Powers, *Faces Along the Bar,* 54.

39. Charters and Kunstadt, *Jazz,* 261, 265; Benny Goodman and Irving Kolodin, *The Kingdom of Swing* (New York: Stackpole Sons, 1939), 101.

40. Klein interview, tape 1, side 1.

41. Thanks to Karl Hagstrom Miller for this suggestion.

42. Egan, "Oasis of Swing."

43. Douglas, "Oh Say Can You Swing," 39.

44. Goodman and Kolodin, *Kingdom of Swing,* 123.

45. Egan, "Oasis of Swing."

46. Douglas, "Oh Say Can You Swing," 39.

47. Peretti, *Creation of Jazz,* 92. A similar argument is made in Leonard, *Jazz and White Americans,* 52–68. Also see Neil Leonard, "Some Further Thoughts on Jazzmen as Romantic Outsiders," *Journal of Jazz Studies* 2, no. 2 (June 1975): 43–46, for a comparison of the values of white Chicago musicians of the 1920s and those of literary modernists such as Hart Crane and E. E. Cummings.

48. Peretti, *Creation of Jazz,* 91–93, 126.

49. Shaw, *52nd Street,* 75; liner notes for Mosaic CD MD8-213, 43.

50. Shaw, *52nd Street,* 75. Another "underground" record made by "Joe Venuti & Friends" includes a parody of "Rudy Smelly" (*Onyx Club Record,* matrix TO 1389, March 6, 1934). Other such recordings made by this group of musicians include

Non Skid Manure, a scatological satire of radio advertising (matrix TO 1293, April 8, 1933), and *Venuti's Pagliacci No. 2,* a satire of opera (matrix 14444-A, December 12, 1933). All of these recordings are reissued on Mosaic CD MD8–213.

51. On crooning and masculinity, see Allison McCracken, "'God's Gift to Us Girls': Crooning, Gender, and the Re-Creation of American Popular Song, 1928–1933," *American Music* 17, no. 4 (Winter 1999): 365–91.

52. In *Venuti's Pagliacci No. 2, St. Louis Blues* is pitted against high culture rather than middlebrow entertainment. The recording opens with the band playing *St. Louis Blues,* until Venuti, portraying a pompous opera singer, interjects, "Gentlemen, please! You're playing the wrong kind of music! . . . What is this? . . . Gentlemen, you're playing the wrong music for me! I want to sing my *Allegro con brio!*"

53. On the blues craze in New York, see Charters and Kunstadt, *Jazz,* 83–92. Louis Armstrong & His Orchestra, *St. Louis Blues,* Okeh 41350, matrix W.493495-B, recorded December 13, 1929, New York, reissued on *Louis Armstrong, Vol. 6: St. Louis Blues* (Capitol CD CK46996). John Edward Hasse, *Beyond Category: The Life and Genius of Duke Ellington* (New York: Simon & Schuster, 1993), 106. On the recording session at which Miley played with members of the Onyx circle, see Oliphant, *Early Swing Era,* 5–8.

54. Irving Mills and His Hotsy Totsy Gang, *Deep Harlem,* matrix E-32949-A, Brunswick 4983, recorded June 6, 1930, New York, reissued on *Benny Goodman and Jack Teagarden, B.G. and Big Tea in NYC* (Decca/GRP CD GRD-609); The Dorsey Brothers' Orchestra, *Old Man Harlem,* matrix B-13426-A, Brunswick 6624, recorded June 8, 1933, New York, reissued on *The Essential Dorsey Brothers 1928–1935* (Collectors' Choice Music CD CCM-098-2).

55. The composition is credited to Irving Mills, Frank Signorelli (pianist on the recording), and Matt Malneck (violinist on the recording) (liner notes, Decca/GRP CD GRD-609).

56. Louis Armstrong & His Hot Five, *West End Blues,* matrix W 40096-B, Okeh 8597, recorded June 28, 1928, Chicago, reissued on *Louis Armstrong Volume IV: Louis Armstrong and Earl Hines* (Columbia CD 45142).

57. Irving Mills, under whose name this record was issued, was Ellington's manager.

58. Louis Armstrong & His Orchestra, *Muggles,* matrix W.402200-B, Okeh 8703, recorded December 7, 1928, Chicago, reissued on Columbia CD 45142.

59. Howard Allan Spring argues that the four-to-the-bar rhythm was inspired initially by the movements of the Lindy Hop, a dance that became popular in Harlem in 1928. Howard Allan Spring, "Changes in Jazz Performances and Arranging in New York, 1929–1932," (Ph. D. diss., University of Illinois at Urbana-Champaign, 1993), 293.

60. Douglas, "Oh Say Can You Swing," 39.

61. Hobson, "Fifty-second Street," 250; Douglas, "Oh Say Can You Swing," 39.

62. Douglas, "Oh Say Can You Swing," 39; Hobson, "Fifty-second Street," 250.

63. Several of the musicians who frequented the Onyx had participated in "mixed" recording dates such as the session with Bubber Miley cited previously. For example, Eddie Lang, Jack Teagarden and Joe Sullivan all played on Louis Armstrong's celebrated *Knockin' a Jug* in 1929, and Lang recorded a series of duets with African American guitarist Lonnie Johnson in 1928 and 1929. On mixed recordings, see Peretti, *Creation of Jazz*, 201–2; on hiring discrimination against blacks, see ibid., 184–86.

64. Ibid., 87–90, 206–8; Sudhalter, *Lost Chords*, 189–90; David Levering Lewis, *When Harlem Was in Vogue* (New York: Penguin, 1997), 162–65; Kenney, *Chicago Jazz*, 102–16. On similar interactions in other cities, see Burton W. Peretti, *Jazz in American Culture* (Chicago: Ivan R. Dee, 1997), 57.

65. Shaw, *52nd Street*, 62; Bud Freeman, interview by Helen Oakley Dance, [1977 or 1978], tape recording, sides 1–4, transcript, 61, JOHP; Benny Carter, interview by Morroe Berger, 1976, cassettes 1–2, transcript, 68, JOHP.

66. Carter interview, cassettes 1–2, transcript, 69; Klein interview, tape 1, side 1; Carmichael with Longstreet, *Sometimes I Wonder*, 210; Charlie Barnet, interview by Patricia Willard, 1978, tape recording, reel 2, transcript, 3, JOHP.

67. Smith and Hoefer, *Music on My Mind*, 203.

68. Arnold Shaw asserts that Tatum did not become a paid performer at the Onyx until after the repeal of Prohibition (Shaw, *52nd Street*, 56, 64), but Hobson and Shultz each claim that he was paid at the speakeasy version of the Onyx as well (Hobson, "Fifty-second Street," 250; Shultz, "Life and Death of Jazz Street," 7–8).

69. Shaw, *52nd Street*, 67.

70. White pianist Joe Sullivan also was hired to work at the Onyx (Hobson, "Fifty-second Street," 250).

71. Barnet interview, reel 2, transcript, 6.

72. Jon Panish argues that a similar imbalance characterized post–World War II American culture, which he sees as "a particular hybrid culture determined by the traditions, condition, needs, and desires of white people" (Panish, *Color of Jazz*, xv). This dynamic differs from that of the 1960s jazz clubs discussed by Robert K. McMichael, where, although whites made up the majority of the audience, "white affirmation of black authority" enabled black musicians to set the terms of musical and social interaction (McMichael, "We Insist—Freedom Now!" 393). In contrast, as I will suggest, the relative absence of African American musicians at the Onyx led white musicians to develop ideas about jazz that differed greatly from those held by many black performers.

73. Lexicographer Robert Gold writes that *jam* itself was "one of several food terms given a sexual meaning by Negroes . . . and then associated with jazz by Negro jazzmen," and that the term gained currency around 1930 (Robert S. Gold, *A Jazz Lexicon* [New York: Alfred A. Knopf, 1964], 161). Although *jam session* came into use by whites shortly thereafter, the term was still unfamiliar enough in 1935 that *Down Beat* felt obligated to define it for its readership of white musicians

(Glenn Burrs, "Those 'Jam Sessions' at the Onyx Club in New York," *Down Beat* 2, no. 9 [September 1935]: 4).

74. Porter, *What Is This Thing Called Jazz?* 31.

75. Scott DeVeaux, *The Birth of Bebop: A Social and Musical History* (Berkeley and Los Angeles: University of California Press, 1997), 207. DeVeaux refers to Neil Leonard's discussion of "romantic outsiders" (Leonard, "Some Further Thoughts").

76. DeVeaux, *Birth of Bebop*, 208.

77. Ibid., 207.

78. David R. Roediger, *The Wages of Whiteness: Race and the Making of the American Working Class* (London: Verso, 1991), 118.

79. Eric Lott, *Love and Theft: Blackface Minstrelsy and the American Working Class* (New York: Oxford University Press, 1993), 52–53.

80. On early white jazz musicians' involvement with actual minstrel performances, see Peretti, *Creation of Jazz*, 190. Berndt Ostendorf argues that minstrelsy "provided the subsoil of the emerging jazz music" of the 1920s (Berndt Ostendorf, "Minstrelsy and Early Jazz," *Massachusetts Review* 20, no. 3 [autumn 1979]: 574–602).

81. Shaw, *52nd Street*, 75. Lott argues that "white men's obsession with a rampageous black penis" was central to minstrelsy (Lott, *Love and Theft*, 25).

82. Burton Peretti writes that "throughout the North, the racist practices of the commercial world prevented whites from working with blacks, and thus kept them from acquiring more accurate perceptions" of blacks (Peretti, *Creation of Jazz*, 190).

83. I employ the term *playing black* to suggest two related meanings at once: these white musicians were both playing at *being* black and playing instruments in imitation of black musical practices. I draw my inspiration for this phrase from Philip J. Deloria's *Playing Indian* (New Haven, CT: Yale University Press, 1998), an examination of white appropriation of Native American identity. Krin Gabbard, drawing on Lott, argues that what Benny Goodman "found . . . so deeply arresting in the manner of black musicians" included "their expression of masculinity" (Krin Gabbard, *Jammin' at the Margins: Jazz and the American Cinema* [Chicago: University of Chicago Press, 1996], 44). Ingrid Monson has discussed the harmful effect of such stereotypes of masculinity on African American musicians: "The most damaging legacy of the mythical view of the rebellious, virile jazz musician may be perhaps that when African American musicians emphasize responsibility, dignity, gentleness, or courtship, some hip white Americans presume that the artist in question may not be a 'real' African American" (Monson, "Problem with White Hipness," 415–16).

84. Nicholas M. Evans makes a similar point when he argues that "a student of early jazz should . . . know that the 'racial' identities of the music's contributors are not limited to white and black, as those terms are commonly defined in the late-twentieth century" (Evans, *Writing Jazz*, 11).

85. James R. Barrett and David Roediger, "Inbetween Peoples: Race, Nationality and the 'New Immigrant' Working Class," *Journal of American Ethnic History* 16, no. 3 (spring 1997): 4.

86. David A. J. Richards, *Italian American: The Racializing of an Ethnic Identity* (New York: New York University Press, 1999), 187.

87. Matthew Frye Jacobson, *Whiteness of a Different Color: European Immigrants and the Alchemy of Race* (Cambridge, MA: Harvard University Press, 1998), 65.

88. Jacobson cites Italian movie star Rudolph Valentino's image as a "racial exotic" in the 1920s as emblematic of a "fading cultural regime" (ibid., 117–18).

89. Roediger, *Wages of Whiteness*, 117.

90. Michael Rogin, *Blackface, White Noise: Jewish Immigrants in the Hollywood Melting Pot* (Berkeley and Los Angeles: University of California Press, 1996), 100. Nicholas M. Evans makes the related argument that Jewish musicians in the 1920s such as George Gershwin, "in transforming jazz into fine art . . . sought to transform their own racial status, making it more 'proximate' to American whiteness than 'distant' blackness" (Evans, *Writing Jazz*, 97). Robert K. McMichael takes a more affirmative view of white ethnic musicians' motivations, arguing that "the attraction of many white ethnics during the 1920s to 'real' jazz music" was linked to the "potential for class-based alliances across race and ethnicity" in which they could find common ground with blacks through the shared experience of oppression (Robert K. McMichael, "Consuming Jazz: Black Music and Whiteness" [PhD diss., Brown University, 1996], 86). Here, I suggest instead that the culture of the Onyx Club tended to create and reinforce racial boundaries as much as it subverted them.

91. Gayle Wald argues in a discussion of Mezz Mezzrow that a "choice to 'identify' . . . with a racially marginalized population . . . is not inherently at odds with—and may even depend upon—a corresponding wish to preserve the racial authority of white masculinity" (Wald, "Mezz Mezzrow," 119). Eric Lott writes similarly that "homosocial scenarios" linking white and black men "actually found the color line even as they witness the latter's continual transgression" (Eric Lott, "White Like Me: Racial Cross-Dressing and the Construction of American Whiteness," in *Cultures of United States Imperialism,* ed. Amy Kaplan and Donald E. Pease [Durham, NC: Duke University Press, 1993], 475).

92. This was also true of earlier saloons; Powers writes that the saloon was "both brotherly and businesslike, both communal and commercial" (Powers, *Faces Along the Bar,* 22), while Rosenzweig argues that "over the fifty years between 1870 and 1920 . . . the saloon gradually became much more of a conventional commercial enterprise" (Rosenzweig, *Eight Hours,* 184).

93. Egan, "Oasis of Swing."

94. See, for example, the "Mr. and Mrs. W. B. Armstrong" mentioned by Douglas ("Oh Say Can You Swing," 39).

95. Paul Lopes writes of this era that the "hepcat ethos against 'commercial' popular music and middle-class conventional culture became an enduring jazz

ideology that informed future 'rebellions' among professional musicians as well as the self-image and cultural trope of jazz musicians as 'hip' urban artists living and creating outside the American mainstream" (Paul Lopes, *The Rise of a Jazz Art World* [Cambridge: Cambridge University Press, 2002], 135.)

96. Charters and Kunstadt, *Jazz*, 262.

Chapter Two

1. On the broader implications of Prohibition's repeal for American nightlife, see Lewis A. Erenberg, "From New York to Middletown: Repeal and the Legitimization of Nightlife in the Great Depression," *American Quarterly* 38, no. 5 (winter 1986): 761–78.

2. Abel Green of *Variety* pointed out in January 1936 that "none of the West 52d street swing joints has a dance license or dance floor. The appeal is all ear" (Abel Green, "Swing It!" *Variety*, January 1, 1936, 188).

3. Green, "Swing It!" 188.

4. "Guitar, Suitcase, and 3 Tipples," *Metronome* 50, no. 2 (February 1934): 18, claims that the Spirits of Rhythm have been appearing at the Onyx Club for five months. Although Alyn Shipton states that tiples generally have four courses of strings, photographs of the Spirits of Rhythm taken in the late 1930s and early 1940s show five (Alyn Shipton, "Tiple [tipple]," *The New Grove Dictionary of Music Online*, ed. L. Macy [accessed 19 September 2003], http://www.grovemusic.com; Charles Peterson photographs in collection of Don Peterson, Chevy Chase, MD, negative files 233 and 615. I thank Don Peterson for allowing me access to this valuable resource). On the group's early history, see "Guitar, Suitcase and 3 Tipples," 18; National Endowment for the Arts Jazz Oral History Project, housed at the Institute of Jazz Studies, Rutgers University–Newark (hereafter cited as JOHP), Teddy Bunn, interview by Chuck Rosenberg, 1977, tape recording, reel 1, sides 1 and 2, transcript, 37. On the Spirits' opening at the legal Onyx, see Arnold Shaw, *52nd Street: The Street of Jazz* (New York: Da Capo, 1977), 67–68. On the opening of the new Onyx Club, see note 61 to the appendix.

5. The Five Spirits of Rhythm [as The Five Cousins], *Nobody's Sweetheart*, matrix TO 1334, recorded September 20, 1933, New York; The Five Spirits of Rhythm, *I Got Rhythm*, matrix 14095-C, Brunswick 01715, recorded October 24, 1933, New York. All Spirits of Rhythm recordings cited in this chapter reissued on Spirits of Rhythm, *1932–34*, Retrieval-Jazz CD RTR 79004.

6. On Wilson Myers, see Otis Ferguson, "The Spirits: 100 Proof," *New Republic*, February 3, 1941, reprinted in *In the Spirit of Jazz: The Otis Ferguson Reader*, ed. Dorothy Chamberlain and Robert Wilson (1982; repr., New York: Da Capo, 1997), 118.

7. Will Friedwald speculates that unlike the Mills Brothers, who used their voices to imitate an entire band, the Spirits of Rhythm "considered it saner and more satisfying musically to pare the orchestra [imitated by the voices] down to just the saxophone section" (Will Friedwald, *Jazz Singing: America's Great Voices from*

Bessie Smith to Bebop and Beyond [New York: Charles Scribner's Sons, 1990], 177). Although I am unsure which of the Daniels brothers is singing lead in this chorus, Douglas is a likely guess; Teddy Bunn confirmed an interviewer's statement in 1977 that Douglas "did the lead vocals a lot of times" (Bunn interview, reel 2, side 1, transcript, 47), and Otis Ferguson claimed in 1941 that Douglas "is incidentally one of the truest singers in the business" (Ferguson, "Spirits: 100 Proof," 121). The key of A major is an unusual choice for *I Got Rhythm,* which is normally played in B-flat major. The likely explanation is that the band, or at least guitarist Bunn, was playing as if in B-flat major but with their instruments tuned down a half step; Bunn discussed this practice in the 1977 interview (Bunn interview, reel 2, side 1, transcript, 56–57).

8. Again, I am speculating here as to the identity of the tiple soloist: Teddy Bunn recalls that Douglas Daniels "had good knowledge of his instrument" and fought with Bunn over solo space (Bunn interview, reel 2, side 1, transcript, 46). Will Friedwald, however, credits the tiple solo to Watson (Friedwald, *Jazz Singing,* 142). Friedwald points out that the "horses" motive was often used by Watson in his scat singing and was later picked up by Ella Fitzgerald (141–42). *Horses* was composed by Byron Gay and Richard A. Whiting (Leo Feist, 1926).

9. On the formation of the idea of "hot rhythm" as a marker of essential racial difference, see Ronald Radano, "Hot Fantasies: American Modernism and the Idea of Black Rhythm," in *Music and the Racial Imagination,* ed. Ronald Radano and Philip V. Bohlman (Chicago: University of Chicago Press, 2000), 459–80. The *Metronome* quotation is from "Guitar, Suitcase and 3 Tipples," 18; other discussions of Watson include Ferguson, "Spirits: 100 Proof," 120; Leonard Feather, "The James Joyce of Jazz," *Esquire* 23, no. 6 (June 1945): 81.

10. Bob Bach, "52nd Street," *Swing: The Guide to Modern Music* 3, no. 1 (July 1940): 24; Bunn interview, reel 2, side 2, transcript, 71; Ferguson, "Spirits: 100 Proof," 120. On Watson's imitation of a trombonist, also see Feather, "James Joyce of Jazz," 81; Leonard Feather, *The Jazz Years: Earwitness to an Era* (New York: Da Capo, 1987), 96; "Guitar, Suitcase, and 3 Tipples," 18; Shaw, *52nd Street,* 67.

11. Ferguson, "Spirits: 100 Proof," 120; Carlton Brown, *Brainstorm* (New York: Farrar and Rinehart, 1944), 45. Brown's account of the Spirits of Rhythm uses thinly veiled pseudonyms; the group is called "The Six Souls of Swing," while Watson is "Lew the Lion" and Teddy Bunn becomes "Ollie Rolls." The quotation is from George M. Fredrickson, *The Black Image in the White Mind: The Debate on Afro-American Character and Destiny, 1817–1914* (New York: Harper & Row, 1971), 277; on *The Birth of a Nation,* see Donald Bogle, *Toms, Coons, Mulattoes, Mammies, and Bucks: An Interpretive History of Blacks in American Films,* 4th ed. (New York: Continuum, 2002), 10–15.

12. "Five Spirits of Rhythm," *Down Beat* 2, no. 1 (January 1935): 4; "Guitar, Suitcase, and 3 Tipples," 18. Discussions of the Spirits' rhythmic approach include "Five Spirits," 4, which points out "how they swing," and Wally Cheetham, "Try to Stop This Goofy Guy: Here's Looking at Red McKenzie," *Metronome* 50, no. 2

(February 1934): 33, which refers to the group as "a quintet of colored boys just chuck full of rhythm." Mercer is quoted in Shaw, *52nd Street*, 79. John Mercer and Bernie Hanighen, *My Old Man*, piano and vocal score (New York: T. B. Harms, 1933), 5; The Five Spirits of Rhythm [as The Nephews], *My Old Man*, matrix 14426-A, Brunswick 6728, recorded December 6, 1933, New York.

13. Hoagy Carmichael, "The Jazz Pioneers Are Passing: Where Do We Go From Here?" *Metronome* 49, no. 8 (August 1933): 16; Milton "Mezz" Mezzrow and Bernard Wolfe, *Really the Blues* (1946; repr., New York: Citadel Underground, 1990), 151, 158. Mezzrow tells a similar but even more stereotypical story about McKenzie, crediting his interest in music to "a little colored shoeshine boy who used to beat time on the shoes" (ibid., 149). A well-known example of a "mixed" recording session involving McKenzie is a 1929 Mound City Blue Blowers date that included white musicians McKenzie, Glenn Miller, Pee Wee Russell, Eddie Condon, Jack Bland, and Gene Krupa as well as African American musicians Coleman Hawkins and Pops Foster (*One Hour* b/w *Hello Lola*, Victor V-38100, recorded November 14, 1929, New York, reissued on Coleman Hawkins, *A Retrospective, 1929–1963* [Bluebird CD 07863]).

14. Bunn interview, reel 2, side 1, transcript, 74–75; Cheetham, "Try to Stop This Goofy Guy," 33.

15. Ram Ramirez, interview by Stanley Dance, n.d., transcript, 45, JOHP. McKenzie also sang with a later incarnation of the Spirits of Rhythm in 1939 at the 51st Street club Kelly's Stable ("McKenzie Working," *Down Beat* 6, no. 2 [February 1939]: 2). Red McKenzie with the Spirits of Rhythm, *'Way Down Yonder in New Orleans*, matrix 38633-A, Decca 186; *I've Got the World on a String*, matrix 38634-A, Decca 302; *From Monday On*, matrix 38635-A, Decca 186; all recorded September 11, 1934, New York.

16. All quotations from Shaw, *52nd Street*, 68, 105–6. Neither the Jam Club nor the Casino Deluxe proved satisfactory: the former was closed down for its failure to obtain a liquor license, while the owners of the latter "wanted paying crowds rather than jamming cats" (Shaw, *52nd Street*, 105–6).

17. Accounts of the founding of the Famous Door, while they agree on the essentials of the story, often contradict one another. Robert Sylvester, in the most complete account, claims that Colt and Hayton each put in $1,000, while eight other musicians (Glenn Miller, Jimmy Dorsey, Gordon Jenkins, Jack Jenney, Jerry Colonna, James Lanin, Artie Bernstein, and Harry Bluestone) put in $100 each (Robert Sylvester, *No Cover Charge: A Backward Look at the Night Clubs* [New York: Dial, 1956], 73). Arnold Shaw's list of contributors substitutes Manny Klein for James Lanin (Shaw, *52nd Street*, 106). George Hoefer, in contrast, claims that twenty-five musicians, mostly from Hayton's radio orchestra, each put in $100 (George Hoefer, "Tales of 52nd Street: The Famous Door," *Down Beat Music '68*, special issue, *Down Beat* 35 [1968], 73). *Down Beat's* report on the club's opening states only that "Jack Colt, Lenny Hayton's manager, and a couple of prominent New York musicians are the new owners" ("Onyx Club Burns, New Spot Opens Across

Street," *Down Beat* 2, no. 3 [March 1935]: 3). An article from a few months later, however, states that the "club was started by twenty-five musicians from NBC last March" (Lathrop Mack, "Park Ave. Nit-Wits Spoil Jam Nites at 'The Door,'" *Down Beat* 2, no. 6 [June 1935]: 2), while later that year *Billboard* reported that "about 16 musicians" opened the club ([Jerry] Franken, "Famous Door, New York," *Billboard*, November 30, 1935, 13). On the Casino Deluxe, see Hoefer, "Famous Door," 73; Shaw, *52nd Street*, 106.

18. Jack Egan, "Oasis of Swing," in program for Swing Music Concert at the Imperial Theatre, New York, May 24, 1936 (I thank Don Peterson for lending me his copy of this program); "Onyx Club Burns," 3; George Hoefer, "Father of the Street: Onyx Days Recalled," *Down Beat's Music, '66: 11th Yearbook*, special edition, *Down Beat* 33 (1966): 94; Shaw, *52nd Street*, 68–69.

19. Shaw, *52nd Street*, 109; Dick Clark, "New York News," *Down Beat* 2, no. 4–5 (April–May 1935): 2. In 1966, George Hoefer reported that "today [Joe] Helbock has his own ideas about how the fire got started and points out *he* wasn't afraid of competition" (Hoefer, "Father of the Street," 94).

20. "Onyx Club Burns," 3.

21. Shaw, *52nd Street*, 107; Guy Lombardo, "Guy Says 'Average Musician Is Swing Crazy,'" *Down Beat* 3, no. 7 (July 1936): 1, 19; Garry Boulard, *Louis Prima* (Urbana: University of Illinois Press, 2002), 20–21, 27. I derive Prima's year of birth from his biographer Garry Boulard (Boulard, *Louis Prima*, 1); the *New Grove Dictionary*, however, claims that he was born in 1911 (Mike Hazeldine, "Louis Prima," *The New Grove Dictionary of Music Online*, ed. L. Macy, http://www.grovemusic.com [accessed 19 September 2003]), while Arnold Shaw gives the date as 1912 (Shaw, *52nd Street*, 107).

22. For a photograph of the Prima quintet, see Shaw, *52nd Street*, 124. Richard M. Sudhalter, *Lost Chords: White Musicians and Their Contributions to Jazz, 1915–1945* (New York: Oxford University Press, 1999), 81. Sudhalter also applies this description to Wingy Manone's recordings of the same period. For a detailed discussion of Russell's work with Prima, see Sudhalter, *Lost Chords*, 730. Louis Prima and His New Orleans Gang, *In a Little Gypsy Tea Room*, matrix B-17739–1, Brunswick 7479, recorded June 27, 1935, New York; *Swing Me with Rhythm*, matrix 17242–1, Brunswick 7431, recorded April 3, 1935, New York. All Prima recordings cited in this chapter are reissued on *The Complete Brunswick and Vocalion Recordings of Louis Prima and Wingy Manone (1924–1937)*, Mosaic CD MD6–217. The liner notes for this set include a useful essay by Lloyd Rauch that discusses each recording session in detail.

23. Boulard, *Louis Prima*, 13–14; "'My Chops Was Beat,' Says Louie, 'But I'm Dyin' to Swing Again,'" *Down Beat* 2, no. 6 (June 1935): 8; Louis Prima and His New Orleans Gang, *Let's Have a Jubilee*, matrix B-16286-A, Brunswick 7394, recorded November 1, 1934, New York; *Chinatown, My Chinatown*, matrix B-17613–1, Brunswick 7456, recorded May 17, 1935, New York; Louis Armstrong and His Orchestra, *Chinatown, My Chinatown*, recorded November 3, 1931, Chicago, reissued on Louis

Armstrong, *The Big Band Recordings 1930–1932.* Armstrong recorded two masters of this song on this date (matrix numbers 405059–4 and 151886): I am uncertain which is included on this reissue. Armstrong plays *Chinatown* at about 320 beats per minute, while Prima's version is closer to 310.

24. Léon Vauchant, "French Musicians: Impressions of America," *Jazz Hot,* no. 5 (September–October 1935): 17; The Rudy Vallee Show [identified as "The Fleischmann's Yeast Hour" during the broadcast], NBC Red network, November 21, 1935, 8:00 PM, Library of Congress Motion Picture, Broadcasting, and Recorded Sound Division, NBC Radio Collection, RWB 7271 A1–4; Artie Shapiro, interview by the author, March 13, 2002; Glenn Burrs, "Casa Loma, Olsen, Prima, Cugat, Pryor, FioRito, McGrew Open in Ch'go," *Down Beat* 3, no. 10 (October 1936): 2, 13; Herbert Moulton and Leslie Roush, directors and producers, *The Star Reporter in Hollywood,* A National Telefilm Release, U.M. & M. TV Corp., 1937, Ernie Smith Jazz Film Collection, ca. 1930s–1960s, Archives Center, National Museum of American History, 491.268. Garry Boulard suggests Cab Calloway as another possible model for Prima's performances (Boulard, *Louis Prima,* 34).

25. Louis Prima and His New Orleans Gang, *Let's Have a Jubilee,* matrix B-16286-A, Brunswick 7394, recorded November 1, 1934, New York; on the song's prominence as Prima's theme, see Boulard, *Louis Prima,* 44. On *Hallelujah!* see Thomas Cripps, *Slow Fade to Black: The Negro in American Film, 1900–1942* (New York: Oxford University Press, 1977), 243–53. In 1935, when Prima opened at the Famous Door, *The Green Pastures* was in the middle of a successful five-year run on Broadway and elsewhere; it was turned into a feature film in 1936 (Thomas Cripps, ed., *The Green Pastures* [Madison: University of Wisconsin Press, 1979], 20, 25; Cripps, *Slow Fade,* 258–61). Louis Armstrong Hot Five, *Gut Bucket Blues,* matrix 9486-A, Okeh 8261, recorded November 12, 1925, Chicago, reissued on Louis Armstrong, *The Complete Hot Five and Hot Seven Recordings,* Columbia/Legacy CD C4K63527. On "Bayou Pon Pon," see John Broven, *South to Louisiana: The Music of the Cajun Bayous* (Gretna, LA: Pelican, 1983), 31. On Arodin's racial identity, see Sudhalter, *Lost Chords,* 78.

26. Boulard, *Louis Prima,* 28; Feather, *Jazz Years,* 116; Davis quoted in Boulard, *Louis Prima,* 62; "Rise of Jam Bands," *Billboard,* December 28, 1935, 49.

27. Feather, *Jazz Years,* 116; Boulard, *Louis Prima,* xii-xiii, 18.

28. Louis Prima and His New Orleans Gang, *Basin Street Blues,* matrix 17615–1, Brunswick 7456, recorded May 17, 1935, New York.

29. Thomas J. Ferraro, *Feeling Italian: The Art of Ethnicity in America* (New York: New York University Press, 2005), 178.

30. "Is Dixieland Stuff Coming Back?" *Metronome* 51, no. 9 (September 1935): 25, 44; Lathrop Mack, "Mannone and Prima Dig Up Ghost of Dixieland Band," *Down Beat* 2, no. 7 (July 1935): 2.

31. Sylvester, *No Cover Charge,* 75; Clark, "New York News," 2; Vauchant, "French Musicians," 17; "Is Dixieland Stuff," 44; Mack, "Park Ave. Nit-Wits," 2.

32. Abel [Green], "Famous Door (New York)," *Variety* 119, no 7 (July 31, 1935): 47; John Hammond, "N.Y. as Backward as Chicago in Swing Music," *Down Beat* 2, no. 6 (June 1935): 4; Mack, "Park Ave. Nit-Wits," 2.

33. Weiss and Davis quoted in Shaw, *52nd Street,* 109; Boulard, *Louis Prima,* xii.

34. Green, "Famous Door (New York)," 47; Hammond, "N.Y. as Backward," 12; Boulard, *Louis Prima,* 35; Shaw, *52nd Street,* 110; Mack, "Mannone and Prima," 2.

35. Mack writes that "Mannone has a current vogue among musicians and Prima with the nightclubbing public" (Mack, "Mannone and Prima," 2). Unlike most of my primary sources, I use the spelling *Manone* rather than *Mannone,* in accordance with Manone's own request in his autobiography and with current convention. Manone dropped an *n* to change the number of letters in his name after he "got hipped to numerology" (Wingy Manone and Paul Vandervoort II, *Trumpet on the Wing* [Garden City, NY: Doubleday, 1948], 128).

36. "'Wingy' Dodged Bullets," *Down Beat* 3, no. 1 (December 1935–January 1936): 6.

37. "An Old Swing Man," *Down Beat* 2, no. 8 (August 1935): 1.

38. Old Viper, "Licks 'n Riffs," *Hot News and Rhythm Record Review* 1, no. 1 (April 1935): 6.

39. Shaw, *52nd Street,* 106.

40. Lathrop Mack, "Mannone's Music Liked by N.Y. 'Hot' Fans," *Down Beat* 2, no. 8 (August 1935): 2.

41. Manone and Vandervoort, *Trumpet on the Wing,* 114; Shaw, *52nd Street,* 142–45; "Talent Scout," *New Yorker* 39, no. 1 (February 23, 1963): 25. In the latter article, Popkin erroneously remembers that he hired Manone in November 1934.

42. Mack, "Mannone's Music Liked," 2.

43. Manone left the Hickory House for the Famous Door in November 1935 and returned around March 1936 ("The Low Down about the Land of Swing," *Down Beat* 2, no. 11 [November 1935]: 4; Jack Egan, "'Stuff' Smith Does His Stuff at Onyx Club: New York News," *Down Beat* 3, no. 3 [March 1936]: 4). He last appears in *Down Beat*'s band listing for the Hickory House in June 1936; after this, his spot was filled by a band led by Joe Marsala and Eddie Condon ("Where the Name Orchestras are Playing This Month," *Down Beat* 3, no. 6 [June 1936]: 14; John Hammond, "Musicians Desert Gin and Weed to Swing Again," *Down Beat* 3, no. 7 [July 1936]: 1, 22; also see Shaw, *52nd Street,* 145–46).

44. Robert Hilbert also points out the similarity between Prima and Manone, writing that "both modeled their trumpet playing and vocal styles on Louis Armstrong's work and both delivered a showmanship filled with enthusiastic gestures and jivey patter, with its roots deep in the New Orleans tradition that saw no difference between entertainment and jazz" (Robert Hilbert, *Pee Wee Russell: The Life of a Jazzman* [New York: Oxford University Press, 1993], 93). Wingy Manone and His Orchestra, *I've Got a Feelin' You're Foolin',* matrix 18134–1, Vocalion 3070, recorded October 8, 1935, New York. All Manone recordings cited in this chapter are reissued on *The Complete Brunswick & Vocalion Recordings of Louis Prima*

and *Wingy Manone (1924–1937)*, Mosaic CD MD6–217. On the quartet's personnel, see Shaw, *52nd Street*, 145. Leonard G. Feather, "The Lowdown on Signor Mannone: Bananas to Jam," *Swing Music* 1, no. 7 (1935): 217; Green, "Swing It!" 188.

45. Feather, "Lowdown on Signor Mannone," 216; Wingy Manone and His Orchestra, *The Isle of Capri*, matrix 17005–1, Vocalion 2913, recorded March 8, 1935, New York; Warren Scholl, "Record Review," *Down Beat* 2, no. 6 (June 1935): 2. Manone's reference to his mother is in "'Ole Capri,'" *Down Beat* 2, no. 9 (September 1935): 2. On the Spirits of Rhythm's influence on Manone, see Shaw, *52nd Street*, 143. Royalty contract between Milsons Music Publishing Company and Wingy Mannone and Manny Kurtz, April 19, 1935, for OH CAPRA! *Oh, Jam It (All Over the Isle)*, box 1, Wingy Manone Collection, Louis Armstrong Archives, Queens College, City University of New York. "'Ole Capri,'" 2; "Manone's Trumpet Playing Brings in the Shekels," *Down Beat* 2, no. 10 (October 1935): 4.

46. Wingy Manone and His Orchestra, *House Rent Party Day*, matrix 16801–1, Banner 33386, recorded February 20, 1935, New York; Louis Prima and His New Orleans Gang, *House Rent Party Day*, matrix 16540-A, Brunswick 7376, recorded December 26, 1934. "The Low Down about the Land of Swing," *Down Beat* 2, no. 11 (November 1935): 4. Manone appears to pay tribute to Rosenfeld in his 1935 recording of *A Smile Will Go a Long, Long Way*, in which he ad-libs, "The little girl from Ioway is smiling!" (matrix 18020–4, Vocalion 3058, recorded September 13, 1935, New York).

47. Jack Egan, Arnold Shaw, and *Down Beat* all suggest that the group comprised five instrumentalists: Condon, Riley, Farley, and an unnamed pianist and bassist (Egan, "Oasis of Swing"; Shaw, *52nd Street*, 69; "Musicians Flock Back to New Onyx Club," *Down Beat* 2, no. 8 [August 1935]: 2). Recordings made under the name Red McKenzie and His Rhythm Kings in July and August 1935, however, include seven instrumentalists: Condon, Riley, Farley, Slats Long (clarinet, tenor saxophone), Conrad Lanoue (piano), George Yorke (bass), and Johnny Powell (drums) (Brian A. L. Rust, *Jazz Records 1897–1942* [London: Storyville, 1970], 1091).

48. "Musicians Flock Back," 2.

49. Glenn Burrs, "Those 'Jam Sessions' at the Onyx Club in New York," *Down Beat* 2, no. 9 [September 1935]: 4.

50. The NBC broadcast, later issued on Alamac LP QSR2432 (*The Band Goes to Town—1935*), was one of a series called *The Band Goes to Town*. *Down Beat* reported in November 1935 that Riley and Farley, with singer Ella Logan, had a twenty-six-week contract to appear on the program ("Low Down about the Land of Swing," 4), and *Metronome* gave the Sunday night broadcast a positive review in the same month (George T. Simon [G. T. S.], "Pick-Ups," *Metronome* 51, no. 11 [November 1935]: 21). In February 1936, *Metronome* reported that "the N.B.C. finis of those boys came when they skipped out of an N.B.C. artists' bureau contract" (George T. Simon [G. T. S.], "Pick-Ups," *Metronome* 52, no. 2 [February 1936]: 32). During the broadcast discussed here, Red Norvo's band, with Red McKenzie on

vocals, played the first set, and the Riley and Farley band, with Ella Logan singing, played the second. Although Logan sang frequently with Riley and Farley on
the radio, I have not found a source that refers to her performing with them at
the Onyx Club.

51. *Loafin' Time* was composed by Milton Ager and Arthur Altman in 1935.

52. "Musicians Flock Back," 2; George T. Simon [G. T. S.], "Pick-Ups: Roasts
and Toasts," *Metronome* 51, no. 10 (October 1935): 21; Jack Egan, "He Slapped Riley
Across the Face with a Steak," *Down Beat* 2, no. 11 (November 1935): 10; Simon,
"Pick-Ups" (October 1935); Wilder Hobson, "Fifty-second Street," in *Jazzmen,* ed.
Frederic Ramsey Jr. and Charles Edward Smith, 251–52 (1939; repr., New York: Liv-
eright Editions, 1985); Shapiro, interview; Bill Crow, interview by the author, Feb-
ruary 27, 2002. Crow's autobiography includes a sensitive appraisal of Riley (Bill
Crow, *From Birdland to Broadway: Scenes from a Jazz Life* [New York: Oxford University
Press, 1992], 61–67). The circumstances under which Riley and Farley assumed
leadership of the group are not clear. In his review, Simon refers to them as the
"Eddy-Reilly outfit," although he mentions that McKenzie is still singing at the
Onyx (Simon, "Pick-Ups" [October 1935]).

53. Quotations are from Eddie Condon with Thomas Sugrue, *We Called It Music:
A Generation of Jazz* (1947; repr., New York: Da Capo, 1992), 240; also see "The Fa-
mous Door, N.Y . . . ," *Down Beat* 3, no. 3 (March 1936): 12; Shaw, *52nd Street,* 73;
Sudhalter, *Lost Chords,* 501–2.

54. The tune appears actually to have been composed by Chicago musician
Red Hodgson, who sued Riley and Farley for plagiarism and eventually split
credit with the duo for the song's composition. See Red Hodgson, "Red Hodgson
Tells How Round & Round Originated," *Down Beat* 3, no. 2 (February 1936): 1–2;
"Sues over Song Hit," *New York Times,* February 19, 1936; "Two Suits Tie Up the
'Round and Round' Royalties," *Down Beat* 3, no. 4 (April 1936): 3; Shaw, *52nd Street,*
72–73. For the story related here, see "A New Melody Haunts the Air," *New York
Times,* sec. 9, January 12, 1936; "Whoa-ho-ho-ho-ho-ho!" *Time* 27, no. 3 (January 20,
1936): 32; Shaw, *52nd Street,* 69–70.

55. It is unclear what instrument Riley played while performing the song.
Time magazine suggests that it was a flugelhorn ("Whoa-ho-ho-ho-ho-ho!" 32);
the *New York Times* refers to a "bass horn" ("New Melody Haunts Air," 15); *Variety*
claims it was "an old, battered French horn" (Green, "Swing It!" 188); and on the
two studio recordings made of the song, Riley identifies the horn as a "gadget"
(matrix 60006-A) and a "three-valve saxhorn" (matrix 60110-A). A *Metronome* reporter, perhaps mishearing the latter recording, makes an almost certainly erro-
neous reference to a "three-valve saxophone" ("How It All Started," *Metronome* 52,
no. 2 [February 1936]: 31). Because the song's lyrics refer to "push[ing] the first
valve down," it is unlikely that Riley used a slide trombone when performing it,
although a valve trombone would have been appropriate. Discographer Brian Rust
credits Riley with playing mellophone as well as trombone during the sessions

when the song was recorded, which suggests yet another possibility (Rust, *Jazz Records 1897–1942,* 1389). Arnold Shaw writes that the instrument was "a trombone or, perhaps, a battered French horn" (Shaw, *52nd Street,* 69).

56. This recording, matrix 60006-A, is available on an LP reissue (New World 248). Decca also made a second recording of the tune (matrix 60110-A) on October 24, 1935. The latter recording is similar to the version discussed here—the main difference is that Farley interjects spoken comments during Riley's vocal on the latter version.

57. Rudy Vallee Show.

58. "Record News," *Metronome* 52, no. 1 (January 1936): 37; "Account of a Ten-Day Film Career," *New York Times,* sec. 10, February 23, 1936.

59. Barry Ulanov, *A History of Jazz in America* (New York: Viking, 1952), 185; David W. Stowe, *Swing Changes: Big-Band Jazz in New Deal America* (Cambridge, MA: Harvard University Press, 1994), 7.

60. Frank Norris, "The Music Goes 'Round and Around," *New Republic* 85, no. 1104 (January 29, 1936): 335.

61. For example, see Norris, "Music Goes 'Round and Around," 334–35; "'Round and Around," *Literary Digest* 121, no. 14 (April 4, 1936): 26; "Whoa-ho-ho-ho-ho-ho!" 30, 32, 34–35. All three articles refer to black musicians as purveyors of "swing": Norris and "Whoa-ho . . ." mention Louis Armstrong, while "'Round and Around" refers to Duke Ellington. In the November 21, 1935, radio broadcast cited earlier, Rudy Vallee credited Louis Armstrong with inventing "swing" in the course of introducing Riley and Farley.

62. "Whoa-ho-ho-ho-ho-ho!" 32. An association between Riley and Farley and potentially unsavory late-night entertainment was made on radio as well; Rudy Vallee referred to *The Music Goes 'Round and Around* as "Mike Riley's new 3 o'clock a.m. favorite" during the November 21, 1935, broadcast cited earlier, and both he and Austin Croom-Johnson (host of *The Band Goes to Town*) introduced Riley as "Mike 'Insomnia' Riley" (Alamac LP QSR 2432).

63. Jack Egan, "Outside 'Ikkies' Try Squeezing In to Hear Big Noise," *Down Beat* 3, no. 1 (December 1935–January 1936): 6.

64. By February 1936, the ubiquity of *The Music Goes 'Round and Around* led to a backlash against it in the media. Two critics among many were *Metronome*'s Jack Tenney, who asked pointedly, "Why, oh why, did the music *have* to go *round and round,*" and bandleader Paul Whiteman, who played the opening bars of the tune on his radio show only to announce "Ha-ha—don't be alarmed—we are *not* going to play *The Music Goes 'Round and Around*" (Jack Tenney, "West Coast Accidentals," *Metronome* 52, no. 2 [February 1936]: 27; Paul Whiteman's Musical Varieties, NBC Blue network, February 23, 1936, 9:45 PM. Library of Congress Motion Picture, Broadcasting, and Recorded Sound Division, NBC Radio Collection, RWB 5545 A1–3). Whiteman goes on to explain that he is playing the tune only to set the scene of the Onyx Club, where guest star Stuff Smith was then performing (see

chapter 3). This suggests the degree to which the song and the club had become connected in the popular imagination.

65. "Riley and Farley Crack Back at Critics," *Down Beat* 3, no. 8 (August 1936): 1, 3.

66. Crow, *From Birdland to Broadway,* 63.

67. Shapiro, interview.

68. Scott DeVeaux, *The Birth of Bebop: A Social and Musical History* (Berkeley and Los Angeles: University of California Press, 1997), 75–76, 160–61.

69. On this point, also see Paul Lopes, *The Rise of a Jazz Art World* (Cambridge: Cambridge University Press, 2002), 153–54.

70. Johnny Blowers, interview by the author, April 2, 2002.

71. Ibid.

Chapter Three

1. Abel Green, "Swing It!" *Variety,* January 1, 1936, 188.

2. Lathrop Mack, "Brunies Replaces Louis Prima at 'Famous Door,' " *Down Beat* 2, no. 9 (September 1935): 8.

3. Ibid.

4. Anthony Barnett, *Desert Sands: The Recordings and Performances of Stuff Smith: An Annotated Discography and Biographical Source Book* (Lewes, UK: Allardyce, Barnett, 1995), 55–56.

5. On the Trent band, see Gunther Schuller, *Early Jazz: Its Roots and Musical Development* (New York: Oxford University Press, 1968), 299–303.

6. Stanley Dance, *The World of Swing* (New York: Charles Scribner's Sons, 1974), 176–78; Barnett, *Desert Sands,* 57, 61.

7. Stuff Smith, *Pure at Heart 2: Anecdotes and Interviews,* ed. Anthony Barnett (Lewes, UK: Allardyce, Barnett, 2002), 23; Barnett, *Desert Sands,* 67.

8. S. Dance, *World of Swing,* 161–67.

9. Jonah Jones, interview by Anja Baron and Al Vollmer, 1999, for the film *Last of the First* (directed by Anja Baron, Kenja Media Productions, 2004), tape 91, transcript. I thank Anja Baron and Al Vollmer for providing me with this transcript. My estimate of the date derives from S. Dance, *World of Swing,* 167; Barnett, *Desert Sands,* 67.

10. Smith, *Pure at Heart 2,* 24–25; Jones, interview by Baron and Vollmer, tape 91, transcript; Barnett, *Desert Sands,* 67.

11. Jones, interview by Baron and Vollmer, tape 91, transcript; S. Dance, *World of Swing,* 167.

12. S. Dance, *World of Swing,* 167–68; Jonah Jones, interview by Helen Oakley Dance, 1978, tape recording, sides 3–4, transcript, 58, National Endowment for the Arts Jazz Oral History Project, Institute of Jazz Studies, Rutgers University–Newark (hereafter cited as JOHP); Jones, interview by Baron and Vollmer, tape

92, transcript; Barnett, *Desert Sands,* 67. Jones remembered that the Silver Grill's audience was "two thirds or a third Polish people" (Jones, interview by Baron and Vollmer, tape 92, transcript). His reference to the neighborhood as a "Harlem neighborhood" seems to suggest that its position as an African American section of Buffalo was analogous to Harlem's position in New York City.

13. S. Dance, *World of Swing,* 187; Cozy Cole, interview by Bill Kirchner, 1980, cassette 2, transcript, 2–3, JOHP.

14. Jones, interview by Baron and Vollmer, tape 91, transcript [bracketed text in original]; Jack Kassiner, "Buffalo News," *Down Beat* 3, no. 4 (April 1936): 6; "Plays More Fiddle Than Joe Venuti?" *Down Beat* 3, no. 3 (March 1936): 3.

15. Jones, interview by Baron and Vollmer, tape 92, transcript. "[The audience]" is my editorial addition; "[sings]" is in the original.

16. A band led by white trombonist Red Stanley briefly headlined at the Onyx between Riley and Farley and the Smith band (Jack Egan, "'Stuff' Smith Does His Stuff at Onyx Club," *Down Beat* 3, no. 3 [March 1936]: 4). Jack Egan reported that "they play swell sweet stuff, but people don't want that at the Onyx. . . . They swing well too, but not enough" (Jack Egan, "Onyx Club Is Port of Missing Musicians," *Down Beat* 3, no. 2 [February 1936]: 4). I have been unable to determine the exact date on which Riley and Farley left the Onyx Club, but reports indicate that they were there for New Year's Eve but gone by February ("Downbeat," *Metronome* 52, no. 1 [January 1936]: 36; "Music World Goes Round and Round: Down Beat's Pictorial Review," *Down Beat* 3, no. 2 [February 1936]: 12).

17. On the complex negotiations required to bring the Smith band for the Onyx Club, see Jones, interview by Baron and Vollmer, tape 92, transcript; Jones, interview by H. Dance, sides 5–6, transcript, 3–5; *Jonah and the Wail,* VHS, produced and directed by Rebecca Marshall (1999, in private collection); S. Dance, *World of Swing,* 168, 179. Jack Egan, Arnold Shaw, and George Hoefer each state that Smith opened at the Onyx on February 3 (Jack Egan, "Oasis of Swing," in program for Swing Music Concert at the Imperial Theatre, New York, May 24, 1936 [I thank Don Peterson for lending me his copy of this program]; Arnold Shaw, *52nd Street: The Street of Jazz* [New York: Da Capo, 1977], 82; George Hoefer, "Father of the Street: Onyx Days Recalled," *Down Beat's Music '66: 11th Yearbook,* special edition, *Down Beat* 33 [1966]: 96). Jones, however, remembered the date as February 4 (Jones, interview by H. Dance, sides 3–4, transcript, 59; sides 5–6, transcript, 3–5), and also correctly remembered February 4, 1936, as a Tuesday. My list of band members is derived from the personnel of the group's first recording session, which took place on February 11.

18. Egan, "Oasis of Swing."

19. Egan, "'Stuff' Smith Does His Stuff," 4.

20. Egan, "Oasis of Swing"; Jones, interview by Baron and Vollmer, tape 92, transcript.

21. Egan, "Oasis of Swing."

22. Paul Whiteman's Musical Varieties, NBC Blue network, February 23, 1936, 9:45 PM, Library of Congress Motion Picture, Broadcasting, and Recorded Sound Division, NBC Radio Collection, RWB 5545 A1–3.

23. Jack Egan, "Very Few Spots Are Doing Business in New York," *Down Beat* 3, no. 4 (April 1936): 4.

24. "'Jitter-Bugs' Thrill at N.Y. Jam-Session: 17 Bands Swing for 3-Hours in Huge 'Clam-Bake,'" *Down Beat* 3, no. 6 (June 1936): 1, 8; also see Shaw, *52nd Street*, 85–88 and Hoefer, "Father of the Street," 96, 107 for descriptions of the concert.

25. Bob Inman, *Swing Era Scrapbook: The Teenage Diaries and Radio Logs of Bob Inman, 1936–1938*, compiled by Ken Vail (Lanham, MD: Scarecrow Press, 2005), 30–31. While the latter tune may have been a swing version of Mendelssohn's famous theme, a 1936 recording by pianist and singer Bob Howard entitled *Mendel's Son's Swing Song* features a minor-key pop tune with no apparent relation to its namesake (Bob Howard and His Orchestra, *Mendel's Son's Swing Song*, Decca 927, recorded September 2, 1936, New York).

26. "'Stuff' Smith Outdoes the Mad Monks," *Down Beat* 3, no. 10 (October 1936): 1.

27. John Hammond, "Many New Faces in New York Swing Spots," *Down Beat* 3, no. 10 (October 1936): 4; also see Shaw, *52nd Street*, 85; Hoefer, "Father of the Street," 107; John Chilton, *Billie's Blues: Billie Holiday's Story 1933–1959* (New York: Stein and Day, 1975), 39–40.

28. "Famous Onyx Club to Move," *Metronome* 53, no. 3 (March 1937): 18; The "Last of the Moe Egans" [Jack Egan], "Onyx Club Looks Up—Eddie Riley Has Tough Breaks," *Down Beat* 4, no. 4 (April 1937): 22.

29. "Stuff Smith Moves Holiday Joins Count Basie," *Down Beat* 4, no. 5 (May 1937): 1, 5; The Last of the Moe Egans [Jack Egan], "Chercer Chunks of Chatter from the Chowder Front," *Down Beat* 4, no. 6 (June 1937): 21; Shaw, *52nd Street*, 56.

30. Smith was cut from the film because of a salary dispute, and pianist Maurice Rocco appeared instead (The Last of the Moe Egans [Jack Egan], "Choice Chunks of Chatter from the Chowder Front," *Down Beat* 4, no. 7 [July 1937]: 3; Grover Jones, *Fifty-Second Street*, Final Continuity [Walter Wanger Productions, 1937], cinema script, New York Public Library for the Performing Arts, Billy Rose Theatre Collection [collection cited hereafter as NYPL Theatre Coll.]; excerpt from *52nd Street*, directed by Harold Young [United Artists, 1937], Ernie Smith Jazz Film Collection, ca. 1930s–1960s, Archives Center, National Museum of American History, ES 491.3–1).

31. Egan, "'Stuff' Smith Does His Stuff," 4.

32. Egan, "'Stuff' Smith Does His Stuff," 4; Gilbert Seldes, "No More Swing?" *Scribner's* 100, no. 5 (November 1936): 71; Valerie Wilmer, "Stuff Smith: The Genius of Jazz Violin," *Jazzbeat* 2, no. 6 (June 1965): 17.

33. S. Dance, *World of Swing*, 168; Jones, interview by H. Dance, sides 7–8, transcript, 39–40.

34. Whiteman's Musical Varieties.

35. Jones, interview by Baron and Vollmer, tape 93, transcript.

36. Ibid.

37. LeRoy Battle, interview by the author, May 23, 2002. Battle's stint with the Smith band probably took place around 1946, a year in which Battle was a regular performer on 52nd Street and Smith played at the Downbeat (advertisement, *New York Amsterdam News,* 2 February 1946, 21 [clipping in Franz Hoffmann, *Jazz Advertised 1910–1967: A Documentation* (Berlin: Franz Hoffmann, 1997), vol. 1–3, 692]; "Three Deuces—and a Hip Trio!" *Down Beat* 13, no. 12 [June 3, 1946]: 19; LeRoy A. Battle, *Easier Said: The Autobiography of LeRoy A. Battle* [Annapolis, MD: Annapolis Publishing, 1995], 101–2).

38. Stuff Smith and His Onyx Club Boys: *Robins and Roses,* matrix 19239–1, Vocalion 3234, recorded May 12, 1936; *I Don't Want to Make History,* matrix 18817–1, Vocalion 3200, recorded March 13, 1936; *I'se a Muggin',* parts 1 and 2, matrices 18654–1 and 18655–1, Vocalion 3169, recorded February 11, 1936; *Twilight in Turkey,* matrix 62172-A, Decca 1279, recorded May 4, 1937. All of these sides were recorded in New York. All Stuff Smith recordings cited in this chapter reissued on Stuff Smith, *Time and Again* (Proper CD PVCD118).

39. Wilmer, "Stuff Smith," 17.

40. "Stuff Smith Champions Fiddle Swing," *Metronome,* September 1937, 43, cited in Barnett, *Desert Sands,* 78.

41. Wilmer, "Stuff Smith," 16.

42. Herman Autrey, interview by John S. Wilson, 1975, part 3, transcript, 80, JOHP.

43. Smith was using an amplifier as early as 1937 or 1938 (Anthony Barnett, *Up Jumped the Devil: The Supplement to Desert Sands; The Recordings and Performances of Stuff Smith; An Annotated Discography and Biographical Source Book* [Lewes, UK: Allardyce, Barnett, 1998], 42; [Anthony Barnett], "Stuff Smith Pink Sub Page," www.abar.net/smith.html [accessed 9 September 2005]).

44. I have not found a source that provides the precise date on which Cole joined the band, but he was part of the group by their March 13, 1936, recording session.

45. Egan, "'Stuff' Smith Does His Stuff," 4; S. Dance, *World of Swing,* 30; Cliff Leeman, interview by Milt Hinton, 1979, tape recording, reel 4, transcript, 14–15, JOHP.

46. Egan, "'Stuff' Smith Does His Stuff," 4.

47. Timme Rosenkrantz, "Reflections: Stuff Smith at the Onyx Club," *Down Beat* 30, no. 1 (January 3, 1963): 39; *March of Time* vol. 3, no. 7, "The Birth of Swing" (Time/RKO Radio, 1937), excerpt included in *Jonah and the Wail.*

48. Charles Peterson photographs in collection of Don Peterson, Chevy Chase, MD (hereafter cited as Peterson collection), negative files 153 and 98.

49. S. Dance, *World of Swing,* 168.

50. Jones, interview by H. Dance, sides 5–6, transcript, 10; S. Dance, *World of Swing,* 168; *March of Time* 3, no. 7.

51. Wilmer, "Stuff Smith," 17.

52. Battle, interview.

53. A transcription of a 1966 recording of Smith telling this story is included in Smith, *Pure at Heart 2*, 45–46; Smith was performing it on 52nd Street at least as early as 1944 (ibid., 44). Timme Rosenkrantz remembered that Smith would "make the management panic" by performing the story at the Onyx (Rosenkrantz, "Reflections," 39).

54. Al Hall, interview by Ira Gitler, 1978, tape recording, cassette 6, transcript, 24, JOHP. Hall played with Smith in Chicago in 1941.

55. Rosenkrantz, "Reflections," 39. It is unclear from context whether this quote refers to the Onyx Club. If so, this suggests that Smith might have been directing his comments at white women, which would have been a risky and surprising gesture for a black performer at the time. At any rate, this account seems to suggest that Smith was comfortable with the casual sexism that characterized the bachelor subculture of the Onyx (see chapter 1.)

56. George T. Simon [G. T. S.], "Pick-Ups: Roasts and Toasts," *Metronome* 52, no. 3 (March 1936): 23.

57. Jones, interview by Baron and Vollmer, tape 92, transcript; George Simon, "Stuff Smith," *Metronome* 52, no. 5 (May 1936): 19; Egan, " 'Stuff' Smith Does His Stuff," 4.

58. Marshall Stearns and Jean Stearns, *Jazz Dance: The Story of American Vernacular Dance* (London: Macmillan, 1968), 196, 41.

59. Joe Louis Barrow Jr. and Barbara Munder, *Joe Louis: 50 Years an American Hero* (New York: McGraw-Hill, 1988), 52, 252.

60. Jervis Anderson, *This Was Harlem: A Cultural Portrait, 1900–1950* (New York: Farrar Straus Giroux, 1981), 285.

61. "Critics in the Doghouse: Stuff Smith Examines Stuff Smith," *Down Beat* 6, no. 8 (August 1939): 9.

62. Previous commentators on Smith have sometimes made passing mention of the role of humor in his musical style. In 1946, for example, Dixon Gayer wrote that "a musician listening to Stuff will get a laugh out of every few bars, for Stuff knows just how to phrase or shade a tone to make the song sound really outrageously funny" (Dixon Gayer, *Disc* [November 1946; clipping in Stuff Smith file, Institute of Jazz Studies, Rutgers University–Newark]). In a related contention, Matt Glaser claims that "Smith's eccentric behavior . . . was expressed in, and in some ways essential to, his musical style" (Matt Glaser, "Stuff Smith," *New Grove Dictionary of Music Online*, ed. L. Macy, http://www.grovemusic.com [accessed 29 September 2003]).

63. A useful annotated list of scholarly works on humor and music can be found in R. Anderson Sutton, "Humor, Mischief, and Aesthetics in Javanese Gamelan Music," *Journal of Musicology* 15, no. 3 (Summer 1997): 391. As Sutton points out, "most of the writings on humor [in music] have dealt with the devices of particular composers, nearly all of them from the latter half of the eighteenth

century" (391). Theoretical discussions not cited by Sutton include Rosanna Dalmonte, "Towards a Semiology of Humor in Music," *International Review of the Aesthetics and Sociology of Music* 26, no. 2 (December 1995): 167–87; Kendall L. Walton, "Understanding Humor and Understanding Music," *Journal of Musicology* 11, no. 1 (Winter 1993): 32–44; Marion A. Guck, "Taking Notice: A Response to Kendall Walton," *Journal of Musicology* 11, no. 1 (Winter 1993): 45–51. Work on humor in American music includes Robert G. O'Meally, "Checking Our Balances: Louis Armstrong, Ralph Ellison, and Betty Boop," in *Uptown Conversation: The New Jazz Studies*, ed. Robert G. O'Meally et al. (New York: Columbia University Press, 2004), 278–96; Cassandra I. Carr, "Charles Ives's Humor as Reflected in His Songs," *American Music* (Summer 1989): 123–39; Cynthia Mahabir, "Wit and Popular Music: The Calypso and the Blues," *Popular Music* 15, no. 1 (January 1996): 55–81; Miguel Mera, "Is Funny Music Funny? Contexts and Case Studies of Film Music Humor," *Journal of Popular Music Studies* 14 (2002): 91–113.

64. Ingrid Monson, *Saying Something: Jazz Improvisation and Interaction* (Chicago: University of Chicago Press, 1996), 106–21; Samuel A. Floyd Jr., *The Power of Black Music: Interpreting Its History from Africa to the United States* (New York: Oxford University Press, 1995), 125.

65. Guthrie P. Ramsey Jr., *Race Music: Black Cultures from Bebop to Hip-Hop* (Berkeley and Los Angeles: University of California Press, 2003), 21–22; Ronald Radano, *Lying Up a Nation: Race and Black Music* (Chicago: University of Chicago Press, 2003), 38.

66. Jerry Palmer, *The Logic of the Absurd: On Film and Television Comedy* (London: British Film Institute, 1987), 39–44. Several works on humor in music offer formulations similar to Palmer's; R. Anderson Sutton, for example, cites surprise and incongruity as key factors in musical humor (Sutton, "Humor, Mischief, and Aesthetics," 394–95), while Henry F. Gilbert asserts that "in most . . . cases the 'cream of the joke' is that the jarring element, the thing which produces the shock, is both incongruous and unexpected" (Henry F. Gilbert, "Humor in Music," *Musical Quarterly* 12, no. 1 [January 1926]: 41).

67. Egan, " 'Stuff' Smith Does His Stuff," 4.

68. Edgar Greentree, "DISCussion," *Down Beat* 3, no. 3 (March 1936): 12. Greentree gives the date of the session as February 18, which contradicts standard discographies.

69. Egan, "Very Few Spots," 4; The Rudy Vallee Show [identified as "The Fleischmann's Yeast Hour" during the broadcast], NBC Red network, April 23, 1936, 8:00 PM, Library of Congress Motion Picture, Broadcasting, and Recorded Sound Division, NBC Radio Collection, RWB 6644 A1–4.

70. For example, the bands of Andy Kirk and Joe Haymes each coincidentally recorded *I'se a Muggin'* on March 11, 1936.

71. Bassist Mack Walker plays the following line over this progression (numbers represent scale degrees, and each note is played twice): | 1 3 | 2 5 |. An exception takes place during the last four bars of the chorus, when Walker plays

either of the following cadential lines: |1 b7 | 6 b6 | 5 5 | 1 1 | or | 1 3 | 4 #4 | 5 5 | 1 1 |. Above, I have intentionally ignored the extended chords that occur as the musicians improvise over the progression (I^6 instead of I, or ii^7 instead of ii, for example) in order to represent the vamp in its broadest outline.

72. Milton "Mezz" Mezzrow and Bernard Wolfe, *Really the Blues* (1946; repr., New York: Citadel Underground, 1990), 215.

73. George Simon refers to Bennett as "the Red Cap, sir" in a 1936 review (Simon, "Stuff Smith," 19).

74. *Down Beat* reported in April 1936 that "Stuff Smith re-recorded 'I'se a Muggin' " because the "first session erred in putting on wax muggin' things that can't be appreciated unless seen" (Al Brackman, "All's Swingin' on the Eastern Front," *Down Beat* 3, no. 4 [April 1936]: 6; see also Shaw, *52nd Street,* 84; Hoefer, "Father of the Street," 96). Although Anthony Barnett argues convincingly that this incident is apocryphal (Barnett, *Desert Sands,* 70), that it was reported at all suggests that physical comedy was associated with Smith's performances of the song.

75. H. Brook Webb, "The Slang of Jazz," *American Speech* 12, no. 3 (October 1937): 183; Dan Burley, *Dan Burley's Original Handbook of Harlem Jive* (New York: Dan Burley, 1944), 144. Arlene Smith, Smith's fourth wife, recalled in a 1994 interview that Smith defined *muggin'* as "vamping" and was "absolutely astounded" to learn that white audiences associated the term with the faces he made while performing the song (Barnett, *Desert Sands,* 44).

76. Battle, interview.

77. Stuff Smith and His Onyx Club Boys, *Onyx Club Spree,* matrix 62175-A, Decca 1279, recorded May 4, 1937, New York.

78. In response to an interviewer's claim that his music was "revolutionary," Smith replied, "Yes, but . . . always, I'd fall back in that chord somewhere," unlike bebop musicians, whom he claimed "would get out of that chord and stay out there" (Smith, *Pure at Heart 2,* 30). Bars 5–8 of this passage seem to be an example of Smith "falling back" into the chord after a period of playing "out there."

79. Mel Watkins, *On the Real Side: Laughing, Lying, and Signifying—The Underground Tradition of African-American Humor That Transformed American Culture, from Slavery to Richard Pryor* (New York: Touchstone, 1994), 248, 252.

80. Ibid., 276.

81. Cheryl Lynn Greenberg, *"Or Does It Explode?": Black Harlem in the Great Depression* (New York: Oxford University Press, 1991), 5.

82. Greenberg, *"Or Does It Explode?"* 3–5; Watkins, *On the Real Side,* 384.

83. Ralph Cooper with Steve Dougherty, *Amateur Night at the Apollo: Ralph Cooper Presents Five Decades of Great Entertainment* (New York: HarperCollins, 1990), 59, cited in Watkins, *On the Real Side,* 384.

84. Greenberg, *"Or Does It Explode?"* 114–39.

85. Watkins, *On the Real Side,* 384–85.

86. Ibid., 388.

87. Ibid., 390–93, 370–71.

88. Ibid., 394. Watkins writes, however, that "by the mid-thirties, pressure to put an end to blackface was building from organizations such as the NAACP," leading many comedians to abandon the practice (395).

89. Whiteman's Musical Varieties.

90. Watkins, *On the Real Side,* 92.

91. Whiteman's Musical Varieties; Rudy Vallee Show.

92. Watkins, *On the Real Side,* 372.

93. Burley, *Handbook of Harlem Jive,* 71.

94. Webb, "Slang of Jazz," 182.

95. Federal Writers Project of the Works Progress Administration in New York City, *New York Panorama* (New York: Random House, 1938), 159–60; Burley, *Handbook of Harlem Jive,* 141.

96. Descriptions of Harlem "tea-pads" include Burley, *Handbook of Harlem Jive,* 50; Mayor LaGuardia's Committee on Marihuana, *The Marihuana Problem in the City of New York* (1944; repr., Metuchen, NJ: Scarecrow, 1973), 10. On the use of jive talk during the selling of marijuana, see Mezzrow, *Really the Blues,* 216–19. Burton W. Peretti, citing Mezzrow, points out that "drug dealing was often carried out beneath a cloak of thick jive" and argues that drug users were more influential than musicians in perpetuating jive (Burton W. Peretti, *The Creation of Jazz: Music, Race, and Culture in Urban America* [Urbana: University of Illinois Press, Illini Books, 1994], 132–33).

97. Burley, *Handbook of Harlem Jive,* 141.

98. Williams defines a "structure of feeling" as a "quite distinct sense of a particular and native style" shared by members of a given generation within a community and argues that "it is a very deep and very wide possession, in all actual communities, precisely because it is on it that communication depends" (Raymond Williams, *The Long Revolution,* rev. ed. [New York: Harper & Row, 1966], 48).

99. Some members of the 52nd Street audience might have been exposed previously to jive through the recordings and performances of the popular bandleader Cab Calloway, whose *Hepster's Dictionary* was published in 1936 (David W. Stowe, *Swing Changes: Big-Band Jazz in New Deal America* [Cambridge, MA: Harvard University Press, 1994], 36–37).

100. Jones recalled that "I didn't want to know about no place else. Harlem was so great. In the years we were coming up in the '30s and '40s" (Jones, interview by Baron and Vollmer, tape 93, transcript) and that "everybody was rushing to get back uptown in those days" (Jones, interview by H. Dance, sides 5–6, transcript, 11).

101. Stuff Smith and His Onyx Club Boys, *Here Comes the Man with the Jive,* matrix 19733–1, Vocalion 3314, recorded August 21, 1936, New York.

102. Mezzrow and Wolfe, *Really the Blues,* 379; Shaw, *52nd Street,* 84.

103. Stuff Smith and His Onyx Club Boys, *You're a Viper,* matrix 18820–1, Vocalion 3201, recorded March 13, 1936, New York.

104. Harry Edison, interview by Stanley Dance, 1979, tape recording, cassette 4, transcript, 3, JOHP.

105. Smith, *Pure at Heart 2*, 45.

106. Stowe, *Swing Changes*, 37; Burley, *Handbook of Harlem Jive*, 11; Mezzrow and Wolfe, *Really the Blues*, 220; Peretti, *Creation of Jazz*, 131.

107. Claude McKay, *Harlem: Negro Metropolis* (New York: E. P. Dutton, 1940); Peretti, *Creation of Jazz*, 132; Burley, *Handbook of Harlem Jive*, 53.

108. Cole interview, cassette 4, transcript, 13–14.

109. On Venuti's influence on Smith, see Mary Lee Hester, "Hot Stuff!" *Mississippi Rag* 11, no. 6 (April 1984): 8.

110. Jones, interview by Baron and Vollmer, tapes 92, 93, transcript.

111. Cole interview, cassette 4, transcript, 14. I assume that Cole's reference to "Benny" here refers to Goodman.

112. Wilmer, "Stuff Smith," 17; Jean Elliott, "It's a European Stuff Smith," *Crescendo*, October 1967, 15, cited in Barnett, *Desert Sands*, 72.

113. Jones, interview by H. Dance, sides 5–6, transcript, 9; sides 11–12, transcript, 25.

114. Smith, *Pure at Heart 2*, 34.

115. Jones, interview by Baron and Vollmer, tape 92, transcript. Bracketed text in original.

116. Ibid.

117. Leeman interview, reel 4, transcript, 14–15.

118. On March 28, 1936, for example, the *Amsterdam News* reported that "Stuff Smith is still blasting his swing rhythms at the Onyx Club" ("Stage-Screen Nite Spots," *New York Amsterdam News*, March 28, 1936, 8, clipping reproduced in Franz Hoffmann, *Jazz Reviewed: Working Book to Jazz Advertised in the Negropress of New England 1910–1949* [Berlin: Franz Hoffmann, 1995], 197).

119. Leonard Gaskin, interview by the author, June 12, 2002.

120. Milt Hinton, interview by David Berger, 1976, tape recording, part 2, reel 2, transcript, 46, JOHP; Lionel Hampton, "Swing," *Baltimore Afro-American*, April 30, 1938, 10 (clipping reproduced in Hoffmann, *Jazz Reviewed*, 208).

121. Willie the Lion Smith with George Hoefer, *Music on My Mind: The Memoirs of an American Pianist* (Garden City, NY: Doubleday, 1964), 206, cited in Barnett, *Desert Sands*, 74.

122. *Variety*, April 27, 1938 (clipping in "Onyx" file, NYPL Theatre Coll.).

123. Carline Ray, interview by the author, April 24, 2002.

124. Gaskin, interview.

Chapter Four

1. See the appendix for details on these clubs.

2. On Wilson, see George T. Simon [G. T. S.], "Pick-Ups: Roasts and Toasts," *Metronome* 52, no. 3 (March 1936): 23; on White and The Three Peppers, "Stellar

Revue at Yacht Club," *New York Evening Journal,* September 18, 1936 (clipping in Red McKenzie file, Billy Rose Theatre Collection, New York Public Library for the Performing Arts [collection hereafter cited as NYPL Theatre Coll.]).

3. David W. Stowe, *Swing Changes: Big-Band Jazz in New Deal America* (Cambridge, MA: Harvard University Press, 1994), 97–98; also see Arnold Shaw, *52nd Street: The Street of Jazz* (New York: Da Capo, 1977), 91; Gunther Schuller, *The Swing Era: The Development of Jazz, 1930–1945* (New York: Oxford University Press, 1989), 297.

4. Eric Porter argues that Duke Ellington similarly strove to "strik[e] a balance between race consciousness and universalism" (Eric Porter, *What Is This Thing Called Jazz?: African American Musicians as Artists, Critics, and Activists* [Berkeley and Los Angeles: University of California Press, 2002], 39).

5. "Stuff Smith Moves Holiday Joins Count Basie," *Down Beat* 4, no. 5 (May 1937): 1, 5; John Hammond, "A Damned Outrage to Throw Thousands Out of Work!" *Down Beat* 4, no. 6 (June 1937): 9. Watson's switch to drums appears to have resulted in or coincided with Moore leaving the band.

6. Trumpeter Rex Stewart provides a firsthand account of Kirby's tenure with Henderson (Rex Stewart, "Flow Gently, Sweet Rhythm (John Kirby)," in *Jazz Masters of the Thirties* [New York: Macmillan, 1972], 152–55).

7. Advertisement, *Down Beat* 4, no. 7 (July 1937): 26; also see Shaw, *52nd Street,* 89.

8. Maxine Sullivan, interview by Phil Hughes, 1980, transcript, 594, National Endowment for the Arts Jazz Oral History Project, Institute of Jazz Studies, Rutgers University–Newark (hereafter cited as JOHP).

9. Charles Peterson photographs in collection of Don Peterson, Chevy Chase, MD (hereafter cited as Peterson collection), negative file 187; W. Royal Stokes, *Swing Era New York: The Jazz Photographs of Charles Peterson* (Philadelphia: Temple University Press, 1994), 48.

10. Peterson collection, negative file 187; Stokes, *Swing Era New York,* 48. Although this set of photographs is not precisely dated in the Peterson collection, they must have been taken between May, when the band opened at the Onyx, and late September, by which time Newton and Watson, both of whom appear in the photos, had left the band.

11. Peterson collection, negative file 204.

12. The three sessions, which took place on March 5, April 15, and July 13, 1937, and were released originally by Variety, are reissued on Frankie Newton, *1937–1939* (Classics CD 643).

13. Frankie Newton and His Uptown Serenaders, *Please Don't Talk About Me When I'm Gone,* matrix M-175–1, Variety 518, recorded March 5, 1937, New York; *There's No Two Ways About It,* matrix M-404–2, Variety 550, recorded April 15, 1937, New York.

14. The three sessions each include recordings with singers—Clarence Palmer, Slim Gaillard, and Leon LaFell, respectively—none of whom appear to have performed with the band at the Onyx. It is possible that Leo Watson filled this role in live performance.

15. Freddie Moore, interview by Ron Welburn, 1983, transcript, part 2, pp. 42–43, JOHP. Although Moore stated during this interview that he was in the Kirby band for about two years (part 3, 15), it appears that he was actually in the band for only about a month (as discussed in the text); I assume, therefore, that his comments about the band refer to sometime around May 1937.

16. Ibid., part 3, 29; part 2, 42; part 3, 17–18.

17. Frankie Newton and His Uptown Serenaders, *The Onyx Hop,* matrix M-559-1, Variety 647, recorded July 13, 1937, New York.

18. The Old Cow Hand, "Gay White Way Slightly Wilted," *Down Beat* 4, no. 8 (August 1937): 21, 24.

19. Herb Shultz, "The Life and Death of Jazz Street" (typescript, in the collection of the author, n.d.), 4–5.

20. Ibid, 6.

21. Robert Inman, interview by the author, April 8, 2002.

22. "Stuff Smith Moves," 5; Hammond, "Damned Outrage," 9.

23. Helen Oakley, "Frank Newton at Onyx Club," *Jazz Hot* 3, no. 19 (August–September 1937): 11.

24. Chip Deffaa, *Swing Legacy* (Metuchen, NJ: Scarecrow Press and the Institute of Jazz Studies, Rutgers University, 1989), 85.

25. Shaw, *52nd Street,* 96.

26. Ibid., 96–97.

27. Sullivan, interview, 557. The line from *Trees* quoted here is from "Scotch and Tom-Toms," *Stage* 15, no. 7 (April 1938): 23. Sullivan points out that Claude Hopkins's 1935 version of the tune preceded her own (Sullivan, interview, 557).

28. "She's So Good Ethel Waters Listens," *Down Beat* 4, no. 8 (August 1937): 16.

29. Sullivan, interview, 574.

30. The Last of the Moe Egans [Jack Egan], "Choice Chunks of Chatter from the Chowder Front," *Down Beat* 4, no. 12 (December 1937): 36.

31. Maxine Sullivan and Her Orchestra, *Loch Lomond,* matrix 21472-1, Vocalion 3654, recorded August 6, 1937, New York, reissued on Classics CD 963.

32. Sullivan, interview, 13.

33. Dempsey J. Travis, *An Autobiography of Black Jazz* (Chicago: Urban Research Institute, 1983), 454; also see Shaw, *52nd Street,* 98.

34. Sullivan, interview, 572–73, 577–78.

35. Ibid., 43, 30.

36. George T. Simon [G. T. S.], "Roasts and Toasts: In Which Some Get Slapped on the Back and Others in the Face," *Metronome* 54, no. 1 (January 1938): 20.

37. John Hammond, "Predicted Race Riot Fades as Dallas Applauds Quartet!" *Down Beat* 4, no. 10 (October 1937): 4; Jack Gould, "News of the Night Clubs," *New York Times,* sec. 11, December 19, 1937; Simon, "Roasts and Toasts" (January 1938), 20; Lou Layne, "Only Seven Months in Gotham, Maxine Sullivan Soars to Top," *New York Amsterdam News,* January 22, 1938 (clipping in Maxine Sullivan file, Institute of Jazz Studies, Rutgers University–Newark).

38. Layne, "Only Seven Months."

39. Simon, "Roasts and Toasts" (January 1938), 20.

40. George Simon [G. W.], "Best Records of 1937: In Which Tommy Dorsey and Maxine Sullivan Cop Top Honors," *Metronome* 54, no. 1 (January 1938): 21.

41. Sherrie Tucker, *Swing Shift: "All-Girl" Bands of the 1940s* (Durham, NC: Duke University Press, 2000), 6.

42. Sullivan, interview, 576.

43. Ron D. Johnson, "Sullivan Swing," *Mississippi Rag* 5, no. 12 (October 1978): 10. In another interview, Sullivan recalled that "I was calling myself Maxine before I came to New York. But I guess it was Claude's idea to call me Sullivan" (Deffaa, *Swing Legacy*, 88).

44. Chip Deffaa, "Still Gently Swinging," *Mississippi Rag* 12, no. 10 (August 1985): 10.

45. Bristol Myers "Town Hall Tonight," NBC Red network, September 22, 1937, 9:00 PM, Library of Congress Motion Picture, Broadcasting, and Recorded Sound Division, NBC Radio Collection, RWA 2179 A1–4.

46. On record companies' restrictions on black musicians' repertoire and black musicians' attempts to pass as white, see Stowe, *Swing Changes*, 124–25.

47. "Dorsey Cut Off Air from Murdering 'Sacred' Tune," *Down Beat* 5, no. 4 (April 1938): 1; Sullivan, interview, 14.

48. Sullivan, interview, 574.

49. Robert Inman, "New York Jazz, March 19, 1938" (typescript, in the collection of the author, n.d.); The Rudy Vallee Show [identified as "The Royal Gelatin Hour" in the broadcast itself], NBC Red Network, March 24, 1938, 8:00 PM, Library of Congress Motion Picture, Broadcasting, and Recorded Sound Division, NBC Radio Collection, RWA 2391 B1–4; *New York Journal-American*, March 26, 1938, clipping in Onyx file, NYPL Theatre Coll.; "Scotch and Tom-Toms," 23.

50. Shaw, *52nd Street*, 90; Sullivan, interview, 26.

51. *Down Beat*, April 1939, 23, cited in Stowe, *Swing Changes*, 97.

52. I do not mean to overemphasize the significance of this debate to the American public as a whole; as David Stowe points out, "it is tempting to dismiss" the controversy over swinging the classics "as what would come to be known as a pseudo-event, its significance wildly exaggerated by news media, which generally adopted a tongue-in-cheek tone in their reporting of it" (Stowe, *Swing Changes*, 97). Moreover, Sullivan herself later dismissed the importance of race in sparking the original controversy, claiming that "it was just a swing version that mattered. This Neil [*sic*] Fitzpatrick in Detroit didn't know whether I was white or black, he just didn't like the idea of 'Loch Lomond' getting swung" (Sullivan, interview, 583). It is clear, however, that ideas of race played a significant part in Sullivan's reception despite her attempts to distance herself from them.

53. Leonard Feather, "58 Inches of Swing," *Rhythm* 12, no. 128 (May 1938): 13.

54. Ibid., 16.

55. "Maxine Sullivan Denies She's Swing Vocalist," *Down Beat* 5, no. 9 (September 1938): 3.

56. *St. Louis Blues* [aka *Best of the Blues*], directed by Raoul Walsh (Paramount Pictures, 1939), print in collection of Wisconsin Center for Film and Theater Research; Sullivan, interview, 60.

57. Sullivan, interview, 62.

58. Author's transcription from film.

59. Sullivan, interview, 27.

60. Ibid., 62.

61. Oakley, "Frank Newton at Onyx Club," 11. It appears, however, that Watson remained with the group as a trombonist and vocalist for several months thereafter; a photograph published in November 1937 shows both Watson and Spencer in the band, and Watson sang and played trombone with the group during a January 1, 1938, broadcast from the Onyx Club over WNEW (Bob Inman, *Swing Era Scrapbook: The Teenage Diaries and Radio Logs of Bob Inman, 1936–1938,* compiled by Ken Vail [Lanham, MD: Scarecrow Press, 2005], 307).

62. Although Helen Oakley's August–September 1937 article on the group lists Bunn as a member, a publicity photograph of the band taken September 9, 1937, does not include him, and no article that I have seen on the group published after this date mentions Bunn (Oakley, "Frank Newton at Onyx Club," 11; Peterson collection, negative file 204).

63. On Newton leaving the group, see The Last of the Moe-Egans [Jack Egan], "Choice Chunks of Chowder from the Chowder Front," *Down Beat* 4, no. 9 (September 1937), 4; this article does not name Charlie Shavers but refers to "a new nineteen-year-old find of John Kirby's." On the rumored love triangle, see H. E. P., "Altitude Is Too Much for Abe Lyman and Band," *Down Beat* 5, no. 2 (February 1938): 3; Shaw, *52nd Street,* 90. The wedding of Kirby and Sullivan is reported in " 'Rag'-Time Marches On," *Down Beat* 5, no. 4 (April 1938): 10. Kirby and Sullivan divorced in 1941.

64. The description of the Newton-era group as a "jamming band" is by trombonist Snub Mosley: "at that time John Kirby had . . . five of the loudest guys you ever heard in your life. . . . But they didn't have no arrangements, they were just . . . a jamming band" (Leo "Snub" Mosley, interview by Frank Driggs, 1980, transcript, 96–97, JOHP). My reference to the Kirby Sextet as "disciplined" is derived from Gunther Schuller, who in an otherwise negative review of the group points out that "Bailey and Procope were, of course, excellent readers and had the discipline, still rare in those years, to cope with the intricate and technically sophisticated arranged ensembles in which the Kirby Sextet indulged" (Schuller, *Swing Era,* 814). I use the term here to allude to critical reception of the group rather than as a personal value judgment; certainly, masterful improvisers must be at least as "disciplined" as musicians who are adept at reading scores.

65. I compile this list of skills from Jazz Oral History Project interviews with drummers Jo Jones and Cliff Leeman and pianist John Malachi, each of whom praises Spencer (Jo Jones, interview by Milt Hinton, 1973, transcript, 155, JOHP; Cliff Leeman, interview by Milt Hinton, 1979, tape recording, reel 2, transcript, 39, JOHP; John Malachi, interview by Bryant DuPre, 1983, transcript, part 2, p. 15, JOHP).

66. Schuller, *Swing Era,* 813.

67. Russell Procope, "Wonderful, Wonderful Jazz," *Jazz Journal* 20, no. 5 (1967): 6.

68. Sullivan, interview, 593. Shavers discusses his experiences arranging for the sextet in "Charlie Shavers Talks to Sinclair Traill," *Jazz Journal* 23, no 5 (1970): 9.

69. Russell Procope, interview by Chris Albertson, 1979, tape recording, reel 2, transcript, 54; reel 3, transcript, 2, JOHP.

70. Ibid., reel 3, transcript, 3.

71. John Kirby and His Orchestra / John Kirby and His Onyx Club Boys, *It's Only a Paper Moon,* matrix 066897–1, Victor 27598, recorded July 25, 1941; *St. Louis Blues,* matrix 071903–1, Victor 27926, recorded February 11, 1942; *I Love You Truly,* matrix 28000-A, Columbia 36165, recorded July 9, 1940; *It Feels So Good,* matrix 23935–1, Vocalion 6424, recorded January 9, 1939; *Fifi's Rhapsody,* matrix 066898–1, Victor 27598, recorded July 25, 1941. All recorded in New York. All Kirby Sextet recordings discussed in this chapter reissued on The John Kirby Sextet, *Complete Columbia & RCA Victor Recordings* (Definitive CD 11168).

72. Schuller, *Swing Era,* 816; John Kirby and His Orchestra, *Little Brown Jug,* matrix WC-2781-A, Vocalion 5570, recorded October 12, 1939, Chicago; *Coquette,* matrix 28003-A, Columbia 35999, recorded July 9, 1940, New York.

73. Schuller, *Swing Era,* 814.

74. John Kirby and His Orchestra / John Kirby and His Onyx Club Boys, *Sextet from "Lucia,"* matrix 28002-A, Okeh 5705, recorded July 9, 1940, New York; *Bounce of the Sugar Plum Fairy,* matrix 29508–1, Columbia 35998, recorded January 15, 1941, New York. On Singer, see ibid., 815; Alan Williams, *Fall from Grace: The John Kirby Story* (Pensacola, FL: Alcoral, 1996), 66–67; Shaw, *52nd Street,* 101.

75. Stowe, *Swing Changes,* 110–12; Deffaa, *Swing Legacy,* 92–93.

76. Schuller, *Swing Era,* 812–13, 815; John Kirby and His Orchestra / John Kirby and His Onyx Club Boys, *Nocturne,* matrix WC2782-A, Vocalion 5520, recorded October 12, 1939, Chicago; *Drink to Me Only with Thine Eyes,* matrix 24679-A, Vocalion 4890, recorded May 19, 1939, New York.

77. John Kirby and His Orchestra / John Kirby and His Onyx Club Boys, *Dawn on the Desert,* matrix 23938–1, Vocalion 4653, recorded January 9, 1939, New York; *On a Little Street in Singapore,* matrix 26856, Okeh 5761, recorded May 27, 1940, New York; *Bugler's Dilemma,* matrix 066896–1, Victor 27568, recorded July 25, 1941, New York. Versions of the Scott pieces cited are reissued on The Raymond Scott Quintette, *Microphone Music* (Basta CD 30–9109–2).

78. Williams, *Fall from Grace,* 46.

79. See Lathrop Mack, "The 'Famous Door' Is Again Favored by Musicians," *Down Beat* 2, no. 10 (October 1935): 2; Marshall W. Stearns, "The Low Down on the 'Hot' Bands," *Down Beat* 3, no. 1 (December 1935–January 1936): 4. Schuller argues similarly that Norvo's 1936 repertoire "foresee[s] the small-band stylings of the John Kirby Sextet of a few years later" (Schuller, *Swing Era,* 518).

80. Schuller, *Swing Era,* 518–21.

81. George T. Simon [G. T. S.], "Pick-Ups: Roasts & Toasts," *Metronome* 52, no. 2 (February 1936): 23.

82. "The Seven Spirits of Rhythm," *Down Beat* 4, no. 11 (November 1937): 31; The Andrews Sisters "with Maxene at the typewriter," "Three Famous Sisters Tell You About 3 Kinds of Swing," *Swing: The Guide to Modern Music* 1, no. 6 (October 1938): 15. The sisters provide the following examples of their somewhat confusing taxonomy. "Jam" style: Joe Marsala, Count Basie, Louis Prima, Wingy Manone, John Kirby; "for the crowd" style: Bob Crosby, Gene Krupa, Jimmy Dorsey, Chick Webb, Artie Shaw; "lifty" style: Tommy Dorsey. "Jam" style bands, they explain, "are found in the smaller swing clubs along Fifty-second street in New York. Such places as the Hickory House, the Onyx Club, Famous Door and Swing Club are famed for presenting this type of music."

83. McGowan Miller, "Swing Lane," *Swing: The Guide to Modern Music* 1, no. 12 (April 1939): 43. This map also appears in the May and June issues of *Swing.*

84. Jack Gould, "News of the Night Clubs," *New York Times,* August 14, 1938; Barrelhouse Dan, "Hot Off the Turntable . . . Ellington Hits All-Time New High on 'Cotton Tail' Disc," *Down Beat* 7, no. 12 (June 15, 1940): 12.

85. *New York Sun,* April 4, 1939 (clipping in Onyx file, NYPL Theatre Coll.); Bob Bach, "52nd Street," *Swing: The Guide to Modern Music* 3, no. 1 (July 1940): 9; Bob Bach, "Reviews Big Kicks of 1940," *Swing: The Guide to Modern Music* 3, no. 7 (January 1941): 16.

86. *New York Times,* October 23, 1938 (clipping in Onyx file, NYPL Theatre Coll.)

87. *New York Times,* sec. 10, August 27, 1939 (clipping reproduced in Franz Hoffmann, *Jazz Advertised 1910–1967: A Documentation,* vol. 7 [Berlin: Franz Hoffmann, 1997], 145).

88. Ted Toll, "Kirby Unit Congas, Minuets, Rhumbas or Jumps at Will," *Down Beat,* 1939 (clipping in John Kirby file, Institute of Jazz Studies, Rutgers University–Newark).

89. Billy Kyle, "Analyzing Billy Kyle's Piano Style," *Music and Rhythm* 1, no. 1 (November 1940): 24.

90. Toll, "Kirby Unit," 6.

91. Schuller, *Swing Era,* 815.

92. Ibid., 814.

93. Ibid., 816, 812.

94. Ibid., 815.

95. On black concert musicians, see Eileen Southern, *The Music of Black Americans: A History,* 3rd ed. (New York: W. W. Norton, 1997), 408–14. Scott DeVeaux, writing of black jazz musicians more generally, argues that "the most satisfying way to undermine" primitivist stereotypes "was to incorporate elements of what the white world respected as musical knowledge and literacy *into* the cultural practices that fueled the stereotype" (Scott DeVeaux, *The Birth of Bebop: A Social and Musical History* [Berkeley and Los Angeles: University of California Press, 1997], 62–63).

96. Benny Goodman and Irving Kolodin, *The Kingdom of Swing* (New York: Stackpole Sons, 1939), 246; Procope, interview, reel 3, transcript, 6; Miller, "Swing Lane," 43; *New York Times,* August 14, 1938 (clipping in Onyx file, NYPL Theatre Coll.); Heywood Hale Broun, "Piano Man in Harlem," *H.R.S. Society Rag* [no. 9] (January 1941): 23. It is unclear exactly to what year Broun refers here, although the passage seems to suggest that it was around the time Newton left the group.

97. Pauline Williams, "Swing and Society Make the Rounds," *Swing: The Guide to Modern Music* 2, no. 1 (May 1939): 28; Bach, "52nd Street," 9.

98. Al Casey, interview by the author and Al Vollmer, June 27, 2002.

99. Leonard Gaskin, interview by the author, June 12, 2002.

100. Stuff Smith, *Pure at Heart 2: Anecdotes and Interviews,* ed. Anthony Barnett (Lewes, UK: Allardyce, Barnett, 2002), 64, 69.

101. Stanley Dance, *The World of Swing* (New York: Charles Scribner's Sons, 1974), 192.

102. Ibid., 19.

103. Gaskin, interview.

104. LeRoy Battle, interview by the author, May 23, 2002.

105. Leonard Feather, *The Book of Jazz: A Guide to the Entire Field* (New York: Horizon Press, 1957), quoted in George Hoefer, "Hot Box: John Kirby," *Down Beat* 29, no. 26 (October 11, 1962): 27.

106. John Kirby and His Orchestra, *Sweet Georgia Brown,* matrix 24678-B, Columbia 36001, recorded May 19, 1939, New York; *Opus 5,* matrix 24947-A, Vocalion 5048, recorded July 28, 1939, New York.

107. Schuller, *Swing Era,* 813; Alyn Shipton, *Groovin' High: The Life of Dizzy Gillespie* (New York: Oxford University Press, 1999), 130.

108. Shipton, *Groovin' High,* 80.

109. Dizzy Gillespie with Al Fraser, *To BE, or Not . . . to BOP: Memoirs* (Garden City, NY: Doubleday, 1979), 138.

110. Ira Gitler, *Jazz Masters of the Forties* (New York: Macmillan, 1966), 184.

Chapter Five

1. Charles Edward Smith, "The Street," notes for *Swing Street* (Epic LP SN6042, 1962).

2. McGowan Miller, "Swing Lane," *Swing: The Guide to Modern Music* 1, no. 12 (April 1939): 43.

3. Alexander, illustration for Bob Bach, "52nd Street," *Swing: The Guide to Modern Music* 3, no. 1 (July 1940): 8.

4. W. Royal Stokes, *Swing Era New York: The Jazz Photographs of Charles Peterson* (Philadelphia: Temple University Press, 1994), 40.

5. Tax Photographs, 1939–1941, reels C-608, C-755, D-982, G-1987, G-1988, G-1993, G-1995, G-1996, H-2194, H-2206, I-2436, I-2444, New York City Municipal Archives.

6. David W. Stowe, *Swing Changes: Big-Band Jazz in New Deal America* (Cambridge, MA: Harvard University Press, 1994), 94–140. On the "brand-name packaging" of swing, also see Kenneth J. Bindas, *Swing, That Modern Sound* (Jackson: University Press of Mississippi, 2001), 39–75.

7. Stowe, *Swing Changes,* 13, 100.

8. Lewis A. Erenberg, *Swingin' the Dream: Big Band Jazz and the Rebirth of American Culture* (Chicago: University of Chicago Press, 1998), 36, 38.

9. Bindas, *Swing,* 75.

10. Martin Jay, *Adorno* (Cambridge, MA: Harvard University Press, 1984), 119. Both Stowe and Erenberg make reference to Adorno; Stowe explicitly rejects Adorno's notion of the audience as passive consumers (*Swing Changes,* 183–84), while Erenberg implicitly disputes "Adorno's view of swing and the jitterbug as the emotionally bereft product of mass industrial culture and the modern culture industry" (*Swingin' the Dream,* 262).

11. Theodor W. Adorno, "On the Fetish Character in Music and the Regression of Listening" [1938], in Theodor W. Adorno, *The Culture Industry: Selected Essays on Mass Culture,* ed. J. M. Bernstein (London: Routledge Classics, 2001), 30.

12. Ibid., 32–33.

13. Ibid., 52–53.

14. Catherine Gunther Kodat, "Conversing with Ourselves: Canon, Freedom, Jazz," *American Quarterly* 55, no. 1 (March 2003): 5.

15. Ibid., 3–6.

16. Jay, *Adorno,* 124.

17. Adorno, "Fetish Character," 53.

18. Ibid., 39.

19. Ibid., 55.

20. Erenberg, *Swingin' the Dream,* 41.

21. Stowe, *Swing Changes,* 100.

22. Irene Thirer, "Touring '52nd Street' with the Movie Makers," *New York Post,* May 5, 1937 (clipping in Fifty-Second Street (Cinema 1937) file, Billy Rose Theatre Collection, New York Public Library for the Performing Arts [collection hereafter cited as NYPL Theatre Coll.]); also see Grover Jones, *Fifty-Second Street,* Final Continuity (Walter Wanger Productions, 1937), cinema script, NYPL Theatre Coll. I have been unable to locate a print of this film; a short clip is in the collection of the National Museum of American History (excerpt from *52nd Street,* directed by Harold Young [United Artists, 1937], Ernie Smith Jazz Film Collection, ca.

1930s–1960s, ES 491.3–1, Archives Center, National Museum of American History), and a print of the film's trailer is housed at the Library of Congress (Motion Picture, Broadcasting and Recorded Sound Division, FEB5081).

23. Walter Bullock and Harold Spina, *Fifty-Second Street,* piano and vocal score (New York: Leo Feist, 1937), 4, 6, 9.

24. Lyrics transcribed from Andy Kirk and His Twelve Clouds of Joy, *Fifty-Second Street,* matrix 61463-A, Decca 1146, recorded December 9, 1936, New York, reissued on Andy Kirk and His Twelve Clouds of Joy, *1936–1937* (Classics CD 573).

25. Fritz Henle, "Memo to: Walter Wanger; Subject: 52nd Street," *Life,* November 29, 1937, 64–67.

26. The earliest source of which I am aware that refers to a broadcast from a 52nd Street club is *Down Beat*'s August 1936 report that "N.B.C. has alotted [*sic*] the Riley-Farley Band three programs a week from the Hickory House" ("Riley and Farley Crack Back at Critics," *Down Beat* 3, no. 8 [August 1936]: 3).

27. Harold Jovien, "Music on Air—Hot and Sweet," *Down Beat* 5, no. 12 (December 1938): 15.

28. Will Bradley's Famous Door Orchestra, NBC Red network, February 21, 1940, 12:30 AM, Library of Congress Motion Picture, Broadcasting, and Recorded Sound Division, NBC Radio Collection, RWA 2211-A3–4.

29. On the major labels, see Stowe, *Swing Changes,* 113–14.

30. "Names in the Swing News," *Swing: The Guide to Modern Music* 2, no. 1 (May 1939): 7; "Onyx Club, N.Y.," *Variety,* May 10, 1939 (clipping in Joe Helboch [*sic*] file, NYPL Theatre Coll.); "Joe Marsala . . . ," *Down Beat* 6, no. 5 (May 1939): 3; "A Night in the Cradle of Swing," *Swing: The Guide to Modern Music* 2, no. 1 (May 1939): 38.

31. The New York World's Fair, located in Flushing, Queens, ran from April 30, 1939, to October 27, 1940 (Stanley Appelbaum, *The New York World's Fair 1939/1940 in 155 Photographs by Richard Wurts and Others* [New York: Dover, 1977], ix, xiv, xvii).

32. The Andrews Sisters, "Strip Teaser Gives Levant a Black Eye!" *Down Beat* 5, no. 12 (December 1938): 36.

33. On Club 18, see Arnold Shaw, *52nd Street: The Street of Jazz* (New York: Da Capo, 1977), 184–92; J[oseph] Bryan III, *The Merry Madmen of 52nd Street* (Richmond, VA: Whittet & Shepperson, 1968). On Leon & Eddie's, see Shaw, *52nd Street,* 36–51. On Tony's, see Shaw, *52nd Street,* 174–78.

34. "Oomph from the Orient," *Pic,* March 4, 1941, 40–41 (clipping in Club Waikiki file, NYPL Theatre Coll.).

35. Shaw, *52nd Street,* 191.

36. "Bandbox, N.Y.," *Variety,* November 16, 1938 (clipping in Band Box, New York file, NYPL Theatre Coll.).

37. "Bandmaker III: 52nd Street," *Swing: The Guide to Modern Music* 1, no. 12 (April 1939): 10.

38. Ruth Sato, "Could Be," *Swing: The Guide to Modern Music* 3, no. 8 (February 1941): 11.

39. "Oomph from the Orient," 41; "Eurasian Hep Cat," *Down Beat* 6, no. 15 (December 15, 1939): 1; Jack Egan, "Dorsey Horn Ace and Krupa Chirp to Wed," *Down Beat* 6, no. 15 (December 15, 1939): 9; Sato, "Could Be," 11; also see Bert Whyatt, "Obituaries: Ruth Sato Reinhardt," *Jazz Journal International* 46, no. 3 (March 1993): 18.

40. Shaw, *52nd Street,* 178.

41. "Hawaiian Yacht Club (New York)," *Variety,* January 26, 1938 (clipping in Hawaiian Yacht Club (N.Y.) file, NYPL Theatre Coll.).

42. H. E. P., "Altitude Is Too Much for Abe Lyman and Band," *Down Beat* 5, no. 2 (February 1938): 3.

43. Shaw, *52nd Street,* 203–4.

44. Robert Inman, "New York Jazz, March 19, 1938" (typescript, in the collection of the author, n.d.).

45. Malcolm Johnson, ["Café Life in New York"?], *New York Sun,* December 6, 1938 (clipping in Onyx Club file, NYPL Theatre Coll.).

46. "Manager Runs Off with Dough;—H. O. to Record Trumpet Quintet," *Down Beat* 4, no. 7 (July 1937): 2; Shaw, *52nd Street,* 89.

47. "Troc, N.Y.," *Variety,* July 12, 1939 (clipping in Troc file, NYPL Theatre Coll.); Malcolm Johnson, "Café Life in New York," *New York Sun,* January 15, 1940 (clipping in Troc file, NYPL Theatre Coll.); Malcolm Johnson, "Café Life in New York," *New York Sun,* September 20, 1939 (clipping in Famous Door file, NYPL Theatre Coll.).

48. "Night Clubs Find Business Is Good," *New York Times,* January 1, 1938, 3; "Teddy Powell's Band," *Swing: The Guide to Modern Music* 2, no. 9 (February 1940): 33. The latter quotation refers to Teddy Powell's opening at the Famous Door in September 1939.

49. See the appendix for details on these two clubs.

50. H. E. P., "Songpluggers Form a Union; Fifty-Second Street Suffers," *Down Beat* 6, no. 9 (September 1939): 27.

51. "New York News: Bud Freeman's Band in B'way Musical Show," *Down Beat* 6, no. 14 (December 1939): 2; "Picketing Helps Close Onyx Club," *Down Beat* 7, no. 2 (January 15, 1940): 3.

52. Johnson, ["Café Life in New York"?], December 6, 1938.

53. "7 Night Clubs Indicted by U.S.," *New York Post,* May 25, 1939; "Operators of Coq Rouge Fined on U.S. Tax Charge," *New York Herald-Tribune,* June 6, 1939 (clippings in Taxation: Clubs: Night: U.S. file, NYPL Theatre Coll.).

54. Milt Hinton, interview by Tom Piazza, [1974], part 2, tape 4, transcript, p. 13, National Endowment for the Arts Jazz Oral History Project, Institute of Jazz Studies, Rutgers University–Newark (hereafter cited as JOHP).

55. A chronology of bands in Harlem theaters during the 1930s and 1940s reveals that short engagements were the rule there as well (Stanley Dance, *The World of Swing* [New York: Charles Scribner's Sons, 1974], 404–6).

56. Johnny Blowers, interview by the author, April 2, 2002; John Hammond, preface in notes to *Swing Street* (Epic LP SN6042, 1962); Irv Manning, interview by the author, January 9, 2003; Janet Holmes to Ed Kirkeby, September 20, 1938, in Ed Kirkeby Papers, box "FW–Ephemera, Biographies & Assorted," folder "Fats Waller 1938," Institute of Jazz Studies, Rutgers University–Newark; Hinton interview, part 2, tape 2, transcript, 44; H. E. P. , "The Deceased of Carnegie Hall Turn Over in Their Graves as Jazz Lifts the Roof!" *Down Beat* 5, no. 12 (December 1938): 3; "Picketing Helps Close Onyx Club," 3; "Places Being Picketed," *Local 802 A. F. of M. Official Journal* 14, no. 12 (October 1940): 25; "Unfair List of Local 802," *Local 802 A. F. of M. Official Journal* 14, no. 12 (October 1940): 27.

57. Billie Holiday with William Dufty, *Lady Sings the Blues* (1956; repr., London: Penguin, 1992), 97, 99.

58. Lathrop Mack, "Brunies Replaces Louis Prima at 'Famous Door,'" *Down Beat* 2, no. 9 (September 1935): 8.

59. Maurice Waller and Anthony Calabrese, *Fats Waller* (New York: Schirmer, 1977), 137.

60. "Night-Club Roughhouse," *Life,* March 3, 1941, 88 (clipping in Club 18 file, NYPL Theatre Coll.).

61. Shaw, *52nd Street,* 247; "What's New in Jazz," *Jazz Information* 2, no. 12 (January 24, 1941): 3. Although Gabler told Shaw that he "started the jams at Ryan's in 1938–39" (Shaw, *52nd Street,* 246), the club did not open until September 1940.

62. "Bandmaker III," 10.

63. On racial discrimination in hiring of big bands during the swing era, see Stowe, *Swing Changes,* 122–23.

64. Advertisement, *Down Beat* 6, no. 9 (September 1939): 11.

65. "Front Page Items: Woody Herman in N.Y. Attracts Wide Comment," *Swing: The Guide to Modern Music* 2, no. 1 (May 1939): 19.

66. Shaw, *52nd Street,* 137.

67. D. H., " 'You Have to Lose Thousands with a Swing Band before You Can Hit That Big Dough,' Alleges Teddy ($) Powell," *Swing: The Guide to Modern Music* 2, no. 6 (November 1939): 8.

68. Artie Shapiro, interview by the author, March 13, 2002; Blowers, interview; Manning, interview.

69. Shapiro, interview; Manning, interview; Sammy Price, interview by Dan Morgenstern, 1980, transcript, 94, JOHP; Al Casey, interview by the author and Al Vollmer, June 27, 2002.

70. The Last of the Moe Egans [Jack Egan], "Tommy Dorsey Sells Five Dozen of Own Fresh Eggs in Nite Club," *Down Beat* 4, no. 3 (March 1937): 31; The Last of the Moe Egans [Jack Egan], "Choice Chunks of Chatter from the Chowder Front," *Down Beat* 4, no. 7 (July 1937): 3; The Last of the Moe Egans [Jack Egan], "Choice Chunks of Chatter from the Chowder Front," *Down Beat* 4, no. 12 (December 1937): 36.

71. "Another New Band Debuts at the Door," *Down Beat* 6, no. 10 (October 1, 1939): 1; Casey, interview.

72. "Another New Band," 1.

73. Ed J. Harris, "New York Turns Out to Greet the Hawk," *Down Beat* 6, no. 9 (September 1939): 37.

74. On "café society," see Robert Sylvester, *Notes of a Guilty Bystander* (Englewood Cliffs, NJ: Prentice-Hall, 1970), 263–68.

75. "Amateur Hide-Beater," *Down Beat* 5, no. 12 (December 1938): 23.

76. "Barnet Heads West to (??) Marry Lamour," *Swing: The Guide to Modern Music* 2, no. 2 (June 1939): 14; see also "A Night in the Cradle of Swing," *Swing: The Guide to Modern Music* 2, no. 1 (May 1939): 38.

77. Pauline Williams, "Swing and Society Make the Rounds," *Swing: The Guide to Modern Music* 2, no. 2 (June 1939): 26; Pauline Williams, "Swing and Society Make the Rounds," *Swing: The Guide to Modern Music* 1, no. 12 (April 1939): 27.

78. See, for example, Bosley Crowther, "Hi-De-Ho! The Night Clubs Turn 'Em Away," *New York Times Magazine,* March 21, 1937, 14–15, 23.

79. Ted Poston, "Dr. Sausage and the Five Pork Chops Burn Up a Night Club and an In-Law," *New York Post,* December 30, 1938 (clipping in Onyx Club file, NYPL Theatre Coll.). "Dr. Sausage" was the stage name of trumpeter Lucius Tyson.

80. Casey, interview.

81. Wilder Hobson, "Fifty-Second Street," in *Jazzmen,* ed. Frederic Ramsey Jr. and Charles Edward Smith (1939; repr., New York: Limelight, 1985), 251.

82. On jitterbugs, see Stowe, *Swing Changes,* 30–37.

83. Marian Squire, "A Steak-House Goes Voodoo; Jam Session," *Variety,* December 29, 1937 (clipping in Hickory House file, NYPL Theatre Coll.).

84. Stowe, *Swing Changes,* 33.

85. Leonard G. Feather, "New York News: Dorsey to Use Guitar Only on Records in the Future," *Down Beat* 7, no. 7 (April 1, 1940): 2.

86. Scott DeVeaux, *The Birth of Bebop: A Social and Musical History* (Berkeley and Los Angeles: University of California Press, 1997), 277. For a detailed profile of 1930s hot jazz enthusiasts, also see Paul Lopes, *The Rise of a Jazz Art World* (Cambridge: Cambridge University Press, 2002), 159–73.

87. Stowe, *Swing Changes,* 81; Erenberg, *Swingin' the Dream,* 140; Dan Morgenstern, "Steve Smith and the Hot Record Society," in liner notes for *The Complete H.R.S. Sessions* (Mosaic CD MD6–187, 1999), 1–3.

88. Erenberg, *Swingin' the Dream,* 141.

89. Ibid.

90. DeVeaux, *Birth of Bebop,* 277.

91. Ibid., 278.

92. Stowe, *Swing Changes,* 83; Lopes, *Jazz Art World,* 174–77. This is not to say that no women or nonwhite men took an interest in hot jazz. For example, Jean Rayburn (later Jean Gleason), a white woman, played in important role in 52nd Street's jazz community as a cofounder of *Jazz Information,* discussed

subsequently, while famous African American writer Langston Hughes is cited as a hot-record collector in an early essay on the phenomenon ("Editorial: A History of Jazz Information," *Jazz Information* 2, no. 16 [November 1941]: 93; Stephen W. Smith, "Hot Collecting," in *Jazzmen,* ed. Frederic Ramsey Jr. and Charles Edward Smith [1939; repr., New York: Limelight, 1985], 289).

93. Inman, "New York Jazz," 2; Robert Inman, interview by the author, April 8, 2002.

94. DeVeaux, *Birth of Bebop,* 279; Casey, interview; Blowers, interview; Inman, interview.

95. DeVeaux, *Birth of Bebop,* 278.

96. Stowe, *Swing Changes,* 82; Shaw, *52nd Street,* 245; Gilbert Millstein, "The Commodore Shop and Milt Gabler" (1946), in *Eddie Condon's Treasury of Jazz,* ed. Eddie Condon and Richard Gehman (New York: Dial, 1956), 96–97.

97. Shaw, *52nd Street,* 244.

98. Ibid.

99. Ibid.; H. E. P., "Nick Kenny Appoints Self One-Man Committee against Swing," *Down Beat* 5, no. 10 (October 1938): 5; "What's New in Jazz," *Jazz Information* 2, no. 16 (November 1941): 8.

100. "Record Leaders," *Swing: The Guide to Modern Music* 3, no. 9 (May 1941): 29.

101. Shaw, *52nd Street,* 245, 244.

102. Bud Freeman, interview by Helen Oakley Dance, [1977 or 1978?], tape recording, sides 1–4, transcript, 81, JOHP.

103. Bach, "52nd Street," 8.

104. "Editorial: History of Jazz Information."

105. Ibid., 100.

106. Ibid., 94.

107. Fred R. Miller, "The Safety Valve: Get-Off on a Theme by Knockwurst," *Jazz Information* 1, no. 27 (March 29, 1940): 6.

108. "New Records," *Jazz Information* 1, no. 33 (May 24, 1940): 3, 8. Paul Lopes writes that white jazz connoisseurs in this era were absorbed with the issue of "who performed . . . authentic black music and who performed a derivative form of jazz emptied of its vitality and authenticity through either a capitulation to commercialism or a misguided professionalism" (Lopes, *Jazz Art World,* 187).

109. "New Records," *Jazz Information* 1, no. 10 (November 14, 1939): 3.

110. Inman, interview.

111. Milt Gabler, "Milt Gabler," [ca. 1971], typescript, 3, box 3, folder 12, Milt Gabler Papers, Archives Center, National Museum of American History, Smithsonian Institution.

112. "Rabson and General Now Making Discs," *Down Beat* 7, no. 5 (March 1, 1940): 6; Jack Egan, " 'Tunes and Not Bands Get the Requests'—Hart," *Down Beat* 7, no. 11 (June 1, 1940): 3; Barrelhouse Dan, "Wham! Jan Savitt Comes On with Two Jazz Sides!!" *Down Beat* 7, no. 6 (March 15, 1940): 14; also see the "Where to Buy Hot Records" listings in *H.R.S. Society Rag* nos. 5–9 (September–December 1940).

113. "Record Leaders," 29.

114. See, for example, *Jazz Information* 1, no. 10 (November 14, 1939): 3.

115. "Editorial: History of Jazz Information," 100.

116. C. Miller, "Readers' Comments," *Jazz Information* 2, no. 4 (September 6, 1940): 29.

117. Ibid., 30.

Chapter Six

1. Count Basie as told to Albert Murray, *Good Morning Blues: The Autobiography of Count Basie* (New York: Random House, 1985), 217.

2. "Ralph Ellison's Territorial Vantage—Interview with Ron Welburn," *Grackle* 4 (1977–78), reprinted in Ralph Ellison, *Living with Music: Ralph Ellison's Jazz Writings*, ed. Robert G. O'Meally (New York: Modern Library, 2001), 30.

3. Arnold Shaw, *52nd Street: The Street of Jazz* (New York: Da Capo, 1977), 148.

4. Gerald Early, *Tuxedo Junction: Essays on American Culture* (Hopewell, NJ: Ecco Press, 1989), 278.

5. David W. Stowe, *Swing Changes: Big-Band Jazz in New Deal America* (Cambridge, MA: Harvard University Press, 1994), 104.

6. Shaw, *52nd Street,* 127.

7. Ibid., 127–30.

8. Jack Gould, "News of the Night Clubs," *New York Times,* sec. 9, July 17, 1938.

9. Basie, *Good Morning Blues,* 218; Advertisement, *New York Times,* July 12, 1938 (clipping reproduced in Franz Hoffmann, *Jazz Advertised 1910–1967: A Documentation,* vol. 7 [Berlin: Franz Hoffmann, 1997], 115 [hereafter cited as *NYT* ad]); Onah L. Spencer, "Duke Ellington Recovers from Operation in N.Y. Hospital," *Down Beat* 5, no. 8 (August 1938): 2.

10. "Basie to Open Monday," *New York Journal-American,* July 9, 1938 (clipping in Famous Door file, Billy Rose Theatre Collection, New York Public Library for the Performing Arts [collection hereafter cited as NYPL Theatre Coll.]); also see "Swing at Famous Door," *New York Herald-Tribune,* July 30, 1938 (clipping in Famous Door file, NYPL Theatre Coll.).

11. Basie, *Good Morning Blues,* 217.

12. Harold Jovien, "Where to Tune in on the Hot Air," *Down Beat* 5, no. 9 (September 1938): 15.

13. Basie, *Good Morning Blues,* 217–18.

14. Shaw, *52nd Street,* 128–29.

15. "Count Basie . . . ," *New York Times,* July 3, 1938 (clipping in Famous Door file, NYPL Theatre Coll.); "Swing at Famous Door"; Shaw, *52nd Street,* 127.

16. "Notes to You: Cat-tales on the Off Beat," *Swing: The Guide to Modern Music* 1, no. 4 (August 1938): 16; "Bassie [*sic*] to Remain at Famous Door," *New York Daily Mirror,* August 18, 1938 (clipping in Famous Door file, NYPL Theatre Coll.); *NYT* ad.

17. Joel Dinerstein, *Swinging the Machine: Modernity, Technology, and African American Culture between the World Wars* (Amherst: University of Massachusetts Press, 2003), 140–41.

18. Ibid., 171.

19. Ibid., 169.

20. A transcription of this broadcast is reissued on *Count Basie Live! 1938 at the Famous Door NYC* (Jazz Hour CD JH-3003).

21. Dinerstein, *Swinging the Machine,* 174.

22. Eddie Bert, interview by the author, March 19, 2002.

23. The studio version is Count Basie and His Orchestra, *Jumpin' at the Woodside,* matrix 64474, Decca 2212, recorded August 22, 1938, New York, reissued on Count Basie, *The Best of Early Basie* (Decca CD GRD-655).

24. "Count Basie: Some Call the Count the King," *Swing: The Guide to Modern Music* 1, no. 4 (August 1938): 15, 19.

25. Dinerstein, *Swinging the Machine,* 171.

26. Shaw, *52nd Street,* 20.

27. Gould, "News of Night Clubs," 8.

28. Shaw, *52nd Street,* 20–21; John Hammond, preface in notes to *Swing Street* (Epic LP SN6042, 1962).

29. H. E. P., "Blind Musicians Plan Jazz Festival," *Down Beat* 5, no. 8 (August 1938): 28. Kruger's name is spelled variously in contemporaneous sources; here, I follow the spelling used in standard discographies.

30. Gould, "News of Night Clubs," 8.

31. Basie, *Good Morning Blues,* 218. Edison's shouts are audible during Basie's piano solo on *Time Out* from the July 23 broadcast (reissued on Jazz Hour CD JH-3003).

32. Gould, "News of Night Clubs," 8; "Swing at Famous Door."

33. Gould, "News of Night Clubs," 8.

34. "Swing at Famous Door."

35. See, for example, "Where the Bands and Orchestras are Playing This Month," *Down Beat* 5, no. 1 (January 1938): 30; "Where the Bands and Orchestras are Playing This Month," *Down Beat* 5, no. 3 (March 1938): 30; "Wingie Manone at Kelly's Stable," *Jazz Information* 1, no. 17 (January 5 [1940]): 1; "Where the Bands Are Playing," *Down Beat* 7, no. 2 (January 15, 1940): 23.

36. "Hawaiian Yacht Club (New York)," *Variety,* January 26, 1938 (clipping in Hawaiian Yacht Club (N.Y.) file, NYPL Theatre Coll.)

37. Eddie Condon and His Windy City Seven, *Love Is Just Around the Corner,* matrix P-22306–2, first issued on Columbia LP XFL-14427, recorded January 17, 1938, New York, reissued on Pee Wee Russell, *Jazz Original* (Commodore CD CMD-404). All of the horn players on this recording led bands on or near 52nd Street in the mid- to late 1930s: cornetist Bobby Hackett at the Troc in 1939 ("Where the Bands Are Playing," *Down Beat* 6, no. 8 [August 1939]: 30); trombonist Georg Brunis at the Famous Door in 1935 (Lathrop Mack, "Brunies Replaces Louis Prima at 'Famous

Door,'" *Down Beat* 2, no. 9 [September 1935]: 8); clarinetist Pee Wee Russell at the Little Club in 1938 ("Where the Bands Are," *Down Beat* 5, no. 11 [November 1938]: 34–35); and tenor saxophonist Bud Freeman at Kelly's Stable (then on 51st Street) in 1939 (advertisement, *Swing: The Guide to Modern Music* 1, no. 12 [April 1939]: 29). Each member of the rhythm section also had connections to 52nd Street: guitarist Eddie Condon and drummer George Wettling played together at Red McKenzie's in 1937 ("Chicago," *Metronome* 53, no. 1 [January 1937]: 38), while Artie Shapiro was the bassist in Joe Marsala's band at the Hickory House throughout the late 1930s (see, for example, advertisement, *Down Beat* 4, no. 7 [July 1937]: 22). Although pianist Jess Stacy may not have worked on the street in this period, a 1939 photograph shows him eating with other musicians at the Pic-A-Rib, 110 West 52nd (W. Royal Stokes, *Swing Era New York: The Jazz Photographs of Charles Peterson* [Philadelphia: Temple University Press, 1994], 63).

38. Gary Giddins, *Bing Crosby: A Pocketful of Dreams—The Early Years, 1903–1940* (Boston: Little, Brown, 2001), 361.

39. Shaw, *52nd Street*, 144–45.

40. Wingy Manone and Paul Vandervoort II, *Trumpet on the Wing* (Garden City, NY: Doubleday, 1948), 123; John Hammond, "Musicians Desert Gin and Weed to Swing Again," *Down Beat* 3, no. 7 (July 1936): 1; "With 'Down Beat' on 'Ole Broadway,' " *Down Beat* 3, no. 8 (August 1936): 13; Shaw, *52nd Street*, 146–47. A photograph of this band appears in Stokes, *Swing Era New York*, 52. Shaw's account implies that Marsala's band with Allen followed Marsala's stint at Red McKenzie's, discussed earlier; the primary sources cited in this paragraph indicate that the Allen band came first. In calling this the first interracial band on 52nd Street, I am referring to organized ensembles rather than jam sessions, in which collaboration between blacks and whites was already taking place.

41. John Hammond, "Many New Faces in New York Swing Spots," *Down Beat* 3, no. 10 (October 1936): 4; Shaw, *52nd Street*, 146.

42. "Chicago," *Metronome* 53, no. 1 (January 1937): 38.

43. G. T. S. [George T. Simon], "First 1937 Roasts and Toasts," *Metronome* 53, no. 1 (January 1938): 26. My identification of the unnamed club as McKenzie's is confirmed by Simon's recollections in a 1943 profile of McKenzie (George T. Simon, "Simon Says," *Metronome* 59, no. 6 [June 1943]: 6).

44. Joe Marsala's Chicagoans, *Clarinet Marmalade*, matrix M-415–1, Variety rejected, recorded April 21, 1937, New York; *Wolverine Blues*, matrix M-412–1, Variety 565, recorded April 21, 1937, New York. All Marsala recordings cited in this chapter are reissued on Joe Marsala, *1936–1942* (Classics CD 763).

45. Original Dixieland Jazz Band, *Clarinet Marmalade Blues*, matrix 22066–2, His Master's Voice B-8500, recorded July 17, 1918, New York. A more likely model is a 1927 recording of the tune by Frankie Trumbauer, which also includes eight-bar solos (Frankie Trumbauer and His Orchestra, *Clarinet Marmalade*, matrix 80392-A, Okeh 40772, recorded February 4, 1927, New York). Trumbauer preceded Marsala at the Hickory House in 1937 (Kapralik, "Hickory House," *New*

York Daily Mirror, January 31, 1937 [clipping in Hickory House file, NYPL Theatre Coll.]).

46. The Last of the Moe Egans [Jack Egan], "Choice Chunks of Chatter from the Chowder Front," *Down Beat* 4, no. 7 (July 1937): 3.

47. Joe Marsala and His Chicagoans, *Mighty Like the Blues,* matrix M-779-1, Vocalion 4168, recorded March 16, 1938, New York; *Woo-Woo,* matrix M-780-1, Vocalion 4116, recorded March 16, 1938, New York; *Hot String Beans,* matrix M-781-1, Vocalion 4168, recorded March 16, 1938, New York; *Jim Jam Stomp,* matrix M-782-1, Vocalion 4116, recorded March 16, 1938, New York. On Rich playing the latter number, see Shaw, *52nd Street,* 149.

48. Bob Inman, *Swing Era Scrapbook: The Teenage Diaries and Radio Logs of Bob Inman, 1936–1938,* compiled by Ken Vail (Lanham, MD: Scarecrow Press, 2005), 151, 177. Beiderbecke's recordings of *Jazz Me Blues* and *Singin' the Blues* are addressed in Gunther Schuller, *Early Jazz: Its Roots and Musical Development* (New York: Oxford University Press, 1968), 189. Marsala recorded *Jazz Me Blues* at his April 21, 1937, session (Joe Marsala's Chicagoans, *Jazz Me Blues,* matrix M-414-2, Variety 565, recorded April 21, 1937, New York).

49. Tom Herrick, "Musicians Go for Marsala's Band," *Down Beat* 5, no. 2 (February 1938): 12; Lavinia, "Tables for Two," *New Yorker* 14, no. 45 (December 24, 1938): 37–38.

50. Irv Manning, interview by the author, January 9, 2003; Artie Shapiro, interview by the author, March 13, 2002. Shapiro's walking bass lines sometimes caused him trouble with Eddie Condon, who "really liked Dixieland. . . . In fact . . . he was a little annoyed with me at times when I deviated and played four beats, you know, he said, 'Just play two,' you know, play two-two time. But I ignored him, I played what I wanted" (Shapiro, interview).

51. Shapiro, interview.

52. Leonard G. Feather, "'I'm Dividing Up the Work,' Says Krupa; Wells Dropped," *Down Beat* 7, no. 11 (June 1, 1940): 11.

53. See, for example, Bill Burton, "Diggin' the Dirt," *Down Beat* 4, no. 9 (September 1937): 17; "Intimate Clicks," *Swing: The Guide to Modern Music* 1, no. 8 (December 1938): 12; "Hickory House . . . ," *New York Post,* November 13, 1937 (clipping in Hickory House file, NYPL Theatre Coll.); Malcolm Johnson, ["Café Life in New York"?], *New York Sun,* September 25, 1940 (clipping in Hickory House file, NYPL Theatre Coll.).

54. Marian Squire, "A Steak-House Goes Voodoo; Jam Session," *Variety,* December 29, 1937 (clipping in Hickory House file, NYPL Theatre Coll.).

55. Herrick, "Musicians Go for Marsala's Band," 12.

56. Shapiro, interview.

57. Manning, interview; Shapiro, interview; Whitney Balliett, "Jazz: Joe Bushkin," *New Yorker* 59, no. 1 (February 21, 1983): 100.

58. On sexist attitudes toward female musicians, see Stowe, *Swing Changes,* 168–72.

59. Manning, interview; Shapiro, interview.

60. See, for example, Harold Jovien, "Hot Air," *Down Beat* 4, no. 12 (December 1937): 20. On the London broadcast, see H. E. P., "Tough Scrams from Tommy Dorsey's Band and Winchell Kids Critics Who Razz Scott's Screwy Titles," *Down Beat* 5, no. 1 (January 1938): 3–4.

61. Patricia Coburn, "Comments: Wow!," *Swing: The Guide to Modern Music* 1, no. 11 (March 1939): 29.

62. Lavinia, "Tables for Two," 37; Theodore Strauss, "Night Club Notes," *New York Times,* January 8, 1939 (clipping reproduced in Hoffmann, *Jazz Advertised,* vol. 7, 129); "Hickory House . . . ."

63. Bob Bach, "Some Like Them Little," *Swing* 2, no. 10 (March 1940): 13; Art Hodes, interview by Don DeMichael, 1979, tape recording, reel 1, transcript, 31, National Endowment for the Arts Jazz Oral History Project, Institute of Jazz Studies, Rutgers University–Newark (hereafter cited as JOHP); Shapiro, interview; Bach, "Some Like Them Little," 13; Herrick, "Musicians Go for Marsala's Band," 12.

64. Leonard Feather, *The Book of Jazz from Then Till Now: A Guide to the Entire Field* (New York: Horizon Press, 1965), 42–43.

65. Hammond, "Musicians Desert Gin and Weed."

66. Shaw, *52nd Street,* 147.

67. "Dynamite . . . ," *Down Beat* 6, no. 4 (April 1939): 3.

68. Leonard Feather, "Gossip from Gotham," *Down Beat* 7, no. 3 (February 1, 1940): 4.

69. "'Mixed Band in Reverse' at Kelly's Stable," *Down Beat* 7, no. 7 (April 1, 1940): 10.

70. "What's New: New York," *Jazz Information* 2, no. 7 (October 25, 1940): 5; "What's New in Jazz: New York," *Jazz Information* 2, no. 8 (November 8, 1940): 5.

71. Feather, *Book of Jazz,* 44; "What's New in Jazz," *Jazz Information* 2, no. 10 (December 6, 1940).

72. Dave Dexter Jr. [D. E. D.,] "Can a White Man Successfully Lead a Negro Band?" *Music and Rhythm* 2, no. 7 (May 1941): 12.

73. Manone and Vandervoort, *Trumpet on the Wing,* 154; Bob Bach, "52nd Street," *Swing: The Guide to Modern Music* 3, no. 1 (July 1940): 24; Manning, interview.

74. Scott DeVeaux, *The Birth of Bebop: A Social and Musical History* (Berkeley and Los Angeles: University of California Press, 1997), 280.

75. Al Casey, interview by the author and Al Vollmer, June 27, 2002; Shapiro, interview.

76. DeVeaux, *Birth of Bebop,* 277–78.

77. Ibid.

78. Shaw, *52nd Street,* 245–46.

79. See DeVeaux, *Birth of Bebop,* 278; Shaw, *52nd Street,* 22, 113, 246; George Hoefer, "Tales of 52nd Street: The Famous Door," *Down Beat Music '68,* special issue,

Down Beat 35 (1968): 79; Gordon Wright, "DISCussions," *Metronome* 52, no. 3 (March 1936): 27. Although DeVeaux and Hoefer each suggest that Gabler ran a series of sessions at the Famous Door, Gabler himself recalled that he "held one session" there (Shaw, *52nd Street,* 246).

80. The Last of the Moe Egans [Jack Egan], "Choice Chunks of Chatter from the Chowder Front," *Down Beat* 4, no. 9 (September 1937): 4.

81. Manone and Vandervoort, *Trumpet on the Wing,* 121–22; "Joe Marsala Rocks It Solid at Hickory House," *Down Beat* 4, no. 8 (August 1937): 25; Shaw, *52nd Street,* 246. In a 1963 interview, Hickory House owner John Popkin claimed to have started Sunday afternoon jam sessions at the club in 1935; in contrast, Milt Gabler argued that the Hickory House jam sessions were inspired by the Bessie Smith jam session at the Famous Door, which took place in 1936 ("Talent Scout," *New Yorker* 39, no. 1 [February 23, 1963]: 25; Shaw, *52nd Street,* 246).

82. "Bandmaker III: 52nd Street," *Swing: The Guide to Modern Music* 1, no. 12 (April 1939): 10; "On the Downbeat . . . ," *New York Times,* January 29, 1939 (clipping in Swing Club file, NYPL Theatre Coll.). These sources do not make it clear whether these sessions were organized formally.

83. "Freeman Opens at Kelly's Stable," *Jazz Information* 1, no. 19 (January 26, 1940): 1; "Bashes at Stable," *Down Beat* 7, no. 8 (April 15, 1940): 2; Leonard Feather [L. G. F.,] "New York News," *Down Beat* 7, no. 6 (March 15, 1940): 2; Shaw, *52nd Street,* 204.

84. "What's New in Jazz," *Jazz Information* 2, no. 12 (January 24, 1941): 3. Although Gabler told Arnold Shaw that he "started the jams at Ryan's in 1938–39," the club did not open until September 1940 (Shaw, *52nd Street,* 230, 246).

85. Shaw, *52nd Street,* 232.

86. See foregoing paragraph of text for Kelly's Stable and Jimmy Ryan's; on the Hickory House, see "New York," *Jazz Information* 1, no. 31 (May 3, 1940): 1.

87. "Talent Scout," 25.

88. Shapiro, interview.

89. Squire, "Steak-House Goes Voodoo."

90. Shapiro, interview.

91. See, for example, "Freeman Opens at Kelly's Stable," 1.

92. "What's New in Jazz," *Jazz Information* 2, no. 13 (February 7, 1941): 4. These bands shared some rhythm section members in common, including drummer Zutty Singleton and bassist Bill King.

93. Charles Peterson photographs in the collection of Don Peterson, Chevy Chase, MD (hereafter cited as Peterson collection), negative file 608.

94. Hodes, interview, reel 1, transcript, 56. Shaw writes that at Ryan's "the sit-ins outnumbered the so-called house group" (Shaw, *52nd Street,* 232).

95. Otis Ferguson, "Jazz at Random," *New Republic,* February 24, 1941, reprinted in *In the Spirit of Jazz: The Otis Ferguson Reader,* ed. Dorothy Chamberlain and Robert Wilson (1982; repr., New York: Da Capo, 1997), 108.

96. Robert Inman, interview by the author, April 8, 2002.

97. Hodes, interview, reel 1, transcript, 55, JOHP.

98. Shaw, *52nd Street,* 248. Although Shaw punctuates and capitalizes "The Blues" here as if it refers to a specific song, it is possible that Gabler was referring to the twelve-bar blues more generally.

99. Shapiro, interview.

100. "Bashes at Stable," 2.

101. See, for example, "What's New in Jazz," *Jazz Information* 2, no. 14 (February 21, 1941): 3; "What's New in Jazz," *Jazz Information* 2, no. 15 (March 21, 1941): 4.

102. Peterson collection, negative file 608.

103. Shaw, *52nd Street,* 247.

104. Ibid., 234.

105. Bob Bach, "Reviews Big Kicks of 1940," *Swing: The Guide to Modern Music* 3, no. 7 (January 1941): 17.

106. Max Kaminsky and V. E. Hughes, *Jazz Band: My Life in Jazz* (1963; repr., New York: Da Capo, 1981), 122; Jack Egan, "Oasis of Swing," in program for Swing Music Concert at the Imperial Theatre, New York, May 24, 1936.

107. Hodes, interview, reel 1, transcript, 55, JOHP.

108. Shaw, *52nd Street,* 233–34.

109. Ibid., 234.

110. Shapiro, interview.

111. Inman, interview.

112. Shapiro, interview.

113. DeVeaux, *Birth of Bebop,* 281; Kaminsky, *Jazz Band,* 122; also see Shaw, *52nd Street,* 247–48. It is likely that at less-formal public jam sessions, like those at the Hickory House, those musicians who simply walked in to play were not compensated; see subsequent text on the union's grudging tolerance of this practice.

114. For example, a flyer advertising sessions at Ryan's is reproduced in Shaw, *52nd Street,* 247.

115. Vic Dickenson, interview by Dan Morgenstern, 1975, transcript, 118, JOHP.

116. Shapiro, interview.

117. Shaw, *52nd Street,* 149.

118. Zutty Singleton and Marge Singleton, interview by Stanley Dance, n.d., transcript, 119, JOHP.

119. Ibid., 123. Singleton also played frequently at the Sunday jam sessions at Ryan's (see, e.g., "What's New in Jazz," *Jazz Information* 2, no. 13 [February 7, 1941]: 4).

120. Herrick, "Musicians Go for Marsala's Band," 12.

121. Manone and Vandervoort, *Trumpet on the Wing,* 154.

122. "Talent Scout," 125.

123. Shapiro, interview; Squire, "Steak-House Goes Voodoo"; also see "Marsala Rocks It Solid," 25.

124. Inman, interview. Reviews from 1941 state that attendance was high at the Ryan's sessions ("What's New in Jazz," *Jazz Information* 2, no. 12 [January 24, 1941]: 3; "What's New in Jazz," *Jazz Information* 2, no. 14 [February 21, 1941]: 3).

125. Kaminsky, *Jazz Band*, 122.

126. Squire, "Steak-House Goes Voodoo."

127. Inman, interview.

128. Kaminsky, *Jazz Band*, 122–23.

Chapter Seven

1. Ken Vail and Donald L. Maggin both give the date of this opening as October 20, although neither cites a source (Ken Vail, *Dizzy Gillespie: The Bebop Years 1937–1952* [Lanham, MD: Scarecrow Press, 2003], 23; Donald L. Maggin, *Dizzy: The Life and Times of John Birks Gillespie* [New York: Harper Entertainment, 2005], 152). A *New York Enquirer* column published on Monday, November 29, 1943, however, reports that the Gillespie band opened "last Thursday night," and Alyn Shipton suggests that the opening was sometime after November 10 (Johnny Kane, "In Old New York," *New York Enquirer,* November 29, 1943, clipping in box 3, brown scrapbook, Bob Howard Papers, Manuscripts, Archives and Rare Books Division, Schomburg Center for Research in Black Culture, New York Public Library [hereafter cited as Howard Papers]; Alyn Shipton, *Groovin' High: The Life of Dizzy Gillespie* [Oxford: Oxford University Press, 1999], 118).

2. Scott DeVeaux, *The Birth of Bebop: A Social and Musical History* (Berkeley and Los Angeles: University of California Press, 1997), 291. The Gillespie quote is from Dizzy Gillespie with Al Fraser, *To BE, or Not . . . to BOP: Memoirs* (Garden City, NY: Doubleday, 1979), 202. Cursory contemporaneous notices of the group include Kane, "In Old New York," and Jimmy Butts, "Harlem Speaks," *Jazz Record,* no. 15 (December 1943): 7.

3. For a comprehensive survey of the musical style of bebop, see Thomas Owens, *Bebop: The Music and Its Players* (New York: Oxford University Press, 1995).

4. Gillespie and Fraser, *To BE,* 208.

5. Ibid., 231; also see "Dizzy Keeps Street Alive," *Metronome* 61, no. 5 (May 1945): 9; Leonard Feather, "Manhattan Kaleidoscope," *Metronome* 61, no. 8 (August 1945): 10.

6. Leonard Feather, "New York Roundup: Dizzy Gillespie," *Metronome* 62, no. 7 (July 1946): 20.

7. mix [Mike Levin], "Small Combo Jazz Progresses," *Down Beat* 14, no. 13 (June 18, 1947): 17; "Eckstine Back to Onyx Club," *Down Beat* 14, no. 20 (September 24, 1947): 12.

8. mix [Mike Levin], "Diggin' the Discs," *Down Beat* 14, no. 2 (January 15, 1947): 18; Yannick Bruynoghe, "52nd Re-Bop Street," *Hot Club Magazine,* no. 20 (October 1, 1947): 10.

9. DeVeaux, *Birth of Bebop,* 3–29.

10. Ibid., 4.

11. Ibid., 5–8.

12. Ibid., 16.

13. Bernie Savodnick, "Gillespie Great," *Down Beat* 11, no. 13 (July 1, 1944): 10.

14. "Broadway Chatters," *New York Age,* June 2, 1945, 10 (clipping reproduced in Franz Hoffmann, *Jazz Reviewed: Working Book to Jazz Advertised in the Negropress of New England 1910–1949* [Berlin: Franz Hoffmann, 1995], 256).

15. Leonard Feather, "Dizzy—21st Century Gabriel," *Esquire,* October 1945, 91.

16. Quoted in Marshall W. Stearns, *The Story of Jazz* (London: Oxford University Press, 1956), 224–25.

17. The Two Deuces [Barry Ulanov and Leonard Feather], "Record Reviews," *Metronome* 61, no. 6 (June 1945): 14; Dizzy Gillespie Sextet, *Groovin' High,* matrix G 554–1, Guild 1001, recorded February 28, 1945, New York, reissued on Dizzy Gillespie, *Shaw 'Nuff* (Musicraft CD MVSCD-53).

18. Thomas Owens argues that at the time of its composition, *Groovin' High* "was the most complex jazz melody superimposed on a pre-existing chordal scheme" (Owens, *Bebop,* 14).

19. Ibid.

20. DeVeaux, pointing out the presence of musicians "firmly associated with swing" on Gillespie's early recordings, writes that "it is hard not to view some of these names as interlopers—competent, even excellent musicians, but so out of sync with the emergent bop style that their presence in the studio with Gillespie is inappropriate, incoherent" (DeVeaux, *Birth of Bebop,* 413–14).

21. "Dizzy Keeps Street Alive," 9; "I Thought I Heard . . . ," *Jazz Record,* no. 31 (April 1945): 2; "I Thought I Heard . . . ," *Jazz Record,* no. 32 (May 1945): 2; "I Thought I Heard . . . ," *Jazz Record,* no. 33 (June 1945), 2; Jimmy Butts, "Where They're Playing," *Jazz Record,* no. 33 (June 1945): 13.

22. DeVeaux, *Birth of Bebop,* 324; Billy Taylor, interview by the author, August 12, 2002. Taylor cites Don Byas and Art Tatum as other 52nd Street musicians who anticipated the melodic and harmonic practices of bebop (Billy Taylor, interview by the author, October 14, 2003).

23. DeVeaux, *Birth of Bebop,* 308–17; "New York Roundup: The Street," *Metronome* 61, no. 4 (April 1945): 23.

24. See "Tatum Broke Datum," *Metronome* 59, no. 9 (September 1943): 7; "On the Jazz Front," *Jazz* [Forest Hills, NY] 1, no. 10 (December 1943): 4; "I Thought I Heard . . . ," *Jazz Record,* no. 16 (January 1944): 2; "Tax Wants Mum; Slam Likes Hum," *Down Beat* 11, no. 12 (June 15, 1944): 4; "Random Ramblings from Rhythm Row," *Down Beat* 11, no. 18 (September 15, 1944): 2.

25. Barry Ulanov, "3's No Crowd," *Metronome* 59, no. 11 (November 1943): 14–15.

26. "Wartime Dollars Boom Music on Swing Alley," *Down Beat* 11, no. 6 (March 15, 1944): 3.

27. "Act of the Year: Art Tatum," *Metronome* 60, no. 1 (January 1944): 23.

28. "Tatum and Shavers Share Deuces' Stand," *Down Beat* 11, no. 14 (July 15, 1944): 1; DeVeaux, *Birth of Bebop,* 290.

29. Tiny Grimes, interview by Bob Kenselaar, 1983, transcript, 51, National Endowment for the Arts Jazz Oral History Project, Institute of Jazz Studies, Rutgers University–Newark (hereafter cited as JOHP).

30. Leonard Feather, "Act Reviews: Art Tatum; Tatum Ultimatum," *Metronome* 59, no. 10 (October 1943): 57.

31. Art Tatum Trio, *I Got Rhythm,* matrix WN-1360-A, Brunswick 80102, recorded January 5, 1944, New York; *I Ain't Got Nobody,* matrix WN-1362-A, Brunswick 80131, recorded January 5, 1944, New York. All Tatum recordings cited reissued on Art Tatum, *1940–1944* (Classics CD 800).

32. Gunther Schuller, *The Swing Era: The Development of Jazz, 1930–1945* (New York: Oxford University Press, 1989), 489. DeVeaux describes this as a "favorite jam session trick" of the era (DeVeaux, *Birth of Bebop,* 310); it also forms the basis of the Kirby Sextet's 1938 recording *From A Flat to C* (see chapter 4.)

33. "Soft Peddle It," *Down Beat* 11, no. 13 (July 1, 1944): 5.

34. "Random Ramblings."

35. Arnold Shaw, *52nd Street: The Street of Jazz* (New York: Da Capo, 1977), 220.

36. *March of Time* 10, no. 5, "Upbeat in Music" (1943). Excerpt in Ernie Smith Jazz Film Collection, ca. 1930s–1960s, Archives Center, National Museum of American History, ES 491.2–2, "Music in America: an amalgam of snippets."

37. Feather, "Act Reviews," 57; Grimes, interview, 36.

38. On Stewart's abilities as an accompanist for Tatum, see James Lester, *Too Marvelous for Words: The Life and Genius of Art Tatum* (New York: Oxford University Press, 1994), 148–49.

39. Grimes, interview, 14; Stanley Dance, *The World of Swing* (New York: Charles Scribner's Sons, 1974), 364.

40. Art Tatum Trio, *I Would Do Anything for You,* matrix WN-1366-A, Brunswick 80102, recorded January 5, 1944, New York.

41. Grimes, interview, 37; Feather, "Act Reviews," 57; Shaw, *52nd Street,* 305; DeVeaux, *Birth of Bebop,* 370.

42. Leonard Feather, "Manhattan Kaleidoscope," *Metronome* 61, no. 8 (August 1945): 10; Bill Gottlieb, "Posin,'" *Down Beat* 14, no. 19 (September 10, 1947): 6; "Weird Wizard," *Down Beat* 14, no. 19 (September 10, 1947): 1; "File for the Future: Nicky Tagg," *Metronome* 63, no. 11 (November 1947): 27.

43. Bernard Gendron points out that "bebop was only one, and not necessarily the favorite, among many advanced, modernist movements in jazz" covered in *Metronome* between 1946 and 1948; alternatives to bebop included white modernists, such as Lennie Tristano and Stan Kenton, who looked to European art music for inspiration (Bernard Gendron, "A Short Stay in the Sun: The Reception of Bebop [1944–1950]," in *The Bebop Revolution in Words and Music,* ed. Dave Oliphant [Austin: Harry Ransom Humanities Research Center, University of Texas at Austin, 1994], 145–46).

44. tac [Frank Stacy], "Erroll Garner, New 88er, Draws Raves," *Down Beat* 12, no. 4 (February 15, 1945): 2; "Impish Erroll," *Metronome* 61, no. 2 (February 1945): 22; Sharon A. Pease, "Erroll Garner a Self-Trained, Creative 88er," *Down Beat* 12, no. 19 (October 1, 1945): 12.

45. Erroll Garner Trio, *Laura*, matrix S5837, Savoy 571, recorded September 25, 1945, New York, reissued on Erroll Garner, *The Complete Savoy Master Takes* (Savoy Jazz CD SVY-17025–26).

46. Gillespie and Fraser, *To BE*, 294.

47. "Be-bop Be-bopped," *Time*, March 25, 1946, 52; "Diggin' the Discs with Don," *Down Beat* 12, no. 15 (August 1, 1945): 8; Mort Schillinger, "Dizzy Gillespie's Style, Its Meaning Analyzed," *Down Beat* 13, no. 4 (February 11, 1946): 14–15; "New York Jazz Stinks Claims Coast Promoter," *Down Beat* 12, no. 16 (August 15, 1945): 2.

48. Feather, "Dizzy—21st Century Gabriel," 91; Schillinger, "Dizzy Gillespie's Style," 14; Bill Gottlieb, "Posin,'" *Down Beat* 13, no. 12 (June 3, 1946): 3; Gillespie and Fraser, *To BE*, 279; Shipton, *Groovin' High*, 194.

49. Shipton, *Groovin' High*, 148; DeVeaux, *Birth of Bebop*, 434; Gillespie, *To BE*, 229.

50. *Jivin' in Be-Bop*, DVD, directed by Leonard Anderson and Spencer Williams (1946; Storyville Films, 2004).

51. Shipton, *Groovin' High*, 184. DeVeaux and biographer Donald L. Maggin both argue that Gillespie's stage manner was influenced by that of his former employer Cab Calloway (DeVeaux, *Birth of Bebop*, 183; Maggin, *Dizzy*, 102).

52. William P. Gottlieb/Ira and Leonore S. Gershwin Fund Collection, Music Division, Library of Congress, "Portrait of Dizzy Gillespie, Downbeat, New York, N.Y., between 1946 and 1948," call number LC-GLB23- 0323, viewed online at http:// memory.loc.gov/music/gottlieb/03000/03200/03231v.jpg; "Portrait of Ella Fitzgerald, Dizzy Gillespie, Ray Brown, Milt (Milton) Jackson, and Timmie Rosenkrantz, Downbeat, New York, N.Y., ca. Sept. 1947," call number LC-GLB23- 0285, viewed online at http://memory.loc.gov/music/gottlieb/02000/02800/02851v.jpg.

53. DeVeaux, *Birth of Bebop*, 435.

54. Taylor, interview, August 12, 2002; also see Shaw, *52nd Street*, 171.

55. DeVeaux argues similarly that the harmonic and rhythmic ambiguities of bebop gave the new style a striking potential for irony and the unexpected (DeVeaux, *Birth of Bebop*, 268).

56. Ibid., 172; Barry Ulanov, "Band Reviews: Dizzy Gillespie," *Metronome* 63, no. 9 (September 1947): 22; Barbara Carroll, interview by the author, July 29, 2002.

57. "Big Bands May Set New Era for 52 St.," *Down Beat* 13, no. 21 (October 7, 1946): 3; Leonard Feather, "The Street Comes Back to Charlie Ventura," *Metronome* 63, no. 5 (May 1947): 20, 48–49; "Debts Shutter Swing Spot," *Down Beat* 14, no. 21 (October 8, 1947): 3.

58. Leonard Feather, *Inside Be-Bop* (New York: J. J. Robbins & Sons, 1949), 39.

59. Feather, "Street Comes Back," 49.

60. Charlie Ventura and His Orchestra, *How High the Moon*, matrix NSC-163, National 7015, recorded September 6, 1946, New York, reissued on Charlie Ventura, *1946–1947* (Classics CD 1111). While the liner notes for the CD reissue list Stanley Baum as the arranger of *How High the Moon*, Feather credited Hefti in his 1949 book (*Inside Be-Bop*, 39).

61. Feather, "Street Comes Back," 20.

62. "Eckstine Back to Onyx Club," *Down Beat* 14, no. 20 (September 24, 1947): 12; "Where the Bands Are Playing," *Down Beat* 14, no. 21 (October 8, 1947): 17.

63. Ira Gitler, *Swing to Bop: An Oral History of the Transition in Jazz in the 1940s* (New York: Oxford University Press, 1985), 231.

64. Ibid., 230.

65. Babs' Three Bips and a Bop, *Lop-Pow*, matrix BN296–1, Blue Note 535, recorded February 24, 1947, New York; *Dob Bla Bli*, matrix BN302–3, Blue Note 536, recorded May 7, 1947, New York, both reissued on Babs Gonzales, *Weird Lullaby* (Blue Note CD CDP 7 84464 2).

66. Bop [*sic*] Bach, "Babs' Three Bips and a Bop," *Metronome* 63, no. 5 (May 1947): 26.

67. Babs' Three Bips and a Bop, *Oop-Pop-A-Da*, matrix BN297–1, Blue Note 534, recorded February 24, 1947, New York, reissued on Babs Gonzales, *Weird Lullaby* (Blue Note CD CDP 7 84464 2).

68. See, for example, the following sequence of headlines from *Down Beat*: "Wartime Dollars Boom Music on Swing Alley," *Down Beat* 11, no. 6 (March 15, 1944): 3; "New York Biz Dying, 52nd St. May Fold Quick," *Down Beat* 12, no. 6 (March 15, 1945): 1, 11; "52 St. Jumps as Top Jazz Names Return Home," *Down Beat* 12, no. 21 (November 1, 1945): 3.

69. "Wartime Dollars Boom," 3.

70. DeVeaux, *Birth of Bebop*, 285; "Spots Shutter as Panic over Tax Continues," *Down Beat* 11, no. 10 (May 15, 1944): 1.

71. "Curfew!" *Metronome* 61, no. 3 (March 1945): 9.

72. "New York Biz Dying"; "New York Roundup: The Street," *Metronome* 61, no. 4 (April 1945): 23. The quotation is from "Curfew Ends N. Y. Jumps," *Metronome* 61, no. 6 (June 1945): 7.

73. DeVeaux, *Birth of Bebop*, 295–96, 302–3.

74. The Two Deuces [Barry Ulanov and Leonard Feather], "Record Reviews," *Metronome* 61, no. 7 (July 1945): 18.

75. Leonard Feather, "Jazz in Harlem," *Metronome* 62, no. 12 (December 1946): 49; Leonard Feather, "' . . . your boy, Symphony Sid . . . ,'" *Metronome* 63, no. 3 (March 1947): 44–45.

76. "Dizzy Keeps Street Alive," 9.

77. "August Heat Slows Up Biz," *Down Beat* 14, no. 19 (September 10, 1947): 1.

78. DeVeaux, *Birth of Bebop*, 4; Amiri Baraka [LeRoi Jones], *Blues People: Negro Music in White America* (1963; repr., New York: Quill, 1999), 179–81; Ingrid Monson, "The Problem with White Hipness: Race, Gender, and Cultural Conceptions

in Jazz Historical Discourse," *Journal of the American Musicological Society* 48, no. 3 (1995): 411.

79. Gillespie and Fraser, *To BE*, 244.

80. Gitler, *Swing to Bop*, 143.

81. Ibid., 144.

82. John Robinson, interview by the author, January 30, 2002.

83. Gitler, *Swing to Bop*, 140.

84. Robert George Reisner, *Bird: The Legend of Charlie Parker* (New York: Citadel, 1962), 209.

85. John Simmons, interview by Patricia Willard, 1977, tape 5, transcript, 29, JOHP.

86. Shaw, *52nd Street*, 292–93, 328; advertisement, *New York Amsterdam News*, sec. B, September 2, 1944; DeVeaux, *Birth of Bebop*, 370. Although Arnold Shaw suggests that Tondelayo's opened in September 1944, the club was advertised as early as August 19 (advertisement, *New York Amsterdam News*, August 19, 1944 [clipping reproduced in Franz Hoffmann, *Jazz Advertised 1910–1967: A Documentation* (Berlin: Franz Hoffmann, 1997), vol. 1–3, 656]).

87. "Ubangi Club (New York)," *Variety*, April 7, 1937 (clipping in Tondelayo file, Billy Rose Theatre Collection, New York Public Library for the Performing Arts [collection hereafter cited as NYPL Theatre Coll.]).

88. Leon Gordon, *White Cargo: A Play of the Primitive* (Boston: Four Seas, 1925).

89. "Charming Hostess," *New York Daily Mirror*, January 3, 1945; advertisement, *New York Amsterdam News*, August 19, 1944; advertisement, *New York Amsterdam News*, September 23, 1944 (clipping reproduced in Hoffmann, *Jazz Advertised*, vol. 1–3, 658).

90. DeVeaux, *Birth of Bebop*, 370.

91. Ibid., 382.

92. Ibid., 228–35, 290; "Kelly's Stable, N.Y.," *Variety*, October 20, 1943 (clipping in Kelly's Stable file, NYPL Theatre Coll.); Jimmy Butts, "Harlem Speaks," *Jazz Record*, no. 14 (November 1943): 11.

93. Leonard Gaskin, interview by the author, June 12, 2002. On Gaskin with Monroe, see DeVeaux, *Birth of Bebop*, 289–90; with Parker, see Jimmy Butts, "Where They're Playing," *Jazz Record*, no. 38 (November 1945): 13.

94. Gillespie and Fraser, *To BE*, 251.

95. Advertisement, *People's Voice*, January 6, 1945; Jimmy Butts, "Where They're Playing," *Jazz Record*, no. 35 (August 1945): 13; "I Thought I Heard . . . ," *Jazz Record*, no. 41 (February 1946): 2.

96. Advertisement, *People's Voice*.

97. Dan Morgenstern, interview by the author, November 8, 2001; Robinson, interview; Lawrence Lucie, interview by the author, Christina Brown, and Al Vollmer, July 9, 2002; Carline Ray, interview by the author, April 24, 2002.

98. LeRoy Battle, interview by the author, May 23, 2002; also see "Three Deuces—and a Hip Trio!" *Down Beat* 13, no. 12 (June 3, 1946): 19.

99. William P. Gottlieb/Ira and Leonore S. Gershwin Fund Collection, Music Division, Library of Congress, "Downbeat, New York, N.Y., ca. 1948," call number LC-GLB23-0281, viewed online at http://memory.loc.gov/music/gottlieb/02000/02800/02811v.jpg.

100. Monson, "Problem," 400, 397.

101. "I Ran Into . . . ," *Jazz Record,* no. 25 (October 1944): 2.

102. "The Beat and the Hipster," *Down Beat* 11, no. 10 (May 15, 1944): 1; "I Thought I Heard . . . ," *Jazz Record,* no. 25 (October 1944): 2; advertisement, *New York Age,* November 25, 1944, 11 (clipping in Hoffmann, *Jazz Advertised,* vol. 1–3, 660).

103. "Handsome Harry the Hipster Illustrates His Song of That Title," *Down Beat* 11, no. 16 (August 15, 1944): 2; "The Gibson, Girl," *Down Beat* 11, no. 16 (August 15, 1944): 2; Shaw, *52nd Street,* 330.

104. Tom Piper, "Zombies Put Kiss of Death on 52nd St. Jazz," *Down Beat* 13, no. 5 (February 25, 1946): 3.

105. Piper, "Zombies," 3; Monson, "Problem," 401.

106. Davis and Troupe, *Miles,* 72.

107. Maggin, *Dizzy,* 173.

108. Malcolm X with the assistance of Alex Haley, *The Autobiography of Malcolm X* (1965; repr., New York: Ballantine Books, 1973), 129.

109. Abe Hill, "'Swing Lane' Zest Dampened but Continues," *New York Amsterdam News,* July 29, 1944.

110. Ibid.

111. Monson, "Problem," 401; Robin D. G. Kelley, *Race Rebels: Culture, Politics, and the Black Working Class* (New York: Free Press, 1994), 176.

112. Monson, "Problem," 404.

113. Ibid., 414.

114. Teddy Reig with Edward Berger, *Reminiscing in Tempo: The Life and Times of a Jazz Hustler* (Metuchen, NJ: Scarecrow Press and the Institute of Jazz Studies, Rutgers University, 1990), 4–5, 11–15; Bob Porter, liner notes for *The Savoy Story: Volume One—Jazz* (Savoy Jazz CD 92856–2, 1999), 19–22.

115. On Garry, see Leonard Feather, "New York Roundup: Vivien Garry," *Metronome* 61, no. 4 (April 1945): 23; mix [Mike Levin], "Garry Trio Musical—and Commercial," *Down Beat* 14, no. 10 (May 7, 1947): 3. On Osborne, see "Mary in Stable," *Down Beat* 13, no. 16 (July 29, 1946): 17; "Carter Joins Osborne Trio," *Down Beat* 15, no. 21 (October 20, 1948): 2. On Carroll, see "Gal's Trio Provides Kicks on Street," *Down Beat* 14, no. 18 (August 27, 1947): 3. On Dardanelle, see "Whose Goose Is Golden or The Egg and They," *Down Beat* 14, no. 3 (January 29, 1947): 10; "Street Starts to Jump," *Down Beat* 14, no. 14 (July 2, 1947): 2.

116. "Names Change but Street Still Jumps," *Down Beat* 12, no. 4 (February 15, 1945): 3.

117. Sherrie Tucker, *Swing Shift: "All-Girl" Bands of the 1940s* (Durham, NC: Duke University Press, 2000), 56–63.

118. "Garry Trio Musical," 3; "Street Starts to Jump," 2.

119. "Garry Trio Musical," 3; The Two Deuces [Barry Ulanov and Leonard Feather], "Record Reviews," *Metronome* 61, no. 6 (June 1945): 15; "Diggin' the Discs with Don," *Down Beat* 13, no. 6 (March 11, 1946): 8.

120. "Gal's Trio," 3.

121. Carroll, interview.

122. For a brief discussion of racial tension on 52nd Street during World War II, see Shaw, *52nd Street,* 255–56.

123. Leroy "Slam" Stewart, interview by Stanley Crouch, 1979, cassette 4, transcript, 21, JOHP.

124. Gillespie and Fraser, *To BE,* 210–11; also see Shaw, *52nd Street,* 259–60.

125. Simmons, interview, tapes 6–9, transcript, 16–17.

126. White drummer John Robinson, for example, was born in Tennessee and worked in Atlanta before moving to New York and playing with black musicians of the bebop movement (Robinson, interview).

127. "Gendarmes Halt Racial Skirmish," *Down Beat* 11, no. 12 (June 15, 1944): 1; "Racial Hatred Rears Ugly Head in Music," *Down Beat* 11, no. 15 (August 1, 1944): 1.

128. Robinson, interview; Reig and Berger, *Reminiscing in Tempo,* 9.

129. David W. Stowe, *Swing Changes: Big-Band Jazz in New Deal America* (Cambridge, MA: Harvard University Press, 1994), 163–64; also see Shaw, *52nd Street,* 255–56; Abe Hill, "The Magic Wand of Swing Keeps 52 St. Doors Ajar," *New York Amsterdam News,* July 29, 1944; Hill, "'Swing Lane.'" White Rose owner Abe Turkewitz denied that police had forced him to close at midnight, claiming instead that the problem was "a shortage of help" ("Vagrant Chicks Blamed in Part for Racial Row," *Down Beat* 11, no.16 [August 15, 1944]: 12).

130. "Tension Mounts on 52nd Street," *Metronome* 60, no. 8 (August 1944): 7, 28; "Vagrant Chicks," 12.

131. eve [Evelyn Ehrlich?], "Alley Combos Out on Order From Police," *Down Beat* 12, no. 22 (November 15, 1945): 1; also see "'Alley' Back in Business Again," *Down Beat* 12, no. 23 (December 1, 1945).

132. "Alley Combos Out." An alternate suspicion was that the charges were "a political issue, with Rockefeller interests—who control nearby Radio City—wanting possession of the entire block" (ibid.).

133. "Top 52nd Street Clubs Padlocked by Police," *New York Amsterdam News,* November 10, 1945.

134. Davis and Troupe, *Miles,* 71. Although Davis does not give a date for this event, a comparison of his account with contemporaneous sources suggests that he was remembering November 1945 (see, e.g., "52 St. Jumps").

135. Piper, "Zombies Put Kiss of Death," 3.

Chapter Eight

1. Bernard Gendron, "'Moldy Figs' and Modernists: Jazz at War (1942–1946)," in *Jazz among the Discourses*, ed. Krin Gabbard (Durham, NC: Duke University Press, 1995), 32.

2. Ibid.

3. Ibid., 37–38, 40–44.

4. Ibid., 32–33.

5. Ibid., 33.

6. Ibid., 49; Bernard Gendron, "A Short Stay in the Sun: The Reception of Bebop (1944–1950)," in *The Bebop Revolution in Words and Music*, ed. Dave Oliphant (Austin: Harry Ransom Humanities Research Center, University of Texas at Austin, 1994), 149.

7. Gendron, "'Moldy Figs' and Modernists," 51.

8. Scott DeVeaux, "Constructing the Jazz Tradition: Jazz Historiography," *Black American Literature Forum* 25, no. 3 (Fall 1991): 539.

9. Samuel B. Charters and Leonard Kunstadt, *Jazz: A History of the New York Scene* (Garden City, NY: Doubleday, 1962), 320.

10. "Business Spotty Along Swing Lane," *Down Beat* 13, no. 17 (August 12, 1946): 5.

11. George Avakian, "Records—Old and New," *Jazz Record*, no. 21 (June 1944): 3.

12. Art Hodes, editorial, *Jazz Record*, no. 39 (December 1945): 16.

13. Frederic Ramsey Jr., "Frisco and Back," *Needle* 2, no. 1 (1945): 31.

14. Rudi Blesh, "Esquire's Second Swing Concert," *Jazz Record*, no. 29 (February 1945): 8; Rudi Blesh, editorial, *American Jazz Review* 2, no. 10 (October 1946): 2.

15. Arnold Shaw refers to the club as "the fortress of those who were damned as 'moldy figs'" (Arnold Shaw, *52nd Street: The Street of Jazz* [New York: Da Capo, 1977]), 229).

16. William Gottlieb, interview by the author, September 17, 2001; Bill Crow, interview by the author, February 27, 2002; Al Vollmer, interview by the author, March 12, 2002.

17. See, for example, Mary Beckwith, "The Spotlight on Bob Wilber," *American Jazz Review* 3, no. 2 (December 1946): 3; Peggy Hart, "Young Jazzmen Spark Ryan's," *American Jazz Review* 2, no. 4 (February 1946): 5.

18. Vollmer, interview.

19. Crow, interview; also see Bill Crow, *From Birdland to Broadway: Scenes from a Jazz Life* (New York: Oxford University Press, 1992), 38–39.

20. Vollmer, interview; Billy Taylor, interview by the author, August 12, 2002; Billy Taylor, interview by the author, October 14, 2003.

21. Vollmer, interview; "Where to Go in New York," *Jazz Record*, no. 3 (March 15, 1943): 8.

22. Shaw, *52nd Street*, 235–36. On Hodes, see "I Thought I Heard . . . ," *Jazz Record*, no. 20 (May 1944): 2; "I Thought I Heard . . . ," *Jazz Record*, no. 27 (December 1944): 2.

On Mezzrow, see "I Thought I Heard . . . ," *Jazz Record,* no. 28 (January 1945): 2; "I Thought I Heard . . . ," *Jazz Record,* no. 31 (April 1945): 2. On Bechet, see "Sid Bechet Trio at Jimmy Ryan's," *Down Beat* 14, no. 8 (April 9, 1947): 17. On Yaged's trio, see "I Thought I Heard . . . ," *Jazz Record,* no. 33 (June 1945): 2; "I Thought I Heard . . . ," *Jazz Record,* no. 39 (November 1945): 2.

23. Charters and Kunstadt, *Jazz,* 319.

24. William Russell, "Louis Armstrong," in *Jazzmen,* ed. Frederic Ramsey Jr. and Charles Edward Smith (1939; repr., New York: Liveright Editions, 1985), 120; James Lincoln Collier, *The Making of Jazz: A Comprehensive History* (New York: Delta, 1978), 284; Lewis A. Erenberg, *Swingin' the Dream: Big Band Jazz and the Rebirth of American Culture* (Chicago: University of Chicago Press, 1998), 221; Shaw, *52nd Street,* 265.

25. Collier, *Making of Jazz,* 284; Erenberg, *Swingin' the Dream,* 221.

26. Erenberg, *Swingin' the Dream,* 221.

27. The date comes from Ralph J. Gleason, "Bunk's Horn Knocks Out Cats at Ryan's," *Down Beat* 12, no. 7 (April 1, 1945): 1.

28. Lewis Eaton, "Jam Session with Bunk," *Jazz Record,* no. 31 (April 1945): 6–7.

29. Gleason, "Bunk's Horn," 1.

30. Bob Aurthur, "Jazzorama," *Jazz Record,* no. 60 (November 1947): 17.

31. "I Thought I Heard . . . ," *Jazz Record,* no. 7 (May 15, 1943): 2; "I Thought I Heard . . . ," *Jazz Record,* no. 19 (April 1944): 2; Shaw, *52nd Street,* 236.

32. De Paris Brothers Orchestra, *Change O'Key Boogie,* matrix 4712, Commodore 567, recorded February 5, 1944, New York, reissued on *Swing Street Showcase* (Commodore CD CCD 7013); Freddie Moore, interview by Ron Welburn, 1983, transcript, part 3, p. 68, National Endowment for the Arts Jazz Oral History Project, Institute of Jazz Studies, Rutgers University–Newark (hereafter cited as JOHP); R. E. M. W., "Tables for Two: Very Warm for March," *New Yorker* 20, no. 6 (March 25, 1944): 65.

33. Vollmer, interview.

34. Ibid.

35. "Kid Quintet at Ryan's," *American Jazz Review* 2, no. 4 (February 1946): 2.

36. Hart, "Young Jazzmen," 5.

37. Ibid.; "Cavalcade at Town Hall," *American Jazz Review* 2, no. 6 (April 1946): 4.

38. Hart, "Young Jazzmen," 5.

39. Ibid., 6.

40. Peggy Hart, "Introducing: Wilber's Wildcats," *American Jazz Review* 3, no. 2 (December 1946): 3–4.

41. Ibid.; Al Avakian, "Sidney Bechet, Musical Father to Bob Wilber," *Jazz Record,* no. 56 (June 1947): 5; Charles Edward Smith, "The Austin High School Gang," in *Jazzmen,* ed. Frederic Ramsey Jr. and Charles Edward Smith (1939; repr., New York: Liveright Editions, 1985), 161.

42. Hart, "Young Jazzmen," 6; "Cavalcade at Town Hall," 4; George Avakian, "Records—Old and New," *Jazz Record,* no. 56 (June 1947): 22.

43. Bob Wilber and His Wildcats, *Willie the Weeper,* Commodore C-583, matrix A4903–1, recorded February 22, 1947, New York, reissued on *The Commodore Story* (Commodore CD CMD-2–400).

44. Hart, "Young Jazzmen," 6; Bob Aurthur, "Jazzorama," *Jazz Record,* no. 55 (May 1947): 23; Beckwith, "Spotlight on Bob Wilber," 3; Hart, "Introducing: Wilber's Wildcats," 4; G. Avakian, "Records—Old and New" (June 1947), 21–22.

45. "Kids Crowd Oldtimers with Their Jazz Style," *Down Beat* 13, no. 25 (December 2, 1946): 2.

46. Ibid.

47. W. Royal Stokes, *The Jazz Scene: An Informal History from New Orleans to 1990* (New York: Oxford University Press, 1991), 56. For a more detailed account, see Bob Wilber with Derek Webster, *Music Was Not Enough* (New York: Oxford University Press, 1988), 23–34.

48. Wilber, *Music Was Not Enough,* 31.

49. Sidney Bechet with Bob Wilber's Wildcats, *Spreadin' Joy,* Columbia 38320, matrix 37999–1, recorded July 14, 1947, New York, reissued on Sidney Bechet, *Spreadin' Joy: 1940–1950* (Naxos Jazz Legends CD 8.120531).

50. Sidney Bechet, *Treat It Gentle: An Autobiography* (1960; repr., New York: Da Capo Press, 2002), 186. The "one-man band record" was a 1941 experiment with overdubbing in which Bechet played all of the instruments in a quartet and sextet by himself (Sidney Bechet's One-Man Band, *The Sheik of Araby* [matrix BS063875–1] and *Blues of Bechet* [matrix BS 063786–1A], Victor 27485, recorded April 18, 1941, New York, reissued on Naxos Jazz Legends CD 8.120531).

51. A. Avakian, "Sidney Bechet," 5.

52. Ibid., 6.

53. Beckwith, "Spotlight on Bob Wilber," 5.

54. Art Hodes, "I Ran Into . . . ," *Jazz Record,* no. 56 (June 1947): 4; "Mickey Gravine: T D-Brunis of 1956; A Real Comer," *American Jazz Review* 2, no. 10 (October 1946): 3.

55. George Avakian, "Records—Old and New," *Jazz Record,* no. 52 (February 1947): 42; G. Avakian, "Records—Old and New" (June 1947), 22; Aurthur, "Jazzorama" (May 1947), 23.

56. Beckwith, "Spotlight on Bob Wilber," 5; Art Hodes, "On the Cover," *Jazz Record,* no. 56 (June 1947): 4; Wilber, *Music Was Not Enough,* 31.

57. Bechet, *Treat It Gentle,* 186.

58. Like Wingy Manone, Brunis dropped letters from his name (originally George Brunies) in the 1930s on the advice of a numerologist (Gerun Moore, "Unlucky? Maybe Your Name Is Spelled Wrong," *Down Beat* 6, no. 11 [October 15, 1939]: 4). Although his name is spelled variously in both primary and secondary sources, I use the shortened version here.

59. Shaw, *52nd Street,* 110; "An Old Swing Man," *Down Beat* 2, no. 8 (August 1935): 1; Lathrop Mack, "Brunies Replaces Louis Prima at 'Famous Door,'" *Down Beat* 2, no. 8 (September 1935): 8.

60. Mary Beckwith and Joan Lesley, "Ryan's Joint Jumping to Mad Brunis Combo," *American Jazz Review* 2, no. 8 (June 1946): 1.

61. "Brunis at Ryan's," *American Jazz Review* 2, no. 9 (July 1946): 5.

62. Beckwith and Lesley, "Ryan's Joint Jumping," 1, 7.

63. Ibid., 1.

64. Ibid., 1, 7.

65. "Brunis at Ryan's," 1; on Brunis's popularity at Ryan's, also see "Ryan's Snubs Street Trend," *Down Beat* 13, no. 21 (October 7, 1946): 1.

66. "Old Swing Man," 1.

67. Shaw, *52nd Street,* 110.

68. Bob Aurthur, "The Bandbox: Featuring Georg Brunis," *Jazz Record,* no. 48 (September 1946): 14.

69. Ibid.; Charles Miller, "New Orleans in New York," *New Republic* 115, no. 21 (November 25, 1946): 694; Shaw, *52nd Street,* 237.

70. Shaw, *52nd Street,* 237.

71. See "Brunis at Ryan's," 1, 7; Beckwith and Lesley, "Ryan's Joint Jumping," 7; "I Ran Into . . . ," *Jazz Record,* no. 46 (July 1946): 2; "Brunis Dixie on the March," *Down Beat* 13, no. 13 (June 17, 1946): 2.

72. Beckwith and Lesley, "Ryan's Joint Jumping," 7; "I Ran Into . . . " (July 1946), 2.

73. William P. Gottlieb/Ira and Leonore S. Gershwin Fund Collection, Music Division, Library of Congress, "Portrait of George Brunis and Tony Parenti, Jimmy Ryan's (Club), New York, N.Y., ca. Aug. 1946," call number LC-GLB13- 0986, viewed online at http://memory.loc.gov/music/gottlieb/09000/09800/09861v.jpg.

74. Aurthur, "Bandbox: Featuring Georg Brunis," 14.

75. ron [Eddie Ronan], "Tony Parenti's Dixie Combo Bows on Stem," *Down Beat* 13, no. 25 (December 2, 1946): 8.

76. "I Ran Into . . ." (July 1946), 2; Aurthur, "Bandbox: Featuring Georg Brunis," 14.

77. Aurthur, "Bandbox: Featuring Georg Brunis," 14.

78. "Brunis at Ryan's," 1, 5.

79. Bob Aurthur, "The Bandbox: Featuring Nobody in Particular," *Jazz Record,* no. 52 (February 1947): 19.

80. Art Hodes, editorial, *Jazz Record* no. 47 (August 1946): 17.

81. Stokes, *Jazz Scene,* 58. Dan Morgenstern relates a similar story, although he says that "Diz declined" the duel (Dan Morgenstern, "Reflections on the Death of 52nd Street," *Jazz Journal* 16, no. 7 [July 1963]: 8). A *Down Beat* article from July 1946 suggests that police forced Brunis back into Ryan's before he could reach the Spotlite (ron [Eddie Ronan], "Police Avert Clash of Dixieland and Re-bop," *Down Beat* 13, no. 14 [July 1, 1946]: 3).

82. "Jazz Uptown," *American Jazz Review* 2, no. 8 (June 1946): 4.

83. ron, "Police Avert Clash," 3.

84. Dizzy Gillespie with Al Fraser, *To be, or Not . . . to bop: Memoirs* (Garden City, NY: Doubleday, 1979), 294–95.

85. Shaw, *52nd Street,* 305–6.

86. Leonard Gaskin, interview by the author, June 12, 2002.

87. Dan Morgenstern, interview by the author, November 8, 2001.

88. LeRoy Battle, interview by the author, May 23, 2002; John Robinson, interview by the author, January 30, 2002.

89. "Jazz Uptown," *American Jazz Review* 2, no. 8 (June 1946): 4; Peggy Hart, "Davison's Dixielanders, Hodes Open Keyboard," *American Jazz Review* 2, no. 9 (July 1946): 1.

90. Wilber, *Music Was Not Enough,* 31.

91. Stokes, *Jazz Scene,* 55.

92. Ibid., 57.

93. Kenny Clarke, interview by Helen Oakley Dance, 1977, tape recording, sides 1–4, transcript, 108, JOHP. On Tough's controversial conversion, see Bill Gottlieb, "Condon Raps Tough for 'Re-Bop Slop,'" *Down Beat* 13, no. 21 (October 7, 1946): 4, 17.

94. Shaw, *52nd Street,* 171.

95. Taylor, interview, August 12, 2002.

96. Cliff Leeman, interview by Milt Hinton, 1979, tape recording, reel 3, transcript, 31–32, JOHP.

97. Ibid., 32–33.

98. Ibid., 33.

99. Ibid., 42.

100. Ibid., 43, 44.

101. Shaw, *52nd Street,* 283.

102. John Malachi, interview by Bryant DuPre, 1983, transcript, part 1, p. 81, JOHP.

103. Shaw, *52nd Street,* 305–6.

Conclusion

1. Leonard Feather, "The Street Is Dead: A Jazz Obituary," *Metronome* 64, no. 4 (April 1948): 33.

2. [Arthur] Getz, front cover, *New Yorker* 24, no. 10 (May 1, 1948). As Arnold Shaw perceptively notes, the arrangement of clubs in the illustration means that the viewer is facing east and that the sun depicted is thus actually rising; nonetheless, in this historical moment, "for 52d St., it was really a setting sun, or sunrise on a dying street," and "cartoonist Getz was giving visual embodiment to obituaries that had already appeared in *Time* and *Collier's*" (Arnold Shaw, *52nd Street: The Street of Jazz* [New York: Da Capo, 1977], 349).

3. Bill Gottlieb, "Good-Time Street," *Collier's* 122, no. 1 (July 3, 1948): 48.

4. "52nd Street Gasping Last Gasps as Deuces Move Music to Clique," *Down Beat* 15, no. 25 (December 15, 1948): 1.

5. Gottlieb, "Good-Time Street," 24.

6. Feather, "Street Is Dead," 17.

7. *The Strip-Tease Murder Case,* VHS, directed by Hugh Prince, (1950; Harbor Drive-In Theatre, n.d.); author's transcription from film. On Jarwood and Olman, see Shaw, *52nd Street,* 296–97, 320–25.

8. Feather, "Street Is Dead," 32.

9. Gilbert Millstein, "The Twilight of a Zany Street," *New York Times Magazine,* January 1, 1950, 12; also see Shaw, *52nd Street,* 340–41.

10. Feather, "Street Is Dead," 17; also see Shaw, *52nd Street,* 339.

11. See Ira Gitler, *Jazz Masters of the Forties* (New York: Macmillan, 1966), 74. The Hickory House, which featured pianist Marian McPartland throughout the 1950s and pianist Billy Taylor during the 1960s, was replaced by a "music-less fish shanty" in 1968 (Shaw, *52nd Street,* 163, 173, 352). Jimmy Ryan's left 52nd Street for a new 54th Street location in 1962 (Shaw, *52nd Street,* 242).

12. Jack Egan, "Choice Chunks of Chatter from the Chowder Front," *Down Beat* 4, no. 11 (November 1937): 28; H. E. P., "Songpluggers Form a Union; Fifty-Second Street Suffers," *Down Beat* 6, no. 9 (September 1939): 27.

13. Ruth Sato, "Could Be," *Swing: The Guide to Modern Music* 3, no. 9 (May 1941): 16.

14. "Goings on About Town," *New Yorker* 17, no. 15 (May 24, 1941): 4.

15. Dave Dexter Jr., "Swing Street Is Dead," [*Metronome?*], July 1942, clipping in 52nd Street file, Institute of Jazz Studies, Rutgers University–Newark.

16. R. E. M. W., "Tables for Two," *New Yorker* 20, no. 6 (March 25, 1944): 65.

17. Dave Dexter Jr., "East Is East . . . ," *Metronome* 61, no. 11 (November 1945): 24; Rod Reed, "Blue Notes," *Down Beat* 12, no. 20 (October 15, 1945): 1.

18. "Worrisome Days Along the Street; Biz Is Sad," *Down Beat* 13, no. 23 (November 4, 1946): 1; Charles Miller, "New Orleans in New York," *New Republic* 115, no. 21 (November 25, 1946): 694; Eddie Ronan, "Where Will 52nd Street Go?" *Hollywood Note* 1, no. 5 (July 1946): 7, clipping in 52nd Street file, Institute of Jazz Studies, Rutgers University–Newark; Art Hodes, editorial, *Jazz Record* no. 47 (August 1946): 17.

19. Svetlana Boym, *The Future of Nostalgia* (New York: Basic, 2001), xiii.

20. Ibid., 43.

21. Ibid., 354.

Appendix

1. " 'Bandbox' Opens on W. 52d Street," *New York Daily Mirror,* November 9, 1938 (clipping in Band Box, New York file, Billy Rose Theatre Collection, New York Public Library for the Performing Arts [collection hereafter cited as NYPL Theatre Coll.]).

2. The April 1939 issue of *Swing: The Guide to Modern Music* carries conflicting reports, with one article claiming that "the Bandbox closed" while another suggests that a new band is soon to begin work at the club ("Bandmaker III: 52nd Street," *Swing: The Guide to Modern Music* 1, no. 12 [April 1939]: 10; "Notes to You: Cat-tales on the Off Beat," *Swing: The Guide to Modern Music* 1, no. 12 [April 1939]: 8). A *Variety* article from May 3, 1939, confirms that the club was closed by that date ("Club 18, N.Y.," *Variety*, May 3, 1939 [clipping in Club 18 file, NYPL Theatre Coll.]).

3. The club took over the space formerly occupied by the Famous Door, which closed May 10, 1936 (Arnold Shaw, *52nd Street: The Street of Jazz* [New York: Da Capo, 1977], 116).

4. The latest reference to Cafe Maria that I have found is Abel [Green], "Famous Door, N.Y," *Variety*, December 8, 1937 (clipping in Famous Door file, NYPL Theatre Coll.). On December 12, the *New York Times* reported that "the Cafe Maria, site of the old Famous Door, is now the Swing Club" (Jack Gould, "News of the Night Clubs," *New York Times*, December 12, 1937).

5. On Saturday, March 14, 1936, the *New York Times* reported that the Caliente "opened on Sunday night" ("Night Club Notes," *New York Times*, March 14, 1936).

6. The *New York Times* reported on June 5, 1937, that "the word is out that the Caliente Club on West Fifty-second Street, which closed several weeks ago, will reopen on Wednesday evening" ("Night Club Notes," *New York Times*, June 5, 1937). I have found no sources that confirm the predicted reopening, however, and the Famous Door was located at 66 West 52nd Street by November 30 (see note 28). The 52nd Street Club occupied this address between the closing of the Caliente and the opening of the Famous Door (The Last of the Moe Egans [Jack Egan], "Choice Chunks of Chatter from the Chowder Front," *Down Beat* 4, no. 12 [December 1937]: 36.)

7. The address 35 West 52nd Street was the home of the Onyx until around February 1934 (see note 61).

8. The Famous Door, which opened on March 1, 1935, took over the Casino Deluxe's lease (Shaw, *52nd Street*, 106).

9. My estimate contradicts that of Arnold Shaw, who states that the club opened in the "summer of 1935" (Shaw, *52nd Street*, 191). Joseph Bryan III, in a monograph on the club, asserts that it opened in July 1936 (J[oseph] Bryan III, *The Merry Madmen of 52nd Street* [Richmond, VA: Whittet & Shepperson, 1968], 7). This is corroborated by a report in the July 3, 1938, *New York Times* that "Jack White's 18 Club will be two years old this week" ("Jack White's . . .," *New York Times*, July 3, 1938 [clipping in Club 18 file, NYPL Theatre Coll.]). My estimate of June, rather than July, derives from a mention of the club in a *Down Beat* article from that month ("Goodman Sits in with New York Bands," *Down Beat* 3, no. 6 [June 1936]: 3).

10. The latest reference that I have found that suggests a focus on jazz at the club is a report that Red McKenzie played there in August 1936 ("Where the Names [*sic*] Orchestras are Playing This Month," *Down Beat* 3, no. 8 [August

1936]: 15). Although musicians such as Frank Froeba and Gordon Andrews continued to appear there thereafter, the club's emphasis was on the raucous comedy of Jack White, Pat Harrington, and Frankie Hyers (on Froeba, see, for example, The Last of the Moe Egans [Jack Egan], "Choice Chunks of Chatter from the Chowder Front," *Down Beat* 4, no. 9 [September 1937]: 4; on Andrews, see Shaw, *52nd Street*, 191; on the comedians, see Shaw, *52nd Street*, 184–92).

11. "Goings on about Town," *New Yorker* 15, no. 8 (April 8, 1939): 4.

12. The *New York Times* reported on July 20, 1945, that 129 W 52 "and the adjoining building at 131 West Fifty-second Street will be the new home of the '18' Club after alternations [sic] are made in the two buildings" ("2 Groups Extend Realty Holdings," *New York Times*, July 20, 1945).

13. The club became Dixon's (see note 18).

14. The club was formerly Dixon's (see note 19). The first reference to this incarnation of Club 18 that I have found is "Club 18 on Hunt for Music Names," *Down Beat* 14, no. 11 (May 21, 1947): 16.

15. The last reference to the club that I have found is "Variety of Styles Mark 52nd Street," *Down Beat* 14, no. 15 (July 16, 1947): 2. The club became the Troubadour (see note 100.)

16. "Debts Shutter Swing Spot," *Down Beat* 14, no. 21 (October 8, 1947): 3. The club was formerly the Troubadour (see note 101.)

17. "Club 18 Closes Its Doors Again, Maybe," *Down Beat* 14, no. 22 (October 22, 1947): 3.

18. "Mooney Opens on Swing Lane at Fancy Price," *Down Beat* 13, no. 21 (October 7, 1946): 1. The club was formerly Club 18.

19. The latest reference that I have found that mentions Dixon's is "Garry Trio Musical—and Commercial," *Down Beat* 14, no. 10 (May 7, 1947): 3. The club became Club 18 (see note 14).

20. The earliest reference that I have found is "Night Club Notes," *New York Times*, March 27, 1937.

21. The latest reference that I have found is an advertisement in the *New York Times*, May 31, 1939.

22. Shaw, *52nd Street*, 326. The earliest reference that I have found is "Tenors at Downbeat," *Down Beat* 11, no. 10 (May 15, 1944): 7.

23. "Goings on about Town," *New Yorker* 23, no. 4 (March 15, 1947): 6; The Square, "Strictly Ad Lib," *Down Beat* 14, no. 7 (March 26, 1947): 5.

24. "Goings on about Town," *New Yorker* 23, no. 19 (June 28, 1947): 7; "Street Starts to Jump," *Down Beat* 14, no. 14 (July 2, 1947): 2.

25. The latest reference that I have found to the club being open is "Goings on about Town," *New Yorker* 23, no. 50 (January 31, 1948): 6. *Metronome* reported in April 1948 that "the Downbeat folded a couple of months ago and reopened under a new name with a girlie show," and a photo caption explains that "the Downbeat is now called the Carousel and features girls" (Leonard Feather, "The Street Is Dead," *Metronome* 64, no. 4 [April 1948]: 16).

26. "Onyx Club Burns New Spot Opens across Street," *Down Beat* 2, no. 3 (March 1935): 3.

27. "The First Home of 'Jam' Music Is Bankrupt," *Down Beat* 3, no. 6 (June 1936): 3.

28. On Sunday, November 28, 1937, the *New York Times* reported that the Famous Door was scheduled to open on Tuesday after a postponement the previous week (Jack Gould, "News and Gossip of Night Clubs," *New York Times*, November 28, 1937).

29. "Famous Door to Reopen as Monument to Swing," *Metronome* 56, no. 9 (September 1940): 9; Ed Flynn, "Cotton Club, Famous Door Both Fold," *Down Beat* 7, no. 13 (July 1, 1940): 2. Oddly, even as *Down Beat*'s reports made it clear that the Famous Door was closed, its band listings throughout the summer continued to suggest erroneously that bands were performing there.

30. *Jazz Information* predicts a September 25 reopening in its September 20 issue ("What's New," *Jazz Information* 2, no. 5 [September 20, 1940]: 28). The club was definitely reopened by September 30 ("Open Door," *New York Daily News*, September 30, 1940 [clipping in Famous Door file, NYPL Theatre Coll.]).

31. Jimmy Butts, "Harlem Speaks," *Jazz Record*, no. 14 (November 1943): 11; "Cats Fall Out to Open New Famous Door," *Down Beat* 10, no. 22 (November 15, 1943): 1. On October 1, 1943, *Down Beat* reported that the club had already moved, but it appears not to have featured music until the end of the month ("On 52nd St.," *Down Beat* 10, no. 19 [October 1, 1943]: 13).

32. "Door Closes with a Bang," *Down Beat* 11, no. 2 (January 15, 1944): 13.

33. *Down Beat* reported on January 15, 1947, that the Spotlite, formerly at 56 West 52nd, had been called the Famous Door "for the past month" ("Four Spots Left, Jazz Blows Final Breath on 52nd Street," *Down Beat* 14, no. 2 [January 15, 1947]: 3).

34. Shaw, *52nd Street*, 318.

35. I have encountered only two references to this club. Fritz Henle, "Memo to: Walter Wanger; Subject: 52nd Street," *Life*, November 29, 1937, 66, states only that "the club has closed" without providing dates. Egan, "Choice Chunks of Chatter" (December 1937), 36, explains that the "new Famous Door" was "formerly the 52nd Street Club, and before that the Caliente." My dates here are thus based on available information for the Famous Door and the Caliente.

36. "Nightclubs and Other Venues," *New Grove Dictionary of Music Online*, ed. L. Macy http://www.grovemusic.com (accessed 8 November 2003).

37. I thank an anonymous online reference librarian at the New York Public Library's Milstein Division of United States History, Local History and Genealogy for finding this address in the Manhattan white pages for Summer 1939.

38. On April 9, 1939, the *New York Times* reported that the club had recently opened (T. S., "News of Night Clubs," *New York Times*, April 9, 1939).

39. The latest reference I have found is a June 1939 survey of 52nd Street clubs stating only that "Bert Frohman's is swell" ("Fifty-Second Street," *Swing: The Guide to Modern Music* 2, no. 2 [June 1939]: 34).

40. Shaw, *52nd Street,* 141.

41. Lathrop Mack, "Mannone's Music Liked by N.Y. 'Hot' Fans," *Down Beat* 2, no. 8 (August 1935): 2.

42. Shaw, *52nd Street,* 352.

43. Ibid., 230.

44. Ibid., 242.

45. "Newton, Stuff Smith on 52nd Street," *Jazz Information* 1, no. 25 (March 8, 1940): 1; "Nightclubs and Other Venues."

46. "Fire at Kelly's Closes Up Club," *Down Beat* 14, no. 4 (February 12, 1947): 1.

47. Shaw, *52nd Street,* 93; also see "Fifty-Second Street," 34, which refers to "Joe Helobock's [*sic*] New Onyx"; Helbock originally planned to call the club the Onyx but lost legal control of the name (Shaw, *52nd Street,* 93).

48. "Two New Clubs Open in N.Y.," *Down Beat* 6, no. 7 (July 1939): 27; Shaw, *52nd Street,* 93.

49. "New Club for 52nd St.," *Down Beat* 12, no. 22 (November 15, 1945): 2.

50. *Down Beat* reported in January 1947 that the club adopted "a doll policy" around the summer of 1946, after Wild Bill Davison left ("Four Spots Left," 3). Davison was still playing there as late as August 1946, although *Jazz Record* predicted that he would soon leave (Bob Aurthur, "The Bandbox," *Jazz Record,* no. 47 [August 1946]: 18).

51. H. E. P., "Author of 'Hot Jazz' Visits U.S.A," *Down Beat* 5, no. 11 (November 1938): 3, states that the club is expected to open but does not give a date; however, the band listings in the same issue claim that Pee Wee Russell is already working there ("Where the Bands Are," *Down Beat* 5, no. 11 [November 1938]: 34–35).

52. The latest reference to the club's operation that I have found is McGowan Miller, "Swing Lane," *Swing: The Guide to Modern Music* 2, no. 1 (May 1939): 3. McGowan Miller, "Swing Lane," *Swing: The Guide to Modern Music* 2, no. 2 (June 1939): 39, claims that the club is anticipating a "Gala Reopening" in June, but I have found no reference to the club thereafter.

53. The earliest primary source of which I am aware is M. Eliot Freedgood, "Ribald Row's Pioneers," *New York Times,* June 27, 1937.

54. The latest reference that I have found is "Recommended," *New York Amsterdam News,* January 20, 1940, 27 (clipping reproduced in Franz Hoffmann, *Jazz Reviewed: Working Book to Jazz Advertised in the Negropress of New England 1910– 1949* [Berlin: Franz Hoffmann, 1995], 223).

55. Bob Bach, "Three T's Open Jam House as N.Y. Hotels Ring Cash Register; Harlem Hot," *Down Beat* 3, no. 12 (December 1936): 3; "Night Club Notes," *New York Times,* November 21, 1936.

56. Shaw, *52nd Street,* 146. The club was still open in January 1937 ("Chicago," *Metronome* 53, no. 1 [January 1937]: 38), but columnist George Simon implied in

the same month (albeit without naming McKenzie's overtly) that the club was "just about to fold" (G. T. S. [George T. Simon], "First 1937 Roasts and Toasts," *Metronome* 53, no. 1 [January 1937]: 26). My identification of the unnamed club as McKenzie's is confirmed by Simon's recollections in a 1943 profile of McKenzie (George T. Simon, "Simon Says," *Metronome* 59, no. 6 [June 1943]: 6).

57. The earliest references of which I am aware are H. E. P., "Local 802 Launches New Bank System," *Down Beat* 6, no. 5 (May 1939): 11; "'Hold Tight'—Here We Go Again," *Swing: The Guide to Modern Music* 2, no. 1 (May 1939): 35.

58. "Two New Clubs Open in N.Y.," 27.

59. My Roman numerals differ from the system used by Arnold Shaw, who divides the history of the Onyx into three parts; my Onyx IV is thus equivalent to Shaw's Onyx III (Shaw, *52nd Street*).

60. In an early essay on the Onyx Club, Jack Egan claims that it opened on July 30, 1930 (Jack Egan, "Oasis of Swing," in program for Swing Music Concert at the Imperial Theatre, New York, May 24, 1936; I thank Don Peterson for lending me his copy of this program). Years later, however, owner Joe Helbock told Arnold Shaw that "he launched the Onyx in 1927, not in '29–'30, as has been reported" (Shaw, *52nd Street*, 54). This is apparently contradicted by a report of the Committee of Fourteen, an antivice group, which claims that a speakeasy named the Aquarium moved from 27 West 48th to 35 West 52nd, the address of the Onyx, "on January 1, 1929, after being raided" ("Night Clubs and Speakeasies Located on Numbered Streets," [ca. 1929–1930], typescript, 41, box 37, folder "Inv. Reports—Night Clubs on Numbered Streets," Committee of Fourteen Records, Manuscripts and Archives Division, The New York Public Library, Astor, Lenox and Tilden Foundations). It is possible, however, that the Onyx and the Aquarium occupied different parts of the brownstone at number 35 in 1929. Later in his interview with Shaw, Helbock describes an unidentified club that occupied the ground floor of number 35 while the Onyx occupied the second floor. The club lasted less than a month before police raided it (Shaw, *52nd Street*, 54). Helbock mentions the Aquarium in this interview ("I was bootlegging on The Street in '27–'28, when the Aquarium was near Sixth Avenue. . . . That was a speak with a tank of fish behind the bar"), but he does not refer to any relationship between the Aquarium and the Onyx (Shaw, *52nd Street*, 52). If the precise date of January 1, 1929, given in the Committee of Fourteen report is correct, Helbock is mistaken about the dates when the Aquarium was on 52nd Street. He may also be moving back the opening date of the Onyx to give his club a claim to priority over other 52nd Street fixtures like Tony's and Leon & Eddie's.

61. The precise date on which the Onyx at 72 West 52nd Street opened is unclear. A *Metronome* article from February 1934 claims that "the Onyx Club, formerly a rendezvous of well-known musikers, moved on February 1 to its new quarters at 72 West 52nd Street" (Richard B. Gilbert, "Richard B. Gilbert on Broadway and Byway," *Metronome* 50, no. 2 [February 1934]: 15). A month later, however, the same periodical reported that "the Onyx opened its new quarters on 72

West 52nd Street on Saturday, the 17th, as the Radio Musicians Club of New York" ("News in the Trade: Onyx's New Quarters," *Metronome* 50, no. 3 [March 1934]: 40). Secondary sources also offer conflicting dates; George Hoefer claims that the club opened on February 9 (George Hoefer, "Father of the Street: Onyx Days Recalled," *Down Beat's Music '66: 11th Yearbook,* special issue, *Down Beat* 33 [1966]: 93), while Arnold Shaw states that it opened on February 4 (Shaw, *52nd Street,* 66).

62. Egan, "Oasis of Swing"; "Onyx Club Burns," 3.

63. Egan, "Oasis of Swing"; "Musicians Flock Back to Onyx Club," *Down Beat* 2, no. 8 (August 1935): 2.

64. "Goings on about Town," *New Yorker* 13, no. 4 (March 13, 1937): 4; "Goings on about Town," *New Yorker* 13, no. 5 (March 20, 1937): 4.

65. "Picketing Helps Close Onyx Club," *Down Beat* 7, no. 2 (January 15, 1940): 3.

66. Doctor Jazz [Bob Thiele], "On the Jazz Front," *Jazz* 1, no. 1 (June 1942): 5.

67. "Onyx Club Shuttered," *Down Beat* 13, no. 13 (June 17, 1946): 1.

68. "Onyx Revue Still in Doubt," *Down Beat* 14, no. 14 (July 2, 1947): 2; "Variety of Styles Mark 52nd Street," 2.

69. The Square, "Strictly Ad Lib," *Down Beat* 15, no. 26 (December 29, 1948): 6.

70. Shaw, *52nd Street,* 297. The earliest primary source that I have found is "Where the Bands Are Playing," *Down Beat* 16, no. 18 (September 23, 1949): 17.

71. Shaw, *52nd Street,* 299. The club is depicted in a photograph accompanying Gilbert Millstein, "The Twilight of a Zany Street," *New York Times Magazine,* January 1, 1950, 12.

72. The earliest references of which I am aware are Jimmy Butts, "Harlem Speaks," *Jazz Record,* no. 8 (June 1, 1943): 5; "Una Mae Carlisle Has Jam Outfit," *Down Beat* 10, no. 11 (June 1, 1943): 23.

73. Leonard Feather, "52nd Street . . . Jumps Again," *Metronome* 59, no. 7 (July 1943): 12; The Square, "Strictly Ad Lib," *Down Beat* 10, no. 13 (July 1, 1943): 13.

74. Arnold Shaw states that the club opened at 62 West 52nd Street (Shaw, *52nd Street,* 95) but later claims that it was located at 60 West 52nd (Shaw, *52nd Street,* 335). The *New Grove Dictionary of Jazz* gives the 62 West 52nd Street address ("Nightclubs and Other Venues"). While it is possible that the club changed location sometime during the 1940s, Shaw's second reference may simply be a typographical error.

75. Shaw states that the Samoa opened "over a year" after the Onyx at 62 West 52nd Street closed, which suggests that the Samoa opened during or after December 1940 (Shaw, *52nd Street,* 95).

76. "Nightclubs and Other Venues." Arnold Shaw suggests that it began as a striptease club; however, banjoist Elmer Snowden worked there in the early 1940s (Shaw, *52nd Street,* 21; "Nightclubs and Other Venues"; "News in Brief," *Jazz Information* 2, no. 16 [November 1941]: 9).

77. Shaw, *52nd Street,* 340–41.

78. The earliest reference that I have found is an advertisement in the *New York Age,* November 25, 1944, 11 (clipping reproduced in Franz Hoffmann, *Jazz*

Advertised 1910-1967: A Documentation [Berlin: Franz Hoffmann, 1997], vol. 1-3, 660). *Metronome* reported in December 1944 that the Spotlite opened during "the past month" ("The Street," *Metronome* 60, no. 12 [December 1944]: 14).

79. *Metronome* reported in December 1946 that Charlie Ventura was playing at the Spotlite ("Charlie Ventura," *Metronome* 62, no. 12 [December 1946]: 50), and *Down Beat* listed Red Allen at the club on January 1, 1947 ("Where the Bands Are Playing," *Down Beat* 14, no. 1 [January 1, 1947]: 22). On January 15, 1947, however, *Down Beat* claimed that the Spotlite "for the past month has been called the Famous Door" ("Four Spots Left," 3).

80. The Swing Club was formerly Cafe Maria (see note 4).

81. The latest reference of which I am aware is "Places Being Picketed: September 13, 1940," *Official Journal, Local 802 A. F. of M., Associated Musicians of Greater New York* 14, no. 12 (October 1940): 25.

82. In one instance, Arnold Shaw writes that the club was at 70 West 52nd Street (Shaw, *52nd Street,* 338–39): this is either a typographical error or the club moved in the early 1950s after switching to a striptease policy.

83. Feather, "52nd Street . . . Jumps Again," 12; The Square, "Strictly Ad Lib," *Down Beat* 10, no. 13 (July 1, 1943): 13.

84. "Cabaret License Revoked," *New York Times,* August 15, 1953.

85. R. J. M., "The Theatre," *Wall Street Journal,* October 10, 1935, states that the club is opening at 38 West 52nd Street, but other sources make it clear that the Yacht Club was operating at that address during *Through the Looking Glass's* run on 52nd Street (see, for example, "Expansion Moves Feature Leasing," *New York Times,* March 20, 1936).

86. R. J. M., "The Theatre."

87. The latest reference of which I am aware is "Where the Name Orchestras Are Playing This Month," *Down Beat* 3, no. 7 (July 1936): 20.

88. Shaw, *52nd Street,* 155. The earliest primary sources that I have seen are "Goings on about Town," *New Yorker* 11, no. 34 (October 5, 1935): 4; "Five Rhythm Chicks Roost in Tillie's Coop," *Down Beat* 2, no. 11 (November 1935): 2; "Buy 207th Street Site for New Building," *New York Times,* November 14, 1935.

89. The New York musicians' local picketed Tillie's in May 1936, but the club is absent from the union's picketing list for June; the union announced in July that the pickets were "withdrawn when the management discontinued the employment of musicians" ("Picket Lines," *Official Journal, Local 802 A. F. of M., Associated Musicians of Greater New York* 11, no. 7 [May 1936]: 5; "Results of Picketing since January, 1935," *Official Journal, Local 802 A. F. of M., Associated Musicians of Greater New York* 11, no. 9 [July 1936]: 8).

90. The earliest reference that I have found is an advertisement in the *New York Amsterdam News,* August 19, 1944, 10A (clipping reproduced in Hoffmann, *Jazz Advertised,* vol. 1-3, 656).

91. The latest reference that I have found is "I Thought I Heard . . .," *Jazz Record,* no. 31 (April 1945): 2.

92. The earliest reference that I have found is Leonard Feather, "Gossip from Gotham," *Down Beat* 7, no. 3 (February 1, 1940): 4.

93. Jack Egan, "'Fair Is Open but Everything Ain't Quite Oke'—Egan," *Down Beat* 7, no. 12 (June 15, 1940): 5.

94. The *New York Times* reported on September 28, 1933, that "a lease of 9 W. 52d St. was assigned . . . to the New Town Casino Club, Inc" ("Leaseholds Recorded," *New York Times*, September 28, 1933). The earliest reference to the club's operation that I have found is "Goings on about Town," *New Yorker* 9, no. 3 (October 14, 1933): 4. Arnold Shaw calls the club a "former speakeasy," which suggests that it might have opened earlier on an unofficial basis (Shaw, *52nd Street*, 113).

95. Shaw claims that Mamie Smith performed at the club "shortly before" it "folded"; Smith's appearance was in September 1936 (Shaw, *52nd Street*, 113; "Haymes Gets Break Skyrocket Chord Will Chill You," *Down Beat* 3, no. 9 [September 1936]: 3). The club was picketed by the New York musicians' local in September and October 1936 ("Picket Lines," *Official Journal, Local 802 A. F. of M., Associated Musicians of Greater New York* 11, no. 11 [September 1936]: 5; "Picket Lines," *Official Journal, Local 802 A. F. of M., Associated Musicians of Greater New York* 11, no. 12 [October 1936]: 12). The club is not on the union's November list of picket lines.

96. "Notes to You: Cat-tales on the Off Beat," *Swing: The Guide to Modern Music* 1, no. 7 (November 1938): 20.

97. The latest reference of which I am aware is "Where the Bands Are Playing," *Down Beat* 7, no. 5 (March 1, 1940): 22. Jimmy Ryan's opened at 53 West 52nd Street in September 1940 (Shaw, *52nd Street*, 230). Sources from 1939 describing the Troc as "new" may indicate that the club closed and then reopened sometime between November 1938 and July 1939, but I have no direct evidence of this ("New Club," *New York Daily News*, July 5, 1939 [clipping in The Troc file, NYPL Theatre Coll.]; Richard B. Gilbert, "On Broadway and Byway," *Metronome* 55, no. 8 (August 1939): 19; "The Troc Club," *New York Herald Tribune*, September 13, 1939 [clipping in The Troc file, NYPL Theatre Coll.]).

98. Louis Calta, "News around the Night Clubs," *New York Times*, January 31, 1943.

99. *Down Beat* reported on June 1, 1944, that owner Irving Alexander planned to turn "the 52nd St. Trocadero" into a "rib joint" ("A Snack, Jack?" *Down Beat* 11, no. 10 [June 1, 1944]: 14).

100. "Troubadour in Slow Start," *Down Beat* 14, no. 19 (September 10, 1947): 1. The club was formerly Club 18 (II).

101. "Debts Shutter Swing Spot," 3. The club became Club 18 (III).

102. Shaw, *52nd Street*, 253; "Musicians Find Spot to Hang Their Hats," *Metronome* 58, no. 10 (October 1942): 8.

103. Shaw, *52nd Street*, 253–54.

104. Arnold Shaw states that the club was at 38 West 52nd Street "shortly after Repeal" (ibid., 178).

105. "Night Club Notes," *New York Times,* October 2, 1937; Jack Gould, "News and Gossip of the Night Clubs," *New York Times,* October 17, 1937.

106. "On 52nd St.," 13.

107. The latest reference that I have found to the club's operation is "Goings on about Town," *New Yorker* 20, no. 13 (May 13, 1944): 4. On May 15, *Down Beat* reported that the Downbeat had taken over its location ("Tenors at Downbeat").

Index

Adorno, Theodor, 114–15, 145

Adrian Rollini's Tap Room, 49

AFM. *See* American Federation of Musicians

African American musicians: bebop and, 156, 169–70; in 52nd Street audience, 87–88, 109–10, 124, 173, 183–84; jam sessions and, 29; as marginal in early years of 52nd Street, 61–62, 89; at original Onyx, 28–29, 222n11; racial stereotypes and, 6, 10, 58, 60, 135, 204–5; during swing era, 113, 121–22. *See also* Harlem: African American musicians in; racial identity: African American performers and; white musicians: emulating African American musicians; *and names of specific musicians*

Alexander, Irving, 288n99

Alexander, Willard, 125, 135, 136, 137

Algonquin Round Table, 118

Allen, Red (Henry), 24, 141, 147, 151, 196, 287n79

Alvin, Danny, 144, 185, 188

American Federation of Musicians: 120, 148, 168; Local 802, 18, 20, 121, 153, 224n37, 287n89, 288n95

American Jazz Review: on Georg Brunis, 193, 194, 195; on Jimmy Ryan's, 184; on kid bands, 188, 189, 191

American Speech, 82

Amos 'n' Andy, 80

Andrews, Gordon, 282n10

Andrews Sisters, 106, 118

Annie Laurie, 95, 96, 97

anticommercialism: African American identity and, 11, 60, 157–58; African American music and, 25, 35; Count Basie and, 137–38; bebop and, 11, 156, 157; Chicago-style jazz and, 128; Commodore Music Shop and, 130–33; general audience as threat to, 56, 58; Dizzy Gillespie and, 166–67; jam sessions and, 22, 29, 115, 148–49, 151–52, 154; jazz aficionados and, 128–31; *Jazz Information* and, 130–33; jazz war and, 180, 182; jive and, 83–84; John Kirby and, 94, 108; as marketable commodity, 10, 11, 34, 41, 52, 57–58; Joe Marsala and, 11, 144–45; masculinity and, 9, 14–15, 19–20, 24, 52, 98, 166–67; modernism and, 23; musicians' ambivalence toward, 31–32, 67, 96–97;

anticommercialism (*continued*)
New Orleans–style jazz and, 128, 180; Onyx Club and, 20–22, 31–32, 56–57, 72, 113, 151–52; racial stereotypes and, 6, 9, 11, 14–15, 29–30, 34, 35, 128, 134–35, 204; record collectors and, 115, 128, 130–31; Riley and Farley and, 55–58, 72; Gunther Schuller and, 108; during swing era, 10, 113–16, 118, 123–24; Claude Thornhill and, 96. *See also under* audience; entertainment industry; white musicians

Apollo Theatre, 45, 80, 83, 97, 134

Aquarium, 15, 285n60

Arcadia, 16

Armstrong, Lil, 63

Armstrong, Louis: De Paris Brothers and, 199; Dizzy Gillespie and, 157; humor and, 54; influence on kid bands, 188–89; influence on Wingy Manone, 50; influence on Louis Prima, 42–44; influence on Stuff Smith, 68; Bunk Johnson and, 185, 186; original Onyx Club circle and, 24, 25, 226n63; Riley and Farley and, 53; Signifyin(g) and, 73; swing and, 56

Armstrong, Mr. and Mrs. W. B., 19, 228n94

Arodin, Sidney, 44

ASCAP (American Society of Composers, Authors, and Publishers), 105

Asch, 169

audience: anticommercialism and, 56, 58, 128–31; for Count Basie, 136–37; for bebop, 158, 170, 181; celebrities in, 126–27; college students in, 66–67, 129, 183–84; dancing by, 119, 127–28, 136, 184; for Dixieland, 2, 183–84; at the Downbeat, 173; as "hepcats," 128; as "ickies" or "ikkies," 57, 128; interracial, 2, 4, 11, 61, 87–88, 109, 124–26, 139, 158, 170, 172, 173, 174–75, 178–79, 183–84; jazz aficionados in, 2, 3, 115, 128–31, 136–37, 145–46, 148–49, 153–54, 184, 185, 195; at Jimmy Ryan's, 2, 183–84, 192–95; as "jitterbugs," 114–15, 127, 129, 130, 136, 145, 154; jive and, 83; for John Kirby, 92–93, 109–10; for Joe Marsala, 127, 145–46; musicians in, 40–41, 49, 54, 57, 61, 65, 72, 85–88, 92, 109, 124–26, 137, 173, 183–84, 203; music-industry professionals in, 31–32, 109, 125; for New Orleans–style jazz, 181; at original Onyx, 32; for Louis Prima, 47–49; for public jam sessions, 153–54; racial stereotypes and, 34, 64, 81, 122, 131; for Riley and Farley, 55–56; for Stuff Smith, 63–65, 72, 81, 82, 109, 242n55; socialites in, 126–27; for Spirits of Rhythm, 40; at Spotlite, 2, 172–73; as "squares," 40–41, 56; for Maxine Sullivan, 97–101; during swing era, 33–34, 52, 58, 124–33; for Art Tatum, 40; at Three Deuces, 2; at Tondelayo's, 172; women in, 19, 47–48, 70, 122, 124, 127, 175, 179, 183, 194, 242n55, 258n92; as "zombies," 174, 176, 179. *See also* hipsters

Aunt Jemima Revue, 62

Aurthur, Bob, 186, 189, 191, 194, 195

Austin High School Gang, 188

Autrey, Herman, 69

Avakian, Al, 190

Avakian, George, 182, 189, 191

Babs' Three Bips and a Bop, 156, 167–68

Bach, Bob, 130, 146, 151, 168

bachelor subculture, 19, 24, 48, 175, 195, 242n55

Baer, Max, 71

Bailey, Buster, 90–95 passim, 103, 107–10 passim, 126, 131, 250n64

Bailey, Mildred, 117, 118

Baker, Houston A. Jr., 8

Baltimore Afro-American, 87

Band Box, 117, 118, 120, 208, 214

Band Goes to Town, The, 235n50, 237n62

Baraka, Amiri, 169

Bargy, Roy, 17, 27, 125

Barne's, 203

Barnet, Charlie: commercial success of, 123; on interracial performance, 28, 29; John Kirby, compared to, 107; Dorothy Lamour and, 126; Cliff Leeman and, 199; Artie Shapiro on, 124

Barnett, Anthony, 244n74

Barrett, James R., 30

Basie, Count: at Famous Door, 120, 123, 126, 134–40, 147; John Kirby and Louis Prima, compared to, 107; musical style of, 137–38, 252n82; racial stereotypes and, 11, 116, 138–40

Basin Street Blues, 45

Basque, 15

Battle, LeRoy, 68, 70, 77, 110, 173, 197

Baum, Stanley, 271n60

bebop: African American identity and, 157–58, 169–70, 182, 204–5; anticommercialism and, 11, 58, 156, 157, 158, 166–67; audience for, 158, 170, 181; evolution vs. revolution in, 156–57, 169; 52nd Street as symbol of, 155–56, 182; Dizzy Gillespie and, 1, 2, 155, 157, 159–60, 164–69, 173, 196; Harlem, origins in, 155, 172; hipsters and, 11, 165, 173–76, 219n2; humor and, 157–58, 165–67; interracial performance and, 170–71; jam sessions and, 155; jazz war and, 2, 12, 179–83, 191, 193, 196–200; John Kirby Sextet, influence of, 11, 110–11, 157; marketing of, 11, 162–69; modernism and, 3, 11–12, 158, 163–65, 169–70, 180–81, 183, 187; musical traits of, 155, 158–59, 166; origin of word, 155; racial stereotypes and, 11, 158, 163, 166–67, 182, 204–5; small-group swing

and, 156–57, 159–60, 268n22; Stuff Smith, influence of, 11, 157; Art Tatum Trio, influence of, 160. *See also names of specific clubs and musicians*

Be-Bop (Gillespie recording), 164

Bechet, Sidney: De Paris Brothers and, 186; at Jimmy Ryan's, 184, 190, 198, 199; Cliff Leeman and, 199; Bob Wilber and, 188–92, 198

Beckwith, Mary, 183, 189, 191

Beethoven, Ludwig van, 8

Beiderbecke, Bix, 17, 25, 130, 143, 144, 189

Benchley, Robert, 15

Benjamin Harrison Literary Club, 94

Bennett, Bobby, 65, 70, 75

Berigan, Bunny, 17, 27, 59, 86, 118

Bernie, Ben, 30, 35, 64

Bernstein, Artie, 231n17

Berry, Chu, 149

Bert, Eddie, 138

Bert Frohman's, 210, 214

Best of the Blues. See *St. Louis Blues* (film)

big bands on 52nd Street: Count Basie, 134–40; commercial opportunities during swing era, 122–24; Dizzy Gillespie, 1–2, 155, 165–66, 172; Charlie Ventura, 167

Big Butter and Egg Man, 63

Billboard, 45

Bindas, Kenneth J., 114

Birdland, 202

Birth of a Nation, The, 37

Birth of Bebop, The (DeVeaux), 58, 155

black. See African American musicians

blackface. See minstrelsy

Black Orchid, 208, 211, 215

Bland, Jack, 231n13

Blesh, Rudi, 182–83

Blowers, Johnny, 58–59, 120, 124, 129

Bluebird, 117

Blues I Can't Forget, 164

Blue Skies, 97

Blues of Bechet, 277n50

Bluestone, Harry, 40, 231n17

Bohlman, Philip V., 5

Bonano, Sharkey, 119, 140

Bop City, 202

Boulard, Garry, 44, 45, 48, 233n24

Bounce of the Sugar Plum Fairy, 105

Bourne, Charlie, 26–27, 28–29, 31, 147, 222n11

Boym, Svetlana, 204

Bradley, Will, 117, 132

break, defined, 53

Bredice, Lou, 188

Bricktop, Madame (Ada Smith), 177

bridge, defined, 76

Broadway: 52nd Street audience and, 47, 109, 153; venues on, 16, 18, 127, 202

Broadway Bellhops, 21

Brooklyn, 87, 152, 190

Brown, Carlton, 37

Brown, Pete, 90–95 passim, 103, 104, 117

Brown, Ray, 155

Brunies, George. *See* Brunis, Georg

Brunis, Georg: at Famous Door, 261n37; humor and, 192–96; jazz war and, 196, 197; at Jimmy Ryan's, 1–2, 191, 192–96; Wingy Manone and, 49; name, spelling of, 277n58; with Louis Prima, 44

Brunswick, 74

Bryant, Willie, 63

Bugle Call Rag, 150, 152

Bugler's Dilemma, 105

Bunn, Teddy, 35–36, 39, 90, 91, 103, 230nn7–8

burlesque: decline of 52nd Street and, 3, 12, 201–2; jazz clubs switching to, 207–8, 282n25, 284n50, 286n76, 287n82

Burley, Dan, 82, 83, 84

Bushkin, Joe, 121, 144, 150

Byas, Don: in brawl, 177; influence on bebop, 163, 268n22; at Jimmy

Ryan's, 151; record industry and, 169, 176; at Three Deuces, 159

cabaret tax, 168

Cafe Maria, 208, 214

café society, 126

Café Society (club), 147

Cahn, Sammy, 116

Caliente, 89, 208, 214

Calloway, Cab, 83, 88, 103, 233n24, 245n99, 270n51

Candy Kids, 187–89

Carmichael, Hoagy, 17, 23, 26, 28, 222n10

Carousel, 282n25

Carr, Mancy, 25

Carroll, Barbara, 163, 167, 176–77

Carroll, Charles, 37

Carter, Benny, 28, 137

Carter, Freddie, 165

Casa Loma Orchestra, 65, 86

Casey, Al, 109, 124–29 passim, 148, 160

Casino Deluxe, 40, 41, 49, 208, 214

Catlett, Sid, 94

Cavanaugh, Inez, 86

CBS, 16, 18, 107, 117, 136

Cézanne, Paul, 22

Change O'Key Boogie, 186

Chaplin, Saul, 116

Charters, Samuel, 20, 32, 181, 223n17

Chase, Frankie, 17, 27

Chicago: Austin High School Gang, 188; jam sessions in, 27, 149; musicians from, at original Onyx Club, 18, 22, 27, 221n3, 224n47; radio audience in, 136

Chicagoans (band). *See* Marsala, Joe

Chicago-style jazz: anticommercialism and, 128; influence on 52nd Street's white musicians, 113, 140; jam sessions and, 152; jazz aficionados and, 128, 130, 182, 183, 184–85; jazz war and, 182–83, 195–96; at Jimmy Ryan's, 184–85, 189; Joe Marsala and,

134, 140, 142, 143, 144, 145, 146. *See also* Dixieland; New Orleans–style jazz; *and names of specific clubs and musicians*

Chickery Chick, 193

Chinatown, My Chinatown, 43

Christopher Columbus, 143

Chrysler Building, 16

Clarinet Marmalade, 142

Clarke, Kenny, 155, 160, 171, 198

classical music. *See* "swinging the classics"

Clayton, Buck, 138, 199

Club Basque, 15

Club 18, 117, 118, 122, 208, 214–15

Club 52nd Street. *See* 52nd Street Club

Club Nocturne, 207

club owners: African American, 11, 158, 170, 171–73; in general, 120, 121, 124, 182, 231n16. *See also names of specific club owners and clubs*

Club Waikiki, 118

Coburn, Patricia, 145

Cole, Cozy, 62–63, 69–70, 85, 87, 110, 159

Cole, Nat "King," 160

Collier, James Lincoln, 185

Collier's, 201

Colonna, Jerry, 231n17

Colt, Jack, 41, 46

Coltrane, John, 73

Columbia (record label), 117, 168, 190

comedy. *See* humor

commercial entertainment. *See* anticommercialism; entertainment industryCommittee of Fourteen, 15, 285n60

Commodore (record label), 117, 130, 131, 132, 169

Commodore Music Shop, 129–33, 149

comping, defined, 159

Condon, Eddie: Georg Brunis and, 194, 195; with Joe Marsala, 124, 141, 142, 147, 234n43, 263n50; Red McKenzie and, 231n13; "mob" of, 150, 151; on Plunkett's, 17; with Riley and Farley, 52, 54–55, 57; with Windy City Seven, 140

Connelly, Marc, 43

Connie's Inn, 71

Connors, Jack, 119

Continental, 169

Cooper, Jackie, 126

Cooper, Ralph, 80

Coquette, 105

Cosco, Joe, 125

Cotton Club, 25, 38

Crane, Hart, 224n47

Crawford, Satch, 126

Creoles, 44, 45

Croom-Johnson, Austin, 237n62

Crosby, Bing, 140

Crosby, Bob, 252n82

Crow, Bill, 54, 57, 183

Cugat, Xavier, 50

Cummings, E. E., 224n47

curfew, 168

Dameron, Tadd, 163, 168

dancing: by audiences on 52nd Street, 119, 127–28, 136, 184; in Count Basie's revue, 136; Dizzy Gillespie and, 167; Hawaiian, 118, 119; John Kirby Sextet and, 98; Louis Prima and, 48; Stuff Smith and, 69, 70, 71; in speakeasies, 16, 221n4; Tondelayo and, 171–72

Daniels, Douglas, 35–36, 39

Daniels, Wilbur, 30, 35, 37, 48

Dardanelle, 176

Dark Eyes, 100

Darling Nellie Gray, 100

Davis, Eddie, 16, 44, 48, 117, 118

Davis, Francis, 7

Davis, Miles, 171, 174, 176, 179, 219n2

Davis, Sammy Jr., 45

Davison, Wild Bill, 182, 195–96, 197, 284n50

Dawn on the Desert, 105

DeArango, Bill, 156

Debussy, Claude, 163–64

Decca, 55, 56, 117

Deep Harlem, 25–26

DeLange, Eddie, 118

Deloria, Philip J., 227n83

DeMarco, Renee, 16

DeMarco, Tony, 16

De Paris, Sidney, 186, 198

De Paris, Wilbur, 184, 186–87, 198

De Paris Brothers, 183–84, 186–87, 198–99

DeRose, Al, 188

Detroit Red (Malcolm X), 174

DeVeaux, Scott: on anticommercialism, 9, 58, 128–29, 148–49; on bebop, 155, 156, 159, 169, 268n20, 270n51, 270n55; on Tiny Grimes, 162; on jam sessions, 29, 148–49, 269n32; on jazz tradition, 4, 181; on racial stereo-types, 58, 166, 253n95

Dexter, Dave Jr., 203

Dickenson, Vic, 152

Dillard, Jenny, 94–95, 96

Dinerstein, Joel, 137–38

Ding Dong Daddy from Dumas, 63, 67–68

Dixie Debs, 147

Dixieland: audience for, 2, 183–84; Italian Americans and, 46; jazz war and, 2, 11–12, 180–83, 196–200; at Jimmy Ryan's, 1, 152, 182–87, 193, 196, 200; John Kirby Sextet as alternative to, 105–6; Joe Marsala and, 143, 145; musical traits of, 140–41; New Orleans–style jazz and, 140–41; Red Norvo as alternative to, 106; revival (1935), 45–46, 49; revival (1940s), 11–12, 180–81, 188–92, 195–96, 205; Riley and Farley and, 53, 54; swing and, 140–41; Ben Web-ster and, 199. *See also* Chicago-style jazz; New Orleans–style jazz; *and names of specific clubs and musicians*

Dixon's, 176, 209, 215

Dizzy Club, 209, 214

Dob Bla Bli, 168

Dodging a Divorce, 105

Dollinger, Artie, 85

Donegan, Dorothy, 176

Donizetti, Gaetano, 105

Dorsey, Jimmy: Andrews Sisters on, 252n82; commercial success of, 123; Famous Door and, 231n17; influence on Johnny Blowers, 59; *Jazz Informa-tion* and, 132; at Onyx Club, 17–18, 27, 32, 85; *Onyx Club Revue* and, 13, 23–25

Dorsey, Tommy: Andrews Sisters on, 252n82; commercial success of, 123; influence on Johnny Blowers, 59; at Onyx Club, 17–18, 26, 32, 52, 85, 125; *Onyx Club Revue* and, 13, 23–25; "swinging the classics" and, 96

Dorsey Brothers Orchestra, 25

double-consciousness (Du Bois), 8

Double Trouble, 52

Douglas, Paul, 19, 21–22, 26–27, 32, 223n22

Downbeat (club): in appendix, 209, 215; audience at, 173; Barbara Carroll at, 167, 176; Dizzy Gillespie at, 166, 167, 169; hipsters at, 174–75; police and, 179; small-group swing at, 159; Stuff Smith at, 68

Down Beat (magazine): on Count Basie, 139; on bebop, 156, 163, 164, 168, 169; on Georg Brunis, 193, 194, 195; on decline of 52nd Street, 201, 203; on Dixieland, 182, 186, 189; on Famous Door, 41, 47; on Dizzy Gillespie, 157, 164; on hipsters, 174; on interracial performance, 147, 151; on jam sessions, 151, 153; on John Kirby, 92, 93, 106, 107; on Wingy Manone, 46, 49, 51; on Joe Marsala, 144, 146; on Louis Prima, 43, 46, 49; on racist violence, 177–79;

on Riley and Farley, 52, 53, 54, 57; on Stuff Smith, 63, 65, 66, 74; on Spirits of Rhythm, 37; on Maxine Sullivan, 95, 97, 99; on swing-era 52nd Street, 117–21 passim, 125–26; on women instrumentalists, 176

Drink to Me Only with Thine Eyes, 105

Dr. Sausage (Lucius Tyson), 127, 131

drugs. *See* heroin; marijuana

Du Bois, W. E. B., 8

Duncan, Hank, 184

Durante, Jimmy, 136, 221n4

Durham, Hobart Crook, 126

Early, Gerald, 135

Eaton, Lewis, 185–86

Eckstine, Billy, 173

Edison, Harry, 83, 138, 139

Egan, Jack: on decline of 52nd Street, 203; on Onyx Club, 22, 31, 125, 151; on Riley and Farley, 57, 235n47; on Stuff Smith, 65–71 passim, 74; on Red Stanley, 239n16; on Maxine Sullivan, 95

Egyptian Barn Dance, 105

18 Club, 117, 118, 122, 208, 214–15

Eldridge, Roy, 62, 113, 118

Ellington, Duke: De Paris Brothers and, 198; at Famous Door, 137; influence on Erroll Garner, 164; influence on Joe Helbock, 18; influence on Riley and Farley, 53; influence on Stuff Smith, 75; "jungle style" of, 25; Irving Mills and, 225n57; racial identity and, 247n4; swing and, 237n61

Ellison, Ralph, 134

Elman, Ziggy, 85, 149

Embraceable You, 68

Empire State Building, 16

Engler, Art, 151

entertainment industry: anticommercialism and, 6, 9, 10, 113–16, 124, 193, 205; during swing era, 113–20, 123, 136

Erenberg, Lewis A., 4, 114, 115, 185, 254n10

Esquire, 165

Europe, James Reese, 18

Evans, Herschel, 134, 138

Evans, Nicholas M., 219n2, 227n84, 228n90

Famous Door: on AFM's unfair list, 121; in appendix, 209, 214–15; Mildred Bailey at, 117, 118; Count Basie at, 118, 126, 134–40; big bands at, 123; Will Bradley at, 117; Georg Brunis at, 261n37; burlesque at, 207; dancing at, 119; Roy Eldridge at, 118; Woody Herman at, 117; Billie Holiday at, 61; jam sessions at, 47, 149; John Kirby at, 103, 109, 118; Wingy Manone at, 34, 50, 61; Red McKenzie at, 55; as musicians' club, 47, 52, 58, 125, 137; Red Norvo at, 106, 117, 118; opening, 33, 41; owners indicted for tax evasion, 120; Louis Prima at, 34, 41–49, 126; racial "mixing" at, 29; Joe Sullivan at, 147; Ben Webster at, 199; Teddy Wilson at, 61

Farley, Ed: Georg Brunis compared to, 194, 195; commercial success of, 34, 52–58, 62; Ella Logan and, 99; musical style of, 53; Stuff Smith and, 64–67 passim, 71, 72

Feather, Leonard: on bebop, 157; on decline of 52nd Street, 201, 202; on Dizzy Gillespie, 157, 165; on interracial performance, 146; on John Kirby, 110; on Wingy Manone, 50; *Mighty Like the Blues*, 142; on Charlie Parker, 163; on Louis Prima, 44–45; on Stuff Smith, 128; on Maxine Sullivan, 100–1; on Art Tatum, 161–62; on Charlie Ventura, 167; on White Rose, 200

femininity, 98

Ferguson, Otis, 36–37, 150, 230n7

Ferraro, Thomas, 45
Fetchit, Stepin (Lincoln Perry), 80
Fifi's Rhapsody, 105
52nd Street (film), 66, 116
Fifty-Second Street (song, Bullock and Spina), 116
Fifty-Second Street (song, Cahn and Chaplin), 116
52nd Street Club, 117, 209, 214
Fiske, Dwight, 16
Fisk University Jubilee Singers, 7
Fitzgerald, Ella, 126, 166, 230n8
Fitzpatrick, Leo, 99, 249n52
Five Pennies, 32, 59
Five Pork Chops, 127, 131
Flamingo, 210, 215
Fleischmann's Yeast Hour, 56
Flow Gently, Sweet Rhythm, 107
Floyd, Samuel A., Jr., 73
Flynn, Errol, 168
Foresythe, Reginald, 105
Foster, Pops, 231n13
Foster, Stephen, 162
four-beat: defined, 26
Fredrickson, George M., 6
Freeman, Bud: in Austin High School Gang, 188; at Commodore Music Shop, 130; with Eddie Condon, 140; influence on Joe Marsala, 144; at Kelly's Stable, 149; musical style of, 113; at Onyx Club, 17–18, 22, 27–28, 52
Friedwald, Will, 229n7, 230n8
Froeba, Frank, 147, 282n10
From A Flat to C, 110, 269n32
From Monday On, 40
Fry, Roger, 7
Frye, Don, 90, 91, 103, 109
Future of Nostalgia, The (Boym), 204

Gabbard, Krin, 227n83
Gabler, Milt, 122, 130–32, 149–52 passim, 179, 265n84
Gaillard, Slim, 159, 247n14

Garner, Erroll, 163–64, 170, 171
Garry, Vivien, 176
Gaskin, Leonard, 87, 88, 109, 110, 172, 196
Gates, Henry Louis, Jr., 73
Gayer, Dixon, 242n62
gay men, 179, 223n21
gender. *See* femininity; masculinity
Gendron, Bernard, 180–81, 269n43
General (record label), 117
Gennari, John, 218n13
Gensler, Lew, 140
Gershwin, George, 35, 228n90
Getz, Arthur, 279n2
Gibson, Harry "The Hipster," 174
Gilbert, Henry F., 243n66
Gillespie, Dizzy: bebop and, 155, 157–60, 163–65, 169, 268n20; big band of, 1–2, 155, 165–66, 172; comedy and, 2, 165–67, 270n51; hipsters and, 173–76 passim; influenced by John Kirby, 110–11; jazz war and, 1–2, 196, 197, 198; modernism and, 3, 163–65; racist violence and, 177; white musicians and, 170–71
Gin Mill Blues, 26
Gioia, Ted, 6, 218n13
Girard, Adele, 142, 143, 144–45
Glasel, Johnny, 188, 189
Glaser, Matt, 242n62
Gleason, Jean, 258n92
Gleason, Ralph, 186
glissando, defined, 42
Goffin, Robert, 7
Gold, Robert S., 226n73
Gonzales, Babs, 156, 167–68
Goodman, Benny: at Famous Door, 137; at Hickory House, 149; influence on Johnny Blowers, 59; interracial performance and, 85, 86, 146–47; John Kirby and, 109; at original Onyx Club, 17–18, 21, 25, 27, 30–31, 32, 227n83; as popular success, 123, 125–26, 132, 145

Gordon, Dexter, 165

Gordon, Leon, 172

Gottlieb, William, 163–66 passim, 173, 175, 183, 194, 201

Gould, Jack, 107, 138, 139

Granz, Norman, 165

Gravine, Mickey, 191

Green, Abel, 47, 50, 61

Green, Charles, 64

Green, Freddie, 137

Green Pastures, The, 43

Greenwich Village: Café Society, 147; gay clientele in speakeasies, 223n21; hipster on, 175; jam sessions in, 149; Nick's, 59, 182; Stuyvesant Casino, 182; Bob Wilber in, 190

Griffin, Chris, 85

Griffith, D. W., 37

Grimes, Tiny, 160, 162, 170, 172

Griselle, Thomas, 105

Groovin' High, 158–59, 166

Gross, Walter, 17

G. Schirmer, 130, 132

Guarnieri, Johnny, 162, 196, 200

Guild, 158

Gut Bucket Blues, 44

Hackett, Bobby, 150, 261n37

Haig, Al, 164, 170

Hall, Al, 70

Hall, Edmond, 151

Hallelujah!, 43

Hammond, John: Count Basie and, 134, 135, 138–39; jam sessions and, 149; on John Kirby, 92, 93–94; on musicians' wages, 120; on Louis Prima, 47, 48; on Maxine Sullivan, 97

Hampton, Lionel, 87, 137, 150, 151

Handsome Harry the Hipster, 174

Handy, W. C., 24

Hanighen, Bernie, 38

Hargail, 169

Harlem: African American comedians in, 80–81; African American musicians in, 122, 256n55; audience members from, 124, 173; bebop in, 155; during early swing era, 20; gay clientele in speakeasies, 223n21; hipsters and, 175; jive and, 61, 72, 76, 82–84, 92; Jonah Jones and Bunny Berigan in, 86; Clark Monroe in, 172; original Onyx Club musicians and, 25–29; politics in, 80; Louis Prima in, 45; Stuff Smith and, 10, 61, 71, 72, 75, 76, 80–84; Maxine Sullivan in, 97; "Symphony Sid" Torin popular in, 169; white musicians in, 27, 28

Harlem (McKay), 84

Harlem Renaissance, 8

Harrington, Pat, 117, 282n10

Harris, Benny, 167, 177

Harris, Ed, 126, 149

Harris, Marion, 62

Hart, Clyde, 79, 159, 186

Hart, Peggy, 183, 189

Hawaiian Yacht Club. See Yacht Club

Hawkins, Coleman: bebop and, 157, 159–60, 165; at Famous Door, 126; influence on Charlie Ventura, 167; with Red McKenzie, 231n13; racial stereotypes and, 58; small-group swing and, 3, 113; at Spotlite, 172

Haymes, Joe, 243n70

Hayton, Lennie, 40–41

head, defined, 158

Healy, Eunice, 125–26

Hefti, Neal, 167

Heifetz, Jascha, 85

Helbock, Joe: African American musicians and, at original Onyx Club, 28–29, 31, 34, 222n11; fire at Onyx Club (1935), 232n19; Key Club and, 284n47; Onyx Club Revue and, 13; opens legitimate Onyx Club, 35; opens original Onyx Club, 15, 17, 285n60; Stuff Smith and, 64, 65, 66; white musicians and, 18–19, 21

Helen Morgan's Summer Home, 15
Hello Lola, 231n13
Hemingway, Ernest, 22
Henderson, Fletcher, 90, 93, 103, 107, 137
Hepster's Dictionary (Calloway), 245n99
Herbert, Hugh, 136
Here Comes the Man with the Jive, 82, 83
Here Is My Heart, 140
Herman, Woody, 117, 123, 199
heroin, 173, 174, 197, 201–2
Herrick, Tom, 146
Hey Ba Ba Re Bop, 193
Hickory House: in appendix, 210,
    214–15; Johnny Blowers and, 58–59;
    Dardanelle at, 176; jam sessions at,
    149–54 passim, 266n113; John Kirby
    at, 103; longevity of, 119, 202; Wingy
    Manone at, 34, 49–51, 59, 141; Joe
    Marsala at, 117–21 passim, 124, 127,
    134, 140–47, 159, 262n37; Red Norvo
    at, 106; opening of, 33; Mary Os-
    borne at, 176; radio broadcasts from,
    255n26; Stuff Smith at, 128; Frankie
    Trumbauer at, 262n45
Higginbotham, J. C., 24
High Society, 193, 194
Hilbert, Robert, 234n44
Hildegarde, 132
Himber, Richard, 21
Hines, Earl, 25, 150
Hinton, Milt, 87, 120, 121
hipsters, 2, 11, 158, 165, 173–77, 205
Hobson, Wilder, 16, 26–27, 54, 127,
    226n68
Hodes, Art: Danny Alvin and, 188;
    on decline of 52nd Street, 203; jazz
    war and, 182, 192, 195; at Jimmy
    Ryan's, 150–51, 184; with Joe
    Marsala, 146
Hodgson, Red, 236n54
Hoefer, George, 223n22, 231n17,
    232n19, 265n79
Holiday, Billie: African American audi-
    ence for, 173; at Downbeat, 159;

at Famous Door, 62, 126; on racial
    discrimination, 121; small-group
    swing and, 3, 113; Stuff Smith and,
    66; at Spotlite, 172
Hollywood Note, 203
Holst, Gustav, 22
homophony, defined, 42
Honeysuckle Rose, 63
Hopkins, Claude, 248n27
Horses, 35
Hot Club Magazine, 156
Hot Club of Scarsdale, 188
Hot Five. *See* Armstrong, Louis
Hot News and Rhythm Record Review, 49
Hot Record Society, 128
Hot String Beans, 142
Hotsy Totsy Gang, 25, 225n55, 225n57
House Rent Party Day, 51
Howard, Bob, 118, 240n25
How High the Moon, 167
H.R.S. Society Rag, 128
Hubble, Eddie, 188
Hughes, Langston, 259n92
Humes, Helen, 136
humor: African American comedians
    and, 80–81; bebop and, 157–58, 166;
    Georg Brunis and, 2, 192, 194–95;
    at Club 18, 118, 122, 282n10; De
    Paris Brothers and, 187; on 52nd
    Street during early swing era, 3;
    Dizzy Gillespie and, 2, 165–67; Tiny
    Grimes and, 162; and jazz, relation-
    ship between, 70–79; and jazz,
    scholarship on, 72–73; at Jimmy
    Ryan's, 192–95; John Kirby and, 91,
    94; Wingy Manone and, 50–51, 54,
    141; Joe Marsala and, 144; and music
    generally, scholarship on, 242n63; in
    Onyx Club Revue, 24; Riley and Farley
    and, 34, 52–57, 194; Stuff Smith and,
    61, 67, 69–81, 128; Spirits of Rhythm
    and, 36, 40; Art Tatum Trio and, 160,
    162; Bob Wilber on, 191
Hunt, Pee Wee, 86

Hutton, Ina Ray, 92, 94, 188
Hyers, Frankie, 282n10

I Ain't Got Nobody, 161
I Can't Get Started, 166
I Don't Want to Make History, 68
I Got Rhythm, 35, 161
I'll Never Have to Dream Again, 13
I Love You Truly, 104
Imperial Theatre, 66
I'm Playing with Fire, 13
In a Little Gypsy Tea Room, 42
Inman, Robert: on audience, 129; on
    Milt Gabler, 131; on jam sessions at
    Jimmy Ryan's, 150–54 passim; on
    John Kirby, 93; on Joe Marsala, 143;
    on Stuff Smith, 66; on Maxine Sul-
    livan, 99
Intercity Network, 145
interracial performance: bebop and,
    170–71; at Famous Door, 62, 139;
    52nd Street's importance to, 12; in
    Harlem, 27–28; at Hickory House,
    141; during jazz war, 200; at Jimmy
    Ryan's, 185; at Onyx Club, 29, 86; at
    public jam sessions, 150–51, 154;
    racial identity and, 6; during swing
    era, 4, 11, 113, 116, 135, 146–51
Ipana Troubadours, 21
I'se a Muggin', 66, 68, 74–76, 78, 81, 87
Isle of Capri, The, 50–51
Italian Americans: Dixieland and, 46;
    racial ambiguity and, 44–45, 48;
    whiteness and, 30–31
*It Don't Mean a Thing (If It Ain't Got That
    Swing)*, 53, 75
It Feels So Good, 105
It's Only a Paper Moon, 104
I've Been Working on the Railroad, 44
I've Got a Feelin' You're Foolin', 50
I've Got the World on a String, 39
I Wish I Could Shimmy Like My Sister Kate,
    194
I Would Do Anything For You, 162

Jackson, One-Round, 122
Jacobson, Matthew Frye, 31
Ja-Da, 193
Jamboree, 169
Jam Club, 40
James, Harry, 139, 149
jam sessions: audience for, 129, 148–49,
    153–54; bebop and, 155; Chicago-
    style jazz and, 152; at Famous Door,
    47, 49, 149; in Harlem, 29; at Hickory
    House, 145, 149–54; interracial,
    150–51, 154, 262n40; at Jimmy Ry-
    an's, 122, 149–54, 179, 185; at Kelly's
    Stable, 149–51; at legitimate Onyx
    Club, 52, 53, 86, 88, 149; at Leon &
    Eddie's, 118, 149; Wingy Manone
    and, 49; Joe Marsala and, 143; min-
    strelsy and, 30; New Orleans–style
    jazz and, 152; at original Onyx Club,
    9, 18, 26–32, 86, 151–52; public,
    148–54; in Scarsdale, 188; Stuff
    Smith and, 63, 86, 88; at Swing Club,
    149; during swing era, 115, 204;
    term, origin of, 226n73; Fats Waller
    and, 148; at Yacht Club, 148. *See also*
    anticommercialism: jam sessions
    and; sitting in; *and names of specific
    clubs and musicians*
Jarwood, Arthur, 202
Jazz Hot, 94
Jazz Information, 128, 130–33, 258n92
Jazz Me Blues, 53, 143, 152
Jazzmen (Ramsey and Smith), 185
Jazz Record, 174, 182–86 passim, 189–94
    passim, 203
Jazz Singer, The, 31
jazz tradition, idea of, 4, 181, 182, 200
jazz war, 12, 180–82, 196–200
Jelly, Jelly, 173
Jenkins, Gordon, 231n17
Jenney, Jack, 119, 231n17
Jewish Americans, and whiteness,
    30–31
Jim Jam Stomp, 143, 153

Jimmy Ryan's: in appendix, 210, 215; audience at, 183–184; Sidney Bechet at, 184, 190, 199; Georg Brunis at, 1, 191, 192–96, 197; De Paris Brothers at, 186–87; Hank Duncan at, 184; Art Hodes at, 184; jam sessions at, 122, 149–54 passim, 179; jazz war and, 182–83, 196–200; Bunk Johnson at, 185–86; kid bands at, 187–92; longevity of, 119–20, 202; Mezz Mezzrow at, 159, 184; Bob Wilber at, 188–92

Jingle Bells, 166

jitterbugs. *See under* audience

jive: African American identity and, 82–84, 174; defined, 82–83; John Kirby and, 92, 93, 106; Stuff Smith and, 61, 70, 72, 76, 82–84, 174

Jivin' in Be-Bop, 165

Johnson, Bunk (Willie), 183, 185–86, 187, 195

Johnson, James P., 150, 189

Johnson, Lonnie, 226n63

Johnson, Malcolm, 119, 120

Johnson, Otis, 147

Jones, LeRoi, 169

Jones, Jo, 137, 160, 171

Jones, Jonah, 62–65, 67–71, 75–76, 83, 85–86, 110

Jumpin' at the Woodside, 137, 138

Jungle Princess, The, 126

Kaminsky, Max, 121, 151, 152, 153, 154

Kassiner, Jack, 63

Kaye, Sammy, 152, 193

Keir, Estelle, 117

Keller, Greta, 13

Kelley, Robin D. G., 175, 224n37

Kelly's Stable: in appendix, 210–15; decor of, 119; Bud Freeman at, 262n37; Vivien Garry at, 176; Dizzy Gillespie at, 160; jam sessions at, 149–53 passim; Red McKenzie at, 231n15; Clark Monroe at, 172; Frankie Newton at, 147; Mary Osborne at, 176

Kenton, Stan, 269n43

Keppard, Freddie, 185

Keyboard, 182, 195, 197, 210, 215

Key Club, 210, 214

Keynote, 169

kid bands, 187–92

Kilmer, Joyce, 95

Kilowatts, 121

King, Bill, 265n92

King Kong, 37

Kirby, John: anticommercialism and, 93–94, 108, 161; audience for, 92–94, 109–10; Club Waikiki and, 118; comedy and, 91–94; influence on bebop, 11, 110–11, 157; Red Norvo and, 105–6; racial identity and, 10, 61, 89–90, 108–9, 111, 205; racial stereotypes and, 106–7, 111; repertoire of, 104–5; Gunther Schuller on, 108; sextet, formation of, 102–4; Spirits of Rhythm and, 90–92; Maxine Sullivan and, 95, 99–100; "swinging the classics" and, 90, 105, 107–8, 131

Kirk, Andy, 243n70

Klein, Manny: Famous Door and, 47, 231n17; on Harlem, 28; at Onyx Club, 17, 19, 21, 26, 31, 65; *Onyx Club Revue* and, 13, 23–25; studio work and, 21

Knockin' a Jug, 226n63

Kodat, Catherine Gunther, 114–15

Kofoed, Jack, 221n4

Kreisler, Fritz, 85

Kress, Carl: at Onyx Club, 17, 19, 26, 65, 119; *Onyx Club Revue* and, 13, 23

Kruger, Jerry, 136, 139

Krupa, Gene, 123, 132, 137, 231n13, 252n82

Kyle, Billy, 103–4, 107, 110, 111

labor: on 52nd Street during swing era, 120–24; minstrelsy and, 7, 30;

standardization and, 20; in studios, 20–22

Ladnier, Tommy, 185, 189

LaFell, Leon, 247n14

Lamarr, Hedy, 172

Lamour, Dorothy, 126

Lang, Eddie, 17–18, 30, 226n63

Lanin, James, 231n17

Lanoue, Conrad, 235n47

Larchmont, NY, 149

La Rocca, Nick, 46

Latin music, 187, 193

Laura, 164

Lazar, Irving, 136

Lead Belly (Huddie Ledbetter), 7

Leeman, Cliff, 69, 87, 199

LeMaire, Jack, 142

Leon & Eddie's: Eddie Davis at, 16, 44, 48, 117, 118; jam sessions at, 149; Louis Prima and, 44; revues at, 33, 118, 119, 207; as speakeasy, 16

Leonard, Neil, 224n47

lesbians, 179

Let's Have a Jubilee, 42, 43–44

Let's Swing It, 52

Levy, John, 171

Lewis, Ted, 136, 194

Liberty Music Shop, 117, 130

Life, 116

Lindy Hop, 225n59

Little Brown Jug, 105

Little Club, 118, 121, 210, 214, 262n37

Little Harlem, 62–63

Little Sir Echo, 143

Livin' in a Great Big Way, 53

Loafin' Time, 53

Local 802. *See* American Federation of Musicians

Loch Lomond, 95–100 passim

Locke, Alain, 8

Logan, Ella, 53, 99, 102

logic of the absurd (Palmer), 74, 76, 77, 79

Lomax, Alan, 7

Lomax, John, 7

Lombardo, Guy, 41, 44

Long, Slats, 53, 55, 235n47

Lopes, Paul, 218n28, 228n95, 259n108

Lopez, Vincent, 16

Lop-Pow, 168

Lord & Taylor, 201

Lott, Eric, 30, 227n81, 228n91

Louis, Joe, 71

Lou Richman's Dizzy Club, 209, 214

Love Is Just Around the Corner, 140

Lucie, Lawrence, 173

Lunceford, Jimmie, 62, 117, 118, 126

Mabel's Dream, 188

Mabley, Moms, 80

Mabon, Peggy, 126

MacDonald, Pete, 66

Mack, Lathrop, 46, 47, 49

Maggin, Donald L., 270n51

Malachi, John, 200

Malcolm X, 174

Malneck, Matt, 225n55

Mama's Chicken Shack, 118, 122, 126, 210, 214–15

Mammy's Chicken Farm/Fry/Koop/ Shack, 118, 122, 126, 210, 214–15

Manne, Shelly, 3, 171

Manning, Irv, 121, 124, 143, 144, 145, 147–48

Mannone, Wingy. *See* Manone, Wingy (Joseph Matthews)

Manone, Wingy (Joseph Matthews): Danny Alvin and, 188; Andrews Sisters on, 252n82; Georg Brunis and, 193; Dixieland revival (1935) and, 46, 49; at Hickory House, 49–51, 149; jam sessions and, 49, 147, 149, 153; jazz war and, 1; at Kelly's Stable, 147, 153; Joe Marsala and, 50, 141–42; musical style of, 50, 140, 232n22; name, spelling of, 234n35, 277n58; popularity of, 10, 34, 50–51, 89, 127;

Manone, Wingy (*continued*)
racial ambiguity of, 34, 46, 51; Teddy
Wilson and, 61–62
Manor, 169
March of the Charcoal Grays, 187
March of Time, 69, 70, 161
Margulis, Charlie, 21
marijuana: Bunny Berigan and, 86; decline of 52nd Street and, 202; heroin
and, 197; hipsters and, 174; Jonah
Jones and, 86; John Kirby and, 92;
police and, 178–79; Stuff Smith and,
75, 82, 83, 92
Markham, Pigmeat, 80
Marsala, Joe: Andrews Sisters on,
252n82; anticommercialism and,
11, 116, 135, 144–45; audience for,
127–28, 145–46; at Famous Door, 137,
139; at Hickory House, 117, 118, 120,
121, 124, 127, 134, 140–53 passim,
159, 234n43, 262n37; interracial performance and, 135, 146–48, 151, 153;
jam sessions and, 149, 151, 152–53;
with Wingy Manone, 50, 141; with
Red McKenzie, 141–42; musical style
of, 113, 134, 140–43; radio broadcasts
by, 117, 145; record labels, 117; sitting
in and, 147–48
Marsala, Marty, 124, 142
Mary Had a Little Lamb, 66
masculinity: anticommercialism and,
9, 14–15, 19–20, 24, 52, 98, 166–67;
hipsters and, 158, 175; and jazz,
scholarship on, 219n2; minstrelsy
and, 30; racial identity and, 9, 14–15,
30, 52, 158, 175; white, 14–15, 195,
228n91; women and, 19
Massaro, Salvatore, 17–18, 30, 226n63
Mastren, Carmen, 50, 144
MCA (Music Corporation of America),
135, 136
McAdams, Garry, 42
McCoy, Norma, 126
McDonough, Dick, 17, 26, 65

McGarity, Lou, 85
McGhee, Howard, 163
McKay, Claude, 84
McKenzie, Red: ambivalence toward
African American musicians, 38–39;
Johnny Blowers and, 59; with Candy
Kids, 187–88; at Club 18, 281n10;
with Joe Marsala, 141; with Red
Norvo, 235n50; at original Onyx
Club, 17; with Riley and Farley, 52,
53, 54–55; Spirits of Rhythm and,
34–35, 38–40, 187–88
McKenzie's, 141–42, 210, 214, 262n37
McKenzie's Candy Kids, 187–89
McMichael, Robert K., 219n2, 226n72,
228n90
McPartland, Jimmy, 17, 188
McPartland, Marian, 3, 280n11
Meadowbrook Club, 123
Melancholy Clown, The, 105
Mencken, H. L., 22
Mendelssohn, Felix, 66
Mendelssohn's Swing Song, 66, 106
Mendel's Son's Swing Song, 240n25
Mercer, Johnny, 38, 86
Merry Macs, 119
Metronome: on bebop, 163; on Don Byas,
169; coverage of 52nd Street, 117;
on curfew, 168; on decline of 52nd
Street, 201, 203; on Erroll Garner,
163; on Dizzy Gillespie, 158, 163,
166, 169; on Babs Gonzales, 168; on
hipsters, 178; jazz war and, 180; on
Wingy Manone, 46, 51; on Red McK-
enzie, 38, 39; on McKenzie's, 141; on
Red Norvo, 106; on Louis Prima, 46,
47; on racial tension, 178; on Riley
and Farley, 54; on Spirits of Rhythm,
36, 37, 39; on Maxine Sullivan, 97;
on Art Tatum Trio, 160
Mezzrow, Mezz: at Jimmy Ryan's, 159,
184; on jive, 84, 245n96; marijuana
and, 75, 245n96; on Red McKenzie,
38, 231n13; scholarship on, 219n2;

white masculinity and, 228n91; Bob
Wilber and, 190
M-G-M, 201
Mighty Like the Blues, 142
Miley, Bubber, 25, 226n63
Miller, C., 132
Miller, Charles, 203
Miller, Eddie, 42
Miller, Fred R., 131
Miller, Glenn, 132, 231n13, 231n17
Miller, Karl Hagstrom, 224n41
Miller, Taps, 126
Mills, C. Wright, 20
Mills, Irving, 25, 225n55, 225n57
Mills Blue Rhythm Band, 103, 147
Mills Brothers, 229n7
minstrelsy: African American responses to, 8, 58, 73, 80–81; during
nineteenth century, 7, 31; original
Onyx Club and, 14, 29–31; Louis
Prima and, 44; Stuff Smith and,
73; Spirits of Rhythm and, 37.
See also under jam sessions; labor;
masculinity
"mixed" bands. *See* interracial
performance
modernism: Erroll Garner and, 163–64;
Onyx Club circle and, 22–23, 224n47.
See also under bebop
"moldy figs," defined, 180
Monk, Thelonious, 155, 199
Monroe, Clark, 172
Monroe's Uptown House, 172
Monson, Ingrid: on bebop, 170; on hipsters, 173–75; on masculinity, 175,
219n2, 227n83; on Signifyin(g), 73;
on whiteness, 219n2
Mood Indigo, 53
Moore, Freddie, 90, 91, 186
Morgan, Helen, 15
Morgenstern, Dan, 173, 196–97,
278n81
Morris, Lloyd, 221n4
Morrison, Chick, 127

Morton, Bennie, 199
Morton, Jelly Roll, 103, 142, 186, 189
Mosier, Gladys, 94–95, 96
Mosley, Snub (Leo), 250n64
Mound City Blue Blowers, 35, 231n13
muggin', defined, 76
Muggles, 25
Mundy, Jimmy, 120
Musical Varieties, 81
Music Box, 132
Music Corporation of America, 135,
136
Music Goes 'Round and Around, The, 53,
55–57, 65, 71–72, 118
music industry. *See* entertainment
industry
Muskrat Ramble, 188, 199
Mutual Broadcasting System, 117
Myers, Wilson, 35
My Favorite Things, 73
My Old Man, 38
My Yiddisher Momma, 100

NAACP, 101
National, 169
NBC, 16, 18, 53, 56, 98, 99, 117, 232n17
Negro a Beast, The (Carroll), 37
Negro and His Music, The (Locke), 8
New Orleans Gang. *See* Prima, Louis
New Orleans Rhythm Kings, 143, 193
New Orleans–style jazz: anticommercialism and, 128–29, 180; Georg
Brunis and, 193, 195; Commodore
Music Shop and, 130; Dixieland and,
140–41; jam sessions and, 152; jazz
aficionados and, 128–30, 185–86;
jazz war and, 180–83, 197–200; at
Jimmy Ryan's, 1, 182–200; kid bands
and, 188–92; Wingy Manone and,
34, 50, 52, 53, 89, 141; Joe Marsala
and, 134, 140, 143; Red McKenzie
and, 38, 52; nostalgia and, 204;
original Onyx Club musicians and,
23–26 passim; Louis Prima and, 34,

New Orleans–style jazz (*continued*)
41–46, 52, 53; racial stereotypes and,
128; revival (1940s) and, 11, 180–81,
188–92, 195–96, 205; Riley and
Farley and, 53, 55; Charlie Shavers
as alternative to, 105; during swing
era, 113; Ben Webster and, 199. *See
also* Chicago-style jazz; Dixieland;
white musicians: New Orleans–style
jazz and; *and names of specific clubs
and musicians*
New Republic, 56, 203
Newton, Frankie, 91–95 passim, 103,
147, 149
New York Age, 157
New York Amsterdam News: advertise-
ments for Tondelayo's, 172; coverage
of 52nd Street, 117; coverage of Stuff
Smith, 87; on hipsters, 174–75; on
racial tension, 179; on Maxine Sul-
livan, 97
New York City Department of Taxes, 112
New York Daily Mirror, 137, 172
New Yorker, 145, 186, 201, 203
New York Herald-Tribune, 139
New York Journal-American, 99
New York Post, 117, 145
New York State Liquor Authority, 202
New York Sun, 119
New York Times: advertisement for
Famous Door, 137; on Count Basie,
135, 138; coverage of 52nd Street,
117; on John Kirby, 107, 109; on Joe
Marsala, 145; on Maxine Sullivan,
97
New York World's Fair, 118
Nichols, Red, 32, 59
Nick's, 59, 182
Nobody's Sweetheart, 35
Nocturne (club), 207
Nocturne (composition), 105
Nolan, Lloyd, 101
Non Skid Manure, 224n50
Norris, Frank, 56

Norvo, Red, 106, 117, 118, 188, 235n50
nostalgia, 12, 204–5
Notes of a Guilty Bystander (Sylvester), 1

Oakley, Helen, 94
O'Brien, Esme, 126
Ochi Chornia, 100, 101, 102
Oh, Dear, What Can the Matter Be, 53
Old Folks at Home, 162
Old Man Harlem, 25–26
Old Viper, 49
O'Leary's Barn, 211, 214
Oliver, King (Joe), 24, 130, 185, 188
Olman, Chauncey, 202
On a Little Street in Singapore, 105
One Hour, 231n13
"On the Fetish Character in Music
and the Regression of Listening"
(Adorno), 114–15
Onyx Club: in appendix, 211, 214–15;
Babs' Three Bips and a Bop at, 167;
celebrities at, 126; closed by fire
(1935), 41, 47, 52; closed by police
(1945), 179; closing of (1939), 120,
121; dancing at, 119; general audience and, 40–41, 56–58, 65–66, 92;
Dizzy Gillespie at, 155, 157, 166;
interracial audience at, 173; Key
Club and, 284n47; John Kirby at,
10, 90–93, 103–4, 106–7, 109; large
shows at, 119; Malcolm X at, 174;
Red McKenzie at, 52; moves to 62
West 52nd, 66; Jimmy Mundy at,
120; as musicians' club, 9, 14–33,
40–41, 52, 55–57, 65, 125, 141;
opening of "legitimate" club, 35;
original speakeasy, 9, 12, 13–33,
113, 125, 129, 151–52, 158, 182, 192,
195, 203; Hot Lips Page at, 117; radio
broadcasts from, 66, 250n61; Riley
and Farley at, 52–57; Stuff Smith at,
61–72, 74, 81, 83, 84–90, 159; Spirits
of Rhythm at, 35–40, 52; Maxine
Sullivan at, 10, 95, 97–101, 119, 126;

Ben Webster at, 159, 160; Lee Wiley at, 117. *See also under* jam sessions

Onyx Club Boys. *See* Farley, Ed; Riley, Mike; Smith, Stuff (Le Roy Gordon)

Onyx Club Record, 224n50

Onyx Club Revue, 13–14, 21, 23–24, 32, 51

Onyx Club Spree, 78–79

Onyx Hop, The, 92

Oop Bop Sh'Bam, 166

Oop-Pop-A-Da, 168

Opus 5, 110

Orchid, 208, 211, 215

Original Dixieland Jazz Band, 46, 142

Original Handbook of Harlem Jive (Burley), 82

Ornithology, 167

Osborne, Mary, 176, 183

Osborne, Will, 23–24

Ostendorf, Berndt, 227n80

Owens, Thomas, 158, 268n18

Page, Hot Lips, 117, 147, 148, 149, 183, 203

Page, Walter, 137

Palmer, Clarence, 247n14

Palmer, Earl, 45

Palmer, Jerry, 73–74, 76

Palmieri, Remo, 158, 165

Panassié, Hugues, 7

Panish, Jon, 226n72

Paramount Theatre, 123

Parenti, Tony, 194

Parker, Charlie: drugs and, 163, 174; Dizzy Gillespie and, 3, 110, 155, 158, 159, 164, 170–71; hipsters and, 176; influence of John Kirby on, 110; modernism and, 3, 163–64; popularity of, 169; at Spotlite, 172, 179; at Three Deuces, 163; at Tondelayo's, 172; Ben Webster and, 160; white musicians and, 170–71; Bob Wilber on, 198

People's Voice, The, 172

Peretti, Burton W.: on gay presence in early jazz, 223n21; on influence of European tradition in jazz, 8; on jive, 84, 245n96; on radio work, 223n17; on white musicians and modernism, 22–23; on white musicians and racial stereotypes, 221n3, 227n82

Performers and Musicians Guild, 213, 215

Pershing, Warren, 126

Peterson, Charles, 70, 112, 151

Pettiford, Oscar, 155, 157, 160, 171, 177

Phillips, Flip, 147

Phil Selznick's, 101

Phyfe, Eddie, 188, 196, 198

Pic-A-Rib, 262n37

Picasso, Pablo, 164

Pinero, Frank, 46

Piper, Tom, 174, 179

Pittsburgh Courier, 117

Plantation Club, 211, 215

Please Don't Talk About Me When I'm Gone, 91

Plunkett's, 17

police: Aquarium, raided by, 285n60; Georg Brunis and, 195, 278n81; Jonah Jones on, 86; Helen Morgan's Summer Home, closed by, 221n4; racial integration, opposition to, 2, 4, 178–79

polyphony: defined, 23

Popkin, John, 49, 149, 153, 265n81

Porter, Eric, 29, 247n4

Powell, Adam Clayton, Jr., 172

Powell, Bud, 111

Powell, Johnny, 235n47

Powell, Teddy, 123, 125–26

Powers, Madelon, 228n92

Price, Sammy, 124, 157

Prima, Louis: Andrews Sisters on, 252n82; audience for, 47–49; Dixieland revival (1935) and, 45–46; at Famous Door, 41–42, 46–49, 126;

Prima, Louis (*continued*)
  influence of Louis Armstrong on,
    42–43; musical style of, 41–42, 50,
    53, 106, 107, 140, 142; popularity of,
    10, 34, 41, 46–49, 52, 62; racial ambi-
    guity of, 34, 41, 43–45, 51, 100
primitivism, 6–7
Primitivist Myth (Gioia), 6
Princippi, Henry, 132
Privin, Bernie, 85
Procope, Russell, 103, 104, 109, 110, 126,
    250n64
Profit, Clarence, 137, 160
Prohibition, 3, 15–16; repeal of, 3, 9, 33,
    129
prostitution, 174–75, 178

Quebec, Ike, 171

Rabson's Music Shop, 132
race: as social construction, 4–5, 30–31.
    See also interracial performance;
    racial ambiguity; racial discrimina-
    tion; racial identity; racial stereo-
    types; racist violence; whiteness
racial ambiguity: Wingy Manone and,
    51; original Onyx Club and, 30–31;
    Louis Prima and, 41, 44–45, 48;
    Maxine Sullivan and, 98–99. *See also*
    racial identity; whiteness
racial discrimination: in employment
    of musicians, 18, 27, 28, 30, 121–23,
    138–39; in European concert music,
    108–9; in Harlem, 80; by police, 2, 4,
    178–79
racial identity: African American per-
    formers and, 60–61, 80, 102, 204–5;
    African American tradition and,
    7–8; anticommercialism and, 11, 60,
    157–58; during bebop era, 3, 157–58,
    169–70, 182, 204–5; blues and, 24;
    constructed through music, 5–6,
    9; 52nd Street's influence on, 12;
    jazz war and, 182; jive and, 84; John

Kirby and, 10, 61, 90, 111, 157; origi-
    nal Onyx Club and, 14, 30–31; Stuff
    Smith and, 10, 61, 62, 85, 102, 111,
    157, 204–5; Maxine Sullivan and,
    10, 61, 90, 102, 111; during swing
    era, 116, 131, 133. *See also* interracial
    performance: racial identity and;
    masculinity: racial identity and;
    racial ambiguity; racial stereotypes;
    whiteness
racial stereotypes: African American
    performers and, 6, 10, 58, 60, 80,
    135, 204–5; of African American
    sexuality, 30, 37, 48, 175; anticom-
    mercialism and, 6, 9, 11, 14–15,
    29–30, 34, 35, 128, 134–35, 204;
    Count Basie and, 11, 134–35, 139–40;
    bebop and, 11, 158, 163, 166–67,
    182, 204–5; Sidney Bechet and, 190;
    Chicago-style jazz and, 128; Club
    18 and, 122; De Paris Brothers and,
    187; Dixieland revival and, 12; early
    history of, 6–7; Dizzy Gillespie and,
    166–67; hipsters and, 174–76; jazz
    aficionados and, 131; *Jazz Information*
    and, 131; jazz war and, 182; Bunk
    Johnson and, 187; John Kirby and, 10,
    61, 89–90, 106–11; Mammy's Chicken
    Farm and, 122; Wingy Manone and,
    51; New Orleans jazz and, 128; in
    1930s entertainment, 80; original
    Onyx Club and, 14–15, 29–31; Charlie
    Parker and, 163; Louis Prima and,
    43–44; "Primitivist Myth" and, 6;
    Stuff Smith and, 10, 61, 62, 64, 73,
    81–82, 84–85, 102, 111; Spirits of
    Rhythm and, 36; Maxine Sullivan
    and, 10, 61, 89–90, 97, 99–102, 111;
    during swing era, 34, 122; "swing-
    ing the classics" and, 90; Tondelayo's
    and, 172; Leo Watson and, 37; white
    critics and, 37–38; white musicians
    and, 6, 10, 38, 89, 128, 135, 175; Bob
    Wilber and, 191. *See also* audience:

racial stereotypes and; minstrelsy; racial identity
racist violence, 2, 4, 122, 177–79
Radano, Ronald, 5, 7, 73, 230n9
radio: broadcasts from 52nd Street clubs, 66, 117, 136, 137, 169, 250n61; networks, 10, 16, 105, 114, 123, 136, 223n17. *See also* studios; *and names of specific networks and stations*
Radio City Music Hall, 18, 274n132
Ramage, Doris, 66
Ramirez, Ram, 39
Ramsey, Frederic, Jr., 182
Ramsey, Guthrie P., Jr., 73
Raskin, Milt, 17
Rauch, Lloyd, 232
Ravel, Maurice, 22, 164
Ray, Carline, 88, 173
Rayburn, Jean, 258n92
record collectors, 10, 115, 128, 130–31, 189, 259n92
record companies, 114, 117, 168. *See also names of specific labels*
Red McKenzie's. *See* McKenzie's
Reig, Teddy, 176, 177, 178
relief acts, 61, 89, 95, 160
Reuss, Alan, 85
Rhythm Club, 29
Rich, Buddy, 143, 144, 152
Richman, Harry, 16
riff, defined, 35
Riley, Mike: Georg Brunis compared to, 194, 195; commercial success of, 34, 52–58, 62; Ella Logan, 99; musical style of, 53; Stuff Smith and, 64–67 passim, 71, 72; at Troc, 117, 118
Rimsky-Korsakov, Nikolay, 96
Roach, Max, 111
Robin, Leo, 140
Robins and Roses, 68
Robinson, John, 170–71, 173, 178, 197, 274n126
Rocco, Maurice, 240n30
Rockefeller Center, 16, 201, 274n132

Roediger, David, 29–31
romantic racialism (Fredrickson), 6
Roosevelt, Eleanor, 100
Roseland Ballroom, 16, 135
Rosenberg, Chuck, 39
Rosenfeld, Connie, 51
Rosenkrantz, Timme, 69, 70, 86, 242n53
Rosenzweig, Roy, 228n92
Rosolino, Frank, 171
Rousseau, Jean-Jacques, 6
Royal Roost, 202
Rushing, Jimmy, 136
Russell, Pee Wee: with Eddie Condon, 140–41; at Jimmy Ryan's, 150; at Little Club, 118, 121, 284n51; with Red McKenzie, 231n13; with Louis Prima, 42
Russin, Babe, 95–96, 100
Ryan, Jimmy, 184. *See also* Jimmy Ryan's
Ryan's. *See* Jimmy Ryan's

Saints Go Marching In. See When the Saints Go Marching In
saloons, 14, 18–20, 24, 228n92
Salt Peanuts, 164, 166, 196
Samoa, 211, 215
Santly, 74
Sato, Ruth, 118, 203
Sauter, Eddie, 106
Savoy (record label), 169, 176
Savoy Ballroom, 134
Scarsdale, NY, 188, 190
Schillinger, Mort, 164–65
Schirmer. *See* G. Schirmer
Scholl, Warren, 50
Schuller, Gunther, 103, 105, 108, 161, 250n64, 252n79
Schutt, Artie, 17–18, 27, 52
Scoggins, Virgil, 35–37
Scott, Raymond, 68, 105, 137
Scott, Tony, 171
Scottish songs, 53, 95, 97, 98, 99, 102
Seldes, Gilbert, 67
Sepia Nephews. *See* Spirits of Rhythm

Sextet from "Lucia," 105

Shapiro, Artie: on audience, 124, 146; with Eddie Condon, 140, 263n50; on jam sessions at Hickory House, 149, 150, 152, 153; Joe Marsala and, 123–24, 142–45, 263n50; on Louis Prima, 43; on Mike Riley, 54, 58; on sitting in, 148

Sharron, Sally, 147

Shavers, Charlie, 103–5, 109, 110, 126

Shaw, Arnold: on Georg Brunis, 194; on decline of 52nd Street, 279n2; on Famous Door, 49, 231n17; on jam sessions, 149, 150, 151, 265n84, 265n94; on Jimmy Ryan's, 150, 151, 184, 265n84, 265n94, 275n15; on Onyx Club, 28, 40, 222n11, 226n68, 285n60; on Riley and Farley, 235n47, 237n55; *The Street That Never Slept,* 3

Shaw, Artie: Andrews Sisters on, 252n82; commercial success of, 123, 145; at Hickory House, 149; Cliff Leeman and, 199; records sold at Commodore, 132; Stuff Smith and, 85

Shaw, Billy, 165

Sheik of Araby, The, 77–78, 188, 277n50

Sherman, Shavo, 136

Shields, Larry, 142

Shim Sham, 71

Shipton, Alyn, 110, 165, 229n4

Shultz, Herb, 28, 92–93

Signature, 169

Signifyin(g) (Gates), 73

Signorelli, Frank, 50, 62, 222n11, 225n55

Silver Grill, 63–64

Simmons, John, 171, 177

Simon, George, 54, 70, 97, 98, 106, 141

Singer, Lou, 105

Singh, Ram, 156, 167–68

Singin' the Blues, 143

Singleton, Marge, 153

Singleton, Zutty, 150, 153, 186, 203

Sister Kate. See I Wish I Could Shimmy Like My Sister Kate

sitting in: American Federation of Musicians and, 153; with Count Basie, 137, 139; during bebop era, 170–71, 172; jam sessions and, 150; with Joe Marsala, 146; at Onyx Club, 85–86; with Stuff Smith, 85–86; during swing era, 113, 147–48, 153

Slave Songs of the United States (Allen et al.), 7

Slim and Slam, 159. *See also* Gaillard, Slim; Stewart, Slam

Smile Will Go a Long, Long Way, A, 235n46

Smith, Arlene, 244n75

Smith, Bessie, 93, 149

Smith, Charles Edward, 112

Smith, Howard, 17

Smith, Mamie, 24, 288n95

Smith, Raymond, 65

Smith, Stuff (Le Roy Gordon): African American audience for, 87–88, 109; in Buffalo, 62–65; humor and, 64, 69–72, 74–79, 81–82, 91, 97, 128, 144; influence on bebop, 11, 157; interracial performance and, 85–86, 147; jive and, 82–85, 92, 174; on John Kirby, 110; musical style of, 63, 67–69, 71–72, 74–79, 106; musicians sitting in with, 85–86, 147; at Onyx Club, 61, 64–72, 74, 81, 83–90, 237n64; popularity of, 65–66, 89, 127; racial stereotypes and, 10, 61, 81–82, 85, 102, 111, 166, 204

Smith, Willie "The Lion," 28–29, 31, 150, 151, 222n11

Snowden, Elmer, 286n76

Soma, Tony, 16

Someone to Watch Over Me, 143

Song of India, 96

Souls of Black Folk, The (Du Bois), 8

speakeasies, 3, 15–16, 223n21. *See also* names of specific speakeasies

Specht, Paul, 18

Spencer, O'Neill, 95–96, 103, 110, 111

Spirits of Rhythm: as headlining act, 61; humor and, 36–37, 90–91; influence on Wingy Manone, 51; John Kirby and, 90–91; Red McKenzie and, 34–35, 38–40, 188; musical style of, 35–36, 91, 97, 106; at Onyx Club, 29, 30, 34–40, 90–91, 222n11; popularity of, 40, 47, 52; racial stereotypes and, 34, 37–38, 106; as Sepia Nephews, 35, 39

spirituals, 7

Spivy, 118

Spotlite: in appendix, 211, 215; audience at, 2; closed by police (1945), 179; Harry "The Hipster" Gibson at, 174; Dizzy Gillespie at, 1–2, 155, 165, 170, 172, 278n81; Al Haig at, 170; Clark Monroe and, 172–73; Charlie Ventura at, 167

Spreadin' Joy, 190

Spring, Howard Allan, 225n59

Spring Song (Mendelssohn), 66

Stabile, Dick, 64

Stacy, Frank, 163

Stacy, Jess, 188, 262n37

Stage, 99

Staigers, Del, 17

Stanley, Red, 239n16

stereotypes. *See* racial stereotypes

Stewart, Luke, 62

Stewart, Rex, 247n6

Stewart, Slam, 159, 160, 162, 163, 170, 177

St. Louis Blues (film), 101

St. Louis Blues (song), 13, 23, 24, 101, 104

Stomping at the Savoy, 67

stop time, defined, 42

Stowe, David: on Adorno, 254n10; on entertainment industry, 114, 116; on jitterbugs, 128; on jive, 83; on racial discrimination by police, 4, 178; on Riley and Farley, 56; on "swinging the classics," 90, 249n52

Stravinsky, Igor, 22

Street That Never Slept, The (Shaw), 3

striptease. *See* burlesque

Strip-Tease Murder Case, The, 201–2

Strong, Denny, 188

studios: labor conditions in, 20–21; musicians' resistance to, 21, 24, 144, 193, 204; original Onyx Club as alternative to, 9, 21–22, 27, 193; racial segregation in, 18, 27; viewed as contrary to jazz tradition, 32, 128

Stuyvesant Casino, 182, 185

Sudhalter, Richard, 42, 44, 220n2

Sullivan, Ed, 178

Sullivan, Joe, 17–18, 26, 31, 147, 226n63, 226n70

Sullivan, Maxine: controversy surrounding, 99–100; gender stereotypes and, 97–98; influence on John Kirby Sextet, 103–4; musical style of, 97, 100, 107; at Onyx Club, 94–95, 97–101, 119, 126; popularity of, 9, 97–98; racial ambiguity of, 98–99; racial stereotypes and, 10, 61, 89–90, 100–2, 108, 111, 205; "swinging the classics" and, 89–90, 96, 105; Claude Thornhill and, 94–96, 98

Sutton, R. Anderson, 242n63, 243n66

Sweet Georgia Brown, 110

swing: Andrews Sisters' classification of, 106; Count Basie and, 134–40; bebop and, 156–57, 159, 167, 169; Dixieland and, 140–41; entertainment industry and, 10–11, 113–24; era, beginning of, 56; jazz aficionados and, 128–29, 136–37, 149, 154; jazz war and, 180–81; Joe Marsala and, 140, 142–45; mass popularity of, 3, 33, 34, 56, 67, 112–16, 127–28, 145, 149; small-group, defined, 113; stereotypes of, 97, 145. *See also names of specific clubs and musicians*

Swing: on Count Basie, 137, 147; coverage of 52nd Street during swing era, 117; on decline of 52nd Street,

Swing (continued)
203; on 52nd Street as "bandmaker," 122; on John Kirby, 106; on Leon & Eddie's, 118; on Joe Marsala, 145, 146; Ruth Sato and, 118, 203; society column in, 126

Swing Club, 121, 147, 149, 212, 214–15, 252n82

"swinging the classics," 90, 96, 105, 108, 249n52

Swing Me with Rhythm, 42

Swing Music, 50

Sylvester, Robert, 1, 15, 46, 231n17

Symphony Sid (Torin), 169

Tatum, Art: and bebop, 268n22; at Downbeat, 159; at Onyx Club, 26, 28–29, 31, 35, 40, 222n11; small-group swing and, 3, 113; Trio, 160–63; at White Rose, 200

Taylor, Billy, 159, 166, 167, 184, 198–99, 280n11

Taylorism, 20

Tchaikovsky, Pyotr Il'yich, 105

Teagarden, Charlie, 17, 26

Teagarden, Jack: Count Basie and, 137, 139; interracial performance and, 226n63; Joe Marsala and, 50; at Onyx Club, 17, 25, 26–27; Stuff Smith and, 85; Johnny Windhurst and, 191

Tenney, Jack, 237n64

Teschemacher, Frank, 130, 144, 188

That's a Plenty, 143, 146, 191

There's No Two Ways About It, 91

They Can't Take That Away from Me, 143

Thornhill, Claude, 44, 94–95, 96–97, 98–99, 100, 105

Three Bips and a Bop, 156, 167–68

Three Deuces: in appendix, 212, 215; audience at, 2; Georg Brunis and, 194; burlesque at, 207; Don Byas at, 159, 169; closed by police (1945), 179; Erroll Garner at, 163, 171; Harry

"The Hipster" Gibson at, 174; Dizzy Gillespie at, 155, 157, 159, 169, 170, 174, 198; Charlie Parker at, 155, 159, 163, 169, 170, 171, 174, 198; Symphony Sid (Torin) at, 169; Art Tatum Trio at, 160–62; Charlie Ventura at, 167; Ben Webster at, 1, 159

Three Little Words, 26–27, 130

Three Peppers, 89

Through the Looking Glass, 89, 212, 214

Thru the Looking Glass, 89, 212, 214

Tillie's Chicken Shack, 89, 212, 214

Tillie's Kitchen, 89, 212, 214

Tillie's Restaurant, 89, 212, 214

Time, 56, 164

Time Out, 261n31

Tin Roof Blues, 193

tiple, defined, 35

Tondelayo (Wilhelmina Gray), 171–72

Tondelayo's, 171–72, 212, 215

Tony's, 16, 118, 127, 207, 285n60

Torch Club, 147, 212, 215

Torin, "Symphony Sid," 169

Tough, Dave, 157, 198

Town Casino, 212, 214

Town Hall Tonight, 98

Traeger, Charlie, 189

Trappier, Trappy (Art), 171

Trees, 95

Trent, Alphonso, 62

Tristano, Lennie, 269n43

Troc, 117–20 passim, 212, 214–15, 261n37

Trocadero. *See* Troc

Troop, George, 17

Troubadour, 212, 215

Truckin', 71

Trumbauer, Frankie, 17, 262n45

Tucker, Sherrie, 98, 176, 219n2

Turkewitz, Abe, 179, 274n129

21 Club, 15, 33, 119, 127

Twilight in Turkey, 68, 105

two-beat, defined, 26

Two O'Clock Club, 213, 215

Ubangi Club, 171
Ugly Chile, 194
Ulanov, Barry, 56, 166–67
Undecided, 109
United Artists, 116
United Hot Clubs of America, 128, 130, 149
Uptown Serenaders. *See* Newton, Frankie

Valentino, Rudolph, 228n88
Vallee, Rudy: *Old Man Harlem*, 26; radio show of, 43, 56, 65, 74, 82, 99, 237n62; satirized by Onyx Club musicians, 23, 24
Variety: on Famous Door, 47, 48; on 52nd Street (1936), 34; on interracial performance, 88; on jam sessions at Hickory House, 150; on Wingy Manone, 50, 61–62; on Louis Prima, 47; on Tondelayo, 171–72
Vauchant, Léon, 43
Vendome Hotel, 62, 63
Ventura, Charlie, 167, 287n79
Venuti, Joe: Carmen Mastren imitating, 144; and *Onyx Club Revue*, 13; at original Onyx Club, 17, 25; Stuff Smith and, 85; "underground" records by, 224n50, 225n52; whiteness and, 30
Venuti's Pagliacci No. 2, 224n50, 225n52
Victor, 117, 168
Vidor, King, 43
violence. *See* racist violence
Vision and Design (Fry), 7
Vocalion, 95, 117
Vollmer, Al, 183, 184, 187
Volstead Act, 15

Waikiki, 118
Wald, Gayle, 220n2, 228n91
Walker, Jean, 126
Walker, Mack, 65, 243n71

Waller, Fats (Thomas): jam sessions and, 88, 148, 150; popularity of, 109; shooting incident and, 122; Stuff Smith and, 88; at Yacht Club, 118, 121–29 passim, 148
Waller, Larry, 122
Waller, Maurice, 122
Walsh, Matty, 194
Ware, Leonard, 160
Washington, John, 65
Waters, Ethel, 95
Watkins, Mel, 80, 82, 245n88
Watkins, Ralph, 161
Watson, Leo: humor and, 36–37, 40, 91; with John Kirby, 90–95 passim, 103; Red McKenzie and, 40; racial stereotypes and, 37; with Spirits of Rhythm, 35–38, 40; vocal style of, 36, 37, 38, 142, 168
Watts, Kenny, 121
'Way Down Yonder in New Orleans, 39
Webb, Chick, 252n82
Webster, Ben, 1–2, 151, 157–60 passim, 165, 172, 199
Weiss, Sam, 30, 40, 48
Weiss, Sid, 50
Wells, Dicky, 138
Wellstood, Dick, 189
West, Harold, 170–71
West End Blues, 25
Wettling, George, 262n37
When the Saints Go Marching In, 187, 194, 196
Whispering, 158
White, Baby, 89
White, Jack, 118, 282n10
White Cargo (Gordon), 172
Whiteman, Paul: at Famous Door, 137; "hot soloists" and, 18; at original Onyx, 19, 30; at Plunkett's, 17; radio show of, 65, 81, 237n64
white musicians: anticommercialism and, 9, 35, 55, 60, 72, 123–24, 204; bebop and, 170–71; big bands and,

white musicians (*continued*)
122–23; Chicago-style jazz and, 113,
140; emulating African American
musicians, 9, 14, 25–31, 38, 40, 43,
45, 51, 52, 53, 61, 188; in Harlem,
27–28; jam sessions and, 9, 29;
modernism and, 22; New Orleans-
style jazz and, 42, 89, 113, 140–41;
"playing black," 30–31, 60, 227n83;
preferential hiring of, 121–23; racial
stereotypes and, 6, 10, 14, 29–31,
34, 38, 89, 135, 175; as romantic
outsiders, 29. *See also names of specific
musicians*
whiteness, 30–31, 45; and jazz, scholar-
ship on, 219n2
White, Sylvia, 126
White Rose, 170, 177, 178–79, 198,
199–200
WHN, 66
WHOM, 169
*Who Put the Benzedrine in Mrs. Murphy's
Ovaltine?*, 174
Who's Sorry Now?, 92
Wilber, Bob, 188–92, 197
Wildcats, 188–92, 197, 198
Wiley, Lee, 117
William Morris Agency, 125
Williams, Alan, 105
Williams, Marietta. *See* Sullivan,
Maxine
Williams, Midge, 98
Williams, Pauline, 126
Williams, Raymond, 82
Willie the Weeper, 188

Wilson, Teddy, 61–62, 86, 89, 137,
146–47
Winchell, Walter, 178
Windhurst, Johnny, 188, 189, 191
Windy City Seven, 140
Wither, Jerry, 136
WMCA, 117, 145
WNEW, 250n61
Wolfe, Bernard, 84
Wolfe, Thomas, 164
Wolverine Blues, 142, 193
women: hipsters and, 175; as instru-
mentalists, 98, 145, 176–77; as jazz
aficionados, 183, 258n92; in Jimmy
Ryan's audience, 183, 194; at original
Onyx, 19; in Louis Prima's audience,
47–48; in Stuff Smith's audience, 70,
242n55
Woo-Woo, 142
World War II, 168

Yacht Club: in appendix, 213–15; audi-
ence at, 124, 127, 129; decor of, 119;
as Hawaiian Yacht Club, 119, 140;
Red McKenzie at, 141; speakeasy,
15; Fats Waller at, 109, 118, 121–29
passim, 148
Yacht Club Boys, 15
Yaged, Sol, 185
Yorke, George, 235n47
Young, Lester, 9, 130, 134, 138
Young, Victor, 13, 23
You'se a Viper, 66, 83

zombies, 174, 176, 179